Zambian Crisis Behaviour

Zambian Crisis Behaviour

Confronting Rhodesia's Unilateral Declaration of Independence, 1965–1966

DOUGLAS G. ANGLIN

McGill-Queen's University Press
Montreal & Kingston • London • Buffalo

© McGill-Queen's University Press 1994
ISBN 0-7735-1219-5

Legal deposit fourth quarter 1994
Bibliothèque nationale du Québec

Printed in the United States on acid-free paper

This book has been published with the help of a grant from the Social Science Federation of Canada, using funds provided by the Social Sciences and Humanities Research Council of Canada.

McGill-Queen's University Press is grateful to the Canada Council for support of its publishing program.

Canadian Cataloguing in Publication Data

Anglin, Douglas G., 1923–
  Zambian crisis behaviour: confronting
Rhodesia's unilateral declaration of independence,
1965–1966

  Includes bibliographical references and index.
  ISBN 0-7735-1219-5
  1. Zambia – Politics and government – 1964 –
  2. Zambia – Foreign relations – Zimbabwe.
  3. Zimbabwe – Foreign relations – Zambia. 4. Crisis management in Government – Zambia. I. Title

DT3113.A64 1994   327.689406891   C94-900376-X

Contents

Tables, Figures, and Maps vii

Preface xi

PART ONE: CRISIS SETTING

I Crisis Decision Making 3

II Zambia and the UDI Crisis 17

PART TWO: CRISIS DECISION FLOW

III Pre-Crisis Contingency Planning I: Initial Response, 26 April–6 August 1965 47
    1 Defiance 49
    2 Copper Airlift 52
    3 Military Base Offer 58
    4 Coal Mining 60

IV Pre-Crisis Contingency Planning II: Securing the Lifelines to the Sea, 7 August–4 November 1965 67
    5 Unified Rhodesia Railways 69
    6 Modernizing Mpulungu Harbour 74
    7 Overture to Portugal 76
    8 British Financial Commitment 82
    9 Anglo-American Airfield Survey 87
    10 Rhodesian Arms Seizure 89
    11 Reconciliation with Zaire 92
    12 Tempering OAU Militancy 95

	13 Common Services Rights 99
	14 Malawi Oil Route 101
V	Crisis Confrontation on Two Fronts I: Military Response, 5 November–2 December 1965 103
	15 Final Warning 104
	16 Troop Deployment 106
	17 Initial Sanctions 109
	18 Kariba Security 114
	19 Opposition to OAU Military Intervention 121
	20 Rebuffing the British Troop Offer 126
	21 RAF Air Cover 135
VI	Crisis Confrontation on Two Fronts II: Economic Survival, 3 December 1965–13 January 1966 140
	22 Shunning OAU Diplomatic Sanctions 143
	23 Diversifying Dependence 147
	24 Oil Sanctions 151
	25 Contingency Aid 157
	26 Rhodesian Coal Royalty 162
	27 Beira Airlift 168
	28 Tanzanian Obstruction 171
	29 Commonwealth Conference 174
	30 The "Quick Kill" 176
VII	Post-Crisis Planning: Trusting Britain, 14 January–27 April 1966 184
	31 Girding for the Crunch 185
	32 Stockpiling Essential Supplies 189
	33 Restraining OAU Militancy 193
	34 The "Long Haul" 197
	Waiting for Wilson 202

PART THREE: CRISIS BEHAVIOUR PATTERNS

VIII	Crisis Components 205
IX	Crisis and Coping 216
X	Stress and Choice 235
XI	Significance 245
	Appendix 1: Content Analysis 257
	Appendix 2: Statistical Analysis 261
	Notes 291
	Index 375

Tables, Figures, and Maps

FIGURES

1 Model of International Crisis Behaviour 7
2 Zambian Imports from Rhodesia and South Africa, April 1965–April 1966 191
3 Levels of Crisis-Induced Stress 210

TABLES

1 Dimensions of Coping Mechanisms in Crisis Decision Making 8
2 Dimensions of Choice in Crisis Decision Making 9
3 Classification of Zambian Crisis Decisions by Policy Objective 14
4 Zambian Crisis Decisions by Period and Issue Area 16
5 Attributes of Zambia as a Crisis Actor, 1965–66 20
6 Zambian Decision Makers: Cabinet Ministers, 1965–66 30
7 Kaunda and Kapwepwe: Idiosyncratic Influences 41
8 Military Options 119
9 British Military Presence in Zambia, 1965: Chronology of Decision-Making Processes and Mechanisms 130

Appendix 2

A1 Trigger Actions by Period 261
A2 Sources of Decisional Trigger Actions by Period 261
A3 Issue Areas of Decisional Trigger Actions by Period 262
A4 Crisis Perceptions as Indicators of Stress by Period 262
A5 Crisis Perceptions as Indicators of Stress by Period and Crisis Component 262
A6 Crisis Perceptions of Threats to Basic Zambian Values by Period and Dimension 263
A7 Time Constraints on Zambian Decision Making by Period 263
A8 Armed Forces of Zambia and Rhodesia, August 1964 263
A9 Pre-Crisis Decision-Making Processes and Mechanisms – Contingency Planning I: Initial Response, 26 April–6 August 1965 264
A10 Pre-Crisis Decision-Making Processes and Mechanisms – Contingency Planning II: Securing the Lifelines to the Sea, 7 August–4 November 1965 265
A11 Crisis Decision-Making Processes and Mechanisms – Confrontation on Two Fronts I: Military Response, 5 November–2 December 1965 267
A12 Crisis Decision-Making Processes and Mechanisms – Confrontation on Two Fronts II: Economic Survival, 3 December 1965–13 January 1966 269
A13 Post-Crisis Decision-Making Processes and Mechanisms – Trusting Britain, 14 January–27 April 1966 271
A14 Information Probe 272
A15 Receptivity to Information 272
A16 Number, Frequency, and Type of Consultative Groups 272
A17 Breadth of Consultations 273
A18 Participation in Consultative Process by Category and Crisis Period 273

ix Tables, Figures, and Maps

A19 Consultative Group and Decision Time 273
A20 Intensity of Consultations by Consultative Group and Crisis Period 274
A21 Consultations: Motivations and Stress 274
A22 Size and Types of Decisional Forums 274
A23 Decisional Authority Patterns 275
A24 Alternatives: Search and Evaluation 276
A25 Search and Evaluation of Alternatives: Decision Time 277
A26 Zambian Hypotheses on Crisis and Coping 278
A27 Levels of Stress and Dimensions of Choice: Pre-Crisis Period 280
A28 Levels of Stress and Dimensions of Choice: Crisis Period 282
A29 Levels of Stress and Dimensions of Choice: Post-Crisis Period 284
A30 Stress and Choice: Core Input Sources 285
A31 Stress and Choice: Costs and Importance 285
A32 Stress and Choice: Complexity 286
A33 Stress and Choice: Systemic Domain 286
A34 Stress and Choice: Process, Activity, Novelty 287
A35 Crisis and Choice: Quality of Decisions 287
A36 Zambian Hypotheses on Crisis and Choice 288
A37 Analysis of Speech Sample by Source, Forum, and Period 289
A38 Intensity of Crisis-induced Stress 289
A39 Frequency of Statements of Perceived Threats to Basic Zambian Values 290

MAPS

1 Zambia xvii
2 Southern Africa, 1965 53

Preface

If the study of foreign policies of underdeveloped countries is underdeveloped, the systematic analysis of their foreign policy decisions is not. It is simply non-existent.

Bahgat Korany[1]

Anyone aspiring to unravel the mysteries of foreign policy decision making under Third World conditions could scarcely be under any illusions concerning the formidable and frustrating nature of the undertaking. Ample evidence exists testifying to the difficulties and delicacy of the exercise. The conceptual and practical problems inherent in analysing the actions of modern states are intractable enough. In the case of developing polities, the task is even more daunting and time-consuming. Accordingly, it is perhaps incumbent on someone intending to embark upon so uncertain an enterprise to justify his presumption in attempting such a seemingly unpromising assignment.

The purpose of this inquiry, in the first instance, is to describe and dissect the decision-making processes in a newly independent Third World developing state confronted with a grave crisis that threatened its basic values and structures. The ultimate purpose, however, is to assess the significance of perceptual changes in the intensity of crisis-induced pressures on the decisional performance of the Zambian leadership in terms of both its procedural practices and the final policy product. The practicality of the first objective has been questioned sufficiently frequently to cause the most audacious to hesitate, while the second quest poses challenges which are even more fundamental. In particular, in developing societies the conceptualization and operationalization of relevant theoretical constructs present special difficulties.

Throughout much of the Third World, basic dates and data on decision making, let alone reliable empirical evidence on the intimate functioning, formal as well as informal, of political systems, are typically not readily accessible, if indeed they exist at all. As Bahgat Korany has cautioned, "the inadequacy of documentary and archival facilities [in Third World states] makes the analysis of past [foreign policy] decisions very hazardous. Even pure information reported by the international and 'elite' press is sometimes of modest quality, low credibility, or just plain incorrect."[2]

To this lament, Christopher Clapham has added that studies which seek to identify regularized patterns of foreign policy making in developing countries frequently "fail simply by virtue of the fact that such regularized patterns can scarcely be discerned ... Familiar techniques such as the detailed reconstruction of decisions or bureaucratic processes cannot be excluded from consideration, but it must be recognized that they may not yield very useful results in states where decision making is idiosyncratic and bureaucracies are unimportant."[3] In the circumstances, it is not altogether surprising that no previous attempt has been made to undertake a systematic study of Zambian decision making.[4]

Nevertheless, there is no need to succumb to defeatism. Reasonable grounds exist for contending that the obstacles to serious and successful inquiry into the decisional processes of Third World actors are by no means as overwhelming as conventional wisdom would suggest. Moreover, the inherent interest and importance of the crisis following Rhodesia's unilateral declaration of independence, both as a case study and in comparative perspective, as well as its continuing relevance, provide compelling incentives to accept the risks entailed. Certainly, the present "barren state of Third World foreign policy studies"[5] cannot be attributed to African decision making being intrinsically less intriguing or instructive than in more developed states.

In assessing the problems associated with in-depth analyses of foreign policy processes in African states, it is important to view them in perspective. The constraints on profitable research in this field are in no way unique to developing countries. "I know only too well," British Field Marshal Lord Carver has recounted on the basis of his personal experience, "how difficult it is, even soon after [controversial and important] events and even when one has been personally involved, to record *why* certain vital decisions were taken. The decisions themselves are usually recorded, but the underlying argument behind them and the factors which tipped the balance in their favour are usually very hard to disinter."[6] Yet these undoubted difficulties have not succeeded in stemming the flood of memoirs and monographs claiming, often with considerable justification, to present intimate and authoritative accounts of decision-maker behaviour.

Nor has the effort been restricted to relatively open Western political systems. Insightful studies exist on closed societies such as the former Soviet Union, where the research environment was, in some respects, comparable to that encountered in many Third World contexts. In both situations, basic documentation and data are frequently non-existent or inaccessible. It is worth noting, too, that restrictions on the range of available research resources in much of Africa has not deterred publication of eminently scholarly analyses of domestic political processes. Certainly, compared with the fragmentary evidence that respected archaeologists and ancient historians routinely rely upon to reconstruct the past, the scope and quality of primary material available to students of contemporary African societies appear relatively rich. The problem is often not so much the "incompleteness and modest quality of data"[7] as the conflicting evidence available from different sources.

Experience suggests that an assiduous pursuit of publicly available sources illuminating African foreign policy behaviour can prove surprisingly rewarding. Clapham even concedes that the "investigation of the psychological environment of [Third World] decision makers is an open field, which because of the greater personalization of decisions could prove more valuable than in more institutionalized systems." Moreover, in contradistinction to Korany, he argues that "there is no reason, other than the paucity of data and the complexion of current academic interests," why "the persistence of stereotypes, the origins of misperceptions, and the nature of behaviour under crisis conditions" cannot be examined as "closely and fruitfully" with respect to developing countries as in the context of major power relations. "The perceptual dimension of foreign policy," he concludes, "exists independently of degrees of modernization."[8]

Despite these promising possibilities, it would be incautious to claim that the evidence marshalled here is exhaustive or that the conclusions based upon it are definitive. Even Michael Brecher, with his unprecedented access to Israeli data, admits to a certain "diffidence" in presenting his detailed findings.[9] Nevertheless, in the social sciences as in politics, it would be unwise to assume that half a loaf is never preferable to no loaf at all. In the circumstances, it is hoped that the present effort will be seen as an instructive and innovative contribution, methodologically and substantively, to a deeper understanding of the dynamics of decision making in one developing country. If so, it will have achieved an important purpose. Beyond this, it would be gratifying if this pioneering study succeeded in inducing or provoking others – including leading players in the UDI drama – to revise, refine, or reinforce the judgments recorded here, or undertake similar analyses of other critical decisions in Zambia or elsewhere in the Third World.

Two other concerns can be anticipated. Both relate to the relevance of the study. To begin with, there may be a disposition in some quarters to question the contribution that single case studies can make to the development of the field of comparative foreign policy. Initially, I had intended to compare Zambia's 1965 UDI crisis with the crisis the country faced in 1972 following the closure of its border with Rhodesia. However, adequate primary source material proved unavailable. Yet, instructive as a comparative approach might have been, its absence does not undermine the external validity of single-case studies in certain circumstances. On the contrary, a persuasive case can be made to justify focusing on a single case. As Bercovitch has argued, "Single cases can provide a powerful impetus to the development of a general explanation as long as they are historically grounded and their description is not couched in purely idiosyncratic terms."[10] Margolian adds that the case considered must be crucial and "the variables of the central hypothesis should be formulated in general terms so that results are replicable."[11] Each of these conditions has been met in the present study.

Secondly, doubts may be expressed as to whether events dating back more than a quarter of a century are of great importance today. Yet, apart from the intrinsic interest in a conflict that gripped the attention of the world at the time, this first major post-independence foreign policy crisis had a continuing impact on subsequent Zambian perceptions and behaviour. For one thing, President Kaunda, the central figure in the drama, continued in office into the 1990s. For him and others, UDI was a seminal and searing experience.

To write a book is inevitably to incur obligations, and never more than in my case. In the process of preparing this study I have accumulated an unusually heavy burden of indebtedness. I have profited enormously from the frank and informed insights and judgments of a wide range of players and participants – political leaders, government officials, businessmen, journalists, academics, and others – who have willingly shared with me their personal knowledge and experience of events recorded here. In addition, as a resident of Zambia during the early UDI years, I benefited greatly from being a privileged observer of the stirring developments of that time. I have felt free to make full use of the information made available to me, but not (with some exceptions) to cite personal sources or even to identify them individually in this preface. My appreciation of their contributions is no less profound for respecting their anonymity. At the same time, it is in no perfunctory sense that I wish to emphasize that I alone am responsible for the interpretations that I have given events and the conclusions that I have drawn. To the extent that my comprehension remains deficient, the blame is mine.

With respect to written records, published and where available unpublished accounts have been sought out wherever they might be found. Unfortunately, few personal memoirs of the period by Zambians have appeared, and none casts any great light on the concerns of this study.[12] Former President Kaunda has been anxious to record for posterity the history of Zambia as he has lived it. Nevertheless, since his resignation as party leader and retirement in 1992, he has found little time to pursue this project. At the same time, none of the relevant archives – Zambian, British, or Rhodesian – is yet officially open for research, though it is uncertain how extensive and significant they will eventually prove to be. What glimpses I have had of British diplomatic documents suggest that they are likely to provide the most detailed, if not always the most reliable, daily diary over the course of the crisis. Only in the case of Canada, whose involvement was admittedly marginal, did I obtain extensive access to invaluable official files, for which I express appreciation to the Historical Division of the Department of External Affairs in Ottawa. Again, I have been free to use the material, but not to cite the source. In addition, I have benefited from the advice and assistance of colleagues and critics, among them Kathleen Kallio, Bahgat Korany, Clyde Sanger, Timothy Shaw, and John Sigler. Above all, Michael Brecher, director of the International Crisis Behaviour Project of which this study may be considered a part, has been unfailing in his support, encouragement, and patience. The efficiency, professionalism, and sound editorial judgments of Marion Armstrong, Joan McGilvray, and Diane Mew are also greatly appreciated, as is the contribution of Christine Earl in preparing the maps.

Finally, I am happy to acknowledge with gratitude that this book has been published with the help of a grant from the Social Science Federation of Canada, using funds provided by the Social Sciences and Humanities Research Council of Canada. During the gestation of this study the SSHRCC and Carleton University also provided generous support on more than one occasion.

On a personal note, while I have striven scrupulously to maintain objectivity throughout, I cannot gainsay my deep sense of solidarity with Zambians in the dilemma they confronted as a consequence of the Rhodesian rebellion. In return for their sacrifices in the common cause, regrettably, they have been treated rather ungenerously at the hands of less committed countries and armchair critics. To the people of Zambia, and to my wife Mary, who shared the excitement and challenges of life in Zambia under the shadow of UDI during its first four years, this book is dedicated with admiration and affection.

Douglas G. Anglin
Carleton University
Ottawa, Canada

A NOTE ON CURRENCY

Unless otherwise indicated, all amounts are quoted in US dollars at the 1965–66 exchange rate. The Zambian pound was at par with sterling. The country switched to the kwacha in January 1968.

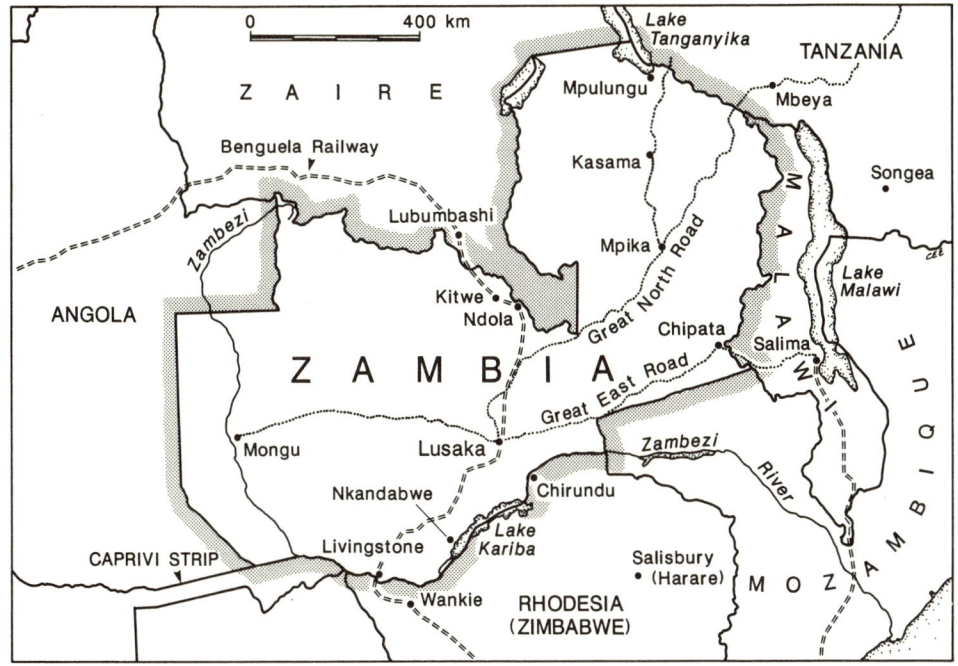

Map 1: Zambia

PART ONE
Crisis Setting

1 Crisis Decision Making

The immediate purpose of this study is twofold. First, it sets out to reconstruct the process of crisis decision making in Zambia during the critical year 1965–66 leading up to and following Rhodesia's unilateral declaration of independence (UDI) from Britain on 11 November 1965.[1] This racially inspired rebellion on landlocked Zambia's southern border and astride her lines of communication with the sea had profound implications for her national security and economic survival.[2] Secondly, the study seeks to assess the impact of rising and declining levels of crisis-induced stress experienced by Zambian decision makers on the mechanisms they employed to cope with the consequences of the conflict.[3] The inquiry is designed not merely to illuminate a Third World crisis of considerable intrinsic interest and importance, but also to contribute to a wider comparative search for knowledge and theory concerning actor behaviour under conditions of crisis.

International crises have long held a powerful fascination for analysts of international relations of many methodological persuasions: diplomatic historians, behavioural scientists, and political economists amongst others. The present study draws somewhat eclectically on several of these traditions. Crisis researchers, however, have been divided as to the most appropriate level of analysis to employ. While much of the burgeoning literature reflects a system-oriented approach, a significant segment has opted for a decision-making focus. The International Crisis Behaviour Project (ICB),[4] of which this volume is a part, shares the latter perspective. The studies comprising the project employ a common framework of analysis developed by its director, Michael Brecher. The model is not so inflexible as to rule out adaptations where required to take account of special circumstances. Nevertheless, modifications have been kept to a minimum to facilitate transnational comparisons.

CRISIS CONDITIONS

The cornerstone of the ICB edifice is the definition of its central concept:

A crisis is a situation with three necessary and sufficient conditions, deriving from a change in its external or internal environment. All three conditions are perceptions held by the highest level decision makers:

1 *threat to basic values*, with a simultaneous or subsequent
2 *high probability of involvement in military hostilities*, and the awareness of
3 *finite time for response to the external value threat.*[5]

This specification departs from Charles Hermann's now classic formulation in several respects.[6] Revisions include the deletion of "surprise" as an essential trait, the broadening of Hermann's "high-priority goals" into "basic values" – encompassing both "core values" and "priority values" – and the recognition that domestic as well as external situational changes might trigger a crisis. The extension of the definition to accommodate crises precipitated by internal instability was initially conceived with Third World circumstances specifically in mind. This is not the situation Zambia faced. Although the UDI crisis gave rise to worrisome domestic concerns, in origin it was clearly externally generated.

In Brecher's opinion, the most important change introduced is his insistence on a perceived "high probability of involvement in military hostilities" as the "pivotal condition of crisis." In its original formulation as a high probability of war, the centrality of this concern was not without its difficulties for the Zambian case study. While there was a distinct military dimension to the UDI crisis, there was less certainty that Zambian decision makers (except possibly in the first weeks of the rebellion) judged that the risk of full-scale military conflict with Rhodesia quite reached the level implied by "high probability." In his subsequent interpretative comments, however, Brecher has effectively dispelled any doubts concerning the applicability of his formula to Zambian circumstances:

5 Crisis Setting

Operationally, "high probability" may be designated as .50 to .99 – that is, at least a 50/50 possibility [but less than certain]. However, a marked change in the probability of war (e.g. from .1 to .3) may be just as salient to decision makers as a move into a high-probability range – especially in cases where protracted conflict predisposes them to expect crisis. What is crucial to the existence of an international crisis is a high – or substantial rise in – perceived war likelihood.

Even a discerned "adverse change in the military balance" – for example, as a consequence of increasing uncertainty concerning an adversary's capabilities – constitutes an acceptable measure of war likelihood.[7]

A seemingly more serious concern arises from the economic implications of the crisis for Zambian security and survival. From the outset, the threat to basic economic values was equally as menacing as the prospect of military destabilization and became, as the crisis evolved, the predominant concern. However, Brecher specifically acknowledges that conceptually an international crisis need not be confined to "the military-security issue area or peace-war continuum." On the contrary, "the source of or trigger to a security crisis may [also] emanate from political-diplomatic, economic-developmental, or cultural-status ... roots." Accordingly, he offers an alternative formulation applicable to an economic crisis. This is conceived of as a situational change which generates:
1 perceived threats to basic material interests;
2 an awareness of finite time constraints on decisions; and
3 an expectation of adverse consequences unless the response is drastic – and effective.[8]

The possibility of treating the UDI crisis as essentially an economic conflict is superficially appealing. Yet, on reflection, it is evident that the Rhodesian rebellion constituted much more than a routine economic challenge. The example of the Indian devaluation crisis, which Brecher analyses as an economic crisis, is qualitatively different in its character and consequences from the multifaceted threat the entrenchment in power in Salisbury of a determined party of white supremacists posed for Zambians. A security crisis is not defined by the value threat that precipitates it. UDI, in its economic and ideological as much as in its military manifestations, put in peril the peace, progress, and purpose of the Zambian nation, and was so perceived in Lusaka. From this perspective, Brecher's initial delineation of the defining characteristics of a crisis as interpreted operationally is clearly more appropriate to the circumstances which confronted Zambia during the difficult year of 1965–66. Thus, the fit of the ICB definition is such as to inspire full confidence in its applicability to the Zambian case.

CRISIS MODEL

The ICB Project adopts a micro approach to crisis research. The model derives from a theoretical framework of the foreign policy system, focusing on the perceptions and behaviour of a single state actor.[9] Briefly, events in the environment, internal as well as external, become inputs into the foreign policy system via a communications network. This involves a subsequent filtering of images through the decision makers' attitudinal prisms. The final choice of foreign policy decisions from among the perceived options involves a continuous interaction between the operational environment, the decision makers' images (psychological environment and predispositions to choice), and the decision-making process (communication networks, organizational and bureaucratic process).

This conceptualization of a foreign policy system as "a ceaseless flow, from the operational environment to implementing acts which create new ongoing stimuli to the various segments of the system,"[10] postulates three major components of the crisis model (Figure 1). These are: stress (the independent variable), coping mechanisms (the intervening variable), and choice patterns (the dependent variable).

The crisis model also specifies a clear time sequence. Environmental change – the trigger action – at t_1 marks the initial breakpoint in interstate relations and serves as a stimulus for the generation of threat perceptions. The full impact of crisis-induced stress occurs at t_2 with a sharp escalation in awareness of threats to basic values and, subsequently, an enhanced sensitivity to limitations on the available time for researching and executing decisional responses as well as greater cognizance of the probability of military hostilities (or of a shift in the military balance). It is the conjunction of these three logically discrete but intimately interrelated perceptions that "makes a situation a crisis and leads to 'crisis-type' decision making."[11]

Threat-induced stress, according to the model, is then mediated, at t_3, through bureaucratic and organizational channels. The coping stage is manifested in a series of analytically distinct but not necessarily sequential processes and mechanisms: the collection and review of information on the environmental stimuli; consulta-

7 Crisis Setting

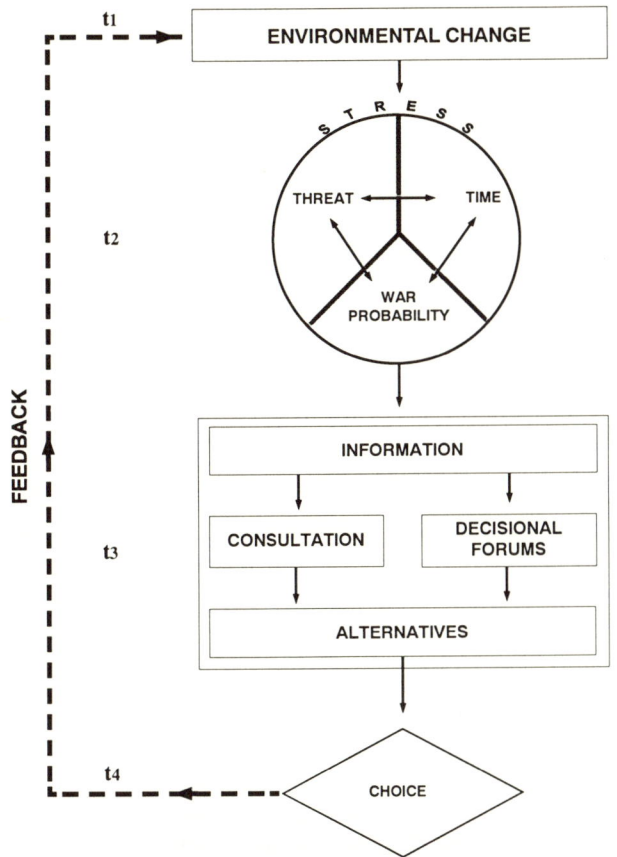

Figure 1: Model of International Crisis Behaviour

tion with expert advisers, interest groups and other high-policy elites, including external agencies; the convening of decisional forums; and the search for and evaluation of policy options. Each of these operations will be explored along a number of instructive dimensions (Table 1)[12] with a view to testing hypotheses drawn from the literature and to formulating fresh ones on state behaviour under differing intensities of crisis-induced stress.

8 Crisis Decision Making

Table 1
Dimensions of Coping Mechanisms in Crisis Decision Making

INFORMATION PROCESSING: the process of seeking, assessing, and sharing information concerning the environmental changes triggering the crisis

> 1 *Extent of information probe* (perceived need and consequent quest): minimal, moderate, or thorough.
> 2 *Receptivity to information* (or evaluative disposition): receptive (open-minded or objective) or unreceptive (distorted by bias, ideological preconceptions, past memories, or wishful thinking).

CONSULTATIVE PATTERNS: information sharing

> 3 *Breadth of consultative circle* (or number of participating groups): minimal, moderate, or extensive.
> 4 *Participation* (interests represented): political (ministerial and UNIP), bureaucratic (including diplomatic and military), corporate (mining and business interests), external (foreign governments and international organizations).

DECISIONAL FORUM: size and structure of choice-selecting group

> 5 *Formal decision-making body*: presidential (small, institutional), senior ministerial (medium-sized, ad hoc), or cabinet (large, institutional).
> 6 *Effective decision-making body*: presidential (small, institutional), senior ministerial (medium-sized, ad hoc), or cabinet (large, institutional).

ALTERNATIVES: search and evaluation

> 7 *Extent of search for alternatives* (exploration and identification): minimal, moderate, or extensive.
> 8 *Perceived range of available options*: limited, modest, or broad.
> 9 *Thoroughness of process of evaluation* (of the relative merits and consequences of perceived alternatives): minimal, moderate, or thorough.

Table 2
Dimensions of Choice in Crisis Decision Making

Dimensions	Coding
Core Inputs: The crucial stimuli to each decision as perceived by the decision makers	
Costs: The perceived magnitude of the losses anticipated from the choice which was made – human, material, political, and intangible	low, medium or high
Importance: The perceived value of the decision at the time of choice	1 – marginal 2 – consequential 3 – important 4 – significant 5 – decisive
Complexity: The number of issues-areas involved in the choice	M–S: military-security P–D: political-diplomatic E–D: economic-developmental C–S: cultural-status
Systemic Domain: The perceived scope of reverberations of the decision	domestic, Southern Africa, black Africa, and/or global
Mental Process: The mental procedure associated with the selected options, as distinct (but not necessarily different) from the procedure attending the evaluation of all other options considered *prior* to choice	*routine*: following established procedures for response to similar challenge *affective*: an assessment dominated by reliance on past experience, ideology, rooted beliefs, emotional preference, etc. *rational*: a calculus based upon the measurement of costs and benefits, qualitatively and/or quantitatively
Activity The thrust of the decision	act, delay or inaction, verbal or physical
Novelty The presence or absence of innovation in terms of reliance on precedent and past choices	yes or no

To facilitate subsequent comparative inquiry, a standardized set of nine research questions will, insofar as the available data permit be utilized as a framework for analysis. In particular, the study will probe the effects of escalating and de-escalating stress experienced by decisions makers on:

Information processing
1. cognitive performance;
2. the perceived need and subsequent quest for information;
3. the receptivity and size of the information-processing group.

Consultative pattern
4. the type and size of consultative units;
5. group participation in the consultative process.

Decisional forum
6. the size and structure of decisional forms;
7. authority patterns within decisional units.

Alternatives
8. the search for and evaluation of alternatives;
9. the perceived range of available alternatives.[13]

The final choice of crisis decision occurs at t_4. This third component of the model focuses on an analysis of the decisions reached under conditions of stress. Once again, the purpose of the exercise is the generation of hypotheses on the basis of designated dimensions of choice (Table 2).[14] Here, crisis decisions are viewed as "patterns of choice" associated with successive crisis phases corresponding to initial rising and declining levels of stress.

According to the model, an international crisis situation exhibits three discernible "time clusters in which stimuli from the environment are conveyed by the communication network to decision makers."[15] During the *pre-crisis period*, stress, while above normal, is nevertheless still comparatively low. In operational terms, its onset is "marked off from the preceding non-crisis period by a conspicuous increase in perceived threat on the part of decision makers." Stress levels associated with the *crisis period* proper, on the other hand, are typically sharply rising or palpably high. This phase is "characterized by the presence of all three necessary conditions of crisis – a sharp rise in perceived threat to basic values, an awareness of time constraints on decisions, and an image of the probability of involvement in military hostilities (or of war likelihood) at some point before the issue is resolved." As with the pre-crisis, the crisis period begins with a trigger event or cluster of events. Finally, in the *post-crisis period*, decision-maker stress moderates, beginning with "an observable decline in intensity of one or more of the three perceptual conditions," until normality returns or, as in the Zambian case, the threat perceptions re-escalate with the emergence of the pre-crisis period of the succeeding crisis phase.[16]

The structure of Part Two of this study reflects this analytical division of a crisis into three periods. For each decision in each period or phase of a period, the decisional flow is, within the limits of the empirical evidence available, dissected in terms of the model, beginning with the initial quest for information and culminating in the evaluation and choice of policy options. The detailed analysis of successive decision-making processes serves a twofold purpose: "First, it illuminates the response behaviour of the crisis actor as decisions and actions through time. Second, it provides the indispensable data for an analysis of coping, or the decision-making process, throughout the crisis and of the dimensions and patterns of choice by one international crisis actor."[17] To accomplish this latter task, it is necessary to accord as much precision as possible, quantitatively and qualitatively, to the crucial if somewhat elusive concept of crisis-induced stress which serves as the independent variable.

Although credible measures of absolute intensities of decision-maker stress are not attainable with available data and methodological techniques, a content analysis of published statements by relevant leaders can provide an acceptable basis of comparison of relative levels at different stages in the evolution of the crisis. This has been attempted using a selection of forty-nine presidential and ministerial speeches delivered over a period of a year (see Appendix 1). Once the changing pattern of stress is established, however hesitantly, the impact of changes in perceived threats, time constraints, and military hostilities on the four coping mechanisms and the subsequent decisional responses can be assessed (in Part Three) on the basis of the various dimensions previously delineated (tables 1 and 2).

CRISIS DECISIONS

The empirical basis for this study is the systematic analysis of thirty-four Zambian decisions spread over a period of a year leading up to and following upon UDI. The list is intended to provide a comprehensive inventory of all relevant and important actions undertaken by the Zambian government in anticipation of or in response to the Rhodesian rebellion. Admittedly, it was not possible to avoid the exercise of subjective judgments entirely. Relevance is a relative matter, and even every relevant decision may not be sufficiently critical to justify inclusion.

A further consideration in the choice of decisions was the adequacy of the available data. Although deficiencies in this respect did pose problems, they did not in the end necessitate the deletion from the list of any known decision that otherwise qualified on its intrinsic merits. It has meant, however, that it has been difficult to document every decision as definitively as would ideally be desirable. In some cases, it has not proved possible to determine even the precise dates of decisions, let alone reconstruct fully the sequence of events and substance of debates involved in the decision-making processes. The principal reason for the restricted data base is that contingency planning for crisis counter-measures was inevitably shrouded in considerable secrecy. In addition, the informality of the embryonic policy-making procedures, the legacy of secrecy stemming from British cabinet traditions, colonial practices, and the exigencies of the nationalist struggle, and the absence of a vigorous and vigilant opposition all contributed to limiting the availability of information. On the other hand, the situation in this respect was somewhat more favourable in the early years after independence than it became later, when the escalating external threat made the government even more security conscious.

The Zambian decisions can be categorized in various ways: in terms of crisis period, policy objective, or issue area. As would be expected, the peak crisis period, which was also the briefest period, accounted for the greatest concentration of decisions, though numerically almost as many are attributable to the extended period of crisis gestation leading up to UDI. The post-crisis period, on the other hand, witnessed a dramatic decline in both the number and frequency of decisions. At times, decisions tended to just happen, without being consciously taken.

With respect to the policy objectives of Zambian decision makers, the most frequent purpose – evident in over two-thirds of the decisions – was to elicit international support. Disengagement from dependence on Rhodesia was a motive in half the cases, while resistance to hostile Rhodesian actions was a factor in only one-third of them. Moreover, the more severe the crisis, the more intense the search for outside assistance and the greater the opposition to Rhodesian animus. On the other hand, concern with disengagement was greatest prior to UDI (Table 3).

In the great majority of cases, the substance of Zambian decisions encompassed more than one issue area.[18] If only the principal issue area is considered, the thrust of decisions appears to be predominantly economic-developmental, with military-security matters the only other concern of any consequence and then only during the crisis period proper. If, on the other hand, account is also taken of issue areas of secondary salience, then the political-diplomatic arena ranks first throughout, suggesting that ultimately economic questions have political implications (Table 4).

Any analysis of Zambian decisions and decision making is bound to reveal several characteristics which, if not uniquely Zambian, can at least claim a certain distinction. In the first place, it was not uncommon for the decision-making process to be protracted, with the result that decisions emerged incrementally or piecemeal over a period of days. Secondly, the effective and the formal decision-making bodies sometimes differed, as did the date a decision was actually taken and the subsequent date of routine ratification. Finally, and perhaps of most significance, the adoption of a decision did not necessarily settle the issue under discussion once and for all. Debate could well be revived on a later occasion, and the same catalogue of arguments and options rehashed. Partisans of one point of view or another might win the immediate battle, yet fail finally to win the war. The practice of keeping certain critical decisions under more or less constant review is perhaps typical of a small, dependent state confronted with a rapidly deteriorating external environment and subject to the vagaries of the major actors over which it can exercise no real influence. Certainly, for Zambia, this was part of the price of finding itself in the midst of a maelstrom not of its own making.

Table 3
Classification of Zambian Crisis Decisions by Policy Objective

Decisions by period, phase and date	Resistance to Hostile Rhodesian Actions	Policy Objectives		
		Disengagement from Dependence on Rhodesia	Search for International Support	

Decisions by period, phase and date	Resistance to Hostile Rhodesian Actions	Disengagement from Dependence on Rhodesia	Search for International Support
Pre-Crisis Period			
Phase I			
1 c. 27 April	1 Defiance		
2 c. 25 May		2 Copper airlift	2 Copper airlift
3 c. 18 June			3 Military base offer
4 c. 14 July		4 Coal mining	
Phase II			
5 10 August	5 Unified Rhodesia Railways		
6 c. 17 August		6 Modernizing Mpulungu Harbour	
7 c. 7 September		7 Overtures to Portugal	7 Overtures to Portugal
8 c. 14 September		8 British financial commitment	8 British financial commitment
9 c. 1 October		9 Anglo-American airfield survey	9 Anglo-American airfield survey
10 5 October	10 Rhodesian arms seizure		10 Rhodesian arms seizure
11 c. 16 October		11 Reconciliation with Zaire	11 Reconciliation with Zaire
12 16 October			12 Tempering OAU militancy
13 26 October	13 Common services rights		13 Common services rights
14 c. 26 October		14 Malawi oil route	14 Malawi oil route

Crisis Period
  Phase I
  15 6 November   15 Final warning
  16 12 November   16 Troop deployment
  17 12 November   17 Initial sanctions   17 Initial sanctions
  18 c. 17 November 18 Kariba security   18 Kariba security
  19 21 November   19 Opposition to OAU military intervention
  20 2 December   20 Rebuffing British troop offer
  21 2 December   21 RAF air cover   21 RAF air cover

  Phase II
  22 6–12 December   22 Shunning OAU diplomatic sanctions
  23 c. 12 December   23 Diversifying dependence
  24 17 December   24 Oil sanctions   24 Oil sanctions   24 Oil sanctions
  25 c. 18 December   25 Contingency aid 25 Contingency aid
  26 22 December   26 Rhodesian coal royalty
  27 c. 23 December   27 Beira airlift   27 Beira airlift
  28 c. 27 December   28 Tanzanian obstruction 28 Tanzanian obstruction
  29 c. 7 January   29 Commonwealth conference
  30 13 January   30 The "Quick Kill"   30 The "Quick Kill" 30 The "Quick Kill"

Post-Crisis Period
  31 c. 24 January   31 Girding for the crunch 31 Girding for the crunch
  32 5 February   32 Stockpiling essential supplies
  33 26 February   33 Restraining OAU militancy
  34 c. 8 March   34 The "Long Haul"

Table 4
Zambian Crisis Decisions by Period and Issue Area

Issue Area*	Crisis Period			Total
	Pre-Crisis	Crisis	Post-Crisis	
Political-diplomatic	1 (13)	2 (15)	1 (4)	4 (32)
Economic-developmental	11 (11)	8 (11)	3 (3)	22 (25)
Cultural-status	1 (7)	1 (7)	0 (1)	2 (15)
Military-security	1 (3)	5 (6)	0 (0)	6 (9)
Total issue areas	14 (34)	16 (39)	4 (8)	34 (81)

*Figures in brackets take account of issue areas of secondary importance.

II Zambia and the UDI Crisis

The prospects [of UDI] were little short of terrifying for Kenneth Kaunda. Zambia had been independent for just over a year and was only starting to settle down with a new black-run administration. It still relied upon white experts in most of the ministries and its army was entirely directed by senior British officers. It was not at all clear where their sympathies might lie if hostilities broke out with the Rhodesians across the Zambezi ... But even more pressing than security matters were the problems of mere survival, because all of Zambia's effective routes ran through Rhodesia.[1]

HISTORICAL OVERVIEW OF CRISIS

Zambia's emergence upon the international stage on 24 October 1964 came amidst much rejoicing, genuine expressions of goodwill, and confident assurances concerning her future prospects, economically, politically, and socially. Internationally, however, the outlook was less auspicious. The storm clouds had already begun to gather south of the Zambezi in minority-ruled Rhodesia. Indeed, there were well-founded fears, following the return of the British Labour party to power earlier that month, that the settler regime in Salisbury was contemplating timing its oft-projected illegal seizure of independence (UDI) to coincide with Zambia's achievement of nationhood.[2]

Although apprehension concerning an imminent rebellion proved premature, Zambians were now amply alerted to the threat they faced. Admittedly, the priority concerns of the fledgling administration in Lusaka were, not surprisingly, nation-building and national development. Coping with the demands of delayed and distorted development and the legitimate – as well as unrealistic – expectations of an impatient public was sufficient to tax the energies and efficacy of even the most experienced government. Nevertheless, the deepening crisis in neighbouring Rhodesia could not be ignored. The prospect of UDI posed a sharp challenge to Zambia's non-racial ideology and an ominous threat to its security. Rhodesia controlled Zambia's rail access to the sea, its hydroelectric power from the jointly owned Kariba dam – one of the major hydro-electric installations in the world[3] – and its supplies of coal and oil. Accordingly, the closer it came to the fateful day, the greater the share of Lusaka's attention UDI came to command.

Barely a year after Zambian independence and following a series of further false alarms, Rhodesia's rulers finally took the plunge and broke with Britain unilaterally. Despite determined efforts, nationally and internationally, to draft contingency plans for Zambia in anticipation of UDI, when the inevitable did occur the country found itself still inadequately prepared for the challenge that lay ahead.

The UDI crisis was triggered by three related developments: Rhodesian proclamation of a state emergency on 5 November 1965, the stationing of troops along the Zambian border, and the formal declaration of independence on 11 November. Zambia responded swiftly to these provocations by moving a detachment of its own troops to the border, instituting limited economic sanctions, and demanding that Britain take immediate military action to crush the rebellion or, at least, intervene to secure the supply of Kariba power. Although London stubbornly refused to employ force against Rhodesia, it eventually did offer a battalion of troops to defend Zambia. The proposal was spurned as designed more to pre-empt any action against Rhodesia than to prepare for it. On the other hand, the offer of an RAF fighter squadron and associated radar facilities was accepted after much hesitation.

With the firm British rejection of a military resolution of the Rhodesian crisis, interest shifted to economic sanctions. Here, the problem was Zambia's vulnerability to Rhodesian reprisals and its dependence on the uncertainties of external, especially British, support to survive a confrontation. Salisbury did, in fact, cut off Zambia's supply of oil in retaliation for a UN embargo, inflated its coal export royalty one hundredfold, and threatened to interfere with Kariba power.

The success of the Berlin-style oil airlift to Zambia and the development of alternative surface supply routes encouraged British

Prime Minister Harold Wilson to believe that, with tightened sanctions, UDI could be ended "within weeks, not months." The key to this strategy was gearing Zambia up to withstand a sudden, total break in relations with Rhodesia. In mid-January 1966 Wilson persuaded President Kenneth Kaunda to join in a "quick-kill" operation a mere month hence. The world would impose sudden, total sanctions on Rhodesia and, at the same time, rush to Zambia's rescue with emergency life-support systems. The questionable assumption on which the whole daring scheme rested was that the rebel regime would collapse before Zambia did. Certainly, few knowledgeable persons considered this timetable realistic. Nevertheless, Zambia made heroic efforts to gird itself for the ordeal.

As the deadline approached, London as well as Lusaka realized that, even with the copper mines reduced to a care and maintenance basis, Zambia's economy could not survive the shock. Accordingly, the "quick-kill" was abandoned in favour of the "long haul." Wilson then led Kaunda to expect a much tougher British stand on Rhodesia following the British general election in March. When, having won a secure parliamentary majority, Wilson chose instead to reopen negotiations with the rebels, Zambians felt sadly betrayed. A new chapter in the protracted UDI saga had begun.

ZAMBIAN ACTOR ATTRIBUTES

The ICB Project employs three boundary-free research typologies to classify the attributes of the crisis actors, the characteristics of the crisis decisional units, and the dimensions of the crisis being dissected.[4] These typologies provide the context within which crisis decision making takes place. They also serve to facilitate cross-case comparisons. Zambian actor attributes are summarized in Table 5 and are amplified upon below. The remaining two typologies are incorporated into subsequent chapters.

Zambia is a small, landlocked developing country in south-central Africa. In area it is larger than Texas though somewhat smaller than Britain and France combined. Its population at the time of UDI numbered under four million, with Africans comprising over 98 per cent of the total. There were some ten thousand Asians, principally of Indian origin, and perhaps sixty thousand Europeans.[5] The latter comprised mainly South African miners, Rhodesian railwaymen, and British colonial officials as well as several hundred commercial (white) farmers. With education under colonialism largely in the hands of mission personnel, a substantial proportion of the population were professing Christians.

Table 5
Attributes of Zambia as a Crisis Actor, 1965–66

Attribute	Classification	Comment
Systemic Context		largely irrelevant
Global configuration	loose bipolar	Rhodesian-South African
Subsystem configuration	loose hegemonial	sub-imperialism
Geographical Context		
Actor location	Southern Africa	
Actor-adversary location	Southern Africa-Southern Africa	
Size		
Area	medium	753,000 sq. km.
Population	small	4,057,000 (1969)
Independent Statehood	contemporary	Independence 1964
Belief Systems	Christian/animist	
Regime Type	dominant party non-communist	UNIP held 55 National Assembly seats to 10 for the ANC (and 10 reserved for whites)
Economic Development	developing	"dual economy" subsistence/modern
Military Capability	small power	3 battalions
External Dependency	high	landlocked

Physically, Zambia's curious figure-of-eight configuration reflects the fierce scramble of rival European colonial powers for control of the strategic central plateau of the continent. Eventually, as British imperialism thrust northward from South Africa during the closing years of the last century, the territory that was subsequently designated Northern Rhodesia gradually came under the administrative and commercial sway of Cecil Rhodes's rapacious British South Africa Company. Chartered rule survived until 1924 when London assumed direct colonial responsibility. Northern Rhodesia remained a Crown Protectorate for the next forty years, though the most pervasive and pernicious influence on its development was not so much Colonial Office paternalism as its proximity to settler-dominated Southern Rhodesia and segregationist South Africa.[6]

21 Crisis Setting

The solemn promises that accompanied the imposition of British "protection" on Northern Rhodesia proved inadequate to prevent its incorporation – much against its will – into the ill-contrived Federation of Rhodesia and Nyasaland from 1953 to 1963. The painful experience of a decade of cohabitation with Rhodesian racists profoundly conditioned the outlook of Zambians towards their southern neighbour. Although federation was originally conceived by the British as a barrier to the northward spread of infectious Afrikaner ideas and influence, power was effectively in the hands of the white minority who made a mockery of the principle of racial partnership enshrined in its constitution. As the Federation's first prime minister, Godfrey Huggins, unashamedly reassured his nervous electorate, the kind of partnership between white and black he envisaged resembled that between a rider and his horse.[7]

Blatant racism was not the only source of hostility to the Federation among Northern Rhodesian blacks. They were also incensed at the systematic siphoning off of the mineral wealth of the Copperbelt for the enrichment of Southern Rhodesia, and especially Salisbury, which was quickly dubbed *bamba zonke* – "the grabber of everything." Over the decade of its involuntary inclusion in the Federation, Northern Rhodesia contributed some US $272 million more in revenue to federal coffers than it received in benefits.[8]

Opposition to the imposition of the Federation and bitterness at what was perceived as a British betrayal were quickly translated into political action. As early as 1948 the Northern Rhodesian African National Congress (ANC) was founded to fight federation. With the failure of its initial campaign, the momentum of militancy slackened temporarily. However, by the late 1950s a resurgence of nationalist fervour set in, in part in response to the independence of Ghana but also in protest against a further British surrender to settler pressure. The intensification of the independence struggle culminated in a split in the ANC in 1958, and the emergence by 1960 of Kenneth Kaunda at the head of the United National Independence Party (UNIP). In 1962 and again in 1964 the first two general elections to be held under universal suffrage confirmed UNIP as the dominant party in the country. In 1972 the Second Republic was inaugurated as a "one-party participatory democracy." One-party rule survived until 1991 when popular dissatisfaction compelled a restoration of multi-party democracy. In the resulting election, Kaunda and UNIP were resoundingly defeated.

At independence in 1964, Zambia's economic outlook appeared decidedly promising. The country ranked third among world copper producers. Its rich Copperbelt astride the border with Zaire provided employment for forty-seven thousand miners, including six thousand expatriates, and contributed 43 per cent of the country's net domestic product, 71 per cent of government revenues, and 93 per cent of export earnings.[9] Admittedly, a majority of the population still lived outside the "line of rail" which bisected the country from south to north, and were engaged in subsistence agriculture. Moreover, educationally the country was inexcusably underdeveloped. With scarcely one hundred university graduates and only a thousand persons with secondary school qualifications, Zambia lagged ten years behind East Africa and twenty-five years behind Nigeria and Ghana. Nevertheless, the developing boom in world copper prices[10] offered the prospect of real progress in the nation's battle against poverty, ignorance and disease.

One salient Zambian attribute that receives insufficient recognition in the ICB typology is the extent of its external dependency, regionally and globally. Despite the dismantling of the Federation, Zambia continued to rely heavily on Rhodesia for essential imports. In the case of energy, 70 per cent of the electricity consumed and 100 per cent of the coal and oil came from or through the south. Moreover, as a landlocked state, Zambia remained totally dependent on its neighbours for access to the sea. With respect to the world economy, the country was more highly integrated into the international system than almost any other African state – as was dramatically demonstrated by its trade dependence index of 98.[11] The intensity of the country's historically conditioned vulnerability to outside pressures greatly compounded the threat that UDI posed, domestically and externally. In addition to its deleterious impact on Zambia's developmental prospects, the country's dependent state had profound implications for its capacity to respond economically, militarily, and even politically. It also added a "dominant bilateral" dimension to the crisis by involving Britain as a central variable in any Zambian calculation of the Rhodesian threat. Accordingly, the dependency factor in the Zambian political economy equation must be considered highly relevant for an understanding of the course of the UDI crisis and the decision-making processes associated with it.

ZAMBIAN FOREIGN POLICY SYSTEM

The Rhodesian rebellion erupted so early in Zambia's existence as an independent state that its foreign policy structures were still far from fully formed. In the fledgling Ministry of Foreign Affairs, a cadre of able but relatively inexperienced officials strove to cope with the complexities of regional and global politics, and to service the country's handful of diplomatic posts elsewhere on the continent and overseas. Moreover, Zambia's modest defence force was only partially trained and still expatriate-led, its intelligence service embryonic, and Parliament and the ruling party preoccupied with domestic priorities. Inevitably, therefore, at this formative stage in the evolution of the institutions and instruments of government, with the normal support structures of the state sadly underdeveloped and a major foreign policy crisis confronting the country, President Kaunda and his ministerial colleagues found themselves with an exceptional burden of responsibility thrust upon them. Almost from the outset, the cabinet and especially the presidency emerged more dominant in decision making than even the constitution envisaged.

Zambia was the first former British colony to opt for republican status and an executive head of state immediately upon attaining independence. Its decision to do so reflected potent indigenous societal and historical influences as well as the character and charisma of the prospective president. Accordingly, the constitution sought to graft a presidential system on to Zambia's (somewhat weak) British inheritance of parliamentary government. Admittedly, in the inter-party consultations leading up to the independence conference in London in May 1964, the vesting of full executive power in the presidency occasioned some concern. To allay opposition fears that a president might assume dictatorial powers, Kaunda conceded that the incumbent should be merely the "chairman of the cabinet of ministers and therefore subject to their advice and influence."[12] Nevertheless, although the president was constitutionally enjoined to consult his cabinet on policy, he was also empowered "to act in his own deliberate judgement" and not "obliged to follow the advice tendered by any other person or authority."[13] In addition, he could appoint (and dismiss) ministers at will. Thus in February 1965 Kaunda simply "entered the cabinet room with a piece of paper in his hand and promptly told his anxious lieutenants which ministries they were to have."[14]

In practice, Kaunda's presidential style was consciously consensual, certainly during his early years.[15] He customarily consulted his cabinet in a genuine search for advice and broad democratic agreement, and encouraged his "colleagues" (as he called his ministers) to voice their views without first trying to impose his on them. When, on occasion, he found it impossible to reconcile sharply opposed opinions – as during the protracted late-night debate on the mineral royalty issue in May 1965[16] – his instincts were to postpone a decision rather than offend a determined minority, especially senior ministers and those with regional power bases. However, such situations were relatively rare. A more common occurrence was for ministers to turn up at cabinet, having neglected to do their homework and therefore ill-prepared to tender informed advice. As a result, issues were not always fully discussed.[17] Moreover, there was a predisposition among ministers, especially when confronted with complex foreign policy issues, to defer to the president's sound judgment and superior knowledge. Accordingly, his opinions normally prevailed.

Once a decision was reached, cabinet members were expected to respect it and, if necessary, defend it in public. Kaunda even reserved the right to veto ministerial pronouncements on sensitive subjects and on at least one occasion intervened to cancel a colleague's speech. With the sudden intensification of the UDI crisis in May 1965, his concern that Zambians "do nothing that might make the situation more complicated" increased. "There must of necessity," he decreed, "be only one commander in the dark days that might lie ahead."[18]

The cabinet held regular scheduled sessions weekly on Tuesday mornings, and at other times as circumstances dictated. As the crisis deepened, the frequency of meetings increased, and appears to have reached a peak during the height of the crisis towards the end of 1965.[19] The president was also accustomed to sounding out ministers individually or in small groups.[20] Unlike formal cabinet meetings which were serviced by a secretariat responsible for circulating agenda papers in advance and recording minutes of the proceedings, these ad hoc sessions typically ended without any written record of conclusions reached – a situation which sometimes gave rise to misunderstandings concerning what precisely had transpired.

The range of presidential consultations was not confined to cabinet members. As one minister explained, "You must realize that the President has many cabinets – we, his ministers, are only one of them."[21] One potential source of policy guidance was the government bureaucracy. However, it suffered from a double disability. In the first place, it was still heavily staffed at its senior levels with former colonial officials whose reputations and past roles tended to inhibit intimate cooperation with them. This was not simply a matter of race, since mutual suspicion did not characterize or constrain relations with the disparate array of expatriate personal advisers recruited to State House.[22] Nevertheless, it was only with the progressive Zambianization of the top civil service posts and the catapulting of a new breed of able, younger administrators into positions of influence and prominence that the impact of the bureaucracy on the formulation of foreign policy slowly came to be felt.[23] The second liability reflected the fact that the fashioning of an effective foreign service was still in its early stages. Both the organization of the nascent Ministry of Foreign Affairs and the development of a network of diplomatic listening posts abroad were inevitably gradual processes, not least because of the keen competition among government agencies and the private sector for the limited pool of qualified personnel.[24] By the time of UDI, Zambia had opened missions in ten capitals, of which only London, Washington, and Moscow as well as the UN in New York were outside Africa. Moreover, not every post was fully operational and in a position to monitor and analyse relevant external developments adequately.

The incipient foreign affairs establishment was far from exercising a monopoly on the provision of information and advice on foreign policy issues. The president maintained extensive personal as well as official contacts with a wide range of influential individuals not only within Zambia but also elsewhere in Africa and overseas, especially in Britain. In the course of the independence struggle he had managed to attract a sizable constituency of British sympathizers – dubbed rather disparagingly the "Dear Kenneth Brigade" – a number of whom subsequently came to hold positions of influence in the Labour government. They proved an uncertain source of support, as Kaunda was to learn to his dismay.

Of more tangible benefit were Kaunda's contacts with the foreign business community, and especially with the heads of the two major mining corporations that dominated the Zambian economy – the Anglo-American Corporation (AAC) and the Roan Selection Trust (RST). Despite initial mutual mistrust, the Zambian government and the copper companies developed a surprisingly cordial and cooperative working relationship based on growing respect and an assumed underlying harmony of interests.[25] Admittedly, the steadily rising world price of copper helped smooth the transition, but the critical contributing factor was the recognition by the companies that their long-term economic interests lay in seeking a realistic accommodation with Zambian political aspirations. As Richard Sklar has explained:

After the sweeping electoral victory of the United National Independence Party in January 1964, both groups of companies adapted with apparent goodwill and sincerity to the new and truly African nationalist political order ... In both groups the top- and middle-level managers who were most intensively engaged in the search for solutions to the economic and logistical problems created by UDI seem to have been also sincerely dedicated to the achievement of Zambian national goals.[26]

Sklar concludes that AAC and RST found it

both necessary and prudent to make numerous concessions to official Zambian conceptions of morality in the conduct of foreign economic relations. From the company standpoint, these constraints, or claims of ideology, have been both costly and distasteful. Nevertheless, the mining industry's record ... is one of compliance and genuine cooperation.[27]

Not that the two companies were always in step politically. Somewhat surprisingly, the South African-based AAC proved distinctly more adroit in adapting to its new environment. The explanation for this, Faber and Potter have hypothesized, is that

within AAC, the major policy decisions seemed to be made by a small group of younger men sent to Lusaka especially for the purpose and enjoying a very large measure of autonomy. Within RST, the decisions appeared to be reached by way of a committee of old-style mine managers on the Copperbelt, and even then their recommendations often needed to be endorsed by London or New York.[28]

These differences in managerial personalities and practices should not be exaggerated. Both companies were considerably more responsive to nationalist imperatives than the great majority of expatriate business concerns throughout the country. A notable exception to the general rule was LONRHO, headed by the maverick British business baron, "Tiny" Rowland. His characteristic gambits to ingratiate himself with President Kaunda were sustained, self-serving and ultimately singularly successful. "To this day," Richard Hall wrote in 1987, "Kaunda remains the most loyal friend LONRHO has in black Africa." UDI did not, however, immediately bring Rowland the contracts he had hoped for.[29]

At the time of UDI there was little in the way of a Zambian entrepreneurial class, though one was to emerge fairly swiftly following the economic reforms of 1968 which opened up vast new opportunities for indigenous business enterprise. More generally, there was as yet little popular consciousness of any embryonic class conflict. Nearly a decade later, Robert Molteno could still assert that "in Zambia, neither leaders nor followers have perceived class membership as a variable relevant to their political behaviour."[30] By the late 1970s there was considerable substance to the trendy claim that the Zambian business class had by then acquired sufficient political coherence and clout to challenge the priority Kaunda had accorded to the liberation of Southern Africa. Although, in the circumstances of the Second Republic (instituted in 1972), a political economy interpretation of Zambian foreign policy offers critical insights,[31] there is little or no empirical evidence to sustain a rigorous class analysis to the study of foreign policy decision making in the first years of the First Republic.

Other Zambian institutions and interest groups were similarly underdeveloped. Most still lacked the organizational capacity to articulate and advance their objective regional and international concerns effectively. The bureaucratic fraction of the Zambian bourgeoisie, which was subsequently to assert its dominance within that class, had barely begun to burgeon. In particular, the parastatals, which were destined in due course to capture the commanding heights of the Zambian economy, at the time controlled only an insignificant segment of industry.[32] Admittedly, the military, whose white officer corps retained strong traditional ties south of the Zambezi, posed a potential problem in the event of open hostilities with Rhodesia, but its opportunities for influencing policy were essentially confined to professional military questions. As for Parliament, its members evidenced little interest in foreign affairs and exercised even less influence. According to one assessment, "neither the National Assembly as an institution nor MPs in their individual capacity have played a crucial role in the Zambian political system," a verdict that has even greater validity in its application to the foreign policy arena. "Throughout 1965 and 1966," Pettman notes, "the National Assembly debates hardly mentioned Rhodesia."[33]

Political parties might have been expected to provide useful channels of communication for tapping the pulse of the nation on developments in the country's external relations.[34] Yet this rarely occurred. Even in the case of the governing party, there were few indications of active grassroots interest in the UDI issue. Only once during the year 1965–66 was there any hint of concern within the ranks of UNIP with Kaunda's handling of UDI. In December, at the peak of the crisis, the parliamentary caucus considered four motions which implicitly criticized the president for alleged excessive moderation in his dealings with the British. Kaunda reacted by intervening swiftly in the proceedings and, in the process, succeeded not only in defusing a potential challenge but also eliciting an impressive vote of confidence. At the same time, the incident proved sufficiently disturbing to prompt him to exercise his constitutional privilege to address Parliament as well as convene a rare extraordinary session of UNIP's National Council, the party's "administrative and directive" body, where his leadership again received solid endorsement.[35] With the National Council meeting only infrequently,[36] the day-to-day conduct of party business was the responsibility of its Central Committee. However, since most members of that important committee were also ministers (Table 6), it tended to leave foreign affairs to be dealt with in cabinet.[37]

At provincial and local levels, it was not uncommon for party bodies or officials to indulge in militant declarations on Rhodesia, Britain, or other contentious issues. However, there is scant evidence to suggest that these spontaneous outbursts had any perceptible impact on government behaviour. The only UNIP branches to provide a significant policy input were those embracing Zambians resident in Rhodesia. These continued to serve as valuable sources of political intelligence even after their formal banning by Salisbury in July 1965.[38]

If the foreign policy input of UNIP was marginal, that of the two opposition parties was negligible. To begin with, the ANC suffered from a series of crippling disabilities: weak leadership and poor organization, a narrow power base almost entirely confined to the Southern Province, and a fiercely confrontational style which was both a consequence of and a contribution to the government's low tolerance level. To the extent that the party had any consistent foreign policy stance, its basic tenet was "Zambia first." In particular, it insisted that Rhodesian problems should be left to Rhodesians, black and white, to resolve.[39] The National Progress Party (NPP), representing the white settler community, was even more equivocal on the issue of UDI. In a bizarre attempt to conceal its true sympathies, its spokesmen maintained a determined "diplomatic silence" on the issue. Despite its proclaimed commitment to constitutionalism, the party steadfastly refused to condemn the Rhodesian rebellion.[40] In the circumstances, the government regularly dismissed the ANC's carping criticisms as ill-informed or irrelevant, and treated the studied silence of the NPP with utter contempt. It did, however, pay close attention to the state of morale of whites, especially that of the miners.

Apart from political parties, Zambian society offered few organized outlets for expressions of popular sentiments on current controversies, and virtually none that articulated public attitudes on foreign affairs. "One looks in vain," Tordoff and Molteno observe, "for a wide range of specifically Zambian ... interest groups which are independent of government."[41] The major exception was the trade union movement and, above all, the Zambia Mineworkers' Union with its immense economic leverage. Yet even trade unions tended to be preoccupied with the immediate material interests of their members. Only when external events adversely affected those concerns – as when sanctions led to increases in the cost of living – did trade unions register much interest in issues beyond Zambia's borders.

The same could be said of the population at large. Despite regular country-wide "meet the people" campaigns, government efforts to educate the public on the domestic implications of changes in Zambia's external environment were not notably successful. As one analyst has argued:

Reports of foreign policy decisions and announcements assume a sound background of knowledge which is largely absent. Explanations need to be couched fairly simply and starkly to have an impact, and the subtleties and sophistications tend to be lost ... Beyond the politically aware among those speaking reasonably fluent English, foreign affairs impinge marginally, if at all.[42]

In the area of foreign policy, therefore, there was little identifiable public opinion that policy makers were compelled to respect, though this did not prevent government spokesmen "pleading the severity of the public pressure" on occasion when it served their negotiating purposes.[43] As long as the world price of copper continued to rise and the costs in terms of deferred development were not excessive, Lusaka's commitment to the liberation of Southern Africa remained broadly acceptable and any incipient dissent politically manageable. At the same time, the absence of significant societal constraints and the low level of political institutionalization meant that the personal belief systems and psychological traits of the Zambian leadership assumed greater salience in the decisional process.

ZAMBIAN DECISION MAKERS

The fifteen ministers who, along with President Kaunda, constituted the Zambian cabinet throughout 1965–66 (Table 6) differed considerably in the domestic constituencies they represented, the political socialization they had experienced, and the influence they

Table 6
Zambian Decision Makers: Cabinet Ministers, 1965–66

Cabinet Members (by seniority)	Cabinet Ministry	UNIP Central Committee	Home Province	Age (Dec. 1965), Profession, Education
1 Kenneth D. Kaunda	President	National president	Northern	41 teacher, parents from Malawi
2 Reuben C. Kamanga	Vice-President	Deputy national president	Eastern	36 businessman, UNIP Cairo repres., 1960–62
3 Simon M. Kapwepwe	Foreign Affairs	National treasurer	Northern	43 teacher, studied in India, 1951–55, leader of the Bemba
4 Mainza M. Chona	Home Affairs	National secretary	Southern	35 first Zambian lawyer 1958, Gray's Inn, London
5 Arthur N.L. Wina	*Finance	(Secretary for international affairs)	Western	36 Makerere (BA) & UCLA (MEd.), UNIP repres. in US, 1959–62
6 Dingiswayo Banda	Transport & Works	Director, Youth Brigade	Eastern	40 bookkeeper
7 M. Justin Chimba	*Justice	†Deputy national treasurer	Northern	44 trade unionist, UNIP repres. in Cairo & Dar es Salaam, 1961–64
8 Solomon Kalulu	Lands & Natural Resources	National chairman	Central	41 teacher, studied in Rhodesia & South Africa
9 Peter W. Matoka	Health	–	North-Western	35 civil servant, Fort Hare (BA) 1955 & American Univ., Washington 1964
10 Elijah Mudenda	Agriculture	–	Southern	38 plant breeder, Makerere, Fort Hare, Cambridge (BSc. in Agric., MA)
11 Nalumino Mundia	*Labour & Social Development	†Deputy national treasurer	Western	38 Delhi Univ. (MA) in Commerce, Stanford Univ.
12 John Mwanakatwe	Education	–	Luapula	39 civil servant, first Zambian graduate 1948, Univ. of SA, lawyer 1964

Cabinet Members (by seniority)	Cabinet Ministry	UNIP Central Committee	Home Province	Age (Dec. 1965), Profession, Education
13 Sikota Wina	Local Government & Housing	(Director of publicity)	Western	34 journalist, expelled from Fort Hare
14 A. Grey Zulu	Mines & Cooperatives	†Deputy national chairman	Eastern	41 bookkeeper, manager
15 Lewis M. Changufu	Information & Postal Services	National trustee (transport secretary)	Northern	38 businessman
16 Mubiana Nalilungwe	*Commerce & Industry	†Deputy national chairman	Western	36 teacher, Delhi Univ. (BEd), Bombay Univ. (MA)

*On 18 January 1966 Mundia resigned and was replaced by Chimba who, in turn, was replaced by Dr D.K. Konoso, Zambia's first medical doctor. Similarly, Nalilungwe resigned and A. Wina took over the Commerce and Industry portfolio temporarily in addition to his own.

†In January 1966 Chimba also replaced Mundia as UNIP deputy national treasurer, and Zulu (till then a national trustee) replaced Nalilungwe as deputy national chairman.

possessed with colleagues. On UDI issues, a majority had only limited direct involvement in the intimate day-to-day formulation of policy. Instead, they served essentially, and usefully, as a sounding-board and legitimizing agency for initiatives originating within an inner cabinet of senior ministers. This ad hoc group was eventually institutionalized as the Foreign Affairs Committee of Cabinet, but at this stage its conduct of business was still entirely informal and its composition somewhat ill-defined. Its core membership comprised the president, Foreign Minister Kapwepwe and Finance Minister Wina, with Vice-President Kamanga and Home Affairs Minister Chona also frequent participants. Others, such as Transport Minister Banda, Commerce Minister Mundia, and Mines Minister Zulu, were coopted as circumstances required. Significantly, each of these ministers, with the exception of Wina, was also a UNIP Central Committee member. Thus the ministers whom the president relied upon as his closest advisers were principally the party old guard.

In the course of their deliberations, decision makers are greatly influenced by the *images* they form of the objective environment within which they are constrained to operate. These perceptions of reality are, in turn, subtly shaped by certain psychological predispositions – Brecher's attitudinal prism – which filter the facts on the basis of ideological convictions, societal traditions and idiosyncratic personality traits.[44] Admittedly, not everyone acknowledges the primacy of the psychological factor in the analysis of foreign policy decision making. Bahgat Korany has been particularly sceptical of the adequacy of "simplistic psychologistic orthodoxy," especially as applied to Third World dependent polities. Yet even he insists that he is "not disputing the relevance of leaders' psychological variables in developing countries' politics." Moreover, he concedes that whereas normally "systemic variables are likely to have greater influence than psychological ones ... the latter would probably rank first when dealing with a foreign policy decision in a crisis situation."[45]

At the onset of the UDI crisis, Kaunda and his cabinet had held office for little more than two years at most[46] and their assumption of responsibility for the conduct of foreign policy extended back barely six months. Nevertheless, they brought to their new appointments rich and varied backgrounds which powerfully conditioned their outlooks on and comprehension of the complexities of international politics and economics. In seeking to delineate the psychological environment that served as a framework for Zambian decision makers, an attempt will be made to identify and assess the significance of, first, the formative influences ministers had experienced in their earlier careers, secondly, previous encounters with crisis situations and, finally, the distinctive imagery that coloured their perceptions of UDI.

Formative Experiences

For most ministers, the dominant influence on their lives had been their absorption in the independence struggle. Their commitment to the liberation cause found expression in fierce opposition to three closely related dimensions of the colonial presence: the denial of self-determination, settler domination as symbolized by federation, and racial oppression. For a majority of the members of the cabinet, full-time service in the nationalist movement as party organizers and freedom fighters had consumed the greater part of their careers, in many instances dating back to the early 1950s.[47] In the course of campaigning, few of them had managed to escape arrest, detention, or rustication on one or more occasions. Admittedly, several of the "new men" had continued in the service of the colonial government as late as 1962, and joined UNIP openly only in the final stages of the struggle. Yet even they had long been imbued with a fervent nationalism that could be traced back to their student days.

Of the diverse manifestations of colonial rule in Northern Rhodesia, the most pervasive and pernicious as well as the most searing in its impact on the nationalist psyche, was the entrenched racialism.

Trains carried "native coaches"; access to cafés was forbidden to all Africans, for whom shopping in the towns meant queuing at "hatches" or "pigeon-holes" where they were liable to be addressed abusively; and there was total racial discrimination in employment by the big mining companies and other commercial and industrial undertakings. Post offices and banks had separate entrances for "natives"; medical and educational services were completely segregated and those available to Africans were minimally financed, equipped and staffed.[48]

In addition to sharing in the daily indignities routinely inflicted on ordinary Africans, nationalist leaders were frequently the victims of unusually vicious racial harassment, if only because increasingly they chose to challenge the iniquities of the colour bar. Moreover, the more educated the African, the greater the supposed threat he posed to white privilege and pride, and the more hurtful the humiliations heaped upon him. The first Zambian graduates to return home typically found themselves denied opportunities for employment or advancement appropriate to their qualifications.[49]

The colonial regime in Northern Rhodesia, reflecting the prejudices of the country's white settler minority, had been notorious in stifling educational opportunities for Africans. It is scarcely surprising, therefore, that the formal academic attainments of the first generation of nationalist politicians should in most cases have been modest in comparison with their counterparts in other former British colonies on the continent. However, there was one positive, unintended consequence of this scandalous legacy; it helped to forge a bond of unity among Zambia's future leaders. Since Munali was the country's first and, for many years, sole African secondary school, all but four members of the cabinet had studied there, in many cases at the same time, and several had subsequently taught there. For Kaunda, who had attended Munali in its early years when it still provided only two years of post-primary instruction, the impact on his outlook was profound. Whereas previously his horizon had been limited to his home village, now "Northern Rhodesia began to make sense to me."[50]

Foreign travel also proved a stimulus to nationalism. Only three members of the cabinet appear not to have had any significant pre-independence exposure to the outside world. In 1957 Kaunda spent seven months in Britain under Labour party sponsorship, and the following year five months in India, while four ministers had served abroad as UNIP representatives in Dar es Salaam, Cairo, London, and Los Angeles. Moreover, a majority had pursued part of their education elsewhere in Africa or overseas. Five had studied in South Africa, three had journeyed to India, and another three to the United States. Uganda and Britain each received two and Rhodesia one. None attended any Soviet bloc institution.

In preparation for independence and with a view to enhancing UNIP's image internationally and domestically with the white electorate, the party leadership had made a conscious effort to recruit a number of parliamentary candidates from the ranks of the incipient Zambian intelligentsia. This enabled Kaunda to construct a cabinet in which seven of its sixteen members possessed university degrees or equivalent qualifications. Among these were Zambia's first African graduate, first lawyer, first agricultural scientist, and (later with the appointment of Dr Konoso) first doctor.

The carefully contrived alliance between veteran party stalwarts and educated newcomers was never easy to sustain, especially as the distinctions in terms of records of service to the party and academic achievements corresponded to some extent with nascent sectional rivalries. Inevitably, those who had borne the brunt of the battle, and in the course of it perhaps sacrificed educational opportunities others had seized, resented seeing recent arrivals moving swiftly and confidently into the seats of power. Thus were sown the seeds of a conflict which subsequently escalated out of control. Nevertheless, at the time of the UDI crisis, and in no small measure because of it, internal divisions among ministers proved manageable – despite one brief, portentous cabinet crisis in late January 1966.[51] Similarly, confronted with the external threat, cabinet members appear to have consciously sought to minimize their ideological differences which, in any case, were largely rhetorical. The only significant divergence in approach to emerge, and this was only a difference in emphasis, was that between those ministers who were temperamentally disposed to urge caution in responding to the challenge of UDI (the nationalists) and those who were more impatient to join in the liberation struggle as well as less deterred by the costs to Zambia.

Crisis Management

UDI was not the first crisis the fledgling Zambian government had to contend with. In the short period Kaunda and his colleagues had been in office in the months leading up to independence, they had accumulated considerable experience in the art of crisis management and had recorded some impressive triumphs. Many of the lessons learned were put to good use in subsequent encounters, but not all. Zambian decision makers had confidently assumed that the British Labour government (which came into office only days before Zambian independence) could be counted upon to behave more sympathetically than its Conservative predecessor, an assumption that proved overly optimistic.

The protracted independence struggle provided Zambian leaders with their baptism of fire in confrontational politics. Although formally a battle of wits with the British colonial authorities, in practice the real opposition came from the white settlers, in Southern Rhodesia as well as Northern Rhodesia. The realization of the goal of independence had required prior action to dismantle the federation, an even more formidable enterprise. Nevertheless, Zambian nationalists proved ultimately successful in both endeavours. They also emerged from their apprenticeship considerably wiser in the ways of the world. Among policy conclusions reached as a result of their experiences were that:
1 The settler community and especially the Salisbury government

were impervious to pleas of justice, or even appeals to their enlightened self-interest; the only way to budge them from their entrenched positions of power was to bulldoze them.

2 The British government, on the other hand, was open to reason and moral suasion; it was anxious to do the right thing but had to be convinced that this was also in its own interest, or inevitable, or at least that there was no practical alternative.

3 The most effective way to pressure the British government was to appeal over its head to the British people; verbal violence and even a modicum of physical violence – the "cha-cha-cha" campaign of 1961 – could prove highly functional since they tended to cause the British acute discomfort.[52]

4 British concessions were not always what they purported to be. Even following a successful conclusion to negotiations, it was still necessary to watch the British like hawks as they were past masters at weaseling out of apparently unambiguous undertakings.

The tough bargaining stance Lusaka adopted in its collision with London over the thorny issue of the British South African Company's mineral rights claims confirmed Zambian instincts concerning the merits of standing firm on vital matters of principle – provided one's position was legally and morally unassailable, as it was in this case. Also, by offering the company a token £2 million as "a show of goodwill" (instead of the £50 million it initially insisted upon), and simultaneously mounting a skilful public relations campaign overseas, Zambia avoided appearing totally intransigent, an important consideration for a country anxious not to impair its reputation with international investors. In the end, in a dramatic last-minute encounter, the company capitulated completely three hours before the midnight proclamation of Zambian independence.[53]

Although Zambian experience suggested that an uncompromising pursuit of principle was a rewarding negotiating technique, the government was not wedded to a single immutable formula to be applied inflexibly in all circumstances. This was apparent from its radically different responses to two major domestic challenges to its authority. The first was an armed uprising by the fanatical followers of a remarkable prophetess, Alice Lenshina, who headed a puritanical Christian separatist sect known as the Lumpa Church. The disturbances were particularly embarrassing to Kaunda, not only because they erupted three months before independence, but also because they were centred on his home district of Chinsali and involved relatives of his on both sides of the conflict. Nevertheless the government reacted, reluctantly but decisively, by meeting

37 Crisis Setting

force with force. The official count of casualties totalled 710 killed and 401 wounded.[54]

By way of contrast, the secessionist threat in Barotseland, a feudal backwater strategically situated on Zambia's western border, was defused with immense skill and delicacy, and in a spirit of conciliation. The issue arose because Barotse traditionalists were keenly sensitive to any infringement of the Protectorate's special privileges and prerogatives enshrined in a 1900 treaty with Queen Victoria. Lusaka, on the other hand, was equally determined that the territory should be fully integrated into Zambia. This Kaunda succeeded in achieving by patient coaxing, with only a judicious measure of gentle coercion, over a considerable number of years. A similar fine sense of touch and timing was evident in the manner Kaunda managed to contain the potentially explosive issue of conflicting sectional claims for cabinet preferment and regional resource allocation.

Zambian decision makers had, over a comparatively short period of time, acquired a not inconsiderable measure of experience in coping successfully with difficult crisis situations. But nothing they had encountered in the past fully prepared them for the demands UDI was to impose on them.

BELIEF SYSTEMS

In the personalized political system prevailing in Zambia at the time, the belief systems of the principal players loomed large as crucial inputs into the decisional process. If anything, their potency was even greater as determinants of foreign policy outcomes than with respect to domestic decisions. A combination of experiential and personality filters contributed to colouring the images which Zambian decision makers held of reality, among them their childhood upbringing and encounters with racism, their trials and tribulations in acquiring an education and earning a livelihood, their tolerance thresholds and predilections for risk-taking, and (of special relevance for this study) their capacities to cope with stress. In no case were such idiosyncratic influences more evident than in the belief system of President Kaunda.[55]

Kenneth David Kaunda

Few national leaders have demonstrated as much moral sensitivity and human compassion as Kaunda, and even fewer who have done so have survived long in office.[56] At the same time, his homilies on the simple virtues and his public displays of weeping were commonly greeted in elite circles with cynicism or dismissed as emotionalism, if not weakness. Certainly, the intensity of Kaunda's Christian faith and his uninhibited profession of it were particularly difficult for the secular Western mind to comprehend. Yet, as Richard Hall has asserted, "Only by constant reference to the way in which religion dominates him can Kaunda's actions be fully understood."[57] Admittedly, Kaunda would be the first to deny that he found it any easier than other mortals to comply fully with the demanding dictates of his conscience, or that he always succeeded. Nevertheless, even as irreverent and redoubtable a critic as René Dumont has testified that "I have met, in my long life, only one head of state who truly tries to live as a Christian ... President Kaunda."[58]

Kaunda was the youngest son of a remarkable Malawian evangelist who had pioneered in northern Zambia as a Presbyterian missionary during the early decades of the century. The religious convictions Kenneth inherited from his parents and subsequently ingested as his own had profound implications for his foreign policy perceptions and prescriptions as president. Morality, he insisted, rather than power provided the only justifiable motivation for political action. Moreover, he viewed individuals and issues in stark terms of good or evil, and foreign policy behaviour as right or wrong. "To us, and to the world," he reassured nervous Zambians, following a dramatic escalation in UDI threat perceptions, "right is on our side ... In any struggle which may come, it is an added strength to know that we are in the right ... Whatever the future may hold, I have no doubt that with God's help we will triumph, right will triumph."[59]

Nothing aroused Kaunda's sense of moral outrage as keenly as the obscenity of racism. His special mission in life, as he saw it, was to eradicate this scourge from the subcontinent, and proclaim the innate and equal worth of every human being.[60]

For Kaunda, the Rhodesian rebellion represented an intolerable personal affront to his most cherished beliefs. The Salisbury regime was not merely illegal, colonialist, oppressive, and exploitative. More fundamentally, it embodied a satanic racialist ideology, which it remained resolutely committed to perpetuate and further entrench. Similarly, Ian Smith as the architect of UDI was conceived as the anti-Christ. What compounded the evil was that Rhodesia also held an economic stranglehold on Zambia.

Kaunda's commitment to non-racialism was not always as passionate at it later became. The turning point appears to have been his sojourn in Britain in 1957 which provided him with a refreshing perspective on white society outside a colonial context. It also introduced him to a number of Labour party leaders, with many of whom he was subsequently to have official dealings in the course of the UDI crisis.[61] Unfortunately, personal friendships forged in the 1950s proved an uncertain basis on which to build sound intergovernmental collaboration in the 1960s. Their cordiality misled Kaunda into placing undue trust in the British government's declared intentions and especially in Harold Wilson's private assurances. As a consequence, he ended up feeling cruelly deceived as well as deeply humiliated. Those ministers who all along had considered him overly deferential to the British now appeared completely vindicated.[62] Nor was this the only occasion on which Kaunda's instinctive loyalty to associates and abiding faith in the inherent goodness of human nature were to cause him acute distress. Colleagues in cabinet and leaders of other African nations were among those who let him down.

A further corollary to Kaunda's Christian humanism was his early conversion to non-violence. On this issue his convictions were powerfully reinforced, even prior to his visits to India, by the preachings of Mahatma Gandhi on the virtues of passive resistance.[63] Throughout Zambia's liberation struggle, Kaunda managed to adhere to his principles and even carry most of the UNIP with him. This restraint was all the more remarkable in view of the provocation of his opponents and the pressures of the more impatient members of his party. However, as he was later compelled to concede, peaceful protest was a viable strategy only if "the people in power have a conscience." When, as in Rhodesia, the "oppressed people cannot touch the hearts of those in power," force offered "the only solution."[64]

Having once reconciled himself to the necessity of military intervention in Rhodesia, Kaunda quickly became its most vigorous and vocal proponent, though he was adamant that only the British could undertake it safely. Here again, his consistent concerns were, first, to minimize the risks of an actual armed clash and, secondly, to avoid any possibility of a racial (or ideological) conflagration erupting, as this would prejudice any prospects of a non-racial Zimbabwe emerging from the ashes and even undermine efforts to maintain a culture of non-racialism in Zambia.[65]

Kaunda admits to having "talked, argued and agonized over this matter of violence" for years before satisfactorily resolving in his own mind the tension between his continuing preference for non-violence and his commitment to justice in Southern Africa. The former he regarded as "the most valuable way of fighting unjust systems," while the latter realistically could only be realized through an armed struggle.[66] Yet conceptual contradictions – of which there were many – typically did not pose as great an intellectual problem for Kaunda as they would have for most Western political leaders, a situation he attributed to "African psychology." In a revealing passage, Kaunda wrote:

... there is a distinctively African way ... of problem-solving and indeed of thinking ... The Westerner has a problem-solving mind whilst the African has a situation-experiencing mind ... Africans ... do not recognize any conceptual cleavage between the natural and the supernatural. They experience a situation rather than face a problem. By this I mean they allow both rational and non-rational elements to make an impact upon them, and any action they may take could be described more as a response of the total personality to the situation than the result of some mental exercise. I think too that the African can hold contradictory ideas in fruitful tension within his mind without any sense of incongruity ... The African mind does not find it easy to think in terms of Either-Or. It is open to influences which make Both-And seem desirable.[67]

This testimony provides important confirmation of the salience of psychological variables in African decision making as well as underscoring the complexities involved in analysing it.

Simon Mwanza Kapwepwe

Foreign Minister Simon Kapwepwe was second only to President Kaunda in influence among Zambian decision makers. His stature reflected not simply the undoubted strength of his personality and the pivotal importance of his provincial power base. He also came to symbolize an alternative, more dynamic projection of the Zambian presence on the world stage. In seeking to assess his distinctive contribution to UDI debates and decisions, it is instructive to compare his operational code of conduct with Kaunda's. At the same time, there is danger in exaggerating the differences, as these were often more matters of style and language than of genuine substance (Table 7).

Kapwepwe and Kaunda were born in the same district in northern Zambia, were products of the same mission school, and had been close friends and political colleagues since childhood. In one respect, however, the two "twins" differed. Kaunda, because of his Malawian parentage, was not as closely identified with traditional society as Kapwepwe, who was the acknowledged leader of the Bemba-speaking peoples who dominated the northern provinces and the Copperbelt.

Table 7
Kaunda and Kapwepwe: Idiosyncratic Influences

Kenneth D. Kaunda	Simon M. Kapwepwe
more an idealist	more a realist
more a humanist	more a nationalist
more emphasis on non-racialism	more emphasis on black consciousness
more internationalist	more pan-Africanist
more willing to sacrifice for sake of Southern African liberation	more emphasis on "Zambia first"
more faith in British	more distrustful of British
more belief in Commonwealth	more sceptical of Commonwealth
more patient and diplomatic	more impatient and undiplomatic
more optimistic	more pessimistic

No Zambian politician was as misunderstood or as misrepresented abroad as Kapwepwe. The conventional wisdom within diplomatic circles was that he was an extremist, a hardline socialist with dubious Chinese connections and a burning desire to supplant Kaunda as president.[68] He was also portrayed as prone to impulsive and irresponsible actions.[69] Admittedly, his proclivity for indulging in rhetorical overkill, his calculated disregard of diplomatic niceties, and his characteristic impatience contributed to his reputation as a radical. As he explained on one occasion, "Kenneth was brought up with a missionary background. I was brought up with a government station background [his father was the District Commissioner's head messenger]. He is thus sometimes very patient and what I consider to be too slow. I sometimes go too fast. The balance has been very good."[70]

In fact, Kapwepwe was pre-eminently a nationalist, a traditionalist, and a pragmatist in practice, despite his predilection for socialist rhetoric. His primary concern was the material well-being of Zambians in general and his fellow Bemba in particular. Whereas Kaunda's mental horizons had been broadened to the point of embracing all mankind,[71] Kapwepwe continued to adhere to a considerably more restricted perception of the national interest. The liberation of Rhodesia, which was so central to Kaunda's concerns, was for Kapwepwe first and foremost the responsibility of the reluctant British colonial authorities and the oppressed Zimbabweans, whose apparent passivity he openly deprecated. Certainly, as an unrepentant proponent of a "Zambia first" game plan, he was loath to call upon Zambians to undertake sacrifices for the sake of "useless" sanctions. Rather, he sought – without any great optimism – to enlist the support of the international community in sharing the burdens which frontline states were fated to bear. For the same reason, he also welcomed the prospect (which he never rated very high) of an army of the Organization of African Unity (OAU) stationed on Zambian soil, as one way of committing the organization to more meaningful participation in the struggle than merely the periodic routine adoption of fiery resolutions.[72]

Both leaders remained proudly African. In this, there was no inherent contradiction with their non-racial convictions, though the balance of emphasis each accorded the two concepts differed somewhat. Publicly, Kaunda appeared rather more concerned to promote a non-racial society, while Kapwepwe placed greater stress on stimulating black consciousness, notably by undertaking an ideological crusade to revive African culture, which he considered a pre-condition for genuine independence. He was also emotionally highly responsive to appeals to pan-African solidarity. At the same time, whereas Kaunda was temperamentally disposed to trust the loyalty of whites in Zambia in the absence of contrary evidence, Kapwepwe's instinctive reaction was to regard them as likely security risks. "Almost every European in Zambia," he warned his OAU colleagues, "with the exception of perhaps a few, have shown, though not openly, that [their attitude to UDI] is a question of kith and kin. This will mean sabotage in our country because these Europeans will be working as agents of the other side of the [Zambezi] river."[73]

Similar sentiments also partially explain Kapwepwe's ingrained distrust of the British. Consequently, he was quicker than Kaunda in detecting Wilson's deviousness.[74] His suspicions found further expression in his marked lack of enthusiasm for the Commonwealth.[75]

Despite the undoubted differences in emphasis that emerged between the two most powerful Zambian decision makers with respect to their crisis perceptions and policy prescriptions, Kapwepwe remained a loyal and valued member of Kaunda's team. Any presidential ambitions he may have harboured earlier he appears to have kept firmly in check throughout the initial phases of the UDI crisis. Only later did they resurface and precipitate an open breach with UNIP in 1971. He died in 1980.

Arthur Nutuluti Lubinda Wina

If Simon Kapwepwe was unjustly regarded as the rogue elephant in the Zambian political system, Arthur Wina provided an assurance of sanity and stability in government. Yet paradoxically the two men, despite their considerable ideological differences and sharp political rivalry, shared a similar nationalist perspective which accorded precedence to Zambia's developmental needs over the pursuit of liberationist goals.

Among Zambian cabinet ministers, Wina could claim both the most renowned customary credentials and the most impressive academic qualifications. He was the son of a distinguished Lozi *Ngambela* (prime minister) of Barotseland as well as a graduate of Makerere College and the University of California in Los Angeles.[76] His unique background as a traditionalist and a modernist enabled him to play a leading role in dragging Barotseland into the twentieth century, securing a foothold there for UNIP, and progressively integrating the province into the national structure. At the same time, he was as fiercely protective of Lozi interests, whenever they appeared threatened, as Kapwepwe was of the Bemba.

Despite his roots, Wina never managed to build a firm personal power base in the country or even, ultimately, in his home province. Alone among senior ministers he held no high party office and had served no period of imprisonment. When he sought election in 1967 as UNIP treasurer, he met defeat. He suffered further humiliation in the parliamentary elections the following year when he lost his seat. Accordingly, he retired into the world of corporate boardrooms without, however, completely shedding his political ambitions. He returned to active politics in 1991 and, upon election to Parliament, was appointed minister of education.

The influence that Wina undoubtedly exercised as a member of the inner circle of Zambian decision makers rested less on his uncertain status within the party and in the country than on his conspicuous competence, which inspired genuine respect in both government and business circles. His most notable triumph was his brilliant brinkmanship in masterminding the takeover of the British South Africa Company's mineral royalty claims without jeopardizing Zambia's international financial standing at birth. Also, as minister of finance for the first four years of independence, he was the principal architect of the country's remarkable economic stability, despite the strains of UDI. As such, he provided an indispensable input into decisions on critical issues of economic policy.

Other Ministers

None of the other members of the cabinet wielded influence on decisions related to UDI comparable to that of Kapwepwe or Wina, let alone Kaunda. This is not to suggest that a number were not significant players at particular times and on particular issues. Politically or ministerially, it might not have been possible or wise to ignore their views. On policy issues, some were instinctively more nationalist in outlook, while others were temperamentally more militant in their opposition to racism in Rhodesia, but none evinced a well-developed belief system. The most prominent was Reuben Kamanga. As one of the original freedom fighters, Eastern Province UNIP leader, and vice-president of the party and the country, he could claim the right to be consulted, and he frequently was. However, his political judgment and private life became causes of increasing embarrassment. Eventually, in January 1966, the president felt compelled to banish him to the United Nations, an order he successfully defied, allegedly by threatening public disorder in the Eastern Province. On foreign policy strategies, Kamanga was not noted for having strong views, beyond a longstanding antipathy to Rhodesia.[77] The same could be said of Mainza Chona, a Southern Province Tonga who, as minister of home affairs, had the delicate task of preserving domestic racial peace. As the country's first black lawyer, he was respected for his legal expertise, but otherwise he had a reputation as an amiable lightweight.

PART TWO
Crisis Decision Flow

III Pre-Crisis Contingency Planning I – Initial Response: 26 April–6 August 1965

Although UDI had long been perceived as a distinct possibility and some contingency planning for that eventuality was initiated shortly after independence, it was not until April 1965 that the Zambian government was forced to face up to the full horror of a settler rebellion in Rhodesia and its implications for Zambia's physical security, racial harmony, and economic survival. Accordingly, the pace of planning was sharply accelerated and the first hard decisions on competing government priorities hammered out.

The pre-crisis period, spanning the six months leading up to UDI, comprised two fairly distinct phases. The first, from April to August, witnessed the beginnings of serious contingency planning to counter the growing threat of Rhodesian economic aggression. The second phase, covering the final three months of political jockeying before Ian Smith took the plunge, found Zambia searching rather desperately for means of survival in a rapidly deteriorating situation which was now beyond the control of even London and Salisbury. By this time, UDI was accepted in Lusaka as both inevitable and imminent. Zambia was also only too well aware that fate had cast it in the unenviable role of economic battlefield in the trial of strength between the principal antagonists. "The one thing that stands out," President Kaunda commented in May 1965, "is that Smith intends to make Zambia pay for any actions by the British government and the rest of the world."[1]

Two related events in April 1965 triggered the sudden and conspicuous increase in threat perceived by Zambian decision makers, and thus signalled the onset of the pre-crisis period. The first was the campaign for the 7 May "general" elections in Rhodesia. In suddenly appealing to the polls, Smith sought (and secured) a decisive mandate from his white electorate to seize independence, illegally if necessary. The campaign also provided an opportunity for the governing Rhodesian Front party to exploit settler prejudices by abusing Rhodesia's northern neighbour. As election day approached and the level of rhetoric escalated, Zambians found themselves increasingly the target of a barrage of threats and provocations as well as ritual accusations of having succumbed to "communistic infiltration." One Rhodesian minister even promised to bury Zambia. "The battle for civilization in Africa," he declared, "is being fought on the ... frontier with Zambia."[2]

A second and more specific challenge was the publication on 26 April of Salisbury's formal reply to London's stern warning, at the time of Zambia's independence celebrations, on the dire consequences of illegal action. In response to Harold Wilson's sombre forecast that a UDI would "inflict disastrous economic damage" on Rhodesia, and the equally pessimistic prognostications of the country's business and farming communities,[3] Smith calmly assured Rhodesians that, "in the long run, they had nothing to lose but all to gain" from breaking the residual colonial chains binding them to Britain. As for the threatened economic sanctions, only "concerted action by all the trading nations of the world" could compel Rhodesia to "capitulate to the demands of the African extremists," a situation he predicted "history has shown ... will not prove successful." To begin with, "countries to the north would have to take into account the crippling effect on their own economies" that collaboration with international sanctions would entail. Moreover, Smith warned ominously,

If, through British government action, the Rhodesian economy was to suffer, even for a short time, an inevitable first step would be the necessity for Rhodesia to consider the repatriation of foreign workers and their families to Zambia and Malawi, in order to protect its indigenous labour force ... The consequences to the countries concerned would be grave indeed and the responsibility would be with Britain alone.[4]

This was not the first indication that Salisbury intended to hold Zambia (and its copper) hostage to ensure Rhodesian immunity from economic sanctions. In August 1964 Kaunda had announced that he possessed a secret document confirming the existence of a Rhodesian-Portuguese plot to strangle Zambia economically in the event of UDI.⁵ Then, in January 1965 in London, on the occasion of Winston Churchill's funeral, Smith had bluntly warned Wilson and others, including Canadian Prime Minister Lester Pearson, that "retaliation" against Zambia might prove a regrettable necessity. Nevertheless, on both occasions Kaunda tended, at least publicly, to dismiss the threats as certain to harm Rhodesia more than Zambia. "I am not worried," he declared in February. "I don't think anyone from Rhodesia would be mad enough" to interfere with the common services, especially Kariba power. In any case "we are fully prepared for any eventuality."⁶ Although this public projection of confidence obscured the considerable concern the president felt privately, Salisbury's decision three months later to publish its white paper, with its explicit threat, shattered any residual complacency and compelled a reassessment of the situation – and a decisional response.

DECISION NO. 1: DEFIANCE (C. 27 APRIL 1965)

Smith's belligerence precipitated hurried consultations between Kaunda and his closest colleagues. Within two days,⁷ the president announced, when questioned, his intention to issue a public statement the following week. This took the form of a radio broadcast on 5 May. Kaunda also took advantage of the presence in Lusaka on an official visit of Prime Minister Seretse Khama of neighbouring Bechuanaland to sound him out on the possibility of severing Rhodesia's rail link with South Africa (which went through Bechuanaland) in the event that Salisbury cut its railway to Zambia. After consulting the British, who were still the colonial authority, Seretse Khama dismissed the idea as tantamount to economic suicide.⁸

In deciding to go public, the government broke sharply with past practice, when Zambia had deliberately maintained a low profile in the Rhodesian dispute. This was partly because the conflict was essentially between London and Salisbury. It also reflected a recognition of the very real injury that Rhodesia was in a position to inflict on Zambia, and a reluctance to invite such painful punishment unnecessarily. Moreover, Harold Wilson was anxious that Zambia should not rock the boat while he was engaged in difficult and delicate negotiations to forestall a break; a curious suspicion lingered in London that Kaunda, not Smith, might prove the more unpredictable and irresponsible. With this in mind, Wilson had extracted a firm undertaking from Kaunda in London in January to submit any public statements on the controversy to him in advance for vetting, and not to initiate any contingency measures (as opposed to merely drafting plans) in case Smith concluded that further delay in declaring independence would be disadvantageous. It was an extraordinary commitment which effectively immobilized Zambia.[9]

Coping

The Zambian decision to break silence was reached swiftly and easily. There was no longer any need to probe Smith's intentions; the Salisbury statement was pointedly unambiguous. Nor is there any evidence of a careful canvassing of alternatives or weighing of consequences; a public declaration of defiance was deemed imperative, if only to counter the psychological shock the Rhodesian *démarche* was designed to administer to Zambian public opinion and the threat that this implied for domestic racial harmony. As President Kaunda explained in his 5 May broadcast, for many months Zambia had remained silent on the question of a UDI. However, "recent happenings [in Rhodesia] have left us no choice [but] to speak out."

When the government of a neighbouring country threatens economic strangulation, when it threatens to hold us to ransom for its illegal acts, when it attacks the democratic foundations of the nation we are attempting to build and makes insinuations about the integrity of our cherished democratic institutions; when, I say, we are subjected to threats and abuse, then I must speak for my nation and my government.[10]

The speedy consensus reached among senior decision makers on the need for a forceful response also helps explain why it was apparently not considered necessary to involve the full cabinet, except perhaps to inform its members.

The lapse of a week between the initial decision to counter the Salisbury challenge and the actual broadcast was partly tactical; by postponing a reply until almost the eve of the Rhodesian elections, it was hoped to maximize its impact on opinion both north and south of the Zambezi. However, the delay also reflected uncertainty as to how much of the government's preliminary contingency planning to disclose. On the one hand, an important domestic objective of the exercise was to reassure the population of all races; the Smith white paper had already generated a certain amount of public disquiet, notably on the Copperbelt. This accounts for Kaunda's promise in his 28 April interview to specify "what action we will take for a start to prepare ourselves for any contingency that may arise." On the other hand, the president was understandably reluctant to reveal too many details and thereby present Salisbury with valuable intelligence. "We should not fall into the trap," he warned, "of declaring what we will or will not do at this juncture."[11]

In resolving this dilemma Kaunda relied on the advice of the small group of senior ministers most directly involved, principally Vice-President Reuben Kamanga, Foreign Minister Simon Kapwepwe, and Mines Minister Grey Zulu. For security reasons, a majority of the cabinet had not been fully taken into the president's confidence and apprised of the precautionary measures already initiated. Similarly, expatriate officials, who still dominated the civil service, were excluded from the consultative process, as many of them were suspected of having Rhodesian connections, if not sympathies.[12] The task of preparing the initial draft of the speech was, therefore, delegated to a small team of increasingly influential Zambian civil servants.[13] Then, after revision, it was submitted to the British prime minister for final vetting. In the excitement of the moment, the obligation to obtain Wilson's prior approval was almost overlooked. However on 4 May the proposed statement was rushed to the British high commissioner who, after suggesting one minor addition, cabled the text to London, where it arrived too late for Wilson to check it prior to its broadcast the following evening.

Choice

In the event, Kaunda's radio broadcast detailed only one point: the creation of district reception committees to cope with the expected flood of Zambian deportees from Rhodesia.[14] With respect to the much greater threat to Kariba power and the other jointly owned services, the president confined himself to announcing that the government, in cooperation with "many other countries in Africa and elsewhere," had undertaken "a detailed study of the consequences for Zambia of economic aggression." He added that "much of the travelling to all parts of the world by ministers and officials" since independence had been concerned with "setting up defences against the possibility of economic aggression in the event of UDI ... I can now assure you that, in the event of Rhodesia committing economic aggression, the support Zambia will receive from all over the world will be tremendous." Kaunda then concluded on a rhetorical note: "We in Zambia," he declared defiantly, "are prepared to hold out to the bitter end against unwarranted aggression ... We are attacking no one, but we will not be attacked without retaliation." If the Salisbury government was "labouring under the false impression that, should Britain impose economic sanctions in the case of UDI, there would be two graves, one in Zambia and one in Rhodesia," he promised that there would be but one, and that in Rhodesia – not Zambia, as one of Smith's ministers assured white voters.[15] It was a forthright and courageous declaration of faith that UDI would collapse before Zambia did. Little did Kaunda realize that, although ultimately his optimism would prove justified, throughout much of the 1970s his confident prediction came perilously close to being reversed.

The force of Lusaka's reaction evidently had a salutary effect on Salisbury for, on 14 May, Smith wrote to Kaunda to "clarify" his intentions and, in particular, to acknowledge Rhodesia's international obligations with respect to the common services and to emphasize that, in the event of UDI, he would "take no initiative to involve Zambia to the latter's detriment." On the contrary, he asserted that "any action taken by Rhodesia adversely affecting Zambia's economic interests could conceivably result only from hostile prior action taken by the Zambian government." Admittedly, this did not really change anything except in tone; the threat of retaliation remained implicit. Nevertheless, taken in conjunction with a cabinet reshuffle in Salisbury a week later, it seemed to presage some weakening of Rhodesian resolve.[16] Accordingly, Kaunda privately revised his estimate of the immediacy of UDI; this was now forecast for September or October – after the tobacco crop was sold – rather than June or July. The few months' reprieve thus granted enabled Zambia to gear itself up for the inevitable ordeal. The first contingency planning decision taken concerned the mounting of an emergency airlift.

DECISION NO. 2: COPPER AIRLIFT (C. 25 MAY 1965)

Preliminary consideration of the economic implications for Zambia of a Rhodesian UDI began shortly after independence in October 1964. It quickly became apparent that, in the worst-case scenario – that is, in the event of a complete severance of road and rail links across the Zambezi and a total cut-off of imports of Rhodesian oil, coal, and electric power – the economy of the country would suffer a crippling and perhaps irreparable blow. This alarming prospect prompted further urgent investigations and the search for specific counter-measures. Planning operated within two time frames.

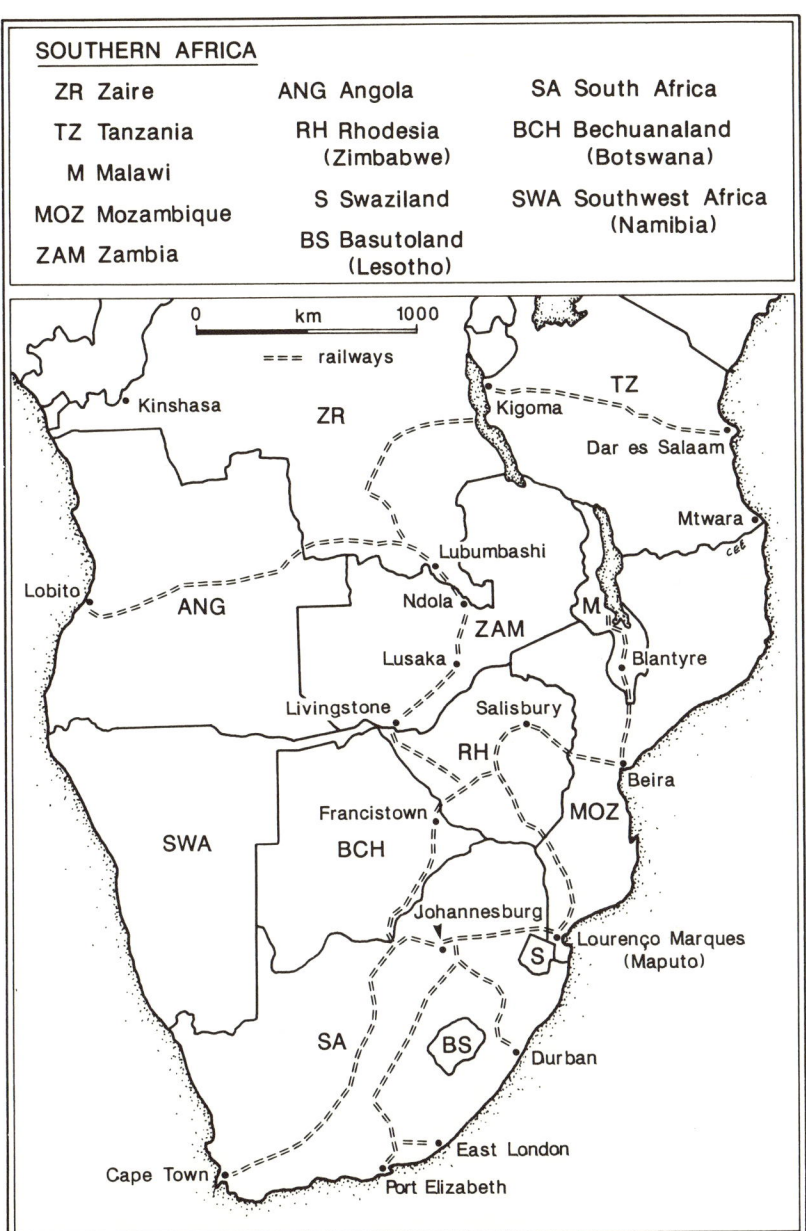

Map 2: Southern Africa, 1965

In the first place, contingency plans were developed to cope with UDI once it occurred; this meant, principally, the identification of alternative trade routes to lessen or eliminate dependence on the southern rail line through Rhodesia. Secondly, discreet precautions were taken in advance of UDI to reduce dependence on Rhodesia, notably through the exploitation of domestic coal deposits (Decision No. 4). This latter course involved greatly accelerating existing government efforts to disengage from Southern Africa, at least with respect to projects that could be implemented within months rather than years; the Tanzania-Zambia railway and the Kafue hydro-electric scheme, for example, did not qualify as contingency measures as their completion schedules stretched over several years.

The various schemes under consideration were both complementary and interdependent; planning in any one sphere – energy, copper production, or transport capacity – depended on progress in the other areas. Thus, if Rhodesia restricted energy imports, copper output would suffer and the pressure to expand the capacity of alternative routes would ease. On the other hand, to the extent that the capacity of available export outlets was limited, copper production would have to be cut back and demands on energy would be correspondingly reduced. This uncertainty made any attempt at realistic contingency planning particularly hazardous; the variables were too numerous, the available data too imprecise, and the post-UDI scenario too problematical. Nevertheless, it was imperative that some attempt should be made to anticipate the consequences, and to cope with them.'[17]

Copper Supply

The first firm decision the Lusaka government reached (on or about 25 May) was to approve an emergency Anglo-American-Canadian airlift to sustain the Zambian economy in the immediate aftermath of UDI (Decision No. 2). This decision had been preceded by four months of careful investigation and consultation.

Initial Zambian calculations suggested that, even if the copper mines were mothballed or production drastically cut back, the available surface routes would be inadequate to cope with the country's minimum essential requirements of coal and other imports, especially during the first few months of the emergency before alternative arrangements became fully operative. Only a Berlin-style airlift would enable Zambia to survive. This distressing conclusion was conveyed to the British prime minister (as well as to President Nyerere of Tanzania) when President Kaunda visited

London in late January 1965. The threat to Britain's supply of copper, with its implications for mass unemployment and the stability of sterling[18] so impressed Wilson that he immediately ordered a thorough study of the feasibility of an airlift. This led to a succession of secret intergovernmental consultations among British and American diplomats and technical experts, culminating in a meeting between the British and American working parties (with a Canadian observer and a Zambian representative) in Washington, 17–20 May, at which a joint Anglo-American paper was painstakingly hammered out for submission to the American president and the British cabinet.[19]

The conclusion of this study was considerably more optimistic – and less realistic – than earlier reports. It argued that even in a worst-case situation, a massive aerial armada operating over a lengthy period at great cost would likely not be necessary; alternative surface routes, in conjunction with energetic measures to limit demands on transport, would probably prove adequate to meet Zambia's critical import needs. Nevertheless, the officials did concede that a supplementary airlift capability might be required in the immediate aftermath of UDI. Accordingly, they recommended that the two governments draft detailed plans for a short-term emergency operation utilizing up to eighty aircraft capable of importing 30,000 tons of oil and other essentials per month and backlifting 17,000 tons of copper – or several times the scale of the operation that eventuated seven months later (Decision No. 24).

The Zambians were not fully convinced of the validity of the premises on which the Washington study was based; in particular, estimates of the capacity of the Benguela Railway through Zaire and Angola to the west coast seemed excessive. At the same time, Lusaka was relieved by the measure of support the country did manage to receive. The recommendation that London and Washington undertake in advance to sustain the Zambian economy, though admittedly at a minimum level of activity, was immensely encouraging. Accordingly, within a week, the Zambian cabinet formally agreed to the mounting of an Anglo-American-Canadian airlift in the event of UDI.

Coping

In seeking to cope with this issue, Zambian decision makers were plagued with immense informational uncertainties. There was simply no way of knowing the scope, intensity, or duration of Rhodesian retaliatory measures. With so many critical variables not susceptible to confident measurement, credible estimates of the shortfall in the capacity of surface routes and, therefore, of the magnitude of the aerial operation required, or even its feasibility, were exceedingly difficult to calculate.

Partly for this reason, the search for options and the data on which to base a judgment was exhaustive. Three broad strategies were available for dealing with the difficulties of marketing copper in the event of Rhodesian restrictions on Zambian access to the southern rail route, or of Zambian efforts to reduce reliance on Rhodesia. These were: production cutbacks, stockpiling, and the development of alternative routes. Each of these possibilities was thoroughly explored. From the first, some reduction in copper production was assumed to be inevitable. Certainly, if Kariba power were interfered with, the lower-grade mines and the Kabwe lead and zinc mine would have to close. In February 1965 Lusaka even attempted to secure the agreement of the two mining groups, the Anglo-American Corporation (AAC) and the Roan Selection Trust (RST), to resort to "highgrading" and pooled production. But RST officials refused to participate in joint contingency planning operations, alleging rather ingenuously that it would violate American antitrust legislation and also involve them in politics, which they considered none of their business.

Another ingenious scheme called for the stockpiling of copper bars in Zambia under American ownership in return for the release of an equal quantity of copper from the US strategic reserve. This, too, encountered formidable legal, political, and technical objections and, after several months of soundings, was ultimately abandoned.[20] It would still have been open to Zambia to have stockpiled copper on its own, but to do so would have deprived both the producer of revenue and the consumer of his copper.

The one remaining possibility, therefore, was the third alternative: to develop new and expanded routes to the sea. Accordingly, explorations concentrated on whether, and when, surface routes might prove adequate to carry whatever copper the country was in a position to produce. It quickly transpired that the crucial variable in determining the *outflow* of copper was the *inward* transport capacity. Even to keep the mines dry on a care and maintenance basis entailed massive imports, principally of coal for the thermal generation of electricity, far in excess of what existing alternative routes could handle. To the extent that limited copper production were attempted, import requirements would rise proportionately. Investigation revealed encouraging possibilities of opening new road and rail outlets and upgrading existing ones. Nevertheless, the most thorough calculations available persuaded British and even American officials by May that, if Zambian copper was to be successfully mined and marketed, provision of a substantial supplementary airlift capacity might be inescapable, at least until alternative routes could be adequately developed.

This conclusion was the result of close and continuous consultation which was essentially externally-oriented. Particularly in the case of the airlift, there was little Zambia could do on its own; it was almost totally dependent on the goodwill and cooperation of London and Washington. The mining corporations too were inevitably involved in the broader aspects of contingency planning, especially AAC which proved far more helpful than RST initially.[21] Within the Zambian government prior to the final cabinet decision, only a handful of key individuals were aware of the network of investigations and negotiations under way. This strict secrecy was partly at the insistence of the British, who were fearful of alarming Salisbury. Formulation of contingency planning policy was effectively in the hands of a small ad hoc cabinet committee set up in February. Initially, it comprised the ministers of Foreign Affairs, of Mines, and of Lands and Natural Resources (the last as UNIP national chairman). Following the president's 5 May broadcast, it was enlarged to include the vice-president and the minister of transport and works. The committee took no specific decisions; rather, its function was to sanction avenues of inquiry, to coordinate and evaluate information, and ultimately to recommend a course of action to the cabinet. Ministers were eventually presented with a formal cabinet paper – the first of many to deal with contingency planning – which they considered on 25 May and adopted virtually without debate.

Choice

The decision to appeal to the West to provide an aerial lifeline to rescue the country and its copper in the aftermath of a UDI generated no controversy at cabinet level. This unanimity was more than a matter of there being no viable short term alternative. Lusaka also had a clear interest in enlisting the widest possible international support in its looming confrontation with Rhodesia; the proposed airlift, therefore, had immense symbolic as well as substantive significance. Moreover, the only political issue of concern to ministers had been satisfactorily resolved at an earlier stage; Zambia was anxious to reconcile the choice of participating countries with the preservation of its image as a non-aligned state.

A purely British operation would have been welcomed as confirming British acceptance of its colonial responsibilities in Rhodesia. However, as early as February, London informed Lusaka that it lacked the necessary airlift capability to undertake the task on its own. Only the Americans and the Russians possessed transport aircraft in the numbers required. However, neither alone was acceptable to Kaunda and a number of his cabinet colleagues.[22] Accordingly, the president authorized exploratory probes to ascertain the possibilities of broader national representation. Effectively, this meant enlisting the Canadians. Ottawa's initial reaction, however, was distinctly unenthusiastic. The Americans too were less than eager, as their air transport fleet was already heavily committed in Vietnam. Moreover, Washington hawks interpreted any suggestion to divert scarce resources elsewhere as a sinister manoeuvre by State Department doves to undermine the war effort. Consequently, it required skilful high-level lobbying with key White House advisers to convince policy makers even to consider American participation in the exercise.

The Zambian request evoked no immediate external response. Lusaka had expected that the Washington meetings would be followed by formal cabinet level agreement between the British and the Americans to sustain the Zambian economy in the event of a crippling Rhodesian blow. This did not happen. London and Washington remained reluctant to accept an open-ended commitment to keep Zambia afloat; there was even a suspicion that, with such a guarantee, Kaunda might be tempted to act "irresponsibly." Instead, investigations into the capacity of alternative routes multiplied and estimates of the gap between essential needs and the available transport in terms of time and tonnages were further refined. In September, with the approach of UDI, the Zambians eventually pressed the three countries for firmer support. The British and Americans reacted by dispatching a thirteen-member technical team to survey the logistical situation on the spot (Decision No. 9).[23] It arrived on 22 October and reported on 12 November, the day after UDI. Five weeks later the airlift became operational (Decision No. 24).

DECISION NO. 3: MILITARY BASE OFFER
(C. 18 JUNE 1965)

Zambia was concerned not only with economic survival in the event of UDI but also with deterring the threatened declaration and ultimately resolving the Rhodesian conflict through the institution of majority rule. Accordingly, it urged Britain repeatedly to exercise its right as the colonial power to intervene militarily. The use of force was first fully debated at the Commonwealth Conference in London, 17–25 June. This was the first summit meeting since Zambian independence and constituted Kaunda's induction into the intricacies of Commonwealth diplomacy. Although the six-point plan for Rhodesia, advanced by President Nkrumah of Ghana on behalf of the African caucus, stopped short of advocating force,[24] a militant minority led by President Nyerere and supported by the "grave pleadings" of President Kaunda condemned the British failure to take pre-emptive military action to forestall a rebellion. When the British protested the difficulties of undertaking a military operation in "a landlocked country five hundred miles from the nearest sea,"[25] Kaunda responded by extending an offer of Zambian territory as a base (Decision No. 3). He argued that the mere stationing of a standby force on the north bank of the Zambezi could serve as a deterrent to rebellion – an assumption the British disputed. London feared that any military initiative, however innocent, could precipitate a UDI.[26]

Coping

The offer of base facilities to the British was very much the personal initiative of the president. The proposal was not in the draft of his 21 June conference statement on Rhodesia discussed with his cabinet prior to his departure for overseas. It was, however, presented to a meeting of the Zambian delegation in London, and readily received its approval; the delegation included several ministers and could, therefore, be considered reasonably representative of cabinet opinion.[27] On the other hand, there was no military member of the delegation, and no evidence of any military input into the decision-making process.

Consultations outside the Zambian team were minimal. The proposal was discussed with Canada's Arnold Smith (soon to be elected Commonwealth secretary general) who was quietly lobbying Wilson on the idea of posting a Commonwealth paratroop battalion in Zambia to deter and, if necessary, crush a Rhodesian rebellion.[28] Whether the issue was also raised in the African caucus is not clear; certainly, Nyerere would have been consulted, and presumably Milton Obote of Uganda and Joseph Murumbi, the Kenyan foreign minister, too.

Choice

Kaunda stipulated only one condition in his offer to the British. This was that, unlike Cyprus, Zambia should retain full sovereignty over any British base on its territory. The form of the offer, however, raised two tactical questions. The first was whether to issue the British with a formal invitation, or to inform Wilson personally that the stationing of British troops in Zambia was a possibility, even though there was little real expectation that he would act on the suggestion. Hence, the principal purpose of the exercise could only be to exert a little additional pressure on him to react to the Rhodesian crisis more energetically. In the event, Kaunda spoke to Wilson privately, rather than present his proposal in the course of his major address to a plenary session of the conference. Secondly, consideration was given to the extent to which the offer should be publicized. The issue was settled when Kaunda took the earliest opportunity to announce his offer publicly in an interview on the BBC the following day.[29]

Wilson's response was predictable; any resort to force, he reiterated, "could plunge Africa into armed conflict going far beyond the borders of Rhodesia."[30] He did, however, keep Kaunda's hopes alive by characteristically hinting to him confidentially that British troops might be ordered into Rhodesia in the event of a breakdown of law and order there, though he neglected to explain that their purpose would be to rescue whites, not protect blacks.[31] Little more was heard of the issue until after UDI, when Kaunda revived his demand for British military intervention in Rhodesia (Decision No. 18).

DECISION NO. 4: COAL MINING
(C. 14 JULY 1965)

Coal was the single most critical variable in Zambia's complex contingency planning equation. Historically, Zambia had depended almost exclusively on inexpensive, high-grade coal railed in from Wankie in Rhodesia. Of the 100,000 tons imported each month, the mines consumed some 60 per cent, and the railways a further 30 per cent, much of it in carrying coal and equipment to the mines. Clearly, any sudden interruption in this coal supply as a result of UDI would have catastrophic consequences for the country. Yet even if some or all the mines were mothballed, this desperate measure would not have eliminated Zambia's dependence on coal. While the need for metallurgical coal would virtually disappear, the simultaneous loss of Kariba electricity would create a huge new demand for coal to fire the standby thermal generators needed to power the mine pumps. In fact, the minimum quantity of coal required to sustain even a "survival economy" amounted to nearly two-thirds the normal level of consumption.[32] An import burden of this magnitude would have been well beyond the capacity of the country's constricted transport routes to bear. In the circumstances, it seemed that the only hope of salvation would lie in locating a local source of coal supply. This was the conclusion to which Zambian decision makers were eventually driven, but only after canvassing every conceivable alternative.

Sizable coal fields had long been known to exist in the Gwembe valley on the north shore of Lake Kariba.[33] However, little interest had been evinced in their exploration as they could not compare with the Wankie field in quality, cost, or accessibility; their low grade and high ash and sulphur content made them difficult and expensive to mine, transport, and use. Nevertheless, two months after independence and with the possibility of UDI very much in mind, the cabinet authorized a modest initial allocation of $364,000 for a "special coal deposits survey." As the Transitional Development Plan explained, "The dangers arising out of the country's complete dependence on imported coal supplies (when coupled with the almost prohibitive cost of alternative sources of supply and the enormous expenditure, in the case of the copper companies, which would be involved in switching to other fuels) need no restatement here."[34]

No immediate action was taken to implement this planning objective as the prospects, based on rather cursory reviews of earlier Geological Survey reports, appeared too unpromising. Zambian energies were concentrated instead on a systematic search for a more auspicious alternative. A satisfactory solution to the problem proved elusive. Numerous ingenious suggestions were explored, but one by one they were discarded as impractical. Interest in domestic coal was eventually revived in April 1965, and further fieldwork by AAC at Nkandabwe authorized.[35] The following month $2 million was inserted into the 1965–66 Capital Fund Estimates for general "coal prospecting" purposes.[36] Finally, in mid-July, the bold decision to embark on a crash open-cast "contingency" mining operation in the "least unpromising" section of the Nkandabwe field was taken (Decision No. 4).[37]

The coal decision was significant in several important respects. In the first place, it constituted a bold attempt to grapple with one of the most intractable contingency planning problems Zambia confronted. Its justification was strategic rather than economic.[38] Secondly, it went beyond mere planning and, for the first time, authorized action in anticipation of UDI rather than as a reaction to it. Thus, it represented the first real breach in Wilson's January ban on "pre-barrier" precautionary measures. Admittedly, during the intervening six months even London had come to realize that the risks of continued inaction outweighed the danger that alerting Salisbury might precipitate UDI.[39] Finally, Nkandabwe was the first contingency decision to cost Zambians money. Other projects, such as the airlift, were expected to attract external financing, or, as in the case of the new Lusaka airport, could be justified on the basis of normal developmental criteria. The coal undertaking, on the other hand, necessitated a redefinition of national priorities and a significant diversion of real resources from economic development to economic defence.[40] It is scarcely surprising, therefore, that the cabinet accorded its final approval only after considerable heart-searching.

Coping

In grappling with this issue, Zambian decision makers suffered from major informational deficiencies. Not only was there uncertainty concerning the timing and consequences of UDI, but reliable estimates of the likely deficits in coal were almost impossible to procure; there were just too many imponderables to contend with. Nevertheless, calculations based on worst-case assumptions were attempted by Zambian officials in January, by the Zambians and the British in March and May, and by the Zambians, British, and Americans later in May.

The selection and analysis of options proved even more time-consuming. The development of Zambia's own coal resources seemed such a costly, protracted, and uncertain enterprise that policy makers searched long and hard for some viable alternative. Two general approaches were explored: reducing the demand for coal, and tapping fresh sources of supply. In terms of consumption, the cutback in copper production was expected to provide the major economy. However, there were limits to the possibilities of savings here; even with the mines on a care and maintenance basis, the heavy pumps had to be maintained in operation to prevent flooding.

An alternative line of inquiry was to search for a substitute for coal which imposed few if any demands on Zambia's already over-extended transportation system. Virtually no idea, however bizarre, escaped the attention of the planners. Two proposals that the mining companies looked into carefully at the request of the government were a charcoal-burning scheme employing an army of forty thousand persons engaged in cutting and burning vast forests[41] and, more promising, the use of local wood as a fuel in place of imported coal, as had been done during wartime and postwar coal shortages.[42] This latter suggestion had the advantage that it could become operational much more quickly. On the other hand, it would have required substantial quantities of diesel fuel, and this would almost certainly have been one of the first casualties of UDI. The same fatal objection applied to the proposals to switch the mine refineries from coal to heavy fuel oil and the railways from steam to diesel,[43] as well as to the imaginative idea of installing aircraft engines on the Copperbelt to generate electricity.[44] There seemed no way of cutting back on coal consumption without creating more problems than it solved. The main effort of the contingency planners, therefore, focused on ways of increasing the supply of coal by stockpiling it in advance of UDI and/or developing alternative sources.

One of the earliest schemes investigated was a proposal to encourage mines to create a strategic reserve of coal on the Copperbelt by importing 100,000 tons a month through the Angolan port of Lobito. Much time and effort were devoted to exploring this possibility but, in the end, the idea had to be abandoned. For one thing, the British were still fearful that an operation on this scale could not be kept secret from the Rhodesians. London conceded that the existence of such a stockpile would serve as a powerful deterrent to rebellion; on the other hand, the process of building it up might just be enough to tip the balance in Salisbury in favour of a UDI.[45] More important, there were doubts in Zambia about the physical capacity of the Benguela Railway to deliver the coal as well as uncertainty concerning Lusaka's legal rights under inherited intergovernmental agreements to divert traffic to this railway without incurring heavy financial penalties.

As appreciation of the formidable problems involved in importing massive quantities of coal from overseas grew, interest shifted to an alternative proposal of openly stockpiling Wankie coal in Livingstone on the Zambian side of Victoria Falls. In May the government appointed a National Coal Supply Commission, headed by the minister of mines and including representatives of the mining companies as the major consumers, to organize the operation. Unfortunately, a genuine railway truck crisis and contrived administration delays by the Rhodesians (who had little incentive to ensure the success of the scheme) combined to compel its abandonment.[46] Not only was the target figure of 350,000 tons of Wankie coal in reserve never realized, but mine stocks actually dropped below the normal minimum of 100,000 tons and, by September, had reached the dangerously low level of 77,000 tons.[47]

In the meantime, one other prospect had been explored: the development of the Songwe-Kiwira coal deposits just across the border in Tanzania. Discussions on this possibility had begun as early as February 1965.[48] First reports on it were encouraging. Moreover, initially the transportation problem appeared manageable. However, production time was estimated at two years – too long to be of much use if, as expected, UDI was only a few months off. Accordingly, the cabinet decided in early May to shelve the scheme[49] and instead take a closer look at local coal sources.

The process of search and evaluation of alternatives was accompanied by fairly continuous consultation with London and Washington. Exchanges on coal took place at three levels, each within the context of a broader consideration of contingency planning as a whole. President Kaunda participated directly through conversations and correspondence with Prime Minister Wilson, notably during visits to London in November 1964 and in January and June 1965. He also forged a close personal relationship with Wayne Fredricks, the US deputy assistant secretary of state for African affairs; the two men conferred at Kaunda's request on at least two occasions, in March in Lusaka and in June in London. Secondly, there were periodic sessions in London (and once in Washington) at which government officials sat down to assess systematically the state of knowledge and planning. Finally, day-to-day contact was maintained through diplomatic missions in Lusaka. Nevertheless, Zambian liaison with the two Western powers on coal was relatively less significant than in the case of the airlift as, in contrast to it, the Nkandabwe project was a commitment which Zambia could largely undertake on its own. On the other hand, coordination of planning with the mining companies, as the principal consumers of coal, assumed greater prominence.

Consultations with the mining groups were confined to a few senior executives and technical experts. These included Sir Ronald Prain, chairman of RST and a resident of Lusaka, and especially Harry Oppenheimer, the Johannesburg-based chairman of AAC of South Africa. The latter had been a party to the clandestine investigations of the possibilities of stockpiling coal imported through Lobito. In April he also readily agreed, despite his interest in the Wankie colliery, to supply a drilling team to prospect for Zambian coal; moreover, he was prepared to finance the search, an offer which Kaunda declined. Relations were less close with RST. It did, however, prepare a technical report on the feasibility of switching its smelters from coal to wood; AAC submitted a similar study on the use of charcoal.[50] Contacts with the mines at the technical level were formalized in May with the establishment of the National Coal Supply Commission with the consulting engineers of the two companies as members. The other major coal customer, Rhodesia Railways, was excluded on principle; it was not consulted, except on the use of the Lobito route and on the Livingstone stockpile, and then only to the extent absolutely necessary. The cabinet as a whole was also only marginally and intermittently involved prior to the final decision. Only the president, members of the ad hoc contingency planning committee of cabinet, and a few officials were kept fully informed of developments.

Security requirements dictated the need to confine detailed knowledge of the contingency planning operation to a narrow circle of policy makers around the president. The political implications of the coal decision, on the other hand, demanded that responsibility for it should be shared as widely as possible. Hence, the necessity to secure full cabinet approval. In the marathon debate that ensued in the special late night session on 14 July, two issues predominated: whether to commit capital funds to the project, and whether to permit AAC to undertake it.

Choice

The natural reluctance of ministers, especially those responsible for social services, to acquiesce easily in a distortion of the nation's established developmental priorities was reinforced by the fact that a majority of ministers appear to have come to the subject inadequately prepared, factually and psychologically, to face up to the harsh realities behind the threat that UDI posed for the country. The basic explanation for this was again the excessive secrecy that surrounded the exercise. For example, supporting documentation was not circulated in advance as was normal, but was given to ministers at the actual meeting. The significance of these two circumstances has been well expressed by Robert Good, the American ambassador at the time:

The hard fact was that all contingency planning projects took resources away from Zambia's new development plan. Not surprisingly each minister resisted cuts in his department ... Contingency planning suffered too from the secrecy surrounding it ... The result was not only that things were left undone but that officials and political leaders were often never informed as to why these preparations were important.[51]

Nevertheless, the case for a secure supply of coal proved unanswerable. At one stage in the debate, a compromise that would have closed Nkandabwe down once a 300,000 ton reserve of coal had been accumulated was advanced,[52] but in the end the original proposal received approval.[53] It was also agreed that the Anglo-American Corporation should be asked to undertake the task, despite its ownership of the Wankie mine. Qualms concerning a possible conflict of interest were overcome when ministers were assured that the award of a drilling contract did not commit the government to subsequently granting AAC the right to mine any coal discovered, though this in fact was what happened. Opposition also appears to have been eased by AAC's offer to share the cost of the undertaking, though the cabinet was apparently unwilling to allow it to assume the full cost.[54]

Once the decision to proceed was reached, it was carried out with "impressive speed."[55] By June 1966 open-cast mining at Nkandabwe was in full production, and a higher quality, longer-life deposit discovered nearby at Maamba was in process of development. In the circumstances, Rhodesia decided not to interfere with the supply of Wankie coal; imports continued, though on a diminishing scale, up to and after UDI.

IV Pre-Crisis Contingency Planning II – Securing the Lifelines to the Sea: 7 August–4 November 1965

Throughout August UDI fever mounted steadily. Salisbury's blatantly provocative announcement in July of the appointment of a separate diplomatic representative to Lisbon in open defiance of British constitutional authority led to speculation that Ian Smith might pursue a strategy of "creeping independence."[1] However, his tough talk at the Rhodesian Front Congress on 7 August made it abundantly clear that he was still intent on snatching independence frontally rather than nibbling at it piecemeal. Barring a last-minute British sellout, UDI was now only a matter of time. Moreover, the prospect that the timing would be earlier rather than later was greatly enhanced when, a few days later, the British publicly promised not to use force to suppress a rebellion – an excess of honesty which relieved Salisbury of the one constraint that might conceivably have deterred it.[2] Any lingering doubts concerning Rhodesian determination to act unilaterally were finally dispelled by Smith's frank confession on 1 September that "we are going to have independence ... in the near future and nothing will stop us." UDI was no longer merely inevitable; it was also "imminent."[3]

Prior to this, the Rhodesian Front cabinet had resolved that "UDI should be taken unless independence were negotiated before the end of the year."[4] Accordingly, it agreed to play out one "final and conclusive" round in the hollow pretence of seeking a peaceful settlement with the British. In the subsequent talks in London, Smith performed with consummate skill, demonstrating once again his mastery of the art of "talking without negotiating." When the charade ended on 8 October, Smith cheerfully declared that UDI was now the logical next step.[5] The point of no return had been reached, though the actual date of independence was delayed a further few weeks to ensure that adequate stocks of essential supplies were on hand – and to run down Zambian inventories, especially of oil, coal, and building supplies.[6]

The Zambian government viewed each fresh lurch towards the precipice by Smith with ever-deepening concern. Salisbury's decision in mid-July to ban UNIP branches in Rhodesia[7] not only constituted the first concrete hostile action directed specifically against Zambia, but also served as clear confirmation that Rhodesian goodwill could not be taken for granted. Subsequently, Rhodesian Intelligence sought to cool passions by systematically feeding false information to the president regarding Salisbury's intentions.[8] Nevertheless, Kaunda was under no illusions concerning the certainty, seriousness, and immediacy of the crisis threatening to engulf the nation. He was also increasingly conscious of the severe time constraints under which he laboured as he scrambled to shore up the shaky defences of his vulnerable political economy. The government could no longer afford, as in the past, to await the results of careful investigations into the full range of policy options. Rather, the time had come to act – both on its own and in concert with other governments in a position to assist economically and logistically.

Zambia's most pressing priority was to secure its lifelines to the sea. Although the government was anxious to lessen dependence on the southern rail route through Rhodesia, and ultimately dispense with it entirely, there was no early prospect of this. Nevertheless, it was essential that Zambia act energetically to reinsure itself against the loss or disruption of its traditional lines of communication southward by developing alternative outlets to east and west coast ports as quickly as possible.

In assessing the range of routes, actual or potential, that might be utilized, Lusaka was initially as much concerned with security as with availability. In order of preference, Tanzania ranked highest as an outlet and Rhodesia lowest, with other neighbouring states falling somewhere in between. In practice, this basis of choice was not easy to sustain, as it was found that the political acceptability and reliability of routes generally bore an inverse relationship to their accessibility and capacity. Thus, although the northeast route through Tanzania alone posed no political problems, it was also at the time the least developed alternative. Admittedly, Lusaka was vigorously promoting the cherished UNIP dream of a Tanzania-

Zambia railway.[9] Yet this could offer a solution only in the long term. In the short run and in response to the immediate crisis demands, the country had to rely on expanding the capacity of existing road and rail facilities.

A number of these alternatives bypassed Rhodesia. However, none was entirely problem-free. Access was still dependent on the goodwill of neighbours – Banda's Malawi, Tshombe's Zaire, and Salazar's Angola and Mozambique – and in each case relations were at best strained. Moreover, collectively they could not hope within the immediate future to handle more than a fraction of Zambia's import and export traffic. Consequently, however much the country might strive to dispense entirely with the southern rail route, it stood condemned for the foreseeable future to a continued, if diminishing, dependence on Rhodesia for access to the sea. In fact, Lusaka's immediate preoccupation was to preserve to the full its existing transit rights based on international conventions and joint ownership of Rhodesia Railways in the face of a determined drive by Salisbury to break up the unified rail system.

DECISION NO. 5: UNIFIED RHODESIA RAILWAYS (10 AUGUST 1965)

In the course of the negotiations for the dissolution of the Federation of Rhodesia and Nyasaland in 1963, the Zambian representatives (who at that stage served merely as advisers to the Northern Rhodesian colonial authorities) acquiesced in a measure of continuing economic integration as the price for securing the political separation of the two Rhodesias.[10] In particular, common service organizations, jointly responsible to Lusaka and Salisbury, were established in three separate spheres: power, airways, and railways. In the case of Rhodesia Railways, provision was made for a Higher Authority for Railways at ministerial level to formulate broad policy directives and for a Board of Management comprising senior officials of the two governments to exercise more direct supervision.[11] Such a set-up would have been difficult enough to operate in the best of circumstances because of the sharply divergent economic interests of the partners; in the political and racial climate of Central Africa in the mid-1960s it became virtually impossible. In the contest of wills across the Zambezi, the jointly owned railway served as a lightning rod for a series of contentious issues, some only indirectly related to railway administration. As a result, the attempt at joint decision making ultimately proved totally unworkable. Accordingly in 1967, after much bitter controversy, the pretence of unification was finally abandoned in all but name. Legally, Rhodesia Railways lives on. More than a quarter of a century later, there is still no agreement on a division of its assets.

The first suggestion for a breakup of the railway came from Salisbury in April 1965 during the heady days leading up to the Rhodesian "independence" election. The Rhodesian minister of transport wrote confidentially to his Zambian opposite number requesting a meeting of the Higher Authority for Railways to consider, among other matters, the question of division. Caught off guard, Lusaka countered with a proposal that the Railways Board should first initiate an expert study to assess the implications of dismantling the joint undertaking.[12] Subsequently, with a view to probing Salisbury's intentions further, President Kaunda warned publicly that any unilateral interference with the railway would render Rhodesia an "international outlaw," while Arthur Wina, the minister of finance, characterized such action as tantamount to a declaration of war. This open challenge elicited from Ian Smith the assurance that Rhodesia would honour her international obligations "as long as Zambia does likewise."[13]

Nothing further was heard of the idea until early August, when the issue was suddenly and forcefully brought into the open. As momentum for a UDI was once again building up in Salisbury, the suspicion was created in Lusaka that a breakup of the railway was planned as a preparatory step to political independence. On 9 August, two days after Smith's fighting speech to his party's annual congress, the Rhodesian deputy chairman of the Railways Board launched a carefully orchestrated campaign designed to precipitate a dissolution.[14] The next day the minister of transport joined in by calling for an "immediate meeting" of the Higher Authority to discuss "all aspects of the unitary system."[15] Although both spokesmen hinted darkly at the desirability of division, they sought to achieve their objective more by capitalizing on specific grievances as a means of discrediting the existing system than by pressing for dissolution directly.

Two alleged injustices were cited as evidence that the intergovernmental rail agreement was functioning to the detriment of Rhodesian interests. These were the dissatisfaction among certain white railway workers and their families at their continued "enforced transfer" to "hostile" Zambia, and the increased running costs of the northern sector of the line as a result of the provision of inducement pay for whites and of training programs for blacks. Neither complaint had much substance. While many Rhodesian whites undoubtedly had difficulty in adjusting to a non-racial society, the alternative to compulsory transfers was a drastic cutback in pay and employment – as the union leadership soon came to appreciate. Moreover, far from the Zambian sector of the railway being a financial liability to the system, high-rated Zambian traffic was heavily subsidizing Rhodesian traffic, much of which was carried at sub-economic rates entrenched under the 1963 agreement.[16]

Nevertheless, Rhodesia's claims were easily exploitable emotional issues ideally suited to serve as a smoke screen for her true intentions. These were transparently to gain sole control of Zambia's vital rail artery with a view to maintaining a communications stranglehold over the country. From Lusaka's perspective, the whole crisis bore the appearance of being a calculated political move designed to enhance Salisbury's leverage at Zambia's expense. Accordingly, the government declined to play the Rhodesian game, and insisted instead that the intergovernmental agreement be fully respected. The most it was prepared to concede was that any specific issues in dispute should be investigated (Decision No. 5).

Coping

The Zambians were uncertain how to respond to the initial Rhodesian approach in April 1965. According to one observer, they "did not know what to make of it and stalled."[17] The information available to them for rational decision making was inadequate on two important points: on the precise political motivation which inspired the initiative, and on the economic costs involved. With respect to the former, some rather vigorous probing of Rhodesian intentions – employing the technique of public warnings by Kaunda and Wina in May – succeeded in inducing satisfactory assurances that no unilateral action was contemplated, at least not immediately.[18] When the issue was revived in August in conjunction with other ominous developments, however, Zambian leaders were no longer in any doubt concerning Rhodesian strategy or the threat it implied for Zambian security and survival. As *The Economist* explained, "A division at the border would enable Rhodesia to strangle Zambia economically at will, by imposing crippling freight rates, or holding up freight from Zambia. Thus the underlying threat to Zambia is: 'Be good boys or we take your trains away. Be especially good boys should we decide to declare our independence.'"[19]

On the costs of splitting the railway, Lusaka insisted that the board should first commission a team of consultants to undertake a detailed study before intergovernmental discussions were contemplated. This remained the consistent Zambian position: dissolution was a technical matter, to be dealt with by experts and officials, rather than a political question to be debated at ministerial level. When no action was taken to institute an inquiry, the Ministry of Transport embarked on its own departmental assessment. Informal consultations also took place with the Zambian members of the Railways Board[20] as well as with its independent chairman.[21]

At the ministerial level, those most closely involved in the consultative and ultimately the decision-making process were the ministers of transport and finance – the two Zambian members of the Higher Authority – along with the minister of labour (with respect to compulsory transfers).[22] The president was also inevitably kept closely informed, though he maintained a low public profile, apparently deliberately in order to emphasize the Zambian perception of the technical character of the issue. His first public comment during the August crisis was delayed more than two weeks and then came at a press conference in response to a question.[23] Similarly, there is little indication that the minister of foreign affairs or the cabinet collectively were significant participants in the policy process. On the other hand, it appears probable that the cabinet, at its regular weekly meeting on 10 August, was brought up to date on developments, and was accorded an opportunity to comment before routinely ratifying the government's general stand.

Zambian decision makers were faced with four broad options. These were: to accept the inevitable and cooperate in an orderly dismantling of the joint system; to reserve judgment pending clarification of the costs and consequences; to reject a breakup of the railway, but to offer to investigate any specific Rhodesian complaints; or to insist on strict maintenance of the status quo.

In other circumstances, the first option would have held considerable appeal on nationalistic grounds. It was, in fact, the Zambian (and Rhodesian) preference during the federal dissolution debates.[24] It was also the outcome Lusaka came to accept "in principle" on the eve of UDI (without admitting this to the Rhodesians) and in practice a year later.[25] With UDI imminent, it was obvious that the machinery of joint decision making was bound to break down completely. Moreover, contingency planning for the development of alternative routes was more advanced by then. In August 1965, however, Zambia was still obsessed with the awesome consequences of placing the fate of the nation at the mercy of the malevolent men in Salisbury. Even the prospect of compensation, which Zambia might have been entitled to claim under the 1963 railway agreement,[26] offered little comfort. Once the Zambian veto was removed, Rhodesia could quickly recoup any losses by discriminatory increases in freight rates. But the major deterrent to the Zambians indulging their nationalist emotions and abandoning the unified rail system was the virtual absence of repair and maintenance facilities in the country, and the inability to acquire any quickly. Accordingly, the first response was ruled out.

The fourth option was also dismissed as it, too, carried unacceptable risks. Too intransigent a stand could have provoked a unilateral break and much mutual recrimination. Dissolution in such circumstances would have been even less conducive to the safeguarding of Zambian interests than an orderly division by agreement. Similarly, the second alternative was eventually discarded. Although it had been tentatively adopted in April, once the political motivation underlying Rhodesia's strategy was exposed, it was no longer necessary to delay a decision. That left only the third option: to attempt to meet the legitimate demands of the Rhodesians.

Choice

The decision to try as far as possible to make joint operation of the railway workable was a satisficing alternative, as the Rhodesians were not openly calling for dissolution even though this was their clear intent. Accordingly, the Zambian minister of transport wrote to his Rhodesian opposite number formally agreeing to consider the complaint concerning compulsory transfers (and any other grievance). He also indicated a willingness to attend a meeting of the Higher Authority, though only after the Board of Management had completed its current study of the dispute and recommended a considered course of action.[27]

These concessions were insufficient to satisfy Salisbury. Two weeks later the Rhodesian transport minister reiterated his demand for a ministerial meeting "as a matter of urgency." At the same time, he cautioned Zambians "not to underestimate the seriousness" of the situation, and hinted ominously at "unfortunate consequences" if the problem were not resolved soon. His warning was reinforced three days later when Ian Smith rejected any attempt "to continue to force this [unified rail] system to be kept going."[28] Nevertheless, the Zambians refused to be stampeded. A month later, following receipt of the Railways Board's report and recommendations, Lusaka finally agreed to a meeting of the Higher Authority.[29] This eventually opened in Victoria Falls on 8 November. However, the next morning, before the sessions resumed and in the midst of negotiations, the Rhodesian ministerial team was suddenly recalled to Salisbury without explanation.[30] Two days later, UDI was proclaimed.

Although Zambia succeeded in staving off the immediate challenge to its contractual rights to an equal voice in the running of Rhodesia Railways, Lusaka soon recognized that joint control could not survive indefinitely. The only real answer to dependence on the south was to develop adequate alternative outlets. Much thought had already been given to the various possibilities. Yet, despite its limited potential, the first route to be reactivated was the costly and circuitous road-water-rail route through Mpulungu and Kigoma on Lake Tanganyika to Dar es Salaam.

DECISION NO. 6: MODERNIZING MPULUNGU HARBOUR (C. 17 AUGUST 1965)

Zambia's decision to modernize her northern port of Mpulungu at the southern tip of Lake Tanganyika and establish an oil depot there constituted the second occasion – the coal decision being the first – on which the government undertook an insurance-type exercise in advance of UDI. Although the proposal had been under active consideration for some months, the impending rebellion in Rhodesia gave it added urgency and clinched the case in its favour. Initially, the project had been presented as a routine scheme to strengthen communications links with East Africa in keeping with the declared intention of diversifying the country's trade routes.[31] Its real rationale, however, had always been strategic. That Zambia was prepared to invest resources in such an unpromising route through the heart of the continent was a measure both of its determination to develop alternative outlets and its desperation in the face of limited options.[32]

Mpulungu was Zambia's sole international port. Originally built at the behest of Cecil Rhodes as the projected terminus of the Rhodesian section of his Cape-to-Cairo railway,[33] it had long served as a somewhat tenuous link with the other lacustrine states. At this time the shipping connections were infrequent, the flow of trade infinitesimal, the freight rates high, and the port facilities meagre and in a state of disrepair. Although provision for improving Mpulungu harbour was formally written into the Transitional Development Plan as early as December 1964,[34] the proposal received little interest until early February 1965 when President Kaunda suddenly came to regard expansion of the capacity of the port as a matter of considerable importance. As a result, the ad hoc cabinet committee on contingency planning looked into the question and a sum of $170,000 was inserted in the 1965–66 Capital Fund Estimates to provide for the "complete rehabilitation of the harbour and port area."[35] In May a local Kitwe firm of consultants was retained to plan new facilities, and in June a Canadian team, in the course of a comprehensive investigation into the capacities of alternative transportation possibilities, detailed the inadequacies of the port.[36] The depressing tenor of the team's conclusions as well as the gathering storm south of the Zambezi spurred the government into early action to remedy Mpulungu's deficiencies. Accordingly, in mid-August the signal was given to upgrade the harbour and resurface its access road (Decision No. 6). A crash program of improvement was quickly instituted; by mid-1966 the essential facilities to enable the port to handle a vastly increased, but still modest, volume of traffic were in place.

Coping

In planning its transport strategy, the Zambian government undertook an exhaustive survey of every conceivable politically acceptable alternative route, however obscure or improbable. In practice, this meant exploring the network of roads, railways, and waterways in Zaire and Tanzania. In this process of search and evaluation, Lusaka turned for assistance to its own Public Works Department and to local consulting firms, enlisted the cooperation of the mining companies and to some extent the railway, and commissioned a series of transportation studies,[37] all in the interests of procuring hard data on which to base a rational decision. As a result, it was possible to eliminate a number of routes which were clearly unsuitable, or which could not be upgraded in time, or which lacked substantial spare capacity. Although the evidence was often incomplete or conflicting, the government did succeed in accumulating a vast bank of information. This was processed through the cabinet subcommittee which eventually submitted its recommendation to cabinet for final formal approval.

Choice

The initial decision involved not so much a choice between competing claims as agreement on a checklist of alternative routes which were viable or could be rendered viable reasonably quickly. Once this technical task had been completed, wider considerations influenced the outcome.

What is surprising, perhaps, in view of the limited use subsequently made of the Lake Tanganyika route, is the priority the reconstruction of Mpulungu harbour received as compared to other routes with far greater potential. Three factors tipped the scales in its favour. In the first place, apart from Mpulungu itself, the route had considerable spare capacity for the transport of oil, which was of critical concern to contingency planners.[38] The route, therefore, provided a reassuring supplement to the (as yet) untried oil airlift. Secondly, it was the only alternative route requiring no expenditure outside Zambia – an important consideration with nationalist-minded ministers. Finally, the transit territory was politically acceptable. For the president, an outlet to the sea which did not require collaboration with the Portuguese held an obvious appeal. However, as UDI approached and the harsh realities of the logistic nightmare Zambia faced sank home, the government came to realize that it could not pursue all its political objectives simultaneously. As a corollary to its decision to accord primacy to the confrontation with Rhodesia, Zambia was compelled in the interest of survival to suppress some of its ideological inhibitions to cooperation with its other neighbours. Specifically, the price of ensuring access to Angolan and Mozambican ports was a measure of accommodation, however reluctantly conceded, with Kamuzu Banda in Malawi (Decision No. 14), Moise Tshombe in Zaire (Decision No. 11), and, most distasteful of all, the Portuguese colonial authorities (Decision No. 7).

DECISION NO. 7: OVERTURE TO PORTUGAL (C. 7 SEPTEMBER 1965)

The underlying causes of Zambian antipathy to Portugal were the colonial power's reactionary and repressive policies and its close collaboration with other white minority regimes in Southern Africa. Although historically Zambia's contacts with Angola and Mozambique on its western and eastern borders, had never been as close – politically, economically, or culturally – as with Rhodesia and South Africa, Lusaka was equally uncompromising in its commitment to majority rule in all colonial territories and joined eagerly in the general chorus of condemnation of Lisbon's intransigence in the UN, OAU, and other international forums. President Kaunda was particularly vocal in denouncing the "unholy alliance" of Salazar, Smith, and Verwoerd of South Africa, even alleging the existence of a secret pact among them to strangle the Zambian economy.[39] This animosity went beyond mere rhetoric; beginning even before independence, Zambia signalled its displeasure in actions. Unlike Malawi, it rejected a Portuguese request to open a consulate in the country, yet permitted nationalist movements from neighbouring Portuguese territories to establish branch offices there – though not, at this stage, guerilla camps.[40] In May 1965 the government offered hospitality to the touring UN Committee of 24 investigating colonial practices in Southern Africa, and the following month hosted a conference in Lusaka of Mozambican revolutionary parties in a vain attempt to fashion a single united liberation movement.[41]

Portugal proved exceedingly sensitive to these persistent pinpricks, and reacted to them by vigorously defending its historic mission in Africa in public and quietly remonstrating with Zambian spokesmen in private. More important, it instituted stern retaliatory measures, notably by interfering with Zambian rail traffic in transit through Mozambique. Although these disruptions were officially ascribed to "technical" problems, such as a temporary shortage of rolling stock, Lisbon intimated that Zambian acceptance of a Portuguese consul would help to overcome the difficulties. The most blatant act of piracy was the open seizure in February 1965 – in the aftermath of a high-level conference of Portuguese, Rhodesian and South African security chiefs in Salisbury – of a consignment of arms and ammunition destined for the Zambian army.[42] This action was in flagrant violation of the Beira Convention of 1950 which guaranteed freedom of transit for landlocked states.[43] The excuse proffered – that the weapons might find their way into the hands of FRELIMO (Front for the Liberation of Mozambique) guerillas – while superficially plausible, lacked substance. The arms embargo was successfully circumvented by diverting subsequent shipments to Dar es Salaam and sending them on by road or air.[44] Nevertheless, the message Lisbon intended to convey registered in Lusaka: the Portuguese authorities were quite capable of interdicting Zambian transit traffic and certainly willing to do so at any time in pursuit of their own political objectives. This realization had profound implications for Zambian contingency planning for UDI. If Portugal were to join Rhodesia in squeezing Zambia economically, or were even to maintain a benevolent neutrality in favour of the rebel regime, Zambia would stand in double jeopardy.

Right from the outset of the crisis, the Benguela Railway through Angola to the port of Lobito had been identified as the major alternative route to which Zambia would have to turn in the event of UDI. Early in 1965 a team had been quietly dispatched to Lobito to assess the import capacity of the railway,[45] and in March further discussions were held with Benguela Railway officials in London.

Over the next several months, Anglo-American-Zambian contingency planners consistently stressed the vital importance of Benguela to Zambian survival, and urged an approach to the Portuguese to enlist their cooperation. This Kaunda was not yet prepared to contemplate. Resistance to the inevitable continued until August. Then, with the imminence of UDI an increasing certainty, as well as the pessimistic tone of the Hoganson-Bright report concerning the capacity of other routes, Zambia was forced to resign itself to the necessity of seeking assurances from Lisbon concerning access to Lobito (Decision No. 7).

Coping

There was no shortage of information confirming the crucial importance of the Lobito factor in Zambia's contingency equations. This had been highlighted in the successive planning exercises undertaken during the first half of 1965 (Decisions No. 2 and 4). What was still unclear was Lisbon's likely reaction to UDI. Initially, Lusaka was inclined to rationalize its reluctance to appeal to Portugal by arguing that intelligence on this point was irrelevant. Either the Portuguese would support Rhodesian independence in which case they would not come to Zambia's rescue, or they would oppose UDI in which case there would be no rebellion; Ian Smith would scarcely risk a break with Britain without an assurance that his rail link with Beira in Mozambique would be secure. These scenarios assumed – wrongly as it turned out – that Lisbon would be compelled to make a clear choice between Salisbury and Lusaka.

Early indications of Portuguese leanings were not encouraging. Reports circulated in August that Rhodesia had reached "a definite understanding with the Portuguese over limiting the use of the Benguela railway if Zambia turned nasty over a UDI."[46] Moreover, Portugal "warmly welcomed" the appointment of a separate Rhodesian "diplomatic representative" in Lisbon, despite British protestations concerning its impropriety.[47] However, as these signs of sympathy for Salisbury coincided with a revival of UDI fever, the effect was to spur Zambia on to seek a clarification of Portuguese intentions.

The attempt to retrieve the arms seized six months earlier provided Zambia with its first opportunity to test the Portuguese political climate. Accordingly, the government asked the British and a number of other friendly governments to intercede in Lisbon on its behalf. As a result, in mid-August the Portuguese relented and agreed to release the shipment, subject only to a formal assurance that the arms would not be turned over to FRELIMO for use against them.[48] Their decision was no doubt influenced by Zambia's success in beating their embargo. Nevertheless, the outcome, and the satisfactory nature of the subsequent detailed negotiations conducted by the respective diplomatic missions in London, encouraged Lusaka to approach the Portuguese on the more critical issue of access to the Benguela rail route.

Consultations on the advisability of this initiative preceded its formal consideration by several months. Representations were made to the government by the British and American officials involved in Zambian contingency planning, and by the mining companies, who were concerned that there be no interruption in the export of their copper to overseas customers. In addition, contacts were established with the Benguela Railway in London and in Lobito and with its Zambian agents, Leopold Walford Limited. The extent to which senior civil servants were involved in the consultative process is unclear. It seems likely, however, that in the later stages the secretary to the cabinet, Valentine Musakanya, and the (expatriate) permanent secretary of transport and works, Ewen Thomson had a significant input, particularly in urging an early decision.

Although there was unanimity among the diverse interests tendering advice to the government, the issue was essentially political rather than administrative or technical, and could only be resolved definitively at the highest level. A decision, therefore, had to wait until the president and his senior ministerial advisers were convinced that an approach to the Portuguese, though "frankly awkward,"[49] was unavoidable. Once that stage was reached, in early September, the proposal was quickly submitted to the cabinet for formal approval, apparently at its regular meeting on 7 September 1965. In surmounting this final hurdle, one rationalization that proved helpful in easing the residual misgivings of Zambian decision makers was the contention that all that was involved was a commercial arrangement with a private (British-owned) railway, not a political deal with the Portuguese government.

The options open to the government were simple and straightforward: to negotiate directly with the Portuguese authorities, or indirectly through an intermediary, or to delay until after UDI. Not much time was expended on canvassing these fairly obvious alternatives, or on evaluating them. As UDI was considered only a matter of weeks away, further delay was ruled out as too risky. On the other hand, direct dealings with the Portuguese were more than some ministers were prepared to accept. In any case, it would merely invite them to bargain for consular representation or other political concessions. Besides, experience with international brokers in the arms case had suggested that working through a middleman might again prove an efficacious formula.

Choice

The actual decision appears to have comprised four elements:
1 that a diplomatic approach be made to Portugal to seek an acceptable assurance that it would not obstruct Zambian efforts greatly to expand transit traffic on the Benguela Railway;
2 that the approach be made through British diplomatic channels or other governments able and willing to assist;
3 that a direct approach be attempted only if all other efforts failed;[50] and
4 that care should be taken to avoid provocative actions that might prejudice a favourable Portuguese response on the issue of access to the Benguela Railway.

The inclusion of this final provision appears to have been prompted by two incidents that threatened to sour relations with Portugal. The first was the confiscation a few days earlier of a substantial cache of arms at Kapiri Mposhi north of Lusaka, and the consequent arrest of three FRELIMO freedom fighters. Although the Portuguese in their recent agreement with the Zambians had not required Lusaka to withhold support from Mozambican liberation movements, President Kaunda was fearful lest the incident might upset the proposed negotiations with Lisbon. Accordingly, he made use of his fortnightly press conference (on 9 September) to reiterate government policy that "the use of our country as a transit route for the transport of arms must cease." Although his attorney general had, in conformity with established practice, secured the release of the three suspects only two days earlier by arguing that their actions did not constitute a "danger to the safety of Zambia or its people," Kaunda publicly took a much more serious view of events. "In the interest of Zambia and its people," he declared, largely for Portuguese consumption,

we cannot tolerate the presence of unsupervised arms in the country. It is highly dangerous ... from now on it is government policy that this traffic should be stopped. I have given fair warning to organizations who indulge in this activity ... they will contravene this at their own peril ... No country whatsoever anywhere in the world can allow free traffic of arms within its country.[51]

The second issue that threatened to embarrass Zambia in its efforts to improve relations with Lisbon arose out of the presence of Portugal at the World Health Organization Regional Committee for Africa meeting in Lusaka. At the first working session on 7 September, several delegations, led by the Guineans, objected to the seating of the Portuguese representatives. They were even more outraged when the Zambian minister of health and conference chairman contended that "health transcends politics." In language guaranteed to arouse the indignation of militant nationalists, he boldly declared that "it would be very stupid of us to say that Portugal should not come here"; he was, of course, preoccupied with the danger of disease migrating across Zambia's borders from Angola and Mozambique. The clamour eventually subsided when the minister intervened the next day to apologize to the delegates for the "inconvenience" he had caused them – even though, on instructions from the president, he pointedly avoided withdrawing the offending remarks.[52]

Once the Zambian government had succeeded in threading its way through these two diplomatic minefields, it set about seeking Western intermediaries to carry its case to Lisbon. As part of its effort to reactivate the Anglo-American contingency planning discussions (Decision No. 8), appeals were made to both London and Washington. Neither responded with an unqualified yes. The British argued that their relations with the Portuguese were currently so strained that any approach at that time would prove counterproductive. Moreover, at the time of their earlier intervention to secure the release of the seized Zambian arms, Lisbon had questioned why London was still acting on Lusaka's behalf. The British were, however, prepared to reconsider the matter once the point of no return on UDI had been reached. The Americans showed more enthusiasm but proposed that the railways and mining companies be sounded out first. There were also suggestions that the cooperation of the Canadians or the Zairiens be enlisted, but the former wielded even less influence in Lisbon than the British did, and the latter were thought unlikely to respond as long as Prime Minister Moise Tshombe remained in office.

In the circumstances and with UDI anticipated in mid-October, Zambia concluded that it now had no alternative but to attempt a direct approach; until the question of access to the Benguela Railway was clarified, no realistic contingency planning would be possible. Accordingly, in early October, Foreign Minister Kapwepwe met his Portuguese counterpart at the United Nations and reached an understanding whereby Lisbon undertook to do all it could to assist Zambia in the event of UDI as long as Lusaka continued to deny operational facilities to Angolan rebels. This agreement was followed up, at the end of October, by a visit to Lusaka by the general manager of Benguela Railway to work out the details of cooperation. Thus, by the time UDI was finally declared, the basis had been laid for the diversion of a significant proportion of Zambia's transit traffic to the Benguela route.[53]

DECISION NO. 8: BRITISH FINANCIAL COMMITMENT (C. 14 SEPTEMBER 1965)

At the conclusion of the Anglo-American consultations on contingency planning in Washington in May 1965, the participating officials confidently assumed that their wide-ranging recommendations would receive the prompt and careful attention of the British cabinet and the White House. This did not happen; even President Kaunda did not receive his personal copy of the report until July. Moreover, periodic Zambian inquiries elicited no encouraging evidence that any follow-through, let alone the joint action originally envisaged, was contemplated. As Robert Good, the US ambassador at the time, has observed, "it is remarkable how slender were the real accomplishments deriving from all this activity."[54] "One of the great difficulties," the permanent under-secretary in the British Foreign Office at the time recalls,

was the idea prevalent in the summer of 1965 that, if the British government were too obviously working on what would happen should Mr. Ian Smith unilaterally declare independence, this might incite him to do so. This doctrine tended to be quoted ["at a high political level"] when we in the Foreign Office worried about inadequate information and we had to suspend worrying.

In the circumstances, it is not surprising that the Zambians revealed "an occasional display of exasperation,"[55] Eventually, in August, with the tempo of the UDI crisis escalating, Lusaka began to consider what steps might be taken to rekindle international interest in preparing a salvage operation to rescue Zambia from the consequences of Rhodesian vengeance.

The inspiration for this initiative appears to have come from Valentine Musakanya who, as secretary to the cabinet, had on 15 August assumed administrative responsibility for contingency planning matters on the departure of the president's expatriate economic adviser. Musakanya was appalled to discover that active planning in Western capitals had effectively ceased, and so quickly set about seeking political support for a renewed appeal to London and Washington. He was also surprised to find that, after all the talk of contingency planning, no comprehensive set of plans existed to cope with the range of dire threats confronting the country. He worked solidly for the next six weeks preparing a "war book."

The potential for harm at the disposal of a Rhodesian regime bent on punishing a Zambian government that joined in resisting its illegal designs was awesome. Even without resorting to military means, Ian Smith could close his northern border to road and rail traffic, bar the export of Wankie coal to the Copperbelt, impose prohibitive charges on Zambian copper in transit to overseas markets, and cut off the supply of Kariba power. Any one of these hostile (and illegal) measures would cripple Zambia's plans for national development, close and possibly flood the mines (in some cases within minutes), and bring the economy to a grinding halt. In combination, they posed a prospect almost too ghastly to contemplate. The only hope Zambia had of escaping some retribution by Rhodesia was to opt out of the Anglo-Rhodesian conflict completely – as Dr Banda in Malawi was proposing. This was a temptation that Smith repeatedly dangled before Kaunda,[56] but it was not one to which the Zambian president could succumb and remain true to his deeply held Christian humanist principles.[57]

To meet its minimum requirements for survival, Zambia sought three forms of assistance from the West:

1 *diplomatic support*, especially in persuading the Portuguese to be cooperative (Decision No. 7);
2 *material support* in organizing an emergency airlift (Decision No. 9), in upgrading the Great North Road in Tanzania and expanding the capacity of the port of Dar es Salaam, and in recruiting standby teams of railway operating personnel in anticipation of a mass exodus of expatriate Rhodesian workers; and
3 *financial support* to meet the costs of contingency projects outside Zambia, principally in Tanzania, undertaken in self-defence in anticipation of being caught in the crossfire between Britain and Rhodesia (Decision No. 8).

In this case, an attempt to analyse the decision-making process is especially difficult as the precise sequence of developments is not entirely clear. What is known is that on 14 September, when passing through London on his way to the United Nations, Foreign Minister Simon Kapwepwe conveyed Zambia's concerns to Arthur Bottomley, the British secretary of state for Commonwealth relations. The Zambian government subsequently formulated two separate but related requests for transmission through diplomatic channels to Britain. The first sought British financing for external expenditures (item 3 above), while the second called for early resumption of joint planning on the first two items. As a result, before the end of the month a Zambian team headed by Valentine Musakanya journeyed to London for contingency planning talks covering all three topics. These were held with British and American officials (and a Canadian observer) from 30 September to 7 October.[58]

Coping

The information deficiencies Zambian decision makers suffered from related principally to the nature and extent of the Rhodesian threat as well as the scale of external support that they would need and could reasonably expect. As it was impossible to predict what might happen in either Rhodesia or Zambia under the pressure of events, it was only prudent to prepare for a worst-case scenario. Fortunately, much of the homework for this had already been undertaken. Apart from the need to update and in certain cases supplement the earlier studies, the basic data were available and, in general, further extensive probing was not required. The urgent need now was not for more surveys but for firm decisions.

The one sphere of contingency planning in which the available information was still inadequate concerned the financial aspects of the operation. These had received no real attention to date. At the time the decision was taken to appeal to the British for funds, only the sketchiest figures existed on the costs of the proposed projects. Even by the time the Zambian delegation reached London, estimates, where they existed at all, were exceedingly crude; estimating the costs of projects in neighbouring states was especially hazardous. Nevertheless, some attempt had been made to calculate costs and also to sound out the views of interested groups within the country and outside. In the process, the Zambian government ascertained that the mining companies were prepared to absorb the substantially higher costs of coal obtained from alternative sources. Consultations with Shell (Zambia) Limited also proved helpful in determining the kinds and costs of equipment required to transport a major proportion of the country's oil imports down the Great North Road from Dar es Salaam.

Kaunda also broached the whole question of contingency planning in general terms with Nyerere (evidently during their talks in Dar es Salaam on 27 and 28 September[59]) and elicited a definitive reply that, whatever assistance Tanzania might be able to extend in other respects, it could in no circumstances finance infrastructural improvements for the benefit of Zambia. This response was not unexpected. Nevertheless, it reinforced Zambian anxiety to press ahead for a clear understanding in advance of UDI on the financial commitments Britain was prepared to assume.

The proposal to seek assurances of British financial support was drafted by Musakanya in consultation with the recently created contingency planning secretariat. The resulting recommendations were approved by the president and his senior ministers before submission to the cabinet for routine ratification at its regular weekly session on 14 September – after the foreign minister had left for London. There was little hesitation among Zambian decision makers in opting for immediate action rather than further delay, as they were impelled by an increasing sense of urgency as well as frustration. The only point in debate was the substance of the request. In the absence of firm figures on costs, Zambia sought to secure British acceptance of the principle of financial responsibility. Three possible formulas were envisaged:

1 that Britain should fully finance all contingency planning projects, on the grounds that the Rhodesian crisis was not of Zambia's making and that it had become involved only as a result of its willingness to support Britain's quarrel with Rhodesia;
2 that Britain, at a minimum, should finance the cost of projects beyond Zambia's borders, on the grounds that, whereas expenditures within the country – even if not fully conforming to its developmental priorities – might have some beneficial domestic spin-off, external expenditures would clearly have none; and
3 that Britain should accept responsibility for external expenditures (as in 2), but that these costs, or some portion of them, should constitute a first charge on Britain's $28 million post-independence contribution to Zambia's First National Development Plan.

The third alternative was rejected out of hand – if it was ever seriously considered except as an option to be avoided; it amounted to shifting all or most of the consequences of British blundering onto Zambian shoulders and, in addition, would have created unacceptable precedents for Zambia subsidizing transit facilities in neighbouring states. The first alternative, on the other hand, although viewed as the only just and logical solution, was bound to be rejected by Britain. Hence, it was agreed to propose the second formula as a reasonable compromise. It was, in fact, an extraordinarily generous gesture, as the estimated cost of internal commitments currently totalled $19 million, or considerably in excess of any likely external expenditures. Moreover, Zambia could only defray its share by diverting scarce funds from urgent development needs.

Choice

Extracting a firm financial commitment from London was regarded as a matter of major importance in Lusaka – the true touchstone of British sincerity. Hence, the government's willingness to pay a considerable price for that promise. Nevertheless, the Zambian delegation returned home virtually empty-handed. The British spokesman dismissed the carefully argued Zambian case with the curt reply that he had no ministerial authority to commit funds. In any case, consideration of payments, even in principle, was premature, if not unnecessary and positively dangerous. The most the British officials were prepared to concede was that the whole question should be studied urgently, though only on the basis of comprehensive proposals yet to be formulated rather than individual projects considered in isolation. This was one reason for rejecting the urgent Zambian appeal for petrol tankers. It was not the first shock the British had administered to the Zambians, nor would it be the last, but the unexpectedly negative response came as a shattering revelation of British political blindness.

The fact was that the British government, and especially Prime Minister Harold Wilson, was so preoccupied with preventing UDI – Ian Smith arrived in London the day the financial talks with Zambia began – that they had little time for or interest in strategies designed to cope with "hypothetical situations."[60] There was also a lingering suspicion in London that the real threat to peace in Central Africa was the possibility that Kaunda might commit some provocative act that would wreck the prospects of an eleventh-hour deal with Smith, and that to offer to underwrite Kaunda with retaliation insurance would only increase the temptation to indulge his supposed instincts for rash reactions. Even less than six weeks before the Rhodesian rebellion the British were still arguing that "the possibility of UDI remained remote" and, if it did occur, it would quickly collapse, certainly before any of the proposed projects could be operational.[61] As a result, UDI day came without any understanding having been reached between Britain and Zambia on the division of financial responsibilities for implementing contingency plans – not even the proposed airlift. The only positive results to flow from the otherwise profoundly disillusioning journey to London, apart from a much clearer understanding of what would be involved in an airlift, was an undertaking by Shell to send out an expert to help with the technical planning and cost estimating of the airlift.

DECISION NO. 9: ANGLO-AMERICAN AIRFIELD SURVEY (C. 1 OCTOBER 1965)

The one sphere in which the British and Americans were disposed to press ahead swiftly with contingency planning arrangements was in preparing the groundwork for a Berlin-style airlift. Specifically, they undertook to assess on the ground the capacity of airfields in Zambia and East Africa to sustain a large-scale air transport operation. Their concern here was less with the fate of the Zambian copper mines than the maintenance, if possible, of at least a limited flow of the vital metal to overseas industries. London and Washington were categorical in insisting that their willingness to participate in this exercise implied no commitment to implement an airlift in an actual emergency. Clearly, they were as anxious as ever to avoid provoking Salisbury into precipitate action or encouraging Lusaka to behave recklessly.

The comparative optimism concerning Zambia's prospects for survival that prevailed at the time of the Washington consultations in May was shattered by the much more realistic conclusions of the Hoganson-Bright report in July. In May the available evidence, though admittedly tentative and sketchy (and challenged by Zambia) had suggested that the country might just manage to sustain itself at a minimal level of economic activity (with the mines in mothballs) without resort to an airlift, if all possible alternative surface routes were fully exploited.[62] The July figures, on the other hand, provided substantially lower estimates of the surplus capacity available on these routes. Nevertheless, it was not until mid-September that Britain reacted to the gloomier prognostications.

Confronted with the obvious imminence of UDI, the British cabinet, acting on a recommendation made four months earlier, authorized the Ministry of Defence to undertake a ground survey of the airfield situation in Zambia and neighbouring states. London also appealed to Washington and Ottawa to join in the study. The Americans, although preoccupied with Vietnam and wary of creating expectations that might result in additional demands on their already overtaxed air transport capabilities, eventually agreed to participate. The Canadians, however, declined; although their presence was sought primarily for public relations purposes, they were suspicious that their involvement might not easily be confined simply to the survey.

It is not entirely clear whether Lusaka was tipped off concerning the British offer in advance of the contingency planning talks in London at the end of September. Certainly, details of the proposal were not spelt out until the opening session. Nevertheless, the immediate reaction of the Zambian delegation was enthusiastic acceptance.

Coping

The response from Lusaka was also prompt and predictable. Ever since the idea of an emergency airlift was first mooted, Zambians had viewed it as something of a panacea for all their transport worries – without, however, always fully appreciating the magnitude of the organizational, operational, and financial effort involved. The British proposal, therefore, though falling short of the full commitment Zambia would have wished, was warmly welcomed as an indispensable first step in providing the country with the security it sought.

In contrast to the normal decision-making process in the case of other issues of comparable importance, the various reactive stages in this instance were uncomplicated. There was no necessity to seek additional information, or to consult widely, or to explore other options. The London talks provided Lusaka with ample opportunity for full briefing on the scope and timing of the inquiry, the composition of the team, and the diplomatic formalities to be followed. Moreover, the various interested parties in Zambia – the mines, the ministries, and the ministers – could be counted on to lend their support. Kaunda did contact Nyerere by telephone to discuss the subject; however, this was not to seek his advice but rather to secure his agreement (which he gave in principle) to the mission including Tanzanian airfields in its survey. Consequently, it was possible, in the interests of speed and without risking subsequent dissent, for Kaunda to act on his own authority. This is what appears to have happened; there is no evidence to suggest that the decisional group extended beyond the president and his closest colleagues.

Choice

The airfields survey was discussed initially at the opening sessions in London on Thursday, 30 September. By the following Monday the

Zambian delegation was in a position to report that Lusaka would formally request the assistance of an Anglo-American team of air transport experts. It appealed to the British and Americans to mount the mission as a matter of urgency and this they agreed to do. The terms of reference required the team to assess the feasibility of supplying Zambia with oil by air at an annual rate of 100,000 to 200,000 tons, beginning within a matter of weeks, and of back-carrying a similar quantity of copper. Admittedly, the scale of the operation specified was more modest than the 200,000 to 400,000 tons per annum envisaged at an earlier stage, presumably because it was now assumed that Ian Smith would not sever all his economic ties with Zambia simultaneously. Nevertheless, the project represented a formidable undertaking.[63]

Until this point the whole exercise had been characterized by extraordinary secrecy – though it is unlikely that there was much that Rhodesian intelligence did not succeed in divining. However, a hint that major contingency counter-measures were contemplated was given when the Zambian minister of finance, on his return from London on 11 October, reported that "very promising" plans were under discussion for an "international insurance cover" to enable Zambia "to maintain some degree of economic viability" in the face of Rhodesian economic aggression. Four days later the government announced that, as part of its review of "future transport requirements," an Anglo-American team had been invited to "analyse Zambia's air freight requirements" along with the associated problems of "logistics and routing," with a view to ensuring the "most effective service possible to meet all foreseeable needs."[64]

The next day the British leader of the team arrived in Lusaka to see Kaunda, at his request, before his departure for the OAU summit. The balance of the team followed a week later. The nine RAF officers and four US Federal Aviation Agency civilians comprising the mission completed their investigations by the end of the month, and submitted their final report on 12 November, the day after UDI.[65] Five weeks later Zambia's oil supply was cut off. The airlift was instituted and the first oil plane reached Zambia within days (Decision No. 24).

DECISION NO. 10: RHODESIAN ARMS SEIZURE (5 OCTOBER 1965)

If any additional evidence were required to confirm Rhodesia's resolve to finalize preparations for UDI and its intention to draw Zambia into the conflict, this was provided by the systematic steps

Salisbury took to ensure that, on the appointed day, the Rhodesian economy would be in the strongest possible position to cope with the consequences and the Zambian economy would be at its most precarious. In pursuit of this goal, determined efforts were made to run down Zambian stockpiles of coal, reserves of oil, and inventories on store shelves, to ration the number of railway trucks allocated to the Zambian sector, and to delay as far as possible financial transfers across the Zambezi.[66] Most of these unilateral measures were implemented gradually and furtively, and hence their impact did not immediately become apparent. One action, however, was instituted openly and brazenly: the impounding of 232 cases of arms and ammunition in transit by rail through Rhodesia and destined for the Zambian army. This was the same luckless consignment that had only recently been released by the Portuguese authorities in Mozambique (see Decision No. 7).[67]

In a diplomatic Note dated 5 October 1965 and delivered in Lusaka the same day, the Ministry of External Affairs in Salisbury formally announced the imposition of a ban on the movement of military supplies across Rhodesian territory. This provoked a stiff Zambian protest directed not to Rhodesia but to Britain as the legal administering power. In a carefully worded reply, the Zambian Ministry of Foreign Affairs argued persuasively that the arms embargo constituted a flagrant violation of Zambian rights to freedom of passage under the 1950 Beira Convention as confirmed by the 1963 Rhodesia Railways agreement. Accordingly, it requested the British government to "take all such steps as it may deem requisite to remedy the breach."[68] The embarrassed British hurriedly passed the protest on to the Rhodesians who, predictably, ignored it. Their ban was clearly a calculated act intended to warn and weaken Zambia in anticipation of an early final break with Britain.

As far as Zambia was concerned, the issue at stake went far beyond the loss of the arms shipment. Its real significance lay in portending Rhodesian action to deny Zambia access to the jointly owned Rhodesia Railways and, by implication, to call in question its legal rights under the other common services agreements. An arms ban could be circumvented by an airlift, as it had been in the case of the Portuguese embargo earlier in the year, but any general disruption in transit traffic would constitute a much more menacing threat. Security for Zambia's lifeline to the sea was a vital national interest. Although Salisbury insisted that it continued to recognize its international obligations in this respect, its cavalier disregard of them in this instance scarcely inspired confidence in its assurances, especially as Ian Smith and his colleagues were loudly proclaiming their willingness to contemplate the ultimate act of illegality: rebellion.[69]

Coping

As with the airfields survey, Lusaka did not agonize long over its response to the Rhodesian challenge. Interference with the railway had been anticipated in previous contingency planning. In the circumstances, therefore, Zambian decision makers felt no necessity to consult the opinions of others, not even the advice of the British who were held legally responsible for their unruly Rhodesian subjects. Nor was any attempt made to seek clarification of Rhodesian intentions. The question whether the arms had been simply denied entry or, as ultimately happened, confiscated outright was from a policy perspective of secondary concern.

The substance of the Zambian reply appears to have been settled by President Kaunda personally, after hasty discussions with some of his closest advisers. Part of the reason for this was that the Rhodesian Note evidently arrived after the Tuesday morning cabinet meeting had concluded, and shortly before Kaunda's departure for Livingstone for a UNIP dinner engagement. Besides, at least four ministers, including the ministers of foreign affairs and of finance were absent overseas. The decision represented no departure from the broad lines of Zambian policy; the actual drafting of the Zambian Note was presumably left to Foreign Affairs officials, with the president checking it next day before its dispatch.

Choice

Although the search for policy alternatives appears to have been fairly fleeting, the outcome comprised choices from three sets of options. Zambia decided to focus on the immediate issue rather than its broader implications; to protest to London rather than to Salisbury; and to air the issue publicly rather than confine it to confidential diplomatic channels.[70]

The first elements in the decision reflected Zambia's anxiety to direct international attention to the violation of its legal rights rather than the wider issues of minority rule and social injustice. With respect to the second aspect, the motive for appealing to the British was not simply to administer a diplomatic snub to Rhodesia, though there was an element of this present. Rather, the objective was to force Britain to face up to its colonial responsibilities in Rhodesia generally, and especially in the event of UDI. The same reasoning explains the decision to break with tradition and deliberately set out to embarrass Britain publicly.

Nevertheless, the stratagem failed. There is no evidence that the British did anything more than pass Lusaka's communications on to Salisbury. Following the first Zambian Note, there were a number of confidential diplomatic exchanges with the British, in the course of which Lusaka repeated the assurance that had satisfied the Portuguese earlier, namely, that the arms were solely for the use of the Zambian army and would not be used against Rhodesia, at least as long as it was not in rebellion against Britain. This was not good enough for Smith whose concern, despite his public pretences, was less with the threat the arms posed than with the precedent he was establishing. The British, too, with the Smith-Wilson negotiations in London at a critical stage, were too preoccupied with averting UDI to be distracted by what seemed to them a peripheral issue. In any case, they professed to be helpless. As a result, nothing effective was done and the ultimate fate of the consignment has never been disclosed.[71]

DECISION NO. 11: RECONCILIATION WITH ZAIRE[72] (C. 16 OCTOBER 1965)

Zambia's search for alternative outlets to the sea to reduce its dependence on Rhodesia was complicated by the ideological convictions of UNIP leaders. The only "black" route that was politically fully acceptable was the Great North Road – an endless, mainly gravel track that wound its way northeast to Tanzania, where the road surface was even less adequate to the punishing demands that were later imposed on it. The equally grandly-named Great East Road to Malawi and the railway westward through Zaire each suffered from double disabilities. Not only did they terminate in Portuguese ports, but President Kaunda's personal relations with Prime Minister Banda of Malawi and especially with Prime Minister Moise Tshombe of Zaire were far from harmonious. Nevertheless, in the weeks leading up to UDI, Zambia was compelled to appeal to each of its neighbours in turn for assistance in resolving its transport dilemma. The first to be approached were the Portuguese (Decision No. 7), then the Zairiens (Decision No. 11) and lastly the Malawians (Decision No. 14).

The decision to seek Zairien support followed closely upon Tshombe's replacement as prime minister on 13 October. Prior to this, the Zambian government recoiled instinctively from any direct dealings with him. As one observer has noted, the prospect of negotiations with Tshombe was "perhaps even more distasteful" than collaboration with the Portuguese. The reason for the intense personal animosity was Tshombe's notorious neocolonialist record and his potential for harming Zambia. Ever since Tshombe's ill-fated attempt to engineer the secession of Katanga, Kaunda had shared the general African nationalist perception of him as "the white man's stooge and the black man's burden."[73] Moreover, as the ally of Rhodesia, in the past Tshombe had actively meddled in Northern Rhodesian politics in opposition to UNIP and, Zambians suspected, was still doing so. Among the disruptive activities he was accused of promoting in Zambia were the financing of the opposition African National Congress, the smuggling of arms into the country, and the fanning of industrial discontent on the Copperbelt as well as harassing Zambian traffic on the Pedicle road across the Katanga salient between the Copperbelt and northern Zambia.[74] In addition, Zairien politicians and their press had a habit of periodically levelling fabricated charges at Lusaka, such as the allegation that it was preparing to invade Katanga and annex the Pedicle.[75]

The Zambian government had difficulty concealing its contempt for the Tshombe regime. Although Kaunda publicly acknowledged the right of Zairiens to choose their own leaders, he refused to allow Tshombe to represent his country at Zambia's independence ceremony – on the pretext that his presence would have provoked a boycott on the part of other African leaders. Moreover, without openly siding with the insurgents during the 1964–65 Zaire rebellion, Zambia's sympathies clearly lay on their side, especially at the time of the Western powers' controversial Stanleyville (Kisangani) rescue operation.[76] Yet, confronted with the looming threat of a Rhodesian rebellion, Lusaka could ill afford to ignore the real assets Zaire was in a position to offer, notably access to three ocean ports – Lobito in Angola, Matadi at the mouth of the Zaire River, and Dar es Salaam via Kalemie (Albertville) on Lake Tanganyika. Zaire could also boast several strategically located airfields capable of sustaining an oil airlift and a surplus of electricity if Kariba supplies were cut off.

Throughout much of 1965 Zambian spokesmen confined themselves to refuting Zairien accusations and periodically assuring Kinshasa of Lusaka's good neighbourly intentions.[77] In March, Zambia accepted an invitation to nominate two officials to observe the conduct of the Zairien elections; in June, Kaunda appealed to his Commonwealth colleagues to assist in restoring peace and stability to Zaire, still wracked by rebellion; and, in September, he wrote to President Kasavubu to reaffirm Zambian goodwill.[78] Despite these gestures, the Zambian government found the attempt to normalize relations with Zaire extremely disagreeable as long as Tshombe remained prime minister. Admittedly, when the Anglo-American contingency planning exercise highlighted the vital importance of the rail routes through Zaire, Zambian ministers decided that the time had finally come to seek a reconciliation, but their brave intentions were quickly abandoned as a result of a rumour suggesting (somewhat prematurely) that Tshombe would shortly be dismissed.[79]

By October the painful decision could no longer be postponed; but, just as Kaunda and his colleagues were bracing themselves to swallow the bitter pill, General Mobutu intervened militarily and Tshombe conveniently fell from grace. With the major impediment to a reconciliation removed, a healing of the breach now became politically possible. Lusaka moved swiftly to forge close brotherly ties with the military regime that succeeded Tshombe, thus opening the way to effective cooperation in coping with the expected consequences of UDI for both countries.

Coping

Zambia's sources of information on Zairien developments were inevitably inadequate. Although Lusaka had opened an embassy in Kinshasa and a consulate general in Lubumbashi (in Katanga) in early 1965, the country was too vast and its problems too complex to expect a handful of diplomats to report extensively on domestic and foreign affairs.[80] Moreover, the legacy of past conflict between UNIP and Tshombe's Katanga party rendered the Zambian government less receptive to fresh intelligence that challenged its preconceived notions. Despite his reincarnation as a national leader in July 1964, Tshombe never managed to shake off his early image as a tribalist, a traitor, and a tool of mercenary interests and multinationals. Consequently, there was little inclination in Lusaka to test or temper his intentions in his new role.[81] Fortunately, while Zambia's ideological inhibitions on dealings with Tshombe delayed the decision to initiate overtures, his abrupt dismissal greatly facilitated a rapid reconciliation. Pressure for a reassessment of the situation had been building up for several weeks. The mining companies, in particular, expressed increasing anxiety concerning the security of their coal and power supplies and especially their transport routes. They urged the government to act expeditiously to adopt a more realistic policy on alternative routes. The Zambian officials who had recently returned from the London talks on contingency planning were impelled by a similar sense of urgency. Finally, the successful conclusion of the Kapwepwe–Franco Nogueira discussions at the United Nations concerning access to the Benguela Railway made an approach to Zaire with respect to the use of its section of the line an inevitable corollary.[82]

The dramatic political developments in Zaire occurred at a time when President Kaunda was on holiday and his ministers were scattered throughout the country on an extended "Meet the People" campaign. Immediately upon his return to the capital, Kaunda recalled his cabinet into emergency session late on the evening of 16 October.[83] The decision to promote close neighbourly relations with Zaire provoked little controversy. The president and his senior colleagues had already reached the point in their thinking when they were almost ready to reconcile themselves to the inevitability of relying on the Zaire railway system; the only question under debate was the timing of the approach. In the new political climate, there was no further reason for delay.

Choice

The actual decision the cabinet reached appears to have been fourfold: to seek political clearance in Kinshasa for the use of Zaire's rail routes in the event of UDI; to request priority on the Lobito line for Zambian traffic; to support measures to expand the surplus carrying capacity of Zaire railways; and to avoid any action that might undermine efforts to cultivate cordial bilateral relations with Zaire.

Ironically, despite the urgency of the issue, there was little follow-up of the decision prior to UDI, beyond sounding out opinion in Kinshasa through diplomatic channels and establishing contact with railway officials in Zaire (and Angola). The new government in Kinshasa was too preoccupied with maintaining itself in office to engage in negotiations on an issue of relatively peripheral concern to it. A ministerial delegation did, however, accept an invitation to Zambia's independence anniversary celebrations.[84]

DECISION NO. 12: TEMPERING OAU MILITANCY
(16 OCTOBER 1965)

The principal agenda item at the special night session of the cabinet that President Kaunda convened 16 October, on the eve of his departure for the OAU summit in Accra, was the formulation of an agreed strategy in response to the militant rhetoric on Rhodesia which he expected to encounter there, especially from states far from the front line. Kaunda was anxious to avoid an OAU commitment to a policy of economic and military confrontation with Rhodesia which would expose Zambia to fierce reprisals without any assurance – beyond fine words – that the external support essential for national survival would be forthcoming. This was at a time when it was still accepted, certainly in Lusaka, that OAU resolutions were intended to be taken seriously.

Early indications were that there might be a concerted effort at Accra, spearheaded by Ghana, to demand sweeping OAU economic sanctions and the mounting of a military invasion – based, presumably, on Zambia – in response to a Rhodesian rebellion. As early as June 1965 the OAU secretary general had declared that, if obliged to use force, African states were "ready to take up the challenge." In August and again in October the Kenyan foreign minister, who was also chairman of the OAU Council of Ministers, announced that "the time had come" for the OAU to "speak in terms of war" rather than simply in resolutions.[85] How significant these and other calls for action were, and how widespread the support for them was, were questions Zambian decision makers were anxious to assess.

Coping

Evidence of the extent to which Lusaka felt the need for fuller information on the likely substance and course of debate at the Accra conference was provided by the sudden recall for consultations of Zambian diplomats in Cairo, Dar es Salaam, and Kinshasa as well as London, Moscow, and the United Nations. The presence in Lusaka of a senior official from the UN mission reinforced the feedback Foreign Minister Kapwepwe was providing from New York on African opinions there.[86] Despite these efforts to tap additional sources of information, an element of uncertainty still remained concerning the intentions of other OAU members. The best the cabinet could hope to do, therefore, was to draft general guidelines to assist the Zambian delegation in the conduct of negotiations at the conference. Even these were not easy to formulate.

There were three broad schools of thought in cabinet concerning the appropriate Zambian response to the approaching Rhodesian crisis:

1 the *confrontationists*, who considered that the government should stick to its principles, regardless of the consequences;

2 the *realists*, who tempered their militancy with a recognition of the practical implications involved; and
3 the *nationalists*, who advocated a strict "Zambia First" policy, even to the extent in some cases of opting out of contingency planning arrangements.

Some ministers also continued to argue that the confrontationist and nationalist strategies were not irreconcilable, that the price of principles was not as high as was sometimes contended.[87]

The lines of division between the different schools were not sharply drawn. The views of individual cabinet members tended to vary over time and even with issues. Moreover, in the interests of maintaining morale, the public pronouncements of government spokesmen did not always fully reflect their inner convictions and concerns.[88] Finally, to compound the confusion, Kaunda and many of his cabinet colleagues harboured grave doubts concerning the efficacy of economic sanctions to ensure the overthrow of the Smith regime, at least before the Zambian economy collapsed. Yet sanctions were the instrument on which Britain was placing exclusive reliance, and the contingency for which Zambia was preparing. Consequently, cabinet ministers periodically questioned whether continued Zambian participation in contingency planning exercises was not simply encouraging British illusions at Zambian expense. So severe were these misgivings in the pre-UDI period that the Zambian attitude appeared to one informed observer as "ambivalent to the point of apparent contradiction."[89] It was in an attempt to reconcile the conflicting imperatives of liberation support and national security that Kaunda placed such emphasis on the argument that the Rhodesian problem was a British responsibility which only Britain could settle.

If there was uncertainty concerning the implications of British policy for Zambia, there was even greater apprehension about possible OAU initiatives. Although it is not clear how thoroughly ministers explored the three alternatives outlined above, the cabinet reached a consensus on the need to urge the OAU to exercise caution. While there was agreement in principle on the desirability of coordinating policies among African states, there was also a determination to resist the imposition of a militantly interventionist strategy on the country, at least until the risks of confrontation could be calculated with greater confidence. As the government-owned *Zambia Mail* warned editorially the previous day, "there are many in the OAU, less acquainted than we are with the realities of living next door to SR [Southern Rhodesia], who might clamour for some foolhardy adventure against SR."[90]

Choice

The instructions the Zambian delegation carried to Accra were to work for a common African approach to the challenge of Rhodesia but, in doing so, to press for agreement on a resolution which avoided any embarrassing commitment to an immediate, total severance of Zambia's economic relations with Rhodesia in the aftermath of a UDI; refrained from recommending the stationing of an OAU army in Zambia; and stressed Britain's primary responsibility to deal decisively with the Salisbury regime and with the spill-over effects of rebellion on neighbouring states.

The delegation's brief was argued principally in private.[91] However, Kaunda's address to the opening session of the summit gave expression to the government's economic concerns. While insisting that "we shall not be deterred from supporting the cause of right," he warned that Zambia's position was "fraught with dangers."[92] His reservations concerning an OAU expeditionary force were not publicly explained until his return to Lusaka. At that time, referring to "a number of would-be solutions" put forward by "well-meaning people," he declared:

If you want to take military action without bloodshed, then you must agree that the only country that can do so is the United Kingdom ... That is why we have in the past – as we do now – offered Zambia as a base for British troops.[93] I am equally convinced that if this were left to ... the United Nations or the Organization of African Unity, then you would have a major conflict which would affect not only the rest of the African continent but the world as a whole.[94]

Although the Zambian delegation in Accra was not as outspoken as Malawi's maverick Prime Minister Banda, it was more effective in winning acceptance for its counsel of caution. After a dramatic and divisive debate, the Council of (Foreign) Ministers' recommendations, already severely qualified as a result of Zambian lobbying, were watered down further. The final published resolution made no specific mention of economic sanctions against Salisbury and only a vague reference to the possible use of force. Britain was singled out as the target for diplomatic sanctions in the event it failed to deal resolutely with a Rhodesian rebellion.[95] And there matters stood for the moment. Nevertheless, following UDI, each of these issues came to the fore again in an even more acute form. Meanwhile the Smith regime, no doubt encouraged by Kaunda's moderate stand in Accra, was launching its final effort to detach Zambia completely from any anti-UDI front.

DECISION NO. 13: COMMON SERVICES RIGHTS
(26 OCTOBER 1965)

As the final showdown with Britain approached, Ian Smith decided to follow up his letter of the previous May with a further personal appeal to President Kaunda to opt out of the coming conflict. On 21 October he wrote to reassure Kaunda that the Rhodesian government remained "willing and anxious to honour its obligations towards Zambia," especially in relation to the three jointly owned common services. It also had no wish to "interfere with normal commercial relations," including the provision of coal and oil for the mines, "no matter what the political relationship between our two countries might be." Rhodesian restraint, however, was not unconditional; it was subject to an explicit understanding that Zambia did not "initiate measures calculated to cause positive harm and damage for political purposes to the economy and stability of Rhodesia."[96] In the process of appearing to project a cooperative Rhodesian image, Smith thus managed to underscore Zambia's economic dependence on its southern neighbour and its vulnerability to retaliation. Then, to emphasize further the precarious position Zambia was in, he generously suggested that, despite his April threat to expel Zambians working in Rhodesia, his government had "no present intention" of adding to Zambia's unemployment problem in this way.[97]

Coping

The Smith letter was timed to coincide with Kaunda's return from Accra,[98] but it did not receive immediate attention as the president was quickly caught up in the celebration of the nation's first anniversary of independence. On the other hand, as with the arms interception issue three weeks earlier, there was little necessity to probe Rhodesian motives or intentions extensively, or to consult widely inside or outside the government. When the issue did come before cabinet at its regular meeting on 26 October, Kaunda was able to report on the temper of African opinion as reflected in the Accra conference, and pressure from this source provided an important input into the decision-making process. In particular, it served to stiffen Zambian resolve to resist any temptation to succumb to Salisbury's seductive suggestions.

The search for an appropriate riposte posed no serious problems, especially as the recent arms issue had provided a partial precedent. In theory, three options were available: acquiescence, protest, and retaliation. Submission to Smith's implied threats was ruled out almost instinctively. Two arguments were subsequently cited by Kaunda as decisive.[99] The first was the practical consideration that Smith's promises were worthless: "If the Rhodesian Premier seizes independence illegally, then can we trust the words of such a man? In any case, his words to us are so full of 'ifs' and 'buts' that they may not be worth the paper they are written on." Then, referring to the fact that Smith had already seized Zambian arms illegally, Kaunda added:

Does this act inspire confidence? Do we have any reason to believe that he will behave differently if and when he is illegally fully independent? My own conviction is that, as long as our economic relationship continues to suit Mr. Smith, we will be all right. But, when he feels strong enough to do without our market, then he will strike at us.

Secondly, Kaunda expressed the moral revulsion ministers felt at any suggestion of collaboration with racists and rebels: "How justified are we going to be in continuing to deal with the Rhodesian government when we know that the rest of the thinking world condemns it, when we know that our own conscience dictates that Smith is a rebel?"

Choice

As finally formulated on 27 October, the Zambian reply differed in some respects from the earlier note in response to the arms seizure. On this occasion, the Rhodesian communication was a personal letter from Smith, rather than a diplomatic Note; the issue posed was a prospective breach of Rhodesia's legal obligations rather than on actual violation; and the content of the letter extended beyond their common services to broader questions of trade. As a result, although the Zambian Note was again formally channelled through the British, in substance it was addressed to Smith. Also, in addition to asserting Zambia's legal rights vigorously, it warned Rhodesia that Zambia too was in a position to retaliate.

With respect to the common services, Kaunda reminded Smith gently but firmly that they were not only "common services but ... jointly owned." Consequently, neither government had "any right to speak as if any of the services belonged to it alone." As for the continuation of trade between the two countries, the president hoped that "nothing will happen that might break the relations between Her Majesty's Government in Britain and the Colony of Rhodesia which might make the Zambian government reconsider its present position."[100]

The warning fell on deaf ears. The drive for independence was now in high gear and nothing could stop it. All Zambia could do at this stage was to scramble to prepare its defences in anticipation of the inevitable. At this eleventh hour, it turned to Malawi in desperation.

DECISION NO. 14: MALAWI OIL ROUTE (C. 26 OCTOBER 1965)

The delay in recognizing the potential of Malawi as an alternative route can be attributed in part to political inhibitions. Despite the many striking similarities in the backgrounds and beliefs of Kenneth Kaunda and Kamuzu Banda, personal relations between the two leaders had been sour for some years.[101] More important was the fact that Malawi was equally landlocked, and dependent for her access to the sea on the Portuguese port of Beira. To complicate matters, the Trans-Zambezia Railway in Mozambique, unlike the Benguela Railway in Angola, was state-owned, thus necessitating direct dealings with the Portuguese authorities. Nevertheless, the political constraints were not the only reasons the Malawi route was overlooked. Initially it did not appear an attractive alternative, physically or economically. It was slow, circuitous, and costly; the Great East Road was long and tortuous, and the Luangwa River bridge inadequate; Malawi Railway had only limited surplus capacity, in part because its track was in desperate need of upgrading; and transshipment at the Salima railhead involved added expense and delay. Still, at a time when every conceivable alternative was being explored, Zambia could ill afford to continue to ignore such an obvious possibility.[102]

The first occasion on which the Malawi route received serious attention was during the contingency planning talks in London in early October. The matter was investigated further upon the Zambian officials' return home, but it was not until after Kaunda's visit to Accra for the OAU summit that any definite action was decided on.

Coping

The Zambian government appears to have been curiously ill-informed concerning the facilities available in Malawi. It was well aware of the limitations of the railway in terms of equipment and axle weights, especially on the Balaka-Salima sector, but it did not appreciate the significance of Malawi's surplus oil storage capacity until local Shell oil company officials drew its attention to this important factor. This revelation appears to have been decisive in alerting Lusaka to the potentialities of Malawi as an emergency route for the import of oil.

Part of the reason for the Zambian hesitation in drawing Shell Zambia into the planning process was the assumption (which was undoubtedly sound) that any information exchanged would be automatically shared with the company's Rhodesian subsidiary. However, with the approach of UDI and following the London talks at which the British and American officials urged an approach to Malawi, the security constraints seemed less compelling. Although President Kaunda did not raise the issue in his conversations with President Banda in Accra, his OAU experience undoubtedly reinforced his determination to press ahead vigorously with the development of alternative routes through Malawi as well as through Tanzania.

Choice

Shortly after Kaunda's return from the OAU summit the question of access to Malawi's rail outlet to Beira was taken to cabinet where clearance was quickly given to seek Banda's cooperation as a matter of urgency. Within two days of the decision, a Zambian ministerial mission was on its way to the Malawian capital with a personal letter from Kaunda. Despite the recent closure of Malawi Party Congress offices in Zambia and the expulsion of party officers, Banda's response was prompt and positive; Zambia's problem, he said, was Malawi's problem. He stipulated, however, that Zambia meet the full costs of its facilities in Malawi.[103] To underscore his support, he dispatched two ministers to Lusaka to pursue matters further. Their visit was reciprocated by a delegation of Zambian officials who inspected Malawian facilities on the ground.[104] Within a day of their return, Rhodesia declared independence illegally. Somewhat surprisingly, the Malawi route turned out to be the only one to exceed expectations.

V Crisis Confrontation on Two Fronts I – Military Response: 5 November–2 December 1965

During the three months prior to UDI, Salisbury provided abundant evidence of its determination to proceed with all deliberate speed, step by step, towards a decisive break with Britain. Although the long-anticipated announcement did not come until 11 November 1965, the actual decision "to go for UDI at the first favourable opportunity" was taken at a planning session of the Rhodesian Security Council on 19 October 1965. That first favourable opportunity was provided by Prime Minister Wilson's inexplicable action in announcing that Britain would not resort to force to suppress Rhodesian rebellion – an admission that his defence minister later characterized as a "classic strategic blunder" and "insane."[1] The next day (1 November), the Smith cabinet acted swiftly to initiate a state of emergency. Its proclamation on 5 November served to signal that the die had been cast firmly and finally.

The proclamation of a state of emergency and its attendant regulations accorded the government sweeping powers, including, ominously, the right to exercise the powers of the governor "in circumstances in which [he] is not available."[2] The official explanation for this grave measure was the existence of a "threat to security posed by numerous trained saboteurs ... who have either already returned to the country ... or are poised in territories north of us." This allegation was obviously a mere pretext; the liberation movements at that time were in no position to endanger Rhodesian security to any significant extent. It was, in fact, a carefully calculated public relations ruse. As the minutes of the 1 November meeting of the Rhodesian cabinet explain, "the gradual assumption of independence after a declaration of a state of emergency was likely to minimize the impact overseas. It would have the additional advantage of not disclosing until the last minute Rhodesia's hand."[3] Certainly, as far as Zambian decision makers were concerned, the real motive for the decision was to clear the deck dramatically as a prelude to UDI.[4] As a consequence, the declaration produced a sharp increase in Zambian threat perceptions, and provided the trigger marking the onset of the crisis period proper. Although the formal confirmation of Rhodesia's independence bid the following week further intensified the crisis-induced stress, it was essentially an escalation of an existing situation. In the case of Lusaka, despite a lingering incredulity that Salisbury would openly court what was seen as certain disaster, the actual UDI proclamation created no great surprise, and was even greeted, after the months of suspense, with a measure of relief.

The crisis period spanned a little more than two months, and embraced two reasonably well-defined phases. During the first four weeks the emphasis was on pressuring London for a military response to the rebellion. By early December it was evident that the campaign had failed. Over the next six weeks, therefore, the focus shifted to economic warfare and, in particular, to measures to ensure national survival in the face of Rhodesian retaliation against Zambian participation in British economic sanctions.

DECISION NO. 15: FINAL WARNING
(6 NOVEMBER 1965)

Announcement of the Rhodesian state of emergency broke while President Kaunda was on his way to Dar es Salaam for discussions with President Nyerere on contingency planning. The news added urgency to their deliberations. Yet so serious did this development appear to Kaunda that he felt compelled to cut short his visit and rush back to Lusaka. The following evening, 7 November, he broadcast to the nation, appealing for national unity and warning Smith of the dire consequences of his actions.

Coping

The signal that reached Lusaka was loud and clear, but there was little that Zambia could do to stave off the inevitable. For this reason, it was not felt necessary to consult widely. Kaunda did take the opportunity of his presence in Dar es Salaam to impress his host with the full implications for Zambia of the impending events. Up to this point, Nyerere had been inclined to dismiss UDI as irrational and therefore improbable. What advice he proffered Kaunda concerning an appropriate Zambian response is not known, but it seems likely that he urged caution.

For immediate counsel, Kaunda turned to the three ministers who accompanied him to Tanzania: Arthur Wina (Finance), Grey Zulu (Mines and Cooperatives), and Dingiswayo Banda (Transport and Works).[5] On their return to Lusaka the presidential party was joined by Vice-President Kamanga, Foreign Minister Kapwepwe and, in all probability, Home Affairs Minister Mainza Chona. It was this ad hoc group of senior cabinet members who pondered the limited options available to the government and sketched the broad outlines of the president's broadcast. There is no evidence that the cabinet as a whole was consulted.

In view of the unsettling effect of the Salisbury announcement on the Zambian population, both black and white, silence was quickly ruled out as inadequate. On the other hand, there were limits to the actions Zambia might initiate without running the risk of precipitating UDI, or at least appearing to do so. This was a sensitive matter with the British. London was desperately anxious that Lusaka should avoid any action that might conceivably be interpreted in Salisbury as provocative. This effectively required that the Zambian response should be merely verbal. Within these constraints, the president sought to speak out as forcefully as possible.

Choice

In addition to praising Zambians for continuing to remain "calm, dignified and non-racial," Kaunda issued one final appeal to Smith to save his country from "a lasting catastrophe." He then went on to reassure Zambians, in words that he hoped Rhodesians would also hear, that Zambia was "not an easy country for them to handle. We provide a market ... for more than one-third of Rhodesian trade and industrial production. Indeed, without this, their foreign exchange position is very shaky."[6] Kaunda scarcely expected his warning to persuade Smith to draw back from the brink.[7] Rather, like Harold Wilson, he wanted to ensure that he had done everything humanly possible to avert disaster by leaving Rhodesian settlers in no doubt that Zambia too was able and determined to defend itself and still strike back. Within a week Kaunda was called upon to make good his brave words.

DECISION NO. 16: TROOP DEPLOYMENT (12 NOVEMBER 1965)

"Zambia has been living with the prospect of UDI next door for so long," the editor of the *Times of Zambia* wrote on the morrow of the independence proclamation, "that the reality is being treated almost with indifference ... there is no sign of tension. Civil aircraft are still flying out of [Ndola] and Lusaka for Salisbury, and trains are still running normally on the jointly-owned Rhodesia Railways, which connect Zambia with the sea through [Rhodesia and] Mozambique."[8]

There was certainly no panic, no public disorder, no sense of impending disaster, and little appreciation of the long ordeal in store for the nation. Yet beneath the deceptive calm lay deep concern in Lusaka: concern for the fragile racial harmony in the country (with many of the whites on the mines and the railway, in government offices, the army and the police in open sympathy with the rebels);[9] concern for the precarious dependence of the economy on Rhodesian power and communications; and concern for the physical security of the state in view of its obvious military vulnerability. The deployment a few days earlier of two battalions of Rhodesian troops along the border was particularly provocative and ominous.[10]

Despite the multiple perils confronting the country, the immediate reaction of the government was remarkably cautious. Its overt action was to post a company of troops adjacent to each of the border crossing points (Chirundu, Kariba, and Livingstone) as a symbol of defiance (Decision No. 16).[11] Even that decision was not announced in the course of the president's broadcast to the nation on UDI evening. Then he confined his remarks to a further appeal for calm, an explanation of the emergency regulations promulgated as a precautionary measure earlier in the day, an expression of determination to ensure that "treason does not prosper and that the act of rebellion is brought to an end," and a forthright warning that, "if Zambia is invaded or if our territory is violated in any way, we will not hesitate to meet force with force."[12] How it was intended that Rhodesian aggression should be resisted, or the liberation of the country achieved, carefully went unexplained. Nor was there any hint of sanctions beyond the obvious refusal of recognition.

Confronted with the fact of UDI, President Kaunda turned to his cabinet as the principal information-processing, consultative, evaluative and decisional forum. Over the next several days members of the cabinet met daily, if not twice a day, in lengthy sessions. In addition, for certain specific purposes, Kaunda sought the advice and assistance of his State House staff, senior civil servants and military officers, and Zambian and foreign diplomats as well as fellow heads of state in East Africa.[13]

Zambia's caution in the immediate aftermath of UDI reflected the "appalling uncertainties" with which its decision makers had to contend. Not only was Rhodesian behaviour unpredictable; so were British (and South African and Portuguese) reactions. This was a recurring constraint throughout much of the crisis; but whereas Zambian leaders would come to cope as best they could despite the crippling informational deficiencies, at the outset the tendency was to delay decisions pending further developments. If, as has been reputed, Kaunda had a "fear of the unknown," he now had plenty to cause him anxiety.[14]

It was difficult to fathom the Smith regime's intentions, especially with the presence in State House of John Brumer, a Rhodesian spy, advising the president. Although Salisbury's enmity could scarcely be in doubt, the economic impoverishment or military destruction of Zambia hardly seemed in Rhodesia's interest. On the other hand, the evidence of UDI seemed to suggest that irrational behaviour in Salisbury could no longer be ruled out. Certainly Lusaka's instincts were to suspect the worst.

Assessing Britain's (and Wilson's) intentions ought to have been easier; it was not. Part of the problem was that, despite the months of effort expended on contingency planning, it was "remarkable how slender were the real accomplishments deriving from all this activity."[15] The fundamental difficulty, however, centred on Britain's political will. This was crucial in view of the persistent Zambian perception that the Rhodesian rebellion was first and foremost a British problem. For this reason, one of the earliest actions of the Zambian government following the UDI announcement was to seek information on how Britain proposed to crush the rebellion and to protect Zambia in the event of Rhodesian retaliation. That same evening Kaunda telephoned Simon Katilungu, the Zambian high commissioner in London, and also summoned the British high commissioner, Sir Leslie Monson, to State House. Neither was in a position to provide a satisfactory explanation of British intentions, though both undertook to make urgent inquiries. The replies, when they came, characteristically proved less than fully informative. As one minister complained on a later occasion with some bitterness, "Our queries are met with a conspiracy of silence."[16]

Immediately following the radio announcement of Rhodesian independence at 1:15 p.m., Kaunda called his cabinet into emergency session.[17] In the course of the next four hours, ministers thrashed out many of the issues and options that were to recur in one form or another over the next several weeks: the use of force and economic sanctions, alternative routes and international contingency support, and possible appeals to the OAU and the UN. The consensus that emerged from this initial exploration of alternatives was that the Zambian government should press Britain, as the responsible colonial power, relentlessly to adopt a maximalist response to the UDI challenge. At the same time, pending clarification of the intentions of other actors, Zambia should itself pursue a minimalist policy.

Coping

Zambian military intelligence concerning Rhodesian army activities, if not Smith's intentions,[18] was quite efficient. "During the past forty-eight hours," Kaunda was able to report in his broadcast on the evening of 11 November, "there has been an increase in troops movements on the Rhodesia/Zambia border. It is now clear that there is the equivalent of two battalions of European troops along the border."[19] In the circumstances, there seemed no real alternative but to respond in kind. The cabinet concurred in this assessment, though the decision as to the precise size, character, and deployment of the token force appears to have been left to the president as commander-in-chief and minister of defence to determine, following further consultations with his expatriate military advisers the next morning (12 November). Although the army commander was understandably unenthusiastic about interrupting vital training schedules, he fully appreciated the political and psychological significance of the gesture, and cooperated wholeheartedly.

Choice

Apart from a certain rhetorical licence and the proclamation of a limited state of emergency, Zambia contented itself with a show of force along its Zambezi river border, more to reassure the nervous residents of the area than to intimidate or deter the Rhodesians. Before the decision could be implemented, however, John Brumer claims to have persuaded Kaunda to institute a buffer zone between the armies, ostensibly to minimize the danger of an unwelcome incident. As a result, unarmed Zambia police were assigned to patrol the border crossings, while the three companies of troops –

only a third the strength of the opposing Rhodesian forces – took up positions a mile or so inland.[20] Moreover, to avoid any possibility of misunderstanding in Salisbury, the president publicly emphasized the limited nature of the operation and its purely defensive purpose.[21] Less than two weeks later the troops were withdrawn, after London had persuaded the rebel regime to pull some of its troops back from the Zambezi. When questioned, Kaunda denied that the Rhodesian military threat had receded. "We have merely found a new way of organizing ourselves."[22]

DECISION NO. 17: INITIAL SANCTIONS
(12 NOVEMBER 1965)

Two days after UDI, a second defensive measure was introduced. In anticipation of a collapse in the value of the Rhodesian pound, instructions were issued that Rhodesian currency and money orders would no longer be negotiable in Zambia. As the president explained, somewhat optimistically, "the Rhodesian pound is not worth the paper it is written on. [It] is completely useless and we have no intention of supporting [it] at all." At the same time several other rather routine economic and financial measures were instituted. Commonwealth tariff preferences were withdrawn; Rhodesia was excluded from the Sterling Area for exchange control purposes; and a ban was placed on Zambian residents dealing in securities through the Salisbury Stock Exchange. It added up to a modest package of penalties, none of which was likely to cause Smith much distress. In fact, Kaunda made a point of emphasizing that "the financial measures we have taken are not of an aggressive nature," but designed simply "to protect Zambian currency."[23] Nevertheless, they represented a beginning, and the debate that preceded their adoption constituted the opening round in a continuing controversy that raged on for as long as UDI lasted.

Coping

A major deterrent to a more forceful Zambian response was the profound scepticism prevailing in Lusaka concerning the depth of Britain's commitment to crush the rebellion. Initial indications were not encouraging. "With the possible exception of Ian Smith himself," Robert Good suggests, "no one studied Wilson's catalogue of sanctions, issued immediately after UDI, more carefully than did President Kenneth Kaunda." His immediate reaction was that, as weapons to topple the Smith regime, they were "hopelessly deficient." He was particularly critical of Wilson's deliberately gradualist approach. Nevertheless, he was prepared to reserve final judgment for a few more days to allow Britain time to intervene in Rhodesia energetically. How Britain lived up to its responsibilities in this respect would, in Lusaka's eyes, constitute the litmus test of its sincerity.[24]

Although the uncertainty surrounding British strategy was the major handicap Zambian decision makers laboured under, they also felt a need to look over their shoulders at what the Afro-Asian majority at the United Nations was doing. As chairman of the African (as well as the Commonwealth) group in New York that month, the Zambian permanent representative to the UN pressed for an emergency meeting of the Security Council immediately UDI was declared. Although his efforts were frustrated as a result of British pressure, the council did meet the following day and quickly adopted a short resolution as an interim measure. This merely condemned UDI, urged non-recognition of the illegal regime, and appealed to states "to refrain from rendering any assistance" to it. For the moment, therefore, there was nothing in UN policy seriously limiting Zambian freedom of action.[25]

Within the government, the initiative in preparing a specific program of sanctions came from the civil service. Some of the planning had no doubt been anticipated prior to UDI, though how much is not clear. Various proposals were debated in the Economic Committee of Cabinet, which several senior officials attended as advisers, among them the permanent secretary of finance and the governor of the Bank of Zambia. The general thrust of official advice was to urge caution and to avoid risks to the Zambian economy; other things being equal, their strong preference was for "business as usual" with Rhodesia. There does not appear to have been any consultation with interests outside the government at this early stage.

The issue of sanctions came up in cabinet in the course of two lengthy sessions on 12 November. It precipitated a wide-ranging discussion which was interrupted but not finally settled by the interim decision to impose only limited sanctions immediately. In its survey of the alternative courses of action available to it, the cabinet identified four broad possibilities. These were (1) to opt out of international sanctions; (2) to postpone a decision; (3) to accept token participation; or (4) to institute a total severance of all economic relations with Rhodesia immediately.

The first option held a powerful appeal for Zambian nationalists. Why, argued Foreign Minister Kapwepwe amongst others, should

Zambians suffer for the sake of Rhodesian Africans, many of whom seemed unwilling to make the necessary sacrifice to liberate their own country? In any case, Article 50 of the UN charter was specifically designed as an escape clause for states such as Zambia "confronted with special economic problems."[26] Had Lusaka sought relief, there is little doubt the request would have been sympathetically received.

The most compelling argument, however, concerned the costs of confrontation. These were impossible to calculate with any precision. At a minimum, sanctions would swell the import bill and fuel inflation for consumers. They would also inevitably result in a diversion of funds from priority projects in the First National Development Plan to alternative routes and other emergency measures. If, in addition, Zambian action or the Rhodesian reaction interrupted essential supplies of Kariba power, Wankie coal or Feruka oil, the economy could be crippled for an uncertain period. The spectre of the mines in mothballs, a mass exodus of whites, racial riots, mass unemployment, empty government coffers, and depleted foreign exchange reserves was not a prospect any government could lightly contemplate. Moreover, there was always the threat of direct Rhodesian military intervention in the form of aerial bombardment, a "Stanleyville-style" rescue operation, or commando raids. It is scarcely surprising, therefore, that many Zambian ministers hesitated to invite national disaster, and were even inclined to accuse their less cautious colleagues of "sacrificing" the interests of the country for an ideal.[27] Ironically, the British government also urged Zambia to seek exemption from UN sanctions under Article 50. London was genuinely alarmed at the possibility that, under pressure from the "extremists" in his cabinet, Kaunda might react rashly and thereby endanger Britain's critical copper supply.

The nationalists were not alone in their reluctance to embark on a complete economic breach with Rhodesia. The Zambian government had consistently argued prior to UDI, and continued to reiterate subsequently, that economic sanctions alone would not work, at least not quickly enough, especially if they were voluntary and less than comprehensive.[28] Its misgivings were evident in the ambivalence, already noted, in its attitude to pre-UDI contingency planning. Moreover, Lusaka feared that to cooperate in implementing sanctions would serve to encourage Britain in its pursuit of a fundamentally unsound strategy, and reduce correspondingly the chances of it adopting the more effective alternative of military enforcement action. Consequently, even those ministers who were predisposed to accept some sacrifices in the interests of African liberation insisted on some guarantee that the Smith regime would collapse within a reasonable period of time – say, three months – and also that in the meantime adequate steps would be taken to ensure Zambia survived the ordeal. Neither the British government nor the United Nations was prepared to offer such assurances, and without them it would have been irresponsible of the Zambian government to act precipitously.

Yet compelling as was the Zambian case for pleading *force majeure*, the arguments for declining to join in sanctions were not conclusive. To begin with, there were moral principles involved, notably respect for Zambia's international obligations and its commitment to the liberation of the continent. Moreover, a refusal to reduce or sever its economic ties with the rebel colony could expose Zambia to the twin charges of sabotaging sanctions and, even more damaging, collaborating with the enemy. Kaunda was especially sensitive to the risk he might run of tarnishing his enviable reputation as a militant pan-Africanist. As he confessed in the course of a press conference, "I feel very guilty about [continuing to trade with Rhodesia], very guilty indeed ... It is my duty as one of the present-day leaders of Africa to contribute to the downfall of a rebel government to the south of us ... for us to remain out would obviously have been a sell-out action."

Kaunda was also conscious of the danger that, as other states cut back on their trade with Rhodesia, Zambia's continuing links across the Zambezi would loom ever larger. His defensiveness in the matter of Zambia's image elsewhere in Africa was evident when, in addressing a national rally three days after UDI, he appeared almost apologetic in explaining the government's apparent inaction. Whereas other African leaders, he declared, could be "contented with shouting slogans thousands of miles from here," Zambia had to proceed cautiously as it had vital interests to protect.[29]

Each of the policy alternatives Zambian decision makers faced posed grave difficulties for the country. Yet the problem as they perceived it was not to search for some moderate intermediate course between the Scylla of unconditional commitment to sanctions and the Charybdis of total abstention, but rather to choose between them. Half measures would be hopeless, as they would mean running risks without reaping any reward. The inability of Zambia – principally because of the ambivalence of others – ever to decide between these two alternatives firmly and finally largely accounts for its subsequent behaviour in oscillating between extremes.[30]

Choice

For the moment, however, the Zambian dilemma was not as acute as it later became. Neither the British nor the United Nations had yet formulated a coherent sanctions strategy. It was possible, therefore, while accepting in principle the obligation to impose sanctions, to delay their implementation until the collective response of the world community had clarified and the prospects of providing the projected alternative routes and sources of supply were more adequately assessed. Perhaps by then the sharp differences that had emerged within the cabinet over the issue would also have attenuated. Certain interim measures were required in the meantime both to contain the spill-over effects on Zambia of the expected crisis in the Rhodesian economy and as an earnest of Zambian determination and intent. Accordingly, Kaunda succeeded in securing the support, however reluctant in some cases, of a majority of his colleagues for a package of proposals which cleverly combined the second, third, and fourth policy options identified above.[31] Specifically, the cabinet resolved:

1. to postpone any final decision on a complete severance of economic relations with Rhodesia;
2. to appeal urgently for international support to enable Zambia to participate fully in comprehensive sanctions at as early a date as possible; but, in the meantime,
3. to adopt a limited list of fiscal and financial measures designed to defend the Zambian pound and deny Rhodesia foreign exchange; and simultaneously
4. to take other appropriate fiscal measures to minimize the economic (and political) impact of the initial sanctions on the Zambian population.

The consensus reached in this preliminary skirmish over sanctions policy amounted to instituting a holding operation. Nevertheless, the government was not content to sit back complacently and wait for others to respond. In announcing the cabinet's interim measures, Finance Minister Arthur Wina warned that these constituted "only initial steps," and hinted at other "measures of a far-reaching nature" which might be adopted "if and when appropriate." He also declared – in advance of any UN action on trade sanctions – that it was "the duty of all [Zambian] importers to seek alternative sources of supply ... vigorously and without delay."[32] Moreover, in a hard-hitting address in the UN Security Council, the Zambian ambassador strongly endorsed a tough African draft resolution calling upon all states to enforce "a complete interruption of economic relations, including an embargo on supplies of oil and petroleum products, and of rail, sea, air, postal, telegraphic, radio and other means of communication."[33]

Finally, on 14 November, Kaunda dispatched an urgent appeal to Wilson for "swift and sizeable British aid to get Zambia ready" to withstand oil sanctions. This bombshell – attributed mistakenly to pressure from Kapwepwe and other alleged extremists in Kaunda's cabinet – created consternation in London. In its view, the Zambian initiative was both "unnecessary and imprudent." Plans to assist Zambia had been conceived previously as precautionary measures in anticipation of possible Rhodesian economic aggression. Now the assumptions were suddenly being reversed. As Good has explained perceptively:

Kaunda was now suggesting that the object of contingency planning was to do everything possible to position Zambia to take hostile action against Rhodesia. It was apparent that Zambia was going to push the British hard to move swiftly and decisively against Rhodesia even at some considerable risk to Zambia itself.

Accordingly, as the Foreign Office later acknowledged, Zambia "had to be constrained."[34]

Even the modest measures introduced immediately were not without their cost. In particular, they threatened to have serious inflationary effects on the cost of living. Consequently, at the same time as Commonwealth preferences on Rhodesian goods were withdrawn, the general tariff level on a range of "consumer-sensitive" goods – many of them traditionally imported from Rhodesia – was lowered by an equal or greater amount. The net effect, therefore, was that less than half of its export trade with Zambia was adversely affected.[35]

No further action was taken to strengthen Zambian sanctions until early December. During the intervening three weeks, Lusaka's major diplomatic preoccupation was the attempt to persuade Britain to resolve the Rhodesian crisis through military means.

DECISION NO. 18: KARIBA SECURITY
(C. 17 NOVEMBER 1965)

Although Kaunda came to embrace wholeheartedly the British strategy of employing economic pressure to effect political change in Rhodesia, unlike Harold Wilson he did not pin his faith exclusively on sanctions. On the contrary, he never abandoned his belief in force as the only swift, sure, and bloodless way to crush the rebellion. Despite repeated British statements categorically rejecting force and his own Gandhian convictions on nonviolence, Kaunda persisted in pressing London relentlessly to intervene militarily in Rhodesia. Over the years, Zambian advocacy of force as the panacea for the Rhodesian problem became so ritualistic that it tended to be dismissed as just a tiresome idiosyncrasy of the president. In the immediate aftermath of UDI, however, his frantic pleas for decisive action could not be dismissed so readily. Frustrating Kaunda's obsession – without precipitating his overthrow – became one of Wilson's major preoccupations.[36]

In arguing his case for military intervention with the British, Kaunda focused on two key elements in his attempt to render it politically more palatable to London. The first was his longstanding contention that any armed incursion into Rhodesia should be confined to action by Britain. London alone possessed the legal authority to assert control in the colony, and – more crucial, if more debatable – alone could expect to do so without firing a shot. "I know positively well," Kapwepwe declared confidently, "that, if the British troops went into Southern Rhodesia, not a single shot would be fired."[37] The alternatives – an African, a United Nations, or a Communist expeditionary force – even if successfully mounted, positioned, and supplied, would undoubtedly encounter much greater resistance and consequently inflict heavier casualties in addition to precipitating an exodus of white skills from Zambia and conceivably provoking a counter-intervention by South Africa. Above all, their presence would transform a local rebellion capable of being dealt with by a limited police action into a major racial or ideological conflict of regional and conceivable global dimensions. As Kaunda explained a few weeks before UDI, action by other than British forces "might answer the present problem," but in the longer run would "certainly create many more complex problems not only for Rhodesia, but for the entire continent."[38] Kaunda's eminent reasonableness undoubtedly impressed Wilson and ensured that his urgent entreaties received more serious attention than might otherwise have been the case. On the other hand, to the extent that Kaunda ruled out alternative scenarios involving other actors, he weakened his own bargaining posture and handed Wilson a virtual veto over any military action.

The second salient feature in Kaunda's pitch to the British only emerged after UDI. Force was initially conceived of as a means of liberating Rhodesia and imposing majority rule. Although this remained the ultimate goal, within a week of UDI the immediate objective of the campaign had subtly shifted to securing control of the electricity generating station at Kariba. This ingenious attempt to legitimize an operation on the south bank of the Zambezi by extending the concept of the "defence of Zambia" to include seizure of the jointly owned facilities there failed to move the British. They suspected (with some justification) that the Zambians secretly hoped that, once a bridgehead had been firmly established in Rhodesia, it would serve as a launching pad for an occupation of the rest of the country. Kaunda even appeared to believe at one stage that if only the British could be coaxed to station a deterrent force in Zambia, the battle to persuade them to cross into Rhodesia would be half won. This explains the frequency with which he urged Britain to establish military bases on Zambian territory (Decision No. 3). It also accounts for his rejection after much hesitation of a later British offer to provide troops for the purely defensive purpose of countering an unprovoked Rhodesian attack (Decision No. 20).

UDI triggered a sustained and intense debate among Zambian decision makers on the merits of alternative means of mobilizing effective military pressure on the Smith regime. As with economic sanctions, Zambian insistence on military intervention predated UDI, but it was only with the onset of open rebellion that differences in approach concerning the composition of the force, the capabilities of competing schemes, and their consequences for Zambia erupted into controversy. Moreover, as the issues were never satisfactorily resolved either within the cabinet or in negotiations with other African states or outside powers, they persisted as subjects of almost constant debate during the critical weeks following UDI and periodically over the next decade or more.

Coping

The major difficulty confronting Zambian decision makers continued to be their inadequate information base. This deficiency was particularly acute when it came to military matters, a sphere in which Zambian leaders had limited experience and less expertise. Within a few days of UDI the defence chiefs did present the president with a comprehensive and realistic military "sitrep," and close consultations continued with East African colleagues. Both Vice-President Kamanga and Foreign Minister Kapwepwe represented Kaunda at the hastily summoned 15 November summit in Nairobi, at which the security of Kariba was the central concern.[39] Nevertheless, on the crucial questions of Rhodesian and British intentions, Lusaka was feeling its way largely in the dark.

With respect to Rhodesia, the Zambian government feared the worst. The cabinet was fully convinced that Salisbury perceived its northern neighbour as a threat to its perpetuation of white supremacy and would therefore seek every opportunity to cripple Zambia economically and even militarily. The successful sabotage of the strategic Kariba-Kitwe power line two weeks after UDI merely confirmed Zambia's instinctive suspicions concerning Rhodesian malevolence.[40] Although London recognized the sincerity of Lusaka's concerns and Wilson later conceded that Zambia had had reason to be worried about the dangers of "a possible Rhodesian pre-emptive [air] strike against Lusaka and the mines,"[41] the British, for their own reasons, tended to dismiss the alleged threats to Kariba power as irrational. Whereas Lusaka considered the presence of Rhodesian troops "guarding" Kariba generating station ominous, London found it reassuring. Certainly, the unsympathetic reception Zambia's security plight received within British government circles only added to Lusaka's growing doubts concerning British determination to move decisively to unseat the rebels.

Britain jealously maintained that Rhodesia continued to be its exclusive colonial responsibility, and for a time there were indications that it might be prepared to take these obligations seriously. Immediately following the proclamation of UDI, the Rhodesian governor, Sir Humphrey Gibbs, acting on royal instructions, formally dismissed the Smith cabinet. The following day London announced its intention of taking legal steps to exercise direct executive and legislative authority in its rebellious colony.[42] Although Kaunda was greatly encouraged by these promising portents, he made it clear that he expected Britain to follow them up by either arresting Smith as a traitor or otherwise enabling the governor as titular commander-in-chief to assume full control of the Rhodesian armed forces and police. His immediate concern was to secure the withdrawal of Rhodesian troops from the Zambezi border.[43] Nevertheless, Kaunda decided to "wait until Monday [15 November] to see if Wilson is going to make the powers of Gibbs really effective before deciding to do anything else." He also pointed to the impending enabling legislation when explaining to an impatient Zambian public "why we have been silent" in the absence of any drastic British response to UDI.[44] However, it quickly became apparent that the flurry of British legal activity was mere window-dressing and of no practical significance.[45]

With the British abandonment of his preferred scenario, Kaunda set about canvassing alternative courses of action (Table 8). His options were rapidly narrowing. To begin with, on the basis of the military briefings he had received, he quickly concluded that any independent army initiative was out of the question. For one thing, it would almost certainly have brought South Africa and possibly Portugal to Rhodesia's side. There were also doubts about the efficiency of Zambia's young army and the political commitment of some of its officers, over half of whom were Rhodesian or South African.[46] Accordingly, Kaunda announced publicly that he had "no intention of crossing the Zambezi into Zimbabwe," adding later, "We knew we had a right to protect Kariba with our troops, but being realists we came to the conclusion that ... if we sent in troops to Kariba, which belongs to us, ... we would allow ourselves to be provoked into ... not only a shooting war, but a racial war. This, we did not like history to record against us."[47]

Similar calculations, as well as his belief that Wilson should be compelled to honour his solemn undertakings, caused Kaunda to ignore the many offers of help he claimed to have received from other African countries and overseas.[48] In any case, these were perceived as mere political gestures; militarily, they were meaningless.

Finally, President Kaunda hoped that the Zimbabwe nationalist parties, ZAPU and ZANU, would rise to the challenge of UDI and create the internal disorder in Rhodesia that alone might have required a British military intervention.[49] Yet once again his illusions were quickly shattered. Despite much fiery oratory, the long-heralded master plans of Zimbabwean freedom fighters to liberate their country failed to unfold. So intense was Kaunda's disappointment, even sense of betrayal, that three days after UDI he exploded in anger. Responding to a UNIP regional conference resolution urging the Zimbabwean liberation movements to go into action, he launched into a bitter public denunciation of their leaders, whom he characterized as "stupid idiots" for their high living, arrogance and passivity. "What is required," he instructed them, "is simply the paralysing of Smith's economy." Yet "there is not a single strike there today; nothing is happening." Instead of shouting from the capitals of the world, he advised them to "go back and fill Smith's jails, as we filled Welensky's jails here."[50] For similar reasons, he rejected any idea of hosting a nationalist government in exile – greatly to the relief of London.[51]

With the elimination of these four options – decisive intervention by Governor Gibbs, Zambia, the OAU, or the liberation movements – there remained only two broad possibilities: strengthened

Table 8
Military Options

Instrument	Decision	Liberation of Rhodesia	Security of Kariba	Defence of Zambia
			Objective	
1 British coup	No. 16	Governor to arrest Smith	—	—
2 Zambia Defence Force		—	rejected (Nov. 13)	troops to border (Nov. 12–23)
3 ZAPU/ZANU		strikes/sabotage urged	—	—
4 OAU army	Nos. 12, 19	discouraged	opposed	accepted in principle?
5 UN/Commonwealth force		opposed	considered (but never a serious possibility); rejected World Bank guard proposal	—
6 Great Power intervention		firmly rejected (despite public hints)	firmly rejected (despite public appeal)	—
7 British force	Nos. 3, 18, 20	suppression of rebellion advocated vigorously and repeatedly	pre-emptive occupation advocated strongly	accepted RAF air cover; rejected British battalion

sanctions including full Zambian participation, and the use of force by the British, at least to safeguard essential Zambian services. Both involved serious risks for Zambia, and both required commitments on the part of the British which, up to this point, they had firmly resisted. Both issues were also raised in a vigorous critique of British policy contained in Kaunda's first letter to Wilson in the immediate aftermath of UDI.[52] In an overly optimistic defence of his policy (on 16 November), the British prime minister pleaded for Zambian understanding of and support for a policy of severe but not punitive sanctions which, he confidently predicted, would, even without the added complication of Zambian involvement, topple the Smith regime swiftly and without bloodshed.[53] At the same time he painted a grim picture of the death and destruction that would result throughout the region from unleashing a full-scale war in Rhodesia.

Shortly thereafter[54] the president met with his senior colleagues to review the developing situation. They were greatly concerned that measures should be taken to prepare Zambia to withstand the shock of a total economic break with Rhodesia and the imposition of oil sanctions. However, they were even more insistent on a British military guarantee of the security of supply of Kariba power to the Copperbelt, as Rhodesian action to cut it off was considered the more current threat. Besides, the Zambians were looking beyond their immediate preoccupation with security to the ultimate liberation of Zimbabwe. Accordingly, the ministers declined to be deterred by the known opposition of the British to their proposals. Even so, the final decision was by no means easy or automatic. Whereas some members were even more militant in their demands than the president, Kapwepwe, who represented a significant minority in the cabinet, had no faith in the British and was emotionally attracted to an African initiative.[55] However, the Nairobi summit, from which Kapwepwe as well as Kamanga had only recently returned, gave Kaunda valuable backing. While not ruling out a military contribution to the defence of Zambia, the East African heads of state agreed to press for a British (or United Nations) "diplomatic guarantee, supported by the use of military force if necessary," to safeguard Zambia's stake in the common services it shared with Rhodesia.[56]

Choice

Kaunda conveyed his government's decisions to London in a personal appeal to Wilson on 17 November. He also outlined them publicly at a press conference later that day. The essential demand was for a firm British commitment to occupy the Kariba power installations militarily in the event Rhodesia interfered with Zambia's electricity supply. Specifically, Lusaka urged "immediate action to airlift British troops to Zambia and to station RAF fighters and bombers at Zambian air bases." Nevertheless, according to one informed source, the letter to Wilson contained no suggestion that "British ground and air units should be flung into action against the rebel Rhodesians as soon as they have taken up their positions along the Zambezi frontier line. Quite the opposite, for the object of the exercise would be diplomatic and psychological."

Diplomatically a British military presence would "wipe out the present deep distrust and bitterness towards Britain," and psychologically it would have "a traumatic effect on settler politics inside the rebellious colony."[57] At the same time, to emphasize the seriousness with which Lusaka viewed the matter and to appease the minority in his cabinet, Kaunda warned publicly that, "should Kariba power be cut off by rebel Smith and the British government does not see its way to sending troops to guard Kariba, ... then I ... reserve the right to invite any power to come and help us protect Kariba."[58] Although this threat was largely a bluff, it acquired sufficient credibility in the course of a meeting of the OAU Defence Committee (otherwise known as the Committee of Five) two days later to alarm Wilson thoroughly. As a result, on 21 November, he dispatched his top African expert and diplomatic troubleshooter, Malcolm MacDonald, to Lusaka to do what he could to avert catastrophe.[59]

DECISION NO. 19: OPPOSITION TO OAU MILITARY INTERVENTION (21 NOVEMBER 1965)

The timing of Kaunda's appeal to the British on the eve of an OAU Defence Committee meeting gave the appearance of a Zambian attempt to pre-empt any independent African military initiative in Rhodesia. Whether or not this conjuncture was deliberate, there is little doubt that the Zambian government and especially President Kaunda harboured grave reservations concerning the hosting of any OAU expeditionary force (as opposed to OAU observers whom he favoured) at a time he feared Rhodesian border incursions. However, outright rejection of the idea would have been politically embarrassing in terms of continental relations. Besides, the threat to call in the Egyptians, the Ethiopians, and the Algerians was perhaps the weightiest stick Lusaka could wield in its running battle with the British.

UDI unleashed a flood of martial oratory across the continent as African statesmen competed in the virulence of their denunciations of Rhodesia's affront to African dignity.[60] On this central issue of racism there were no "moderate" African opinions, though the degree of passion exhibited tended to correspond to the distance of African capitals from the Zambezi. In most instances this amounted to little more than "shouting slogans," as Kaunda noted disdainfully.[61] In other cases the rhetoric was accompanied by vague offers of troops for an African liberation army. In addition, President Nkrumah of Ghana wrote to Kaunda and six other heads of state on 19 November proposing a Treaty of Mutual Defence and Security, essentially to ensure assistance to Zambia in the event of Rhodesian aggression.[62] The first concrete step to organize a concerted African response to UDI was taken with the meeting that same day of the OAU Defence Committee in Dar es Salaam. Originally set up in secret at the OAU summit in Accra in October with representation from Egypt, Kenya, Nigeria, and Tanzania as well as Zambia, it had been assigned responsibility for the "immediate and effective implementation" of the organization's military strategy on Rhodesia.[63] Its mandate now was to translate African outrage over events in Rhodesia into a considered and coherent plan of action. This did not prove easy or ultimately successful, as wide differences of opinion emerged even among militants on the appropriateness or practicality of specific measures considered.

The interventionists, spearheaded by OAU Secretary General Diallo Telli, Tanzanian Foreign Minister Oscar Kambona, and President Nasser's representative, pressed strongly for the mounting of a multinational African army and its positioning on the north bank of the Zambezi with a view to intimidating the rebel regime into surrendering or, failing that, conquering the colony.[64] While Zambia was not disposed to challenge this scenario in principle, it did have serious misgivings concerning many practical aspects of the operation. When no resolution of these crucial issues could be reached, a subcommittee was dispatched to Lusaka to appeal directly to Kaunda. Despite "maximum pressure" brought to bear on him, he remained firm in his insistence on certain essential safeguards and guarantees. In the end, the committee session broke up with little agreement except to refer the question of "the direct use of military force by OAU member states against the minority government of European settlers in Southern Rhodesia" to an extraordinary meeting of the OAU Council of Ministers "in view of the magnitude of the operations involved."[65] By the time it convened in Addis Ababa on 3 December, the RAF was in the process of installing itself at Zambia's three international airfields, and the issue of an African army, though it continued to be the subject of lively controversy, had become largely academic.

Coping

Lusaka had much greater confidence in the adequacy of its political and military intelligence with respect to OAU military intervention in the Rhodesian conflict than on most issues it confronted. In addition to the appreciations prepared by its own military advisers, it had been amply primed by the British – for their own reasons. Nothing it subsequently learned at OAU meetings caused it to revise its earlier judgments in any essential respects. When, therefore, the Zambian minister of home affairs, Mainza Chona, cross-examined his colleagues in the OAU Defence Committee, it was less for his own edification than for their education. Few of them had adequately explored the practical implications of armed intervention either for Zambian security or for Zimbabwean liberation. For Lusaka, therefore, the ensuing dialogue was not so much a genuine effort at consultation as an exercise in gently resisting inopportune political pressures. A critical influence on the course of the debate was President Nyerere's contribution. More than any other African leaders, he recognized Zambia's vulnerability and sympathized with Kaunda's dilemma. In urging Defence Committee members (including his own foreign minister) to heed Zambia's cautionary instincts and provide military assistance only on request, Nyerere proved instrumental in defusing a potentially divisive confrontation.[66]

In turning to Britain for military support (Decision No. 18), the Zambian government had by implication (as Kapwepwe realized and regretted) decided against making military facilities available to the OAU. Nevertheless, within days the issue was forcefully revived when Chona flew home to Lusaka to report on the Dar deliberations to Kaunda and his senior ministers at State House, Sunday evening of 21 November. As a result of this further review, Zambia's previous position of opposition in practice was confirmed definitively, and conveyed to the other subcommittee members when Kaunda conferred with them the next morning.[67]

Lusaka's principal preoccupation remained its dread of precipitating a racial (or ideological) war. Nevertheless, several additional political and military considerations were proving persuasive.[68] To begin with, there was profound scepticism concerning the capacity of OAU members collectively to mobilize the necessary resources to organize, equip, transport, supply, and service an expeditionary force on a scale adequate to deter rebel aggression, let alone liberate Rhodesia. It seemed more probable that any OAU intervention would invite rebel retaliation against Zambia – as occurred in the 1970s with the establishment of freedom fighter bases in Zambia – without offering any effective protection in return. Besides, with OAU troops in occupation, Britain might feel less inclined to come to Zambia's rescue if required, while South Africa might seize the occasion to push her defence perimeter north to the Zambezi. Moreover, without well-disciplined troops under full Zambian operational control, there would be a distinct risk of the force posing a threat to internal security. Certainly, the government was acutely conscious of the danger that the presence of an OAU contingent could exacerbate domestic racial relations and trigger a wholesale exodus of white skills, with calamitous consequences for copper production and the economy. Thus, the conditioning variable of external dependency served as a very real constraint, though not the sole one, on Zambian freedom of action.[69]

As the Zambian position had been debated on at least two earlier occasions, ministers appear not to have spent much time consulting outside opinions or arguing their case again, though the extent to which Kapwepwe reiterated his sympathies with a pan-African approach is uncertain. Instead, they concentrated on refining their position and considering how best to present it without appearing lukewarm in their commitment to liberation and continental cooperation.

Choice

Rather than accept or reject an OAU initiative outright, the Zambian negotiators sought to detail their concerns. Principal among these were the timing of the intervention, the command structure, the force's operational orders, and its logistical organization. Accordingly, Zambia laid down four conditions:

1. Implementation should be postponed pending the outcome of current negotiations with the British, and then take place only following a formal Zambian request.
2. The Zambian government should maintain full operational control of any troops stationed or based on its soil.
3. The role of the force should be purely defensive; to protect Zambia rather than to liberate Rhodesia.
4. Adequate contingency plans would have to be made to provision the force, to meet civilian consumption needs, to develop

alternative sources of oil in the likely event that Rhodesian supplies were cut off, and to maintain copper exports at an acceptable level.

In addition, Lusaka requested that there should be no committee communiqué announcing OAU approval of the proposal, even in principle, prior to a final resolution of the practical problems associated with its implementation.

This formidable list of conditions effectively ruled out any OAU military adventure for the indefinite future. Admittedly, discussion and debate resurfaced periodically over the next weeks and months, principally when negotiations became bogged down with the British; Kaunda found it diplomatically useful to remind London that there were other options open to him.[70] In early December the OAU Council of Ministers thrashed out the issue of force once again in an atmosphere of high emotion. In an effort to instil a note of realism into the proceedings, Kapwepwe urged the adoption of only such resolutions as member states were prepared to implement.

> If we are not going to sacrifice, then do not let us sit here and talk of sending our soldiers half-heartedly to Zambia and fight Smith ... If we do not have full [government] support on this issue, let us take other measures which would suit our pocket ... It is not going to be a war of two weeks or six months; it is going to take us about twelve years; and it is going to cost us ... big, big money.

In the end, the ministers resolved to request members to make available "military advisers ... to study and plan the use of force to assist the people of Zimbabwe."[71] Yet for all practical purposes the project was already dead.

The final *coup de grâce* was administered by an OAU military reconnaissance mission. Following a tour of the border area in February 1966, it concluded that, on military, logistical, and financial grounds, African states could not hope to mount the required invasion force of three to four divisions with the necessary air support for at least another five or six years. The estimated cost of fielding a single battalion for a month was $4 million.[72] Nevertheless, despite the inability of the OAU to undertake an operation on this scale, the exercise was not entirely unproductive. For reasons that were not entirely rational, the spectre of an African (or communist) army on the Rhodesian border struck terror in the hearts of British ministers.[73]

DECISION NO. 20: REBUFFING THE BRITISH TROOP OFFER (2 DECEMBER 1965)

No issue was pressed so persistently or so persuasively as Kaunda's demand for British military intervention in Rhodesia. Even prior to Zambian independence and subsequently during the nation's first year, he had offered hospitality to a British force as the best hope of deterring a UDI (Decision No. 3). When the rebel break with Britain came, Kaunda promptly warned Wilson that he would be held responsible for any failure to send troops to safeguard the Zambian-owned hydro-electric generating station across the Zambezi in Rhodesia. This opening shot in what proved a protracted diplomatic campaign was followed a few days later by a more specific request that the British position adequate army and air force units in Zambia to guarantee the security of its Kariba power (Decision No. 18). Neither appeal evoked a sympathetic response in London. On the contrary, they provoked a barrage of replies ridiculing the whole idea and arguing that military measures were impractical, unnecessary, and undesirable, if not positively dangerous.[74]

Part of the explanation for Wilson's swift and spirited ripostes was his fear that any commitment of troops to Zambia would increase the danger of a military confrontation with Rhodesia. Moreover, he regarded the predilection for military solutions a direct challenge to his own almost fanatical, if misplaced, faith in selective sanctions as the only safe and sure strategy available. The revived Zambian initiative also served to strengthen suspicions in London that Kaunda was emotionally unstable. Even worse, he might be overthrown by the so-called extremists in his cabinet, led by Kapwepwe.[75] Reports reaching London warned of increasing "restlessness" in Lusaka with the inability (or unwillingness) of the British to deal with the Rhodesian rebellion decisively.

Despite his lack of interest in Kaunda's "first informal explorations" of the military option,[76] Wilson now began to treat it more seriously. His awakened interest in the idea, however, came about not so much as a consequence of Kaunda's carefully reasoned arguments, but rather as a frenzied reaction to the spectre of Egyptian MiGs and a "Red Army in blue [UN] berets" massed along the Zambezi.[77] How Wilson succeeded in convincing himself that there was any real prospect of either the OAU getting its act together or the Soviet Union coming to Zambia's assistance,[78] or Kaunda allowing either to happen, is still something of a mystery. Nevertheless, the threat appeared sufficiently credible in London that Malcolm Mac-

Donald was rushed to Lusaka with an urgent message from Harold Wilson appealing to Kaunda to exercise restraint. But the Zambians stood firm on their consistent demand that Britain deploy troops at Kariba without further delay. To reinforce his case, on 26 November, a few hours after the sabotage of the Kitwe power pylon, Kaunda wrote to Wilson. According to Barbara Castle, the letter was

> anguished but stern in tone, asking "exactly what our friends intend to do to help us." It demanded financial help, British troops "to come and protect Kariba," and the granting of powers to [Governor] Humphrey Gibbs to form a legal government in Rhodesia. With great dignity, it dismissed the "kith and kin" argument as "a savage and primitive approach to life in the twentieth century."

The central thrust of the letter, however, was the formal request that British troops be airlifted to Zambia, "not only to man the northern bank of the Zambezi, but to occupy Kariba," preparatory no doubt to restoring law and order throughout Rhodesia.[79]

Following his failure to shake Zambian resolve, MacDonald flew to London to consult with Wilson and the Rhodesia committee of the cabinet, and to urge them to abandon their obstinate opposition to the introduction of British troops into Zambia. He impressed upon them the vital necessity of some dramatic concession to restore Zambia's shattered confidence in British intentions and, equally important, to pre-empt any alternative military initiative that might emerge from the OAU Council of Ministers later that week.[80] MacDonald hurried back to Lusaka armed with a compromise proposal. In essence, it provided for the positioning of a British battalion on Zambian soil as a guarantee to both Lusaka and Salisbury (and also to the Conservative opposition) against external attack. Thus, it succeeded in meeting all London's concerns but few of Lusaka's. In particular, the restriction of the force to a purely defensive role predictably proved totally unacceptable to Kaunda and his cabinet.[81] Even the earnest pleading of Arthur Bottomley, the secretary of state for Commonwealth relations, who was despatched in desperation to Lusaka with a mandate to conclude a firm agreement quickly, failed to assuage Zambian concerns. Lusaka was prepared to host an army in transit to Rhodesia but not in effect an army of occupation designed to frustrate rather than facilitate military action in Rhodesia. After much agonizing debate, the cabinet rejected the conditional British offer on the terms on which it was tendered.

Coping

During the ten hectic days preceding the final decision to reject the British counter-proposals (Table 9), Kaunda was immersed in two sets of interacting consultations – on the one hand with British delegations, and on the other hand with his cabinet colleagues. The Anglo-Zambian talks were conducted in two stages, with an intermission to enable MacDonald to return home bearing the formal Zambian request for British troops. The opening phase comprised three days of intensive exchanges (22–24 November) between Malcolm MacDonald, supported by the British high commissioner, Sir Leslie Monson, and President Kaunda and his three closest ministerial advisers: Reuben Kamanga, Simon Kapwepwe, and Arthur Wina. In the course of several sessions the two parties probed each other's minds over the whole range of issues arising out of UDI, including British policies and constraints, relevant developments within Rhodesia, and their economic consequences for Zambia.[82] Their discussions were interspersed with a parallel series of meetings of the president with his senior ministers as well as his full cabinet.

There is no evidence that the domestic consultative net was cast more widely, though a few top civil servants and presidential aides may have been marginally involved. Kaunda was, of course, careful to keep in touch with key African leaders. These contacts worried Wilson, and led him to attribute "some of the difficulties we face in our discussions" with Kaunda to the "most tremendous pressure" he was subject to from some of his fellow heads of state.[83] Nkrumah and Nyerere, in particular, were apprehensive that Kaunda might succumb to British terms, thereby precluding the hosting of an African liberation army. Significantly, both cabled their congratulations when Zambia rejected the offer of a British defence force.[84]

The second stage (29 November–2 December) was a period of intense negotiation and tough bargaining. On 28 November, in anticipation of an unsatisfactory British reply, Kaunda had conferred in Ndola with his four senior ministers on what action to take in this likely eventuality.[85] Their fears were fully confirmed when, next day, the British high commissioner outlined the British proposals to them. These were debated at length in cabinet during a four-hour session the following morning. Later that day MacDonald returned from London with fuller details, which he at once set out to sell to Kaunda in the course of two tense meetings. The package deal came complete with a joint communiqué ready for Kaunda's immediate signature. However, by evening it was painfully evident that there was "still a lot of argument about ground forces." In fact, the Zambians flatly rejected the "humiliating" British terms.[86] Accordingly Arthur Bottomley, armed with plenary powers, was rushed out from London to bolster British muscle.[87] During the next two days he met with Kaunda and his cabinet on seven separate occasions – all to no avail.[88] MacDonald also conferred separately and at length with Kapwepwe, regarded by the British as the most intransigent of the ministers, on the eve of the foreign minister's departure for the crucial OAU Council of Ministers meeting in Addis Ababa.[89]

One factor complicating the conduct of negotiations was the primitive state of communications between London and Lusaka. Wilson attributed this to abnormal atmospheric conditions, but the cause of his frustrations was more fundamental. According to Whitehall officials, the principal reason for the hold-up in negotiations was "the ludicrously simple problem of communications."

All messages between London and Lusaka must either go by open radio telephone link or by telegram, and both can be tapped by the Rhodesian government. This has forced Mr. Wilson to use time-wasting cyphers ... That is why it was thought necessary to send Mr. Bottomley to Lusaka with full negotiating power. It is hoped that, in this way, the laborious process can be speeded up.[90]

So convinced were the Zambians that force offered "the only chance we have to bring down the rebellion" that scant considerations were given to other possible alternatives. In any case, these had already been fully explored and discarded.[91] As Kaunda explained to the press, while in principle he preferred sanctions to force, in practice they fell "very short of what is required." He also hinted, less convincingly, that with offers of troops "flowing in daily" from Africa and overseas, there were other options available to him. Kaunda again warned that the introduction of foreign forces would inevitably lead to "a very serious racial bloody war or ideological bloody war." In fact, he declared solemnly, "we are certainly very close to a third world war." The search for alternatives, therefore, was confined to the question of how best to respond to the conditional British offer. Three possibilities presented themselves: reluctant acceptance, tactical delay, and outright rejection.[92]

The temptation to settle for half a loaf was considerable. After the determined resistance in London to any military presence at all north as well as south of the Zambezi, any British concession

Table 9
British Military Presence in Zambia, 1965: Chronology of Decision-making Processes and Mechanisms

1965	Events	Communications: Kaunda-Wilson	Consultations with British	Ministerial meetings	Decisions
Nov. 11	UDI			cabinet	
12	Zambian troops to border; Initial Zambia sanctions		Kaunda-Monson	cabinet (2)	Decision No. 16 Decision No. 17
Sun. 13					
14		personal letter to Wilson Wilson message to Kaunda		cabinet	
15	Kamanga/Kapwepwe attend EA summit, Nairobi				
16		Wilson message to Kaunda		cabinet	
17	Kaunda press conference	Kaunda message to Wilson		senior ministers	Decision No. 18
18					
19	Chona attends OAU Defence Committee, Dar es Salaam (to 22)				
20	UN Security Council sanctions				
Sun. 21	OAU Defence Subcommittee in Lusaka	Wilson message to Kaunda		senior ministers	Decision No. 19
22	Subcommittee meets Kaunda and departs. Malcolm MacDonald arrives		Kaunda/Kamanga/Wina/Kapwepwe meet with MacDonald/Monson		
23	border troops withdrawn Rhodesian Railways Board meeting, Salisbury	Wilson message to Kaunda	Kaunda/Kamanga/Wina/Kapwepwe meet with MacDonald/Monson	cabinet senior ministers	
24			Kaunda/Kamanga/Wina/Kapwepwe meet with MacDonald/Monson	senior ministers	
25	Kaunda press conference				

Date	Event	Meeting	Notes
26	Kitwe power pylon sabotaged		
27	MacDonald to London	Kaunda message to Wilson	
Sun. 28	Rhodesia Committee of British cabinet meets		
29	Chona leaves for OAU Defence Committee Addis Ababa	Wilson reply to Kaunda	Monson reports to senior ministers	senior ministers Ndola
30	MacDonald to Lusaka Bottomley to Lusaka		Kaunda-MacDonald Kapwepwe-MacDonald cabinet–Bottomley	cabinet (2) cabinet cabinet
Dec. 1			cabinet–Bottomley	
2	Kapwepwe leaves for OAU Council of Ministers, Addis Ababa	Kaunda message to Wilson		cabinet (2)
3	RAF advance party arrives in Ndola; Bottomley departs; OAU Council of Ministers opens; Kaunda press conference			cabinet	formal request for British troops and air defence
4					
Sun. 5	Kapwepwe returns			cabinet (2)	
6	UNIP caucus			cabinet	
7					
8	Smith coal surcharge threat	Kaunda letter to Wilson			
9	Kaunda addresses Parliament		Kaunda meets MacDonald/Monson		Decision No. 20 Decision No. 21
10	MacDonald to Lusaka		Kaunda meets MacDonald/Monson		

seemed something of a victory. It is scarcely surprising that some ministers found the proposed compromise satisficing. Despite Kaunda's efforts to minimize the threat, the possibility of a Rhodesian military incursion could not be dismissed completely. Moreover, the mere existence of an efficient fighting force on the Rhodesian border would have introduced a measure of uncertainty into rebel calculations. There was always the hope (or, in the case of the British Conservative opposition, the fear) that, with the troops in place, it might be easier at some future date to relax their initial operational restrictions if political or military circumstances changed.[93] Wilson had given Kaunda a categorical "assurance that we shall not stand idly by if Rhodesia cuts off power supplies to the Copperbelt."[94] Nevertheless, the majority view in cabinet was strongly opposed to acceptance. Whatever threat to Zambia existed could be adequately met by air cover (Decision No. 21). "We do not need troops to sit in Zambia," Kaunda explained. "Our own troops can cope with any offensive attacks from Rhodesia."[95] In any case, Lusaka was fully convinced that Wilson's calculated allusions to the contingent use of force were totally disingenuous.[96]

Temporizing offered the prospect of wringing a few more marginal concessions out of Britain. The closer the approach to the OAU council of war in Addis Ababa, the more desperate Wilson became to conclude a quick agreement with the Zambians and beat the Egyptians to the Zambezi.[97] Yet Kaunda was also anxious, though for different reasons, to secure an early British commitment. Whereas Wilson was determined to prevent any effective military intervention and to rely on sanctions beginning to bite in the course of time, "it was precisely Kaunda's objective to deny [Wilson] this time and to force the pace of Britain's response."[98]

While the Zambian government was genuinely anxious to host a British army contingent, it was not prepared to submit to humiliating conditions or to compromise its sovereignty. In the course of negotiations a number of issues that initially caused concern or offence were satisfactorily resolved. These involved the character of the force and the terms under which it would operate within Zambia. Among the points in dispute were:[99]
1 *Command.* London abandoned its insistence on "unequivocal British command" in favour of a compromise arrangement providing for nominal Zambian control on the understanding that no unacceptable orders would be issued.
2 *Exclusivity.* While eventually conceding that the presence of British forces should not "prejudice in any way Zambia's sover-

eign right to obtain assistance from any quarter should the need arise," London reserved the right to pull its troops out at any time and for any reason.

3 *Numbers.* Whereas initially the British hoped to get away with the dispatch of an air force squadron or, at most, a token force of two hundred troops or less, designed more to boost Zambian morale than to serve any real military purpose, they ended up undertaking to send a full battalion.[100]

4 *Location.* Although the British would have greatly preferred to establish their base at Ndola airport for logistical and political reasons, in the end they reluctantly agreed to deploy their troops on the north bank of the Kariba dam.

On a fifth condition – the operational orders of the force – no compromise proved possible. Whereas Wilson was adamant that any troops provided would be "purely for defensive purposes," Kaunda "refused to have them unless they had orders, within days, to occupy Kariba."[101] This was the issue on which the negotiations finally collapsed.

The decision to reject the British offer was not reached without prolonged debate, much heart-searching and considerable division of opinion.[102] It was a measure of the importance of the issue and the intensity of feelings it aroused that the full cabinet was drawn into the discussions. In the final five days of bargaining, the cabinet met at least daily in a series of marathon sessions as ministers struggled with their consciences and the fate of their country.[103] Every aspect of the proposal was exhaustively explored.

One unwelcome intrusion into the debate that made Zambian acceptance psychologically more difficult was Ian Smith's mischievous comment applauding the prospect of British assistance to maintain law and order in Zambia. This calculated taunt added insult to a simmering sense of injury as a result of inspired British press reports alleging that the whole exercise was designed to save Kaunda from his extremists.[104]

Choice

By the morning of 2 December it appeared that a clear majority of the cabinet – reportedly eight of the twelve ministers in attendance[105] – were disposed to delay a decision pending the outcome of the OAU deliberations concerning an African expeditionary force. This would have enabled the president "to hold out for better terms which would not affront African dignity" while at the same time keeping all Zambian options open.¹⁰⁶ However by the afternoon (after Kapwepwe had departed for Addis Ababa) a somewhat different compromise had emerged, presumably as a result of presidential persuasion. The final cabinet verdict provided for: (1) outright rejection of the terms of the British troops offer; (2) continued pressure on the British to occupy the Kariba power station; and (3) explicit reservation of Zambia's right to call in non-British troops.

This formulation had the cardinal advantage of enabling Zambia to project a strong nationalist posture at the OAU conclave in Addis Ababa, without apparently abandoning any of its prime political objectives.¹⁰⁷ In practice, however, this decision, taken in conjunction with the simultaneous acceptance of RAF air cover (Decision No. 21), represented a signal diplomatic coup for the British. Wilson had never been anxious to risk a confrontation with Rhodesia by stationing troops along its border.¹⁰⁸ His overriding concern was to exclude others from intervening, and this he succeeded in doing by RAF occupation of Zambia's three international airfields. For Zambia, on the other hand, the outcome was the worst of both worlds: no British action on Kariba and no available alternative.

In retrospect, it was perhaps never reasonable to expect that Zambia's legitimate security requirements could be realized by reliance on outsiders. This harsh reality was not immediately appreciated in Lusaka. On the contrary, the president wasted no time in resuming his campaign to convince London to provide a protective force for Kariba.¹⁰⁹ This prompted Wilson to send MacDonald on a third mission to Lusaka on 9 December.¹¹⁰ Faced with the imminent threat of mass OAU action to sever diplomatic relations with Britain, Wilson also explored the possibility of a Commonwealth peacekeeping force or a World Bank guard to "quarantine" Kariba; neither materialized. Finally, in mid-January, Wilson revived the idea of stationing British troops in Zambia. Though the ostensible purpose remained the defence of that country, his real concern, in anticipation of an early end to the Smith regime, was to be ready to move into Rhodesia to protect white lives. Kaunda, however, still insisted that the object must be to crush the rebellion and not simply to pick up the pieces after its collapse. Despite the benefit of Wilson's familiar declamation on the futility and folly of such a course of action and the visit of a high-powered British military mission the following week, the Zambians remained unpersuaded even though they were compelled to resign themselves to defeat.¹¹¹

DECISION NO. 21: RAF AIR COVER (2 DECEMBER 1965)

Britain's offer of air cover generated considerably less controversy in Lusaka than its proffered contribution of ground troops and in the end was accepted, though with some misgivings. There are two principal reasons for the different Zambian response to the two parts of the British package, despite their seeming similarity. In the first place, Wilson was desperately anxious to establish dominance of Zambian air space to the exclusion of all competitors, and mounted immense diplomatic pressure to persuade Lusaka to "request" air protection. His primary concern was not the defence of Zambia but, as he frankly confessed, to "do everything in our power to prevent the stationing of other air forces in Zambia."[112] In anticipation of this, London had developed routine contingency plans shortly after UDI to enable it to take over Zambian airfields swiftly. The offer of an infantry battalion was a belated concession, reluctantly pressed, and happily abandoned when the prime goal of air control was achieved.

A second explanation for British success was the considerable apprehension Lusaka felt concerning Smith's aggressive intentions and irrational behaviour. As Kaunda subsequently explained,

> I sometimes even think his actions verge on madness. Or he might be driven to madness when things get more difficult for him. I felt Smith might decide, when he is pulled down, to pull down everyone else with him in a holocaust of violence. Therefore, as our great weakness was in the air, I wanted this protection first of all.

Thus, while a border raid or a conventional ground attack seemed only a remote possibility, and could presumably be contained, the danger of an air assault was judged real (and, in fact, became tragically real in the 1970s). If, as Lusaka hoped, agreement was reached on British troops neutralizing Kariba, Rhodesian retaliation against Zambia's copper mines and airports was considered a certainty. For this reason, the two requests were initially treated as a package deal.[113]

Zambia's acute sense of vulnerability reflected the fact that its air defences were virtually non-existent.[114] Following the breakup of the federation, Rhodesia had inherited the Royal Rhodesian Air Force intact. This comprised a formidable force of Hunter and Vampire jet fighters and Canberra bombers which, ironically, had been largely paid for out of Zambian copper revenues. Zambia received only a few small transport planes and an assurance of financial compensation, which Britain failed to honour.[115] For these reasons as well as perhaps a feeling that it might be politically prudent to appear reasonable and cooperative, Zambian concurrence on an air support agreement proved easier to attain than that on ground forces.

Within hours of the announcement of Zambian cabinet approval, an advance RAF party arrived in Ndola and proceeded to take over operational control of the airport there as well as in Lusaka and Livingstone. When fully deployed, the British force comprised a squadron of ten Javelin all-weather jet fighter-reconnaissance aircraft[116] armed with Firestreak air-to-air missiles, a fleet of supporting aircraft to fly in fuel and other supplies, a sophisticated early warning radar facility and air traffic control centre in Lusaka, and six hundred men of the RAF Regiment to protect the planes and ground installations.[117] In the case of Livingstone, the airfield was occupied with men but not planes, in keeping with a confidential understanding worked out between London and Salisbury to avoid provocative acts in the border area.[118]

Coping

There is no evidence that Zambian decision makers made any great effort to acquire additional information, or indeed that they felt any real need for more. They were fully convinced that, on the basis of long and close association with Rhodesia, they were uniquely qualified to assess the nature and extent of the military and economic threat they faced. Where they did lack expertise, as on matters of military technology, they were generally quite content to accept British advice. Their dependence in this respect occasionally resulted in confusion and suspicion, as when Kapwepwe, on the basis of a misleading report in a pro-Smith London newspaper, charged that the British Javelins were obsolete and inferior to the Rhodesian Hunters.[119]

Consultation, except with the British, was also limited. Even the statutory Defence Council was only marginally involved; its sole role was to advise on accommodation arrangements for the incoming RAF units. Kaunda did attempt to maintain contact with a number of African heads of state, notably Nyerere, but he appears not to have sought out their opinions. On the contrary, when Nyerere telegraphed Kaunda strongly urging him to reject the British offer of a token air force as an "insult in the face of your need and Africa's demand for justice," the Zambian president pointedly ignored the gratuitous advice. Kaunda also appears to have been slightly upset by the decisions of Nyerere and Nasser to ban overflights of their territories by RAF planes en route to Zambia.[120]

Similarly, the search for and evaluation of alternatives to the British offer were perfunctory. Zambians were thoroughly persuaded of the urgent need to acquire an air defence capability and considered that the British had an obligation to provide it. Accordingly, debate focused on the conditions under which the RAF would be required to operate in Zambia. In the course of its deliberations, the cabinet canvassed four possible responses: unconditional acceptance; postponement; conditional acceptance; and linkage with an agreement on ground troops.

There appears to have been no support in cabinet for immediate unconditional acceptance of the British offer. On the other hand, there was some disposition to delay a decision pending the outcome of the OAU meeting. A majority of members, however, were sufficiently impressed with the immediacy of the Rhodesian threat to oppose postponement. Most also shared Kaunda's concern to avoid the risks associated with hosting African or other non-British air contingents. Support for deferral might have gained more favour if Zambian negotiators had not succeeded in clarifying and improving the terms of the initial offer. Certainly, Kapwepwe was not prepared to sacrifice Zambian sovereignty for the sake of security. He was particularly insistent on retaining the unfettered right to appeal for assistance from any quarter whatsoever.[121] Before departing for Addis Ababa, he made clear that his consent was contingent on an unambiguous acknowledgment of this principle.[122] The British eventually recognized the intensity of feelings among Zambians concerning any infringement of their hard-won sovereignty and bowed to their demands not only with respect to freedom of choice of military partners but also the command structure.[123] The formulas devised fully respected the Zambian government's formal authority while enabling Britain to achieve its primary objective of effectively occupying and controlling Zambia's major airfields and dominating its air space.[124]

No immediate agreement proved possible on two issues, and Lusaka finally acquiesced in setting them aside for later discussion. The first was the British contention that Lusaka should accept substantial responsibility for the costs of the RAF operation. The Zambians reacted to this demand with outrage. They pointed out not only that the threat to Zambia came from a British colony, but also that it had been British insistence that had led to the federal air force being transferred to Rhodesia and British perfidy that explained the failure to pay Zambia compensation. So strongly did Kaunda and his colleagues feel on this issue that London eventually backed down and assumed responsibility for all but the local costs of accommodation and transport.[125]

Kaunda appealed for RAF aircraft with an "air strike capability," presumably with a view to disrupting Rhodesian communications; in his letter of 17 November to Wilson, he reportedly specifically mentioned the need for bombers.[126] This request London flatly refused to consider. In fact, Wilson made a point of tipping off the chief of the Rhodesian air staff in advance concerning the dispatch of the Javelins "in order to remove any impression that we were ourselves preparing an attack on Rhodesia."[127] In the end, Lusaka was forced to abandon its demand. It did, however, continue to link its approval of the air agreement to a British commitment of ground forces to the defence of Kariba. Insistence on this package deal proved the fundamental issue in contention between London and Lusaka and, subsequently, within the Zambian cabinet. No doubt some ministers were from the outset disposed to settle for an air agreement alone, on the grounds that RAF air cover was essential to counter the threat of a Rhodesian air strike, protect the proposed oil airlift, and reassure the public. Most members, however, recognized that British anxiety to conclude an immediate agreement offered Zambia the only real leverage it had with London. What appears to have finally persuaded the cabinet to agree to leave the issue of Kariba to subsequent negotiations was Wilson's clever but wholly disingenuous suggestion at a crucial point in the discussions that he might in certain circumstances contemplate a "limited operation" in Rhodesia. Relying on this shaky straw, the cabinet next day agreed reluctantly but unanimously to abandon linkage and, with it, any slim hope of British intervention to protect Kariba. What proved to be a mere crust was judged preferable to no bread at all.[128]

Choice

In the final analysis, therefore, Zambia accepted the British terms, modified to safeguard its sovereignty, for an RAF takeover of Zambian air defences, though on the understanding that discussions would continue on cost-sharing and the defence of Kariba.

Zambian dissatisfaction with the agreement was evident almost from the first. Apart from Kapwepwe's disparaging comments on the capabilities of the Javelins, the discovery that RRAF planes could fly in undetected under the RAF radar aroused public alarm. Some of this was reflected in discontent within the UNIP parliamentary caucus.[129] More important was the wrangling over costs and accommodation as well as the recriminations that resulted whenever RAF personnel expressed sympathy for the rebels or defected to Rhodesia.[130] As time passed, costs mounted and the original reasons for an RAF presence receded. Both London and Lusaka lost interest. Accordingly, in August 1966 Zambia concurred in a British suggestion that the agreement be terminated.[131]

VI Crisis Confrontation on Two Fronts II – Economic Survival: 3 December 1965–13 January 1966

With the effective collapse of diplomatic efforts to convince the British government to mount a military challenge to the rebel regime, or even to defend Zambia's contractual rights at Kariba, Lusaka's Rhodesian strategy underwent a distinct shift in emphasis. Not that its campaign in favour of force was ever finally abandoned; it continued to be promoted as a matter of principle on every conceivable occasion.[1] Nevertheless, faith in the ultimate triumph of reason was no longer as evident in Lusaka as earlier. The actors with the means lacked the will, and those with the will lacked the means. Moreover, the escalation in the intensity of economic warfare with Rhodesia compelled Lusaka to face up squarely to its implications for Zambia as a hostage state. However restrained Zambia's own participation might be, Salisbury was certain to retaliate for the imposition of ever more severe international sanctions, especially the projected oil boycott. This concern in Lusaka for the economic costs of confrontation was not entirely new; a number of issues in the earlier "military" phase of the conflict had had a significant economic dimension, notably the preoccupation with protecting the power supply to the Copperbelt (Decision No. 18). Now, however, the dilemma was posed in an increasingly stark form that precluded any possibility of it being ignored or circumvented.

In the course of the next weeks and months, Zambian decision makers were immersed in a series of debates which replicated essentially the same sets of arguments and alternatives, regardless of the specific issue in contention. Four broad responses were open to the government:

1 *De-emphasis on sanctions.* Zambia would have preferred to abandon reliance on sanctions as the sole instrument of coercion in favour of continued pressure for a military solution. Yet this would have been a counsel of perfection. It would also have been a prescription for inaction.

2 *Accommodation.* The prospect of opting out of the Anglo-Rhodesian conflict and accepting the rebel offers of coexistence on the basis of mutual non-interference in each other's affairs exercised an occasional appeal, especially among some Zambian nationalists who were appalled at the sacrifices their country was being called upon to bear in the interests of others. Yet repeatedly the temptation to take the easy way out was successfully resisted, even by the nationalists.

3 *Limited sanctions.* A more acceptable compromise envisaged a level of participation in international enforcement measures consistent with Zambia's self-respect and economic circumstances. Meanwhile contingency planning would be pushed ahead and external support sought to gear the country up to survive the shock of drastic disengagement from its near-total dependence on Rhodesia.

4 *"Quick kill."* Finally, there were occasional advocates of an early and complete severance of relations with Rhodesia in all spheres, including transport, power, and trade, with little regard for the costs or consequences. At its most extreme, this alternative involved a deliberate act of national suicide with a view to precipitating a crisis in world copper markets and forcing Britain to intervene massively in Rhodesia.[2]

While a showdown with Rhodesia (and Britain) was emotionally appealing to a number of Zambian ministers, the more cautious heads among them counselled some version of the third option. Even this alternative committed the country to a considerable and costly measure of economic reorientation. It also compelled the government to subordinate many of its domestic political priorities to overriding external economic imperatives.

The growing recognition that the Rhodesian rebellion would not be crushed quickly or easily influenced government thinking in two other respects. In the first place, it pointed to the need for more systematic planning procedures and a longer-term perspective. To coordinate the national effort, the president constituted a Contingency Planning Organization (CPO). The roots of the CPO can be traced back to the early post-independence period. In February

1965 a small cabinet committee, headed by Simon Kapwepwe, was set up in great secrecy to keep contingency planning concerns under review. Its role was not to take decisions but rather to supervise the work of Gordon Goundrey, the United Nations economic adviser to the president, who was engaged in collecting statistics, drafting working papers, and suggesting promising initiatives to be explored. Following the president's May broadcast (Decision No. 1), membership of the committee was broadened, as the pace of its activities increased.[3] Meanwhile, with the appointment of Valentine Musakanya as secretary to the cabinet, a parallel official committee within the Cabinet Office became involved in a variety of issues related to contingency planning. On Goundrey's departure, in August, Musakanya assumed overall responsibility for contingency planning under the president. As a result, the ministerial committee ceased to function, though Kapwepwe appears to have retained some responsibility for coordination. Over the course of the next few weeks the informal Cabinet Office committee of permanent secretaries expanded its operations, assembled a modest secretariat, and established a number of functional working groups. By mid-October the CPO was fully operational. Nevertheless, its existence was not publicly revealed until 27 November with the announcement of the secondment "for special duties" of Kenneth Knaggs, permanent secretary of finance, as secretary general.[4]

The CPO was largely staffed by expatriate civil servants seconded from various ministries as well as by specialists drawn from industry and experts recruited under technical assistance schemes. Under its secretary general, it was organized into five divisions dealing with transport and power, commerce and industry, finance, procurement, and relief measures and refugees. Although formally responsible to the committee of permanent secretaries and to a ministerial committee headed by the minister of mines and cooperatives, in practice the crisis conditions required it to work closely with the president, and to report directly to him. During the first couple of months it also of necessity appropriated operational responsibilities independent of the relevant ministries or even ministers, by virtue of the fact that it alone among government organs had access to information on all aspects of the country's economy and development.

Secondly, the government became increasingly conscious of the need to sustain public confidence and morale among both blacks and whites. The stress of UDI was exacting its toll at all levels and in all segments of society. There were already rumblings of discontent within the parliamentary caucus, ugly racial incidents on the mines and on the railway, resentment over the severity of petrol rationing, and rumours of impending food shortages.[5] The president responded to the public unease by mounting a sustained campaign to explain government policies to the people through addresses to the National Assembly, press conferences, party conferences, and political rallies, as well as by dispatching teams of ministers to tour the provinces.[6] As a result, the government largely succeeded in carrying the country with it, and even reassuring the whites.[7] The experience did, however, alert the president to the constraints imposed on policy by an inadequately informed population in a racially divided society.

DECISION NO. 22: SHUNNING OAU
DIPLOMATIC SANCTIONS (6-12 DECEMBER 1965)

The decision of the OAU Council of Ministers on 3 December to call on member states to sever diplomatic relations with Britain if it failed to crush the Rhodesian rebellion by 15 December[8] proved profoundly embarrassing to Zambia. The intention of the resolution – to jolt Britain into acting with greater vigour and determination – was accepted as admirable. But Kaunda was painfully aware of the high costs of compliance; implementation would have meant forfeiture of British contingency and development assistance as well as defence support, including the RAF Javelins and any prospect of a Kariba force. By insisting that Britain bore full responsibility for the spill-over effects of UDI on neighbouring states,[9] Zambia had placed itself in a position of almost total dependence on British goodwill for its economic salvation. For Lusaka to have imposed diplomatic sanctions on Britain while simultaneously demanding full compensation for the costs of confronting Rhodesia would not only have been counter-productive but conceivably suicidal. "If we cut off diplomatic relations with Britain," Kaunda asked rhetorically, "how can we make her meet these obligations?"[10]

In supporting the OAU initiative in Addis Ababa, the Zambian foreign minister, unlike some of his colleagues, was not swept along on a mere tide of emotion. On the contrary, Kapwepwe played a prominent part in promoting it,[11] even to the extent of urging withdrawal from the Commonwealth as an additional act of solidarity.[12] In each case Kapwepwe acted on his own without specific instructions. Whether he ever contemplated the decision to withdraw applying to Zambia is doubtful, since his brief was to emphasize Zambia's special circumstances. On his return home he certainly seemed to suggest that the purpose of the resolution was purely declaratory – a measure of the intensity of African feelings and frustrations. In effect, it represented "what the OAU would like to do if it could, even while knowing it could not."[13]

Although Kaunda might well have felt compelled to support the proposal had he been in Addis Ababa,[14] he had no illusions concerning its awesome implications for Zambia's ability to resist Rhodesian retaliation. Accordingly, following a cabinet session on 6 December at which Kapwepwe reported at length, Kaunda wrote to OAU heads of state to outline his predicament. When he realized that Tanzania was determined to honour its OAU obligations, he hurriedly and anxiously sought out a meeting with Nyerere in Mbeya, across the border in Tanzania, with a view to minimizing the adverse consequences of Tanzanian action for Zambia. Finally, after further cabinet consideration the government announced on 15 December that the peculiar "geographical and economic position of Zambia in South and Central Africa" made it difficult to comply with the OAU resolution at present.[15]

Coping

Information. The instinctive reaction of the Zambian government was to assume that it had little choice but to ignore the OAU resolution. Yet before reaching a final decision to opt out, it sought clarification on four aspects. The first involved its obligations under the OAU charter. Zambia was less concerned with the binding character of the resolution than with its moral obligations. Despite Kapwepwe's claim that defaulters would be "answerable to the Council," the considered opinion in Lusaka was that the "decision" was legally merely a recommendation.[16] More disturbing was Nyerere's eloquent argument that the "honour of Africa" and perhaps the survival of the OAU demanded compliance.[17] The Zambian conscience was to some extent eased when, on further inquiry, it was found that this uncompromising stand was not widely shared, and that OAU pronouncements could not be held to override vital national interests.

Discreet diplomatic soundings also relieved Lusaka of the fear that it might find itself politically isolated from the rest of the continent; Kapwepwe's report that OAU members "really mean business" had been particularly worrying.[18] More serious was the prospect that diplomatic sanctions by neighbouring states, especially Tanzania, might prejudice the willingness or ability of Britain to assist Zambia develop alternative outlets to the sea. Again, Kaunda felt moderately reassured when Nyerere undertook to do his best to limit the damage to Zambian interests.[19]

Finally, Lusaka was interested in discerning whether London might be driven to take some dramatic initiative prior to the deadline to demonstrate its sincerity. It quickly transpired, however, that the British government was "in no mood to be pushed" into adopting "irresponsible actions," particularly after the humiliation Wilson had suffered as a result of the African (and Zambian) walkout on the occasion of his recent address to the UN General Assembly.[20]

Consultation. Kaunda was well aware that daring to defy the OAU and parting company with Nyerere could prove politically sensitive and divisive. Accordingly, he was careful to consult potential critics inside and outside the country more widely than was his custom. He lobbied for support within his parliamentary caucus and the national council of UNIP as well as in cabinet.[21] He also appears to have attempted to reassure the mining companies, who were showing increasing signs of alarm. Kaunda also sought to test the climate of opinion elsewhere on the continent and overseas, sounding out the views of the diplomatic community in Lusaka and recalling several of his ambassadors for consultations.[22]

When Kaunda wrote to the other African heads of state he underscored the unique dilemma his country faced. "As President of Zambia," he declared, in justifying his initiative publicly, "I feel it is my duty to explain to my fellow leaders the difficult position in which Zambia would find herself in the circumstances that would follow" a break with Britain. The response was generally positive. As Kaunda reported, most leaders with "Zambia's interests at heart" appreciated its "peculiar problem."[23] Chief among its public defenders was Nyerere. Privately, however, he was never fully persuaded by Kaunda's "caution." Having pressed Kaunda strongly but unsuccessfully to set an example that the rest of Africa would feel bound to follow, he now sought to minimize the potential contagion of Zambia's dangerous precedent by stressing its unique circumstances. He declared that Zambia was the one OAU member that "no sane person could ask to implement" a diplomatic break, since it was already "bearing enough suffering in Africa's cause."[24] A minority, however, remained unassuaged. Their reproaches caused Kaunda great distress, and led him to lash out angrily. In particular, he denounced as "misleading" and "utterly stupid" the calumny that, "because we haven't broken our relations with Britain, we are being soft."[25] Zambia also opposed convening an emergency OAU summit to reopen the issue, in part no doubt because of reluctance to risk further pillorying.[26]

Meanwhile Kaunda was experiencing counter-pressures from elsewhere. Britain, in particular, gently impressed on him (and other African leaders) the calamitous consequences of succumbing to "misguided emotionalism," and urged him to enlighten the more irrational OAU members on the folly of undermining Wilson's carefully designed strategy on Rhodesia. Ottawa too weighed in on Britain's side with a letter drafted in close concert with the Commonwealth Relations Office. In it, the acting prime minister pleaded with Kaunda not to prejudice his own position or precipitate a Commonwealth crisis by any ill-considered action.[27]

Alternatives. Zambian decision makers were convinced that there was no realistic alternative to maintaining and strengthening their political and economic links with Britain. The only scope for discretion was whether and to what extent Zambia should seek to influence the responses of other OAU members. Their decisions were not a matter of indifference. While Zambia welcomed any pressure that spurred Britain on to greater efforts, there was a danger that a secondary diplomatic sanction might provoke it into reacting negatively. At the same time, Lusaka was reluctant to take any initiative that could be interpreted as undermining the authority of the OAU. In the circumstances, there were four possible postures Zambia could adopt: active dissuasion; selective dissuasion; dissuasion by example; or neutrality. The cabinet appears to have devoted considerable attention to exploring each of these alternatives, and to evolving a consensus – somewhat incrementally over a period of days from 6 to 12 December – that carried unanimous ministerial support. Nevertheless, several members, including Kapwepwe, acquiesced only reluctantly in the ultimate choice.[28]

Choice

The final outcome of the cabinet's deliberations was inevitably something of a compromise. Its essential elements were: no diplomatic break with Britain "at present"; no overt attempt to influence other OAU members except Tanzania; and a forthright defence of Zambian abstention. Kaunda insisted that "it is not within my province to tell other nations whether they should break their ties with Britain or not."[29] Nevertheless, the mere fact of informing them of Zambia's decision was bound to affect their perceptions of the issue. Kenya, in particular, was explicit in citing Zambia's predicament as an excuse to justify its own inaction.[30] In the end only nine of the thirty-six OAU members complied with the OAU appeal and of these, only Tanzania's action imposed serious problems for Zambia.³¹ However, the whole experience drove home to Zambia how excessively dependent it was on Britain and Tanzania in any effort Lusaka might take to disengage from Rhodesia.

DECISION NO. 23: DIVERSIFYING DEPENDENCE
(C. 12 DECEMBER 1965)

There was no easy escape from Zambia's dilemma. The more it sought to extricate itself from dependence on Rhodesia, the more it found itself beholden to Britain and, as a result, the more constrained it felt in its foreign policy behaviour and the less capable of exercising persuasive influence on British policy. Lusaka was particularly anxious to pin primary responsibility for ending the Rhodesian rebellion on London; yet the more Britain succeeded in retaining firm control over the management of the Rhodesian crisis on behalf of the world community, the less punitive were the measures it seemed prepared to permit, especially in the matter of force. Only when there appeared to be some remote threat of OAU or Soviet intervention did it modify – reluctantly, ambiguously, and inadequately – its categorical opposition to any British military pressure in central Africa.

The recent painful reminder of Zambian disabilities as an international actor led the government to explore ways of breaking out of the country's international strait-jacket.

Lusaka now decided it was "necessary and timely" to turn to two of the leading members of the UN for assistance. Accordingly, on 15 December, simultaneously with its statement on the OAU resolution and no doubt as part of the price of unanimity on that decision, the government announced its intention of dispatching "high-powered" goodwill ministerial missions to Moscow and Washington. This surprise initiative represented a dramatic break with tradition which had accorded pre-eminence to Zambia's bilateral relations with Britain.³² It was also unexpected, as Kaunda had warned frequently and fervently of the dangers of introducing Cold War complications into southern Africa. But he had also always been careful to reserve the right to invite in outsiders, and specifically the Americans and, by implication, the Russians (or the Chinese) should this be judged necessary.³³

Coping

It seems probable that the superpower option was first entertained as early as 28 November when Kaunda met with his senior ministers in Ndola to assess the alternatives available to them.³⁴ The actual decision, however, was taken somewhat precipitately in the course of the debate over the OAU recommendation. Since the proposed missions were themselves exploratory, little need was felt for further information beyond the customary inquiries undertaken to confirm that the timing of the visits was convenient. Nor were there extensive consultations. The Zambian ambassador to Washington had previously been summoned home, and his views were no doubt solicited. With respect to the Soviet Union, the permanent secretary in the Ministry of Foreign Affairs, who had only recently returned from Moscow, was able to report on the reactions of Soviet leaders to the Rhodesian issue and especially the widespread misconceptions there concerning Zambian policies.³⁵ It also seems likely that Kaunda sounded out Nyerere's opinion at Mbeya.

The opportunities available to Zambia for diversifying its sources of material support were limited. A sympathetic response from the Commonwealth was assured. For this reason, Zambia had requested that the issue of economic sanctions and their impact on Zambia be raised at a conference of senior Commonwealth trade officials in London at the end of November.³⁶ This proved useful in alerting a broad cross-section of the international community to the perils confronting the country, even if few members were in a position to offer more than token assistance. Only the major powers were capable of intervening significantly. Of the two superpowers, the United States was viewed as a more promising prospect as well as, for some, the preferred partner. Nevertheless, in the interests of non-alignment and cabinet solidarity, simultaneous approaches to Washington and Moscow were considered *de rigueur*.

If the choice of target states was easy and obvious, defining the mandates of the proposed missions was less so. The press announcement was distinctly and no doubt deliberately vague on this point; it merely stated that the ministers would discuss "safeguarding [Zambia's] ownership rights to Kariba power installations" and "other related matters."³⁷ In actual fact, considerable care seems to have been taken, within the limits of the time available, to survey, evaluate, and select from the range of possible purposes. Among the objectives considered were publicizing Zambia's plight and exploring potential areas of cooperative action, especially contingency aid and enforcement measures. Yet it is by no means certain that the terms of reference of the ministerial teams were ever fully clarified. There is also evidence to suggest that the principal purpose of the exercise was to shake the British out of their complacency rather than to secure specific Soviet and American commitments. If so, the tactic was largely, but not entirely, unsuccessful.

The mission to Moscow reinforced Wilson's fears of a Zambian-Soviet conspiracy to deny critical supplies of Zambian copper to British industry. So concerned did he appear that, two days after the announcement on 15 December of the proposed visit to Moscow (and unbeknown to Lusaka), he despatched an urgent "top secret" message to Sir Humphrey Gibbs, the beleaguered governor of Rhodesia, with an alarming report for transmission to Ian Smith. In it, Wilson asserted that

> it is doubtful whether a mandatory military resolution can be delayed more than a few weeks if that ... Smith should realize that it is most unlikely that international military action including inevitably certain big powers can be delayed for more than a very short period and the likelihood of Russian or Eastern European participation is very grave ... In my view you should send for Smith now and give him the full substance of this message and underline the grave responsibility lying on him if Rhodesia is going to become the cockpit of the gravest type of military intervention.

How much Wilson was simply indulging his imagination and how much he seriously expected to shock Smith into abandoning UDI is unclear. The scenario was so improbable that Smith, not surprisingly, simply ignored Wilson's dire warning.[38]

Choice

The decision, as finally ratified by the cabinet (apparently at the same emergency session on 12 December at which the decision to maintain diplomatic relations with Britain was confirmed[39]) involved a two-stage strategy. The ministerial teams would first make one final appeal to Britain to take the necessary measures to safeguard Kariba power from sabotage by the Rhodesians.[40] Since cabinet ministers had little faith that the response would be other than negative,[41] arrangements were then made for the teams to proceed separately to Washington and Moscow.

On his departure overseas, Foreign Minister Kapwepwe spelled out the objectives of the missions as he understood them. These were:
1 To ask the American and Soviet governments:
   – "to use force against Smith,"
   – "to help us to airlift oil into Zambia," and

- "to repair the [Great North] road between Zambia and Tanzania."
2 "To explain our stand why we opposed Smith," namely,
- "that the minority should not impose themselves on the majority,"
- "that it will never help the white population to live peacefully with the Africans in Rhodesia and indeed the whole of Africa,"
- "to avoid the racial war," and
- "to avoid an ideological war."[42]

How closely the ministers adhered to this brief is unclear. According to diplomatic and press reports at the time, the issues they actually pursued were:
1 Securing superpower support for a campaign of increased pressure on Britain to deploy troops on the Rhodesian side of the Kariba dam;
2 assessing the feasibility of mounting a UN force for Kariba and/or imposing comprehensive mandatory sanctions under chapter 7 of the UN Charter;[43]
3 canvassing the prospects of mobilizing adequate contingency aid to enable Zambia to survive a complete economic break with Rhodesia; and
4 clarifying Zambian (and OAU)[44] policy, especially for the benefit of the Soviets whose perception of Zambia was that of a South African neo-colony.

To counter rumours of a cabinet split on ideological lines, Kaunda designated Simon Kapwepwe, with his reputation for radicalism and his alleged suspicion of Americans, to head the mission to Washington, and dispatched the more diplomatic Arthur Wina to Moscow.[45] Neither team returned with much to show for its efforts. By the time the Zambians reached Washington, the Americans had announced their support for oil sanctions and a major commitment to participate in the oil airlift. An American survey team had arrived earlier to explore the possibilities of upgrading the Great North Road to Tanzania as an alternative to reliance on the Rhodesia Railways.[46] Beyond these measures, the Johnson administration, increasingly preoccupied with Vietnam, was not prepared to go at that time. There was certainly no intention of departing from British policy, particularly in the matter of enforcement measures.[47]

The mission to Moscow was even less productive. Despite the clichéd verbiage of the lengthy joint communiqué, according to the Zambian ambassador there the delegation "returned home empty-handed and thoroughly disappointed." In particular, the Soviets curtly refused to join in the oil airlift. Even the negotiations for the purchase of a fleet of trucks and tankers on strictly commercial terms ultimately collapsed.[48] The most that could be claimed was some progress in rehabilitating Zambia's tattered, neo-colonial image within the Kremlin, and in checking Soviet criticism of Zambian policy.[49]

Zambia's brief experiment to diversify its international dependence only served to confirm there was little alternative to increased reliance on Britain. If the British were a large part of the problem, they also offered the one slim hope of an eventual solution. However much Lusaka resisted and resented it, Zambia could only proceed at a pace dictated by London. This lesson was again driven home with particular force when Zambia confronted the issue of severing its economic ties with the south.

DECISION NO. 24: OIL SANCTIONS (17 DECEMBER 1965)

With the passage of time, it became increasingly difficult for Zambia to justify further delay in reaching a definitive decision on whether and to what extent to join in UN sanctions. The initial instalment implemented immediately after UDI (Decision No. 17) was more a holding operation than a promise of things to come. Since then, the UN Security Council on 20 November had called on all members "to do their utmost in order to break all economic relations" with Rhodesia, and specifically to impose an embargo on oil, and Britain on 1 December had extended its sanction list to include virtually all Rhodesian exports. This left Zambia, as Rhodesia's leading market, more politically isolated than ever.[50]

Time did little to resolve Zambia's dilemma. While it had no faith in the efficacy of sanctions to bite swiftly or decisively, realistically it had to recognize that they were Wilson's chosen instrument; the choice was between sanctions and nothing – or worse. In the circumstances, Lusaka had no real alternative but to acquiesce in British policy and press for its energetic enforcement, while at the same time treating it as a test of British sincerity.[51] This implied gearing Zambia up to withstand a complete economic rupture with Rhodesia, and specifically a reciprocal oil embargo. Kaunda was convinced that, if the sanctions option was to succeed, full Zambian participation was essential. Accordingly, three days after UDI in his first *démarche* to Wilson, he appealed for early and adequate contingency support to ensure his country's economic survival. No doubt he also hoped in this way to draw Britain more deeply into conflict with Rhodesia. The British (and the Americans) were appalled at the audacity of the Zambians, and responded quickly with dire warnings that there was no way the country's economy could be sustained in such circumstances. In any case, so supremely confident was Wilson in the soundness of his sanctions strategy that initially he even contended that direct Zambian participation was unnecessary to topple Smith.[52] To reinforce this message, Malcolm MacDonald was dispatched to Lusaka to caution Kaunda against acting irresponsibly.

London's nervousness and naiveté over sanctions enforcement only increased Zambian suspicions that Wilson was more concerned with the risk to the supply of Zambian copper and with the mounting restlessness in the ranks of the Conservative opposition than with any serious commitment to confront the Rhodesian rebellion. Kaunda particularly resented the British using Zambian vulnerability as an excuse for their own inaction. He insisted that the first priority should be "to take firm steps against the rebel regime." In the process, it was inevitable that Zambia was "going to suffer as a result of mistakes committed by successive British governments" but its perilous position ought to be accepted as a challenge to be met by mobilizing British and international aid, rather than as a constraint on policy.[53] In the meantime, Lusaka continued to proceed cautiously.

The next instalments of sanctions measures, announced on 6 and 16 December, involved increased restrictions on financial dealings with Rhodesia. There was not, however, any curtailment of trade. Even the simultaneous introduction of import controls was designed to ration traffic on the overextended Rhodesia Railways on the basis of national priorities rather than by source. The nearest thing to a hint at more drastic measures was the finance minister's appeal to Zambian businesses "still tied to Rhodesia administratively" to dissociate themselves from their parent firms as soon as possible.[54]

Although Zambia continued to urge that international sanctions should be comprehensive as well as coercive, its principal preoccupation was with the problem of oil. This was the really critical economic weapon in terms of its psychological symbolism, its potential impact on the Rhodesian economy, and its repercussions on Zambia. Kaunda stressed that the success of oil sanctions depended on three conditions being met: prompt implementation, effective action to plug the anticipated loopholes through South Africa and Mozambique, and the organization of adequate alternative supply routes for Zambia's oil.[55] With all Zambian oil imported through the south, it was certain that Salisbury would retaliate against any British-organized oil embargo by immediately cutting off Zambian supplies. Even in the absence of sanctions, Zambia's oil stocks were causing Kaunda great anxiety.[56] As a matter of deliberate policy, instituted in October 1965 in preparation for UDI, Rhodesia in collusion with the international oil companies had set about systematically running down Zambian reserves.[57]

No aspect of pre-UDI contingency planning had been studied as thoroughly as the mounting of an Anglo-American emergency airlift (Decisions No. 2 and 9). Nevertheless, Wilson waited five weeks[58] before personally approaching President Johnson on 16 December to secure his agreement both to participate in an aerial rescue operation and to press American oil companies to respect a voluntary oil ban.[59] However, once Washington's support was ensured, events moved swiftly. The following day London sought Zambia's concurrence.[60] There had already been intensive discussions with the British at the official level on the operational aspects of the airlift, but final clearance had yet to be reached at the political level. In the event, cabinet agreement was obtained quickly, if not easily, thus paving the way for an immediate public announcement that same day.

Coping

The decision to endorse oil sanctions was one of the most momentous the Zambian government took in the course of the UDI crisis. As the American ambassador subsequently recounted, "It was an extraordinary situation. Not only the economy of [the] country but quite possibly its political viability were placed in jeopardy in order that a rebellion in a neighbouring country might be defeated and the rights and duties of a third country might be upheld. In all this Zambia was an innocent bystander."[61]

When the cabinet convened on short notice on 17 December to consider its response, it was well aware that an embargo posed grave risks for the nation. "Everyone around the cabinet table knew that at stake was not only the intricate industrial mechanism of the Copperbelt, but the willingness of already edgy whites to stay at their jobs" in government as well as in industry.[62] Before committing itself irrevocably, therefore, it was anxious to obtain the fullest possible information on which to base a considered judgment. In particular, it sought clarification on the depth of global commitments to the enforcement of oil sanctions, the expectation of success in toppling the Smith regime, the estimated duration of the emergency, the forms, sources, and adequacy of international assistance to Zambia, and whether the costs would be commensurate with the results. The answers to these queries were neither easy nor, in all cases, fully reassuring.

Information. Of immediate concern to the assembled cabinet members were the logistical arrangements for the projected airlift. Moving thousands of oil drums over long distances under conditions prevailing in Central Africa was a formidable undertaking. For the operation to prove feasible, it was essential to enlist the cooperation of countries with major air transport capabilities and to secure base facilities on the coast within reasonable range of the Copperbelt. By itself Britain lacked adequate airlift capacity to sustain a rescue operation on the scale required, but with the commitment of the Americans to the enterprise the previous day its viability seemed assured. The prospect that the Canadians might also join in was greatly welcomed, as much for political reasons as for the added payload they could contribute.[63] As for neighbouring states, Nyerere had confirmed that the British could use Dar es Salaam's facilities even if, in the meantime, he had broken diplomatic relations with London (he was later to qualify this offer).[64] Access to airfields in Zaire and especially in Angola and Mozambique was more problematical and, in fact, negotiations with the Portuguese never reached a final conclusion (Decision No. 27). With respect to the new Zairien regime, relations were somewhat delicate as a result of an off-the-cuff comment of Kaunda's describing Mobutu's coup of 25 November as a "sad development." Despite efforts to patch up the "misunderstanding" and general assurances of support from General Mobutu, Zambia was unable to take anything for granted.[65] This uncertainty was serious as Zairien facilities were to prove vital since both the American and Canadian airlifts eventually operated out of Kinshasa.

A major concern of Zambian ministers was to tie the British down to firm figures and dates for oil deliveries. They were particularly anxious to ensure that the planned capacity of the airlift was adequate to meet the country's reasonable, though inevitably reduced, consumption requirements. They also sought assurances that the target level would be reached quickly, before Zambia's dwindling oil stocks were exhausted. To clarify the dimensions of the crisis the country faced, Kenneth Knaggs, secretary general of the recently reorganized Contingency Planning Organization, was called in to testify. He reported the chilling fact that current reserves amounted to less than two weeks' normal needs, and predicted that, even with severe rationing and projected deliveries, stocks would continue to decline to less than two days' requirements before the build-up of supplies met minimum demands. Yet the most the Zambians could get the British to commit themselves to in terms of totals and timetables was a "best endeavour" undertaking.[66]

Equally vital for rational decision making, and even more uncertain, was whether oil sanctions would actually "work." The Zambians were prepared to risk national survival, but only if the agony was not unduly prolonged and there was a reasonable guarantee that their sacrifices would succeed in ridding Rhodesia of minority rule. This was a matter of grave concern, especially to the "nationalist" ministers led by Kapwepwe. In assessing the prospects of an early rebel collapse, Lusaka remained unpersuaded by London's excessive optimism; it knew of no grounds to suggest that Smith would succumb under pressure of sanctions alone. Zambia was also sceptical that an oil embargo would be adequately respected internationally. Wilson's incredibly naive confidence that Pretoria and Lisbon would prove cooperative, or at least hesitate to intervene decisively to bolster Rhodesia, was rightly discounted as mere wishful thinking.[67] Nevertheless, despite their grave misgivings, ministers had yet to recognize just how monumentally incompetent the British sanctions operation would prove.[68] Consequently, they were less distrustful of British intelligence than they had reason to be, and later learned to become. In agonizing over their decision, therefore, they acted on a partially incomplete and faulty information base. The one thing the Zambians did know for certain was that, if Britain imposed oil sanctions, Rhodesia would quickly punish Zambia.

In its search for information and guidance, the Zambian government consulted fairly widely in advance of the final cabinet session. A principal source of advice was its own Contingency Planning Organization. This served as a major coordinating agency, with the mining companies, the oil-marketing companies,[69] and the British and American diplomatic missions all regularly represented on its deliberative bodies. Of these various interests, liaison with the British was the closest and most continuous.[70] Kaunda also conferred with Nyerere and had an opportunity to consult with the Zambian ambassadors to Zaire, the United States, and the United Nations, and the high commissioner to Britain, who had earlier been recalled to Lusaka to report on developments at their posts. The most important consultations Kaunda held, however, were with his cabinet. The decision on oil sanctions was so agonizing that, as he himself explained, it would have been difficult to implement without the full support of his ministers.[71]

Alternatives. When members of the cabinet gathered at State House on 17 December to deliberate on the fate of the nation in the face of the mounting international momentum for oil sanctions, they quickly realized – and resented – how limited their real options had become. In theory they could still decline to participate and hope to escape unscathed. Britain would then have had two choices. It could have overridden Lusaka's objections, proceeded with an oil embargo, and left Zambia to cope with Rhodesian counter-sanctions on its own with little claim to international sympathy or support. Alternatively, it could have acquiesced in a Zambian veto, abandoned the attempt to apply oil sanctions (which Zambia and other African states had consistently clamoured for) and presumably sought a settlement with Smith at the expense of the African majority. Suspicion that the British were secretly anxious to "sell out" was certainly a powerful deterrent to Lusaka giving London the excuse it was assumed to want. As Kaunda explained, "Zambia could hardly afford to say 'No,' ... as this might tempt Britain to lay the failure of its policy at Zambia's door." Accordingly, he resigned himself to the inevitable, though he felt "deeply angered that his friends in London should have placed him in such an unenviable position."[72]

Choice

Once the principle of participation was conceded, the only remaining room for manoeuvre concerned the precise terms of acceptance. There were four conditions ministers wanted the British to agree to: (1) full financial compensation; (2) an increase in airlift capacity as well as a more rapid buildup of fuel stocks; (3) a deadline by which, if the rebellion had not ended, force would be used to supplement sanctions; and (4) an airlift of coal, food, and spare parts in addition to oil.[73]

Although the third condition was, not unexpectedly, once again flatly rejected,[74] as was the fourth, the first two were substantially met. The British undertook to bear the full costs of their airlift (as did the Americans and the Canadians later) and intimated a willingness to be more responsive in the parallel negotiations on contingency aid which were simultaneously under way in Lusaka. The real point of contention turned out to be the target tonnage for oil deliveries. Initially the British promised 10,000 tons a month compared with normal consumption of 17,000 tons but, as a result of firm Zambian insistence, agreed to do their best to airlift in

14,000 tons. Without this concession it is doubtful if the "nationalists" in the cabinet could have been won over. As it was, Kapwepwe characterized the whole oil sanctions charade as an exercise in "slow torture" – for Zambia, not Rhodesia.[75]

Once the Zambian cabinet concurred in the British embargo, events moved swiftly. As anticipated, Salisbury reacted by immediately cutting off oil shipments to Zambia. Its action was followed two days later by the imposition of a punitive surcharge on coal exports destined for Zambia's railways and mines. That same day the first RAF transport aircraft touched down in Lusaka with a cargo of oil drums and on 23 December stringent gasoline rationing was introduced.[76] Within two weeks American and Canadian planes had joined the airlift,[77] thus narrowly averting a total exhaustion of available supplies. Even so, it was many months before the development of alternative surface routes enabled the airlift to end, and nearly three years before rationing could be lifted, following the completion in record time of an oil pipeline from Dar es Salaam to the Copperbelt. In December 1965, however, it was not at all certain that the Zambian economy would survive that long.

DECISION NO. 25: CONTINGENCY AID (C. 18 DECEMBER 1965)

Britain's perverse refusal to face up to the possibility of a determined Rhodesian bid for independence ensured that, when UDI was declared, no provision had been made for financial assistance to Zambia.[78] However, Kaunda wasted no time in pressing Wilson vigorously for substantial support as a matter of urgency. Although his initial approach (on 14 November) was pointedly ignored, Kaunda persisted, and eventually Malcolm MacDonald was sent out to find out what the fuss was all about. He returned to London on 28 November, armed with another forthright letter for Wilson, detailing a lengthy list of Zambian needs. MacDonald, as a result of his experiences in Lusaka, became persuaded that Zambia had a convincing case and that, for psychological as well as political reasons, Britain should respond swiftly and sympathetically.[79] Instead Sir Arthur Snelling, deputy under-secretary of state in the Commonwealth Relations Office, was despatched to Lusaka with a meagre offer of £1 million ($2.8 million) in contingency aid, principally for British-built trucks and railway cars.[80] While the British government prided itself on its generosity, the Zambians scorned the proffered grant as totally inadequate. Following further angry exchanges, however, the British government finally showed signs of comprehending the depth and dimensions of Zambia's concern. In mid-December a large ministerial delegation, headed by Cledwyn Hughes, minister of state for Commonwealth relations, and Maurice Foley, parliamentary secretary for economic affairs and a trusted friend of Kaunda's, descended on Lusaka with a mandate which for the first time enabled constructive negotiations to take place. These culminated on 19 December in an agreement embodying a commitment of £3.5 million ($9.8 million) in British goods and services for the development of alternative surface routes.[81]

A fundamental contradiction which embittered the controversy over contingency aid emerged from the sharply differing assumptions of the two parties. Whereas London confidently expected UDI to collapse within a few months at the most, Lusaka feared that reliance on sanctions alone portended a long, debilitating, and perhaps inconclusive economic confrontation. Kapwepwe's pessimistic prediction that the sanctions struggle could last "at least fifteen years" proved only too perceptive.[82] Secondly, London was anxious to occasion a minimum of disruption to the integrated economies of Central Africa – the proud legacy of the ill-fated Federation – in order to ensure that post-UDI reconstruction could take place quickly and smoothly. Lusaka, by contrast, saw UDI as an opportunity to disengage progressively and permanently from dependence on Rhodesia. As Kaunda explained, "The government is determined to turn this historical mishap into a blessing ... We will use this tragedy to cut our links with the racialist South."[83] Thirdly, London envisaged contingency planning as a shared-cost exercise in which Britain (and hopefully the international community) would supplement Zambia's own efforts to cope with its economic predicament; Lusaka, on the other hand, argued consistently that Zambia was an entirely innocent victim of past and present British policies. Accordingly, Britain was obliged to assume complete financial responsibility for the consequences, especially as it was so insistent on asserting its claim to sole legal responsibility for its errant colony.[84] Finally, London, perceived the contingency planning problem as one of deterring and, if necessary, countering any Rhodesian attempt to cripple the Zambian economy in retaliation for international sanctions, while Zambia conceived its purpose as preparing it to join fully in the economic offensive against Rhodesia.[85] Although the Hughes mission contributed to clarifying these competing perspectives, it only partially resolved the underlying conflicts.

Coping

If the British had been prepared to provide the blank cheque Zambia considered its right, Lusaka would have had few concerns over costs. As it was, there were three areas in which Lusaka felt a substantial need for additional information. The first was the magnitude of the British contribution; this did not prove easy to elicit. Prior to UDI, London had given little thought to the matter and, during the first weeks of the rebellion, perpetuated what one Zambian minister characterized as a "conspiracy of silence."[86] When it did produce a figure in early December, the sum proposed was scandalously inadequate to ensure even minimum life support. Secondly, Lusaka hoped for some indication as to whether and to what extent it could count on material support from neighbouring states and the international community generally. In the case of Tanzania, Nyerere had early made it clear that his government was in no position to assist financially with projects on its territory.[87] What was still uncertain, however, until his meeting with Kaunda at Mbeya, was the extent to which a diplomatic break with Britain would affect British participation in efforts to develop alternative surface and air routes through Tanzania. In the case of the major powers, the despatch of ministerial missions to Moscow and Washington was in part a quest for information concerning their likely responses. As for international organizations, the results of initial appeals to Commonwealth members, individually and collectively, had proved promising.[88] The United Nations, on the other hand, had offered no encouragement. Finally, Zambia needed to be able to quantify, at least in global terms, the anticipated cost of the projected contingency planning exercise, in order to estimate the residual financial liabilities it would be expected to assume. This was the most difficult as well as the most critical calculation.

Although the CPO was set up expressly to collect and process information on the financial and operational aspects of the contingency planning enterprise, it lacked the staff and resources to carry out its mandate on its own. Accordingly, it consulted closely and continuously with mining and commercial interests as well as with the American embassy and especially the British High Commission, both of which strengthened their staffs to ensure effective liaison.[89] In the absence of a Tanzanian mission in Lusaka, the Zambian High Commission in Dar es Salaam maintained direct contact with the Tanzanian Contingency Planning Committee and other government agencies there; a similar arrangement would shortly operate in Kinshasa throughout the airlift. At the political level, Kaunda was in constant communication with both Wilson and Nyerere. On specifically financial concerns, however, the most intimate consultations were with the British. In the four weeks leading up to the 19 December aid agreement, two British ministerial missions journeyed to Lusaka, Malcolm MacDonald paid three visits, and numerous officials and experts descended on the capital, many of whom were involved in contingency aid negotiations.[90]

The precise succession of events leading up to the Zambian decision to accept the British aid package is not entirely clear. Negotiations with the British got off to a shaky start as a result of Cledwyn Hughes's ill-judged interview with the press on arrival prior to meeting the government. The Zambians took great umbrage at both the substance of his remarks and especially the perceived breach of protocol committed. Kaunda refused (or, according to his own account, was "forbidden" by his colleagues, reportedly led by Kapwepwe) to receive the British ministers until the day of their departure.[91] The British did succeed on 16 December in establishing some sort of negotiating arrangements with Finance Minister Arthur Wina and CPO Secretary General Kenneth Knaggs. A broad consensus, subject to cabinet confirmation, appears to have been reached early on a division of financial responsibilities. Maurice Foley then reportedly spent two days signing a "wad of vouchers" covering orders for British road and rail equipment. Subsequent more detailed negotiations proved more difficult, partly as a result of the chaotic state of telephone communications with London but also because Wina had received only sketchy instructions. Nevertheless, progress was sufficient for draft proposals to be considered by cabinet on 17 December, though formal approval apparently came only a day or two later. To what extent the cabinet was involved in this final stage is not clear. The available evidence suggests that the decisional forum was effectively Kaunda and his senior ministers.[92]

The institution of oil sanctions on 17 December and the immediate Rhodesian retaliation against Zambia finally eliminated one Zambian policy alternative: the outright rejection of the British aid offer. With the survival of the nation threatened, neutrality in the Anglo-Rhodesia conflict was no longer an option. Even prior to this, the major issue at stake in the negotiations with the British was the definition of the categories of contingency planning costs for which they were willing to acknowledge financial responsibility. Although Lusaka's bargaining position was weak, it was not hopeless. Three broad possibilities existed – essentially the same alternatives the Zambian government had canvassed prior to UDI (see Decision No. 8):

1 Ideally, Lusaka wanted London to provide comprehensive coverage for the full economic costs of confronting the Rhodesian regime, including the resulting inflation and the consequences of deferred development.
2 Britain, on the other hand, considered its obligations were limited essentially to compensating Zambia for economic damage directly attributable to Rhodesian reprisals, actual or imminent – provided there was no Zambian provocation.
3 As its minimum negotiating position, the Zambian government argued that, in addition to reimbursing it for any direct harm resulting from UDI, Britain should accept responsibility for at least the contingency planning costs necessarily incurred outside Zambia.[93]

Choice

The Zambian negotiators quickly concluded that there was no prospect of persuading Britain to underwrite the Zambian economy and restore it to its former state at the conclusion of the crisis. London flatly refused to consider any commitment that was open-ended in terms of either time or money. Lusaka did, in a rather meaningless gesture, serve notice that it intended to seek redress from Britain "when the emergency is over" for the "economic and financial harm ... arising out of the actions of the illegal regime in Rhodesia." The most the British government was prepared to acknowledge was a vague responsibility to assist the Zambian economy "to the maximum extent in its power ... to meet the contingency created by the rebellion."[94] In practice this meant providing the "external" financing for approved contingency projects – initially some 35 per cent of the total.[95] Even this was subject to two qualifications: that the sums involved did not impose undue strain on the British economy, and that no project should extend beyond three months – the estimated life of the rebellion.[96] Britain also undertook to meet certain costs resulting directly from Rhodesian retaliatory actions, though only in cases where Zambia was economically unable to bear them. Thus the British assumed the full costs of the oil airlift, but declined to compensate Zambia for the massive increase in the Rhodesian coal royalty, presumably because the mining companies and the railway were judged capable of absorbing the additional charges.

The compromise on contingency financing was not what the Zambians had hoped for, but it was the best that could be expected in the circumstances.[97] In any case, it proved only an interim settlement. With the prolongation of the rebellion, controversy over contingency planning costs provided a continuing source of friction and frustration in relations between Lusaka and London.

DECISION NO. 26: RHODESIAN COAL ROYALTY (22 DECEMBER 1965)

Zambia was almost totally dependent on Rhodesian sources of energy. Initially, its greatest fear was the cutting off of Kariba power, but Salisbury chose instead to exercise its leverage over oil and coal supplies. Coal was particularly convenient as a weapon. Unlike power, it was not a common service to which Zambia had clear legal rights and, unlike oil, it was a Rhodesian resource rather than an overseas import. The Zambian market of over one and a quarter million tons of coal annually represented a significant source of foreign exchange, both directly and in rail charges. Accordingly, the Smith regime chose not to impose an export ban, as it had in the case of oil, but to apply a hundred-fold increase in the royalty.[98] This amounted to a price jump of nearly sixfold.

Rhodesian action to exploit Zambian vulnerability with respect to coal was not entirely unexpected. There had long been rumblings among Rhodesian Front backbenchers protesting against the sale of cheap coal to "hostile Zambia." The Salisbury government had resisted these pressures as likely to encourage precautionary countermeasures. Even after UDI it sought to reassure Lusaka that the introduction of export controls would not interfere with the coal trade.[99] Yet within a month, as sanctions began to pinch, a tougher line emerged. On 8 December Smith announced sweeping measures to acquire foreign exchange; in future, exports, including coal, would have to be paid for in advance in US dollars. He also threatened Zambia with increased coal charges as well as higher freight rates and the expulsion of Zambians resident in Rhodesia.[100] The Zambian response was to declare coal an "essential import" and to instruct the Bank of Zambia to make the necessary foreign exchange available, though it took another two weeks before Lusaka countered with similar financial restrictions on exports to Rhodesia.[101]

In the meantime, Smith had again taken to the air. On 19 December, in the aftermath of oil sanctions, he announced that his government had been forced with regret to impose coal and coke surcharges on Zambia. Much of the broadcast was taken up with a routine personal attack on Wilson for "asking Zambia to fight Britain's battle for her."

It is regrettable that Zambia, with whom we have always had good economic relations, to the mutual benefit of both countries has allowed herself to be talked into supporting Britain in the economic war against Rhodesia ... It is to be regretted even more that the greatest hardship will be borne by – not the real culprits, the British Government – but by the people of Zambia. However, ... I hope it will be [appreciated] that the more we are attacked, the more determined, indeed the more defiant, we become.[102]

Although there must have been times when Smith's ritualistic resort to crocodile tears evoked a sympathetic echo among Zambians, the government refused to succumb to his seductive oratory.[103] The issue was too crucial. As Kaunda explained, it posed a threat to "not only our economy but also our sovereign security and national dignity." He pondered his reply carefully before announcing his verdict in a broadcast to the nation on the evening of 22 December. "We cannot and will not cooperate or connive in these illegal efforts at gross extortion," he declared. "Therefore should [Smith] persist in trying to collect these illegal extra charges, we shall take measures to ensure that Smith's effort to threaten and blackmail us will fail utterly." In the words of the American ambassador, it was "an ultimatum without a time limit and a threat without a penalty."[104] Nevertheless, ten days later Smith suddenly backed down and suspended his punitive surcharges.[105] It was a classic example of where Kaunda's instincts for the right decision paid off brilliantly.

Coping

The Zambian authorities considered themselves exceptionally well-informed on Rhodesian actions and intentions. Their confidence had been boosted by the success of their intelligence sources in providing advance warnings of the hostile measures announced in Smith's two broadcasts of 8 and 19 December.[106] Kaunda also felt uniquely qualified, on the basis of long and intimate association, to fathom the workings of the minds of Rhodesian settlers, and hence to detect and interpret their behavioural patterns. (Zambian experience suggested that, in most situations, it was safe to assume the worst.) Where Lusaka did sense a need for additional data – though less acutely than might have been expected – was on the prospects and price of dispensing with Wankie coal entirely. It was also anxious to ascertain the extent to which it could count on the British for political and financial support, and on the multinational mining companies to use their influence in Salisbury to lobby on Zambia's behalf.

The consultative process was essentially a two-way affair. While the Zambians set about systematically sounding out London on its intentions,[107] the British and Americans in turn made urgent representations to the president, directly and indirectly, earnestly imploring him to exercise the utmost caution.[108] Somewhat surprisingly, the government's own CPO seems to have been only marginally involved in the formulation of policy, presumably because the issue was perceived of as more political than economic. On the other hand, the assistance of the mines, and especially of the Anglo-American Corporation, appears to have been actively sought. Certainly, there is every indication that the AAC, which found both its Zambian copper mines and its Rhodesian coal mines threatened with disruption or closure, intervened in Salisbury strongly and possibly decisively.[109] It was joined in this exercise by spokesmen for Rhodesian secondary industries which, though less concerned with the specific issue of coal, feared that further escalation of the conflict with Zambia would lead to the loss of their lucrative markets there. Pretoria too seems to have urged Salisbury to abandon its obvious blunder, and backed up its "advice" with an offer to sell South African coal to Zambia.[110]

In the case of the cabinet, consultation appears to have been less close than was customary for Kaunda. The Rhodesian bombshell was raised at the regular Tuesday morning meeting on 21 December and a number of options explored, including the possibility of a complete ban on Wankie coal imports. The issue seems not to have received the detailed discussion its gravity would appear to have justified, principally no doubt because of the absence overseas of the foreign, finance, and mines ministers, amongst others, all of whom might have exercised a restraining influence.[111] As a result, the final formulation of the Zambian response was very much a personal presidential decision. There is no evidence that the cabinet as a whole played any significant part in the process, or was even briefed on the precise terms of Kaunda's speech prior to its broadcast to the nation.

Alternatives. The president and his immediate advisers canvassed a wide range of policy options during the three days between Smith's initial announcement and Kaunda's public reply. One possible response was simply to give in to the ransom threat, as the government did in practice for ten days at the end of December.[112] The sum demanded was certainly within Zambia's capacity to pay and, even with the added surcharge, the cost of Wankie coal on the

Copperbelt was still, deliberately, kept slightly below that of supplies from any other source. But the issue at stake was the principle, not the price; to succumb to blackmail would have meant providing Salisbury with additional foreign exchange with which to circumvent sanctions. "The government of Zambia," Kaunda declared defiantly, "cannot be a party to any attempt by the illegal regime in Rhodesia to avoid the effects of economic sanctions." An even more compelling argument was the president's firm conviction that, "should we acquiesce now, who can doubt that it will be only a little while before further demands were made upon us" – as, indeed, Smith had already intimated. In Kaunda's mind, Zambia faced a Munich situation; if a clear stand were not taken now against appeasement, Rhodesia would continue systematically to subvert and ultimately destroy Zambia.[113]

A second strategy – and Kaunda's instinctive response on the morrow of the Smith broadcast – was to attempt to shift responsibility to Britain by insisting that it declare the action of the illegal Rhodesian regime illegal. If, then, the British failed to enforce their own edict, Lusaka would feel justified in demanding that they pay the royalty themselves or compensate Zambia fully. However, it quickly became apparent that London had no intention of assuming any legal or financial responsibility for rebel behaviour. Consequently Zambia was forced to consider other approaches.[114]

A third alternative was retaliation. This envisaged paying the coal royalty if necessary, but at the same time reducing Rhodesia's foreign exchange earnings from other sources by 10 per cent more than the increased levy. Kaunda hinted at this course of action when he announced that "any attempt by rebel leader Smith to get extra foreign exchange out of Zambia will be met with a response that will deprive him of rather more than he plotted to gain." The 10 per cent target could be reached by reducing imports from Rhodesia by one-third, and it was hoped in this way to induce Rhodesian businessmen threatened with the loss of their Zambian markets to register their complaints vigorously in Salisbury.[115]

In his fury and frustration, Kaunda's mind turned to contemplate even more daring and dangerous reprisals. The most audacious was a complete severance of trade relations with Rhodesia with the intention of deliberately precipitating a crisis of such monumental proportions – in the world copper market as well as in Southern Africa – that Britain would be forced, for economic if not moral reasons, to intervene decisively to crush the rebel regime. Although this scenario amounted to a calculated act of national economic suicide, it appears nevertheless to have received serious, if somewhat brief cabinet consideration, before being dropped. Kapwepwe, predictably, opposed any action that threatened the livelihood of Copperbelt miners.[116] A slightly less desperate measure was the proposal for a total embargo on the shipment of copper by the southern rail route. As the alternative outlets to the sea in process of development could carry at most only one-third of normal copper production, the balance would have had to be stockpiled. This would have had the advantage of pressuring Britain in addition to penalizing Rhodesia. Restricting the flow of copper to world markets and driving up the world price would have served as a forceful reminder to Britain of its critical dependence on Zambia. On the other hand, the cost to Zambia in deferred income would have been twenty times the freight revenue the Rhodesians stood to lose.[117]

A final trade sanction explored was an outright ban on Wankie coal imports. Direct retaliation against coal held a powerful appeal for Kaunda, who saw it as the most logical response to Rhodesian blackmail tactics. Yet although phasing out dependence on Wankie coal was already an important component in Zambian contingency planning,[118] instituting an immediate rupture in supply without prompting a subsequent shutdown of the Copperbelt posed a formidable logistical challenge. The Nkandabwe coalfield was not yet in production and was of inferior quality; the deposits in southern Tanzania were inaccessible; and a coal airlift, contemplated earlier, was no longer feasible. An experimental consignment of South African coal imported through Lobito confirmed the potentiality of the Benguela route as well as the need for time to develop it adequately. Similarly, various imaginative proposals to conserve coal by converting the mines to oil (itself in short supply) were still in the formative stage.[119] Nevertheless, despite the immense risks involved, Kaunda was reluctant to abandon the option completely.[120] He therefore devised a variant: instead of Lusaka seizing the initiative in banning Wankie imports, it could simply decline to pay the "illegal" impositions and leave it to Salisbury to assume responsibility for pressing its demands to the point of an open breach.

Choice

The actual decision as finally formulated shortly before Kaunda's broadcast to the nation on 22 December[121] combined three elements:

1 A qualified refusal to pay the additional coal royalty and coke tax. "Once [the British government] has pronounced these increases ... as illegal," Kaunda declared, "we shall expect the parties concerned to refuse to pay them."
2 A threat of unspecified substance: "Should the illegal Smith regime persist in trying to collect these extra charges ... we shall be forced to take counter measures."
3 The absence of a deadline for withdrawal. The original intention of issuing a one-week ultimatum was dropped under pressure from the British and Americans; the only hint of a time limit was the assertion that "we shall strike back promptly."

It was a cleverly calculated gamble, a classic exercise in brinkmanship, but one which could still prove a prescription for disaster. If Smith refused to retreat, Kaunda would be left with little option but to back up his brave words with costly deeds. "My countrymen," the president warned, "I cannot hide from you that we shall then knowingly and deliberately be embarking upon a course of action that may have grave repercussions upon the lives of us all."[122]

The dangerous game of bluff paid off in the end, and Kaunda's confidence in the soundness of his insights into rebel psychology was vindicated. Smith and his colleagues – ever ready to expect Africans to react irrationally – evidently took fright at the vagueness of the Zambian threats. They must also have come to recognize the folly of renouncing a major source of foreign exchange earnings. Accordingly, after some initial hesitation,[123] Smith responded on New Year's Day with a dazzling offer to suspend coal royalties for the time being and to resume the transshipment of oil products to Zambia "conditionally."[124] His goodwill gesture, he claimed, was a contribution to a "restoration of normal relationships" between neighbouring countries and "an end to this useless economic war." Kaunda's reaction was immediate and forthright: the offer was a cheap propaganda stunt. "Smith and his fellow rebels," he explained, "have made promises to us before which they have broken. What reason have we to believe that this will be any more genuine than offers he has made before?" At the same time Kaunda reiterated Zambia's determination to press forward toward a "permanent break with Rhodesia." The next day the Rhodesian Ministry of Commerce formally confirmed the suspension of the surcharges.[125] It was a signal and surprising Zambian victory, though scarcely evidence that the Smith regime was "coming down to its knees." A battle had been won, but the war raged on.[126]

DECISION NO. 27: BEIRA AIRLIFT
(C. 23 DECEMBER 1965)

The success of the Anglo-American-Canadian airlift, and hence the survival of Zambia, depended on the availability of adequate port and airfield facilities along the Atlantic or Indian Ocean coasts within reasonable range of Lusaka and Ndola, the two international airports in Zambia capable of handling heavy transport aircraft. The possibilities here were strictly limited, geographically, technically, and politically. The closest, and in many respects the most suitable, base was Beira in Mozambique. Yet the Zambian government still found the prospect of collaboration with the Portuguese politically embarrassing. Prior to UDI, Lusaka had managed to muster the courage to contact Lisbon for assurances concerning access to the Benguela Railway westward to Lobito (Decision No. 7) and to the circuitous road-rail route eastward through Malawi to Beira (Decision No. 14). However, nothing had been done to explore the possibility of operating an airlift from Portuguese colonial ports. Contingency planning to date had been based almost exclusively on the use of Tanzanian airfields. The UK/US survey team did not even mention Beira in its final report submitted on 12 November.[127] It was not until a month after UDI that the full dimensions of the logistical problem the airlift posed began to be appreciated.

Once detailed operational planning for the proposed airlift got under way towards the middle of December, it quickly became apparent how crucial Beira might be to its success, especially in view of the growing uncertainties surrounding the use of Dar es Salaam. Accordingly, the British approached the president, who appears to have accepted the logic of the evidence and authorized them to contact the Portuguese government. Sir Archibald Ross, the British ambassador in Lisbon, brought up the matter in the course of an urgent audience he secured with Dr Antonio Salazar on 17 December, the day oil sanctions were announced. The Portuguese dictator readily agreed in principle to a British oil bridge based on Beira. Armed with this assurance, Ross returned five days later with a formal request to Foreign Minister Franco Nogueira detailing the proposed arrangement and the specific facilities required.[128]

In the meantime, crisis fever was once again mounting in Lusaka. Salisbury had clamped its punitive coal royalty on Zambia and Tanzania had followed with an ominous ban on RAF use of Dar es Salaam.[129] The dwindling stocks of oil were also causing growing anxiety.¹³⁰ Having written to President Mobutu of Zaire on 21 December in a spirit of reconciliation,¹³¹ Kaunda now turned his mind to the need to effect a further rapprochement with the Portuguese. He had already instructed the Zambian mission at the United Nations to avoid any provocative action,¹³² but it appeared that something more positive would be required. Although the British had intervened in Lisbon on Zambia's behalf, the Portuguese had always expressed a preference for dealing with Lusaka directly. Kaunda had hitherto resisted according the Portuguese regime the desired measure of legitimacy. Confronted now with a rapidly deteriorating situation, he felt compelled to abandon his ideological scruples. On 23 December he wrote a personal letter to Dr Salazar.¹³³ That same day, Kapwepwe called on the Portuguese ambassador in Washington in great secrecy to reinforce Kaunda's appeal and amplify on Zambia's specific needs.¹³⁴

Coping

Kaunda was sensitive to the argument that Beira was essential to the economic survival of Zambia, once the hard data were presented to him. He did, however, insist on being persuaded, not just that Beira offered "the quickest and by far the best" route, as he stated in his letter to Salazar,¹³⁵ but that it was indispensable. His principal source of information and expertise was the team of British officials in Lusaka responsible for planning the operation. They, of course, had an interest in utilizing the easiest and cheapest routes, but London also saw a Beira airlift as a way of weaning the Portuguese away from Rhodesia and building up oil stocks in preparation for the final confrontation with the Smith regime.¹³⁶ The decisive factor in Kaunda's conversion appears to have been Nyerere's action, contrary to his assurances at Mbeya less than a fortnight earlier, of suddenly imposing serious restrictions on the British airlift out of Dar es Salaam.

It is not certain how widely Kaunda consulted Zambian opinion outside his immediate circle of State House advisers and the CPO. Pressure of time and the political sensitivity of the issue as well as security considerations seem to have limited the numbers involved. Although in his letter to the Portuguese prime minister, Kaunda referred to the wishes of "my government," there is no evidence of any cabinet participation in the policy process. Even senior ministers, several of whom were overseas at the time, appear not to have been consulted. Kapwepwe was obviously informed of the decision but played no direct part in it. Rather, it appears that in approaching Portugal, Kaunda was exercising his personal prerogative as president to act on his own initiative in the interest of the nation.

Prior to resigning himself to the necessity of a direct appeal to Salazar, Kaunda sought to satisfy himself that no practical alternative to reliance on Beira airport existed. Of the airfields in independent Africa with the potential to serve as coastal bases, only Dar es Salaam and Kinshasa had adequate ground facilities, and their distances from the nearest Zambian airport (over 50 and 100 per cent greater than in the case of Beira) severely limited their daily airlift capacity.[137] Consequently, as Kaunda explained to Salazar, "despite the present airlift which Britain is undertaking from Dar es Salaam and which is to be mounted shortly from the Congo by the Americans, these supplies will not meet all Zambia's requirements even when the airlift arrangements are working to capacity." Kaunda also inquired into the possibility of much greater use of road and rail routes. As he reported to Salazar, although "all possible land routes have been examined ... none offers an immediate solution to the present crisis."[138] The limiting factor here was time. Finally, Kaunda hoped it might suffice to allow London to conduct any negotiations with Lisbon on Lusaka's behalf. It soon became evident that the Portuguese intended to take advantage of Zambia's obvious discomfiture to extract long-sought political gains, notably recognition and respectability. "We wish to deal only with Zambia," Franco Nogueira noted in his diary, "and no one but her."[139]

Choice

Weighed down by the cumulative burden of successive escalations of the crisis, Kaunda found himself once again with no real option but to swallow his pride and his principles, and seek the assistance of the Portuguese colonialists. In the struggle for the liberation of Southern Africa, Rhodesia clearly took priority over Angola and Mozambique. Once Kaunda was convinced of the necessity of action, he seized the initiative swiftly, and penned his appeal to the Portuguese dictator:

It is my wish and that of my Government, to use the Beira/Blantyre land route and, more immediately, the Beira airport for the airlift. It is also my wish to use increasingly the port and air facilities at Lobito Bay ... My government fully realizes that the Portuguese Government may wish to remain neutral in this matter [between Britain and Rhodesia] but I am hopeful that Your Excellency's Government will be able to agree in principle to keep open a line of oil supplies to Zambia through Beira and Lobito Bay. I would greatly appreciate your cooperation in this matter.

On receipt of this, Salazar is reported to have remarked that the situation in Zambia must have been "truly distressing for Dr. Kaunda to take the unprecedented step of approaching" him. In any case, he responded promptly and affirmatively.[140]

During his meeting with the Portuguese ambassador in Washington, Kapwepwe had offered to send a delegation to Angola, Mozambique, or Lisbon to negotiate the physical arrangements for an airlift. Lusaka later had second thoughts on political grounds, and when Portugal opted for a ministerial meeting in Lisbon, Zambia politely refused. Fortunately President Banda of Malawi interceded, possibly at Kaunda's request, and secured Portuguese consent to the holding of talks at official level and in Mozambique. Two meetings did in fact transpire: a preliminary technical session in Beira on 27 January and a full-scale conference in Lourenço Marques, 15–17 February.[141] In the end, agreement proved elusive. The Portuguese were adamantly opposed to a British airlift as, in their paranoia, they suspected it was a clever cover for an invasion of Rhodesia or even the conquest of Mozambique.[142] But they were careful not to refuse the Zambian request outright, imposing instead crippling conditions which they knew would be refused.[143] The Zambians eventually abandoned the attempt to organize an airlift and concentrated on developing rail services, which Portugal (and Malawi) had always considered preferable and certainly more profitable, and which Zambia conceded were "simpler and more economical."[144] Lusaka was not too disappointed at its failure, as nearly two months had elapsed since its first approach to the Portuguese, and the country had since managed to survive the worst period of oil drought in early January. The British, however, were greatly upset, as the Beira airlift had been the cornerstone of Wilson's master plan to prepare Zambia for a complete break with Rhodesia (Decision No. 30).[145]

DECISION NO. 28: TANZANIAN OBSTRUCTION
(C. 27 DECEMBER 1965)

As a landlocked state, Zambia was acutely conscious of its dependence on its more fortunate maritime neighbours. The more it succeeded in disengaging from Rhodesia, the greater its dependency on others became. The dependency was as real, if less apparent, in relation to Tanzania as it was with respect to Portugal; despite the dramatic discrepancy in ideological affinities, both relationships demanded deference and discipline on the part of Zambia. In the case of Tanzania, the highly personalized nature of the Kaunda-Nyerere entente (which did not extend universally to the ministerial or official levels) was both its strength and its weakness. It tempered the clash of interests inevitable in such an unequal relationship, even if it did not fully eliminate them. It also placed Zambia at the mercy of Nyerere's intensely personal, if principled, ideological idiosyncrasies. These occasionally threatened vital Zambian interests when, as with the Dar es Salaam airlift, Nyerere appeared to pursue his quarrel with Britain at the expense of Zambian survival.

Prior to UDI, Zambia experienced some difficulty both in persuading Tanzanians of the imminence of UDI – Nyerere refused to take anything so irrational seriously – and in enlisting their sympathy for Zambia's plight. Their principal interest in strengthening communication ties between the two countries seemed to be the commercial benefits offered. Yet once UDI occurred, any lack of commitment Tanzanians may have had ended, certainly as far as Nyerere was concerned. "We assure you of our wholehearted cooperation," he declared in a telegram to Kaunda on 1 December: "To us, Zambia and Tanzania are one. For whatever assistance is within our power, you have only to ask and it is yours ... Zambia is in the front line but it is not true that it has no outlet to the sea. It has Tanzania. Even while we are politically separated, Zambia, Tanzania, and the whole of Africa, stands or falls together."[46]

Despite this welcome assurance, Zambian unease was not entirely assuaged. Consequently, when Nyerere threatened to sever relations with Britain, Kaunda rushed to Mbeya in some distress on 11 December to impress on him the possible implications for Zambia. Kaunda returned fully reassured by Nyerere's personal pledge that nothing would be done to interfere with British efforts to assist Zambia. Nyerere also specifically authorized, as he subsequently confirmed in writing, the mounting of a British airlift based on Dar es Salaam.[47] Moreover, to speed up the operation, he acquiesced in the deployment of RAF planes, pending the availability of civilian aircraft.[48] However, the sudden arrival unannounced of a British frigate in Dar es Salaam harbour on 22 December – albeit with a cargo of steel drums urgently needed for the oil airlift – proved too provocative, especially as rumours of an imminent British invasion swept the city.[49] Next day the Tanzanian government issued a blistering statement denouncing the RAF and RN presence as "not acceptable" and serving notice that "British military vessels and personnel should not be used in Tanzania for the purpose of the oil airlift to Zambia. The character of these operations must be completely civilian, not military."[50] After delicate negotiations, agreement was eventually reached on a timetable for phasing out RAF participation, but not before Zambians suffered through several anxious days and Kaunda dispatched his vice-president with a personal appeal to Nyerere not to overlook Zambia's vital interests.[151]

Coping

When news of the proposed Tanzanian statement reached Lusaka on 22 December the immediate need was for clarification from Dar es Salaam of the precise action intended, especially with respect to any time limit (on which the statement was silent). Lusaka was also anxious to ascertain the reaction of the British, particularly their ability and willingness to comply with the Tanzanian demands and the consequences for Zambia under various eventualities. Steps were taken, therefore, to pursue these issues urgently through diplomatic channels.[152] This did not prove easy. Nyerere was up-country and the Christmas holiday was approaching. Accordingly, Kaunda decided to attempt a more direct approach.

The president's options were limited. There was no hope of the Tanzanian government rescinding its ban, if only because it had already committed itself publicly. Nor could Zambia withstand an RAF withdrawal if it produced a hiatus in oil deliveries; the loss of even one day's supply – 16,000 gallons at that time – could prove crucial when stocks in the country were already perilously low and still declining. All that Kaunda could hope for was that Dar es Salaam would delay implementation of its order until replacement aircraft could be procured.

Choice

The president's decision involved a two-track approach: appealing to the British not to abandon the airlift exercise, despite their bewilderment at Tanzanian behaviour; and appealing to Nyerere to agree to an orderly transfer from a military to a civilian operation. To reinforce his message, he sent two ministers on short notice to Dar es Salaam bearing a personal letter for Nyerere. The mission was successful in that it returned with a written assurance that Tanzania would "do nothing to interrupt or slow down the air lift of oil to Zambia." Kaunda was delighted and relieved. The British, too, proved surprisingly understanding and cooperative. As a result, by the time the RAF withdrawal had been completed on 3 January the immediate panic had subsided, even if memories of it lingered on.[153]

The incident over RAF landing rights left one unforeseen legacy. It brought into the open the incipient strains that were beginning to emerge in neighbourly relations. Whereas Tanzanians, understandably, felt a certain envy at Zambia's copper wealth, Zambians came to suspect that Tanzanians were more interested in profiting from Zambia's misfortunes than in assisting it to cope with the consequences of UDI. Tanzania was perceived as the country that benefited most from UDI. One Zambian minister was even reported as stating jokingly that Ian Smith deserved a life-size statue in his honour in the Tanzanian capital. Fortunately, the close personal friendship that prevailed between Kaunda and Nyerere ensured that minor mutual recriminations were not allowed to get out of hand.

DECISION NO. 29: COMMONWEALTH CONFERENCE (C. 7 JANUARY 1966)

The initiative of the Nigerian prime minister, Alhaji Sir Abubakar Tafawa Balewa, on 12 December, in offering to host an extraordinary Commonwealth conference on Rhodesia in Lagos evoked little initial enthusiasm in Lusaka. Zambia reacted in a similar negative manner to suggestions of a UN Security Council meeting and an emergency OAU summit. Each of these proposals was perceived as a manoeuvre to undercut the OAU resolution on breaking diplomatic relations with Britain. Kaunda's basic reservation, echoing Nkrumah, was that this was no "time for conferences; it is a time for action."[154] By 7 January 1966 Kaunda's scepticism concerning the usefulness of the conference had modified somewhat, and he began to see some clear economic and political advantages for Zambia in attendance. Although unable to participate personally, he sent his vice-president in his place.[155]

Coping

With only a lukewarm interest in the proposed conference, Kaunda felt little compulsion to seek additional information before formulating a response. But as a number of other Commonwealth leaders were eager for him to participate, he was exposed to a barrage of arguments and pleas urging his attendance. Prime Minister Pearson of Canada was among those who were particularly anxious that Kaunda should attend, and his concern appears to have prompted Prime Minister Balewa to dispatch an urgent mission to Lusaka to appeal to Kaunda personally.[156] Similarly, once Wilson had made up his mind to attend, he sent Malcolm MacDonald on a fresh mission to Lusaka to persuade Kaunda to join him.[157]

There were also restraining influences on the president. Nyerere was no doubt consulted, and the reasons for his planned boycott carefully weighed. Nkrumah too appears to have communicated to Kaunda his determined opposition. At home, there were voices within the cabinet that favoured staying away, among them Kapwepwe, who had argued earlier at the OAU Council of Ministers for withdrawal from the Commonwealth. Admittedly, Kaunda appears to have made up his own mind in the absence of Kapwepwe overseas, for on 30 December he announced that "we will definitely attend" and named his foreign minister as a likely member of the delegation. Yet following Kapwepwe's return next day, the issue seems to have been reopened, with a final decision taken by the president in consultation with his senior ministers at a 3:00 a.m. session at State House on the morning of 7 January. Significantly, Kapwepwe was not included in the delegation.[158]

Once it was confirmed that the conference would definitely be held, Kaunda faced four possible responses: attend or stay away, attend briefly or send a deputy. Joining Tanzania, Ghana, and Australia in a boycott appealed strongly to Kapwepwe and the more militant ministers. Certainly, Kaunda had severe personal misgivings concerning the value of the exercise – as did Wilson and Pearson for their own reasons. His major reservation was the absence of any defined purpose to the meeting. On the other hand, in addition to his public commitment to Zambian participation, his natural instincts inclined him to be cooperative, especially in the case of the Commonwealth which he, unlike Kapwepwe, valued as an institution. More important, he came to realize that Lagos offered a promising forum in which to argue Zambia's case, and he was reluctant to allow Wilson to carry the day by default. It also provided an opportunity to press Zambian claims to significant international contingency assistance; the principal purpose of the Commonwealth, Kaunda asserted, should be "to help Zambia in her battle with Rhodesia."[159] In its present precarious economic state, Zambia could ill afford to miss any opportunity to enlist international sympathy and support. Nevertheless, Kaunda could not see his way clear to absenting himself from Zambia "for very long."[160] Both the external situation and to some extent the domestic scene were too uncertain to permit his departure for even three or four days. He did, however, explore the feasibility of a brief appearance, and even inquired of the British if they could provide a plane for the purpose. As this third option did not prove possible,[161] he was left with the final alternative of sending a deputy in his place.

Choice

The Zambian delegation arrived in Lagos well-briefed, and took full advantage of the Commonwealth platform to present its case forcefully and effectively. Zambia's dilemma emerged as a central concern of the conference, even though, at its conclusion, Kamanga ritualistically pronounced the conference "a useless exercise which did not serve any purpose."[162] It did at least succeed in establishing a committee to monitor sanctions and mobilize aid to Zambia. It also committed Wilson to a resumed session within six months (which typically he later managed to weasel out of). Of more immediate importance was the extent to which some of Wilson's excessive and unwarranted optimism rubbed off on the Zambians, a process which was completed when he flew on to Lusaka on 13 January to confer with Kaunda.

DECISION NO. 30: THE "QUICK KILL" (13 JANUARY 1966)

Prime Minister Harold Wilson's fast talking at the Lagos Commonwealth conference succeeded brilliantly in defusing African anger for the moment,[163] but only at the cost of creating unrealistic expectations that sanctions against Rhodesia "might well bring the rebellion to an end within a matter of weeks rather than months."[164] If faith in British leadership were not to suffer irreparably, it was now essential that Wilson back up his fine words with effective action. His failure to grasp the challenge was later to earn Britain the sobriquet of the "toothless bulldog."

The immediate task was to tighten the net of neighbours around Rhodesia. Portugal, it was correctly surmised, would prove uncooperative. Nevertheless, by shutting down the Beira-Feruka pipeline which supplied all Rhodesia's (and Zambia's) oil imports and, if necessary, mounting a naval blockade of Beira port,[165] it was hoped to neutralize Mozambique's entrepôt trade with Rhodesia. In the case of South Africa, London was reconciled to Pretoria's inevitable rejection of sanctions on principle, but it continued to assume naïvely that Prime Minister Verwoerd's pledge of non-intervention and his commitment to maintain "normal" commercial relations "as in the past" signalled an assurance that there would be no *increase* in trade with Rhodesia, especially in oil – which had not previously been imported through South Africa.[166] That left Zambia – the major consumer of Rhodesian manufactures, coal, and rail services – as the principal remaining gap to plug. Despite the one-third cut in Zambia's imports from Rhodesia achieved to date,[167] the pressure was on Lusaka to end its remaining sanction-busting, or bear the opprobrium of having sabotaged the international effort to crush the Rhodesian rebellion.

As preoccupations nearer home had kept Kaunda from Lagos, Wilson flew to Lusaka immediately following the conference in an attempt to sell his strategy to the president. The Zambian government had never been persuaded that economic sanctions alone would bring about the eventual overthrow of the illegal regime in Salisbury, let alone within a matter of weeks as Wilson had predicted in Lagos. Vice-President Kamanga was among those conference delegates who had voiced grave misgivings in this regard. Zambian spokesmen, and notably Foreign Minister Kapwepwe, never ceased to reiterate that the government's commitment to the military option remained as firm as ever.[168] Nevertheless, Lusaka had to recognize realities: there was no immediate prospect of budging London on this issue. Continuing to insist on force in the face of British intransigence, therefore, was an exercise in futility that could prove counterproductive. The best was becoming the enemy of the possible. "Britain has chosen economic sanctions," Kaunda rationalized,

and we cannot sit down still and say we are not going to participate in this. We've got to. But this does not shift us from our original thinking that this is primarily a military affair. If sanctions can do, obviously no one will be happier than myself because, of course, it is a very much better weapon if it can succeed. We are giving it all the help we can to make it a success.[169]

A further consideration was the deepening suspicion that the alternative to sanctions in London was not force but a sell-out to Salisbury, despite Wilson's categorical assurance that "we cannot negotiate with these men."[170] Besides, Zambia had a vital economic interest in maintaining British goodwill and support.

Resignation to the inevitable was not as disagreeable a decision for the Zambian government as it would have been earlier. The build-up of the oil airlift and the promise of alternative land routes engendered a new mood of confidence. By the turn of the year, Zambian spokesmen were beginning to project a more positive perspective on sanctions, partly no doubt as a morale-building measure. Thus Kaunda interpreted Smith's surprising climb-down on the coal royalty issue as "the first sign of a breakthrough for economic sanctions." Several of his ministers sounded similar optimistic notes, one even declaring, on the basis of "reliable information" in the possession of the government, that the rebel regime would "soon collapse."[171] Zambians, though still sceptical, were thus not entirely unreceptive to Wilson's earnest entreaties when he landed in Lusaka on the morning of 13 January.

The bold scenario which the amateur strategists in Whitehall had worked out in such incredible detail[172] and which Wilson carried to Lagos and on to Lusaka was predicated on the premise of a "quick kill" rather than slow strangulation. The success of the enterprise, however, depended crucially on Zambian cooperation. Once the stiffened sanctions began to bite deeply, Zambia would be called upon to administer the *coup de grâce* by closing its border with Rhodesia.[173] Secondly, it would be asked to accommodate a British battalion which, as soon as the rebel regime showed clear signs of crumbling, would cross the Zambezi to assume direct British control of the country. Wilson's purpose in visiting Lusaka, therefore, was (1) to commit Kaunda to a firm timetable for the application of full Zambian sanctions on imports (apart from coal and power) of Rhodesian origin; (2) to secure his acquiescence in placing the Zambian economy on a care and maintenance basis for the duration of the sanctions regime, estimated at a month or more; and (3) to overcome his objections to a British military presence in Zambia (see Decision No. 20). By marshalling all his extraordinary persuasive powers, Wilson succeeded in achieving his first two objectives, though not his third.

Coping

The Wilson blitz of Lusaka began with a working breakfast at State House, continued with a three-hour session at which Kaunda was joined by his foreign affairs and finance ministers,[174] culminated in a private stroll through the garden of State House during which "Harold" confided some of his most intimate secrets to "Kenneth," and concluded with a half-hour conversation at the airport prior to Wilson's departure before lunch for Nairobi. In between, the two leaders managed, among other things, to squeeze in separate press conferences, to tour Lusaka, and to pay an obligatory visit to the RAF detachment stationed in the city.[175] This tight timetable subjected Zambian decision makers, confronted with issues of grave importance for the fate of the nation, to intense pressures and severe time constraints. In particular, it proved impossible to probe the implications of the British project exhaustively, to consult at length among themselves or ascertain the opinions of other colleagues and advisers, or to explore adequately the availability of alternative policies.

The hectic pace of the schedule had important consequences, especially for the information-gathering and consultative processes. There was little or no opportunity to debrief the Zambian delegation which returned from the Lagos conference with Wilson, and none to seek the expert counsel of officials in the CPO. The Zambians were forced instead to rely for information on the incautious calculations which the British relayed so confidently concerning the anticipated impact of sanctions on Rhodesia (and Zambia). Unfortunately, as one British official later confessed, British "staff work was almost unbelievably bad." By way of contrast, Zambian officials had "a far better grasp of the realities of the Rhodesian situation."[176]

The Zambian decisional group was small, comprising only Foreign Minister Kapwepwe and Finance Minister Wina in addition to the president. Kaunda was very much the dominant voice in the triumvirate. Apart from his constitutional status and personal preeminence, he had been the principal target of Wilson's cunning charm and therefore emerged more thoroughly and intimately briefed than the others. Although the two senior ministers were not insignificant players, they were not present at all sessions and when they were, their predispositions on policy tended to point in opposing directions. Kapwepwe was reluctant to sacrifice the welfare of "my people" in a cause of uncertain cost, duration, and success. Wina, on the other hand, rather welcomed a confrontation as a means of forcing Britain's hand and precipitating an early resolution of the conflict, thus enabling the country once again to direct its energies to the urgent task of national development.

As the initiative in policy had now clearly passed into Wilson's hands, the Zambian search for options had to take into account his idiosyncratic intentions. This automatically ruled out any serious attempt to revive debate on a military solution, though this did not deter the Zambians from reminding Wilson that force was still the preferred course of action. More ominous was Wilson's evident impatience to coax Smith back to the negotiating table as early as possible.[177] With this in mind, he contrived to slip Commonwealth Secretary Arthur Bottomley across the border into Rhodesia, ostensibly to "stiffen" the beleaguered governor, but actually to meet Smith. Although the stratagem was ultimately abortive, it hardly inspired confidence in British integrity.[178] Nevertheless, the mere fact that Wilson would even consider treating with traitors proved a powerful incentive in inducing Zambia to accept Wilson's quick-kill strategy.

Realistically, acquiescence appeared to be the sole recourse open to Zambia. Even postponement of a decision did not seem a practical proposition. The only real element of manoeuvre came with the operationalization of the quick-kill concept. Here, Wilson and Kaunda each sought to impose his own conditions. Wilson's principal preoccupation was to prevent Zambia acting over-precipitately. His concern reflected a basic British misapprehension that Kaunda was pressing for an immediate break, and was sufficiently unstable emotionally that he might jump the gun at any moment, regardless of the consequences for the country or, more importantly, for the British exchequer.[179] For this reason, "instant Wilson" named 15 February – a scant month away – as a compromise cut-off date. The imminence of the deadline left British officials in attendance in a state of shocked silence. The Zambian team was equally staggered, and frankly doubtful that the economy of the country could be geared up in time to survive the siege. April, or even May, would have made more sense; by then, the rains would have ended and the "hell-run" to Tanzania would be less impassable. But once Wilson had committed himself to a definite date, he stubbornly defended it, until Kaunda finally capitulated and agreed to plan accordingly.[180]

This remarkable diplomatic coup succeeded only because Wilson managed to reassure Kaunda, at least in part, on many of the latter's major concerns. The first was some assurance that sanctions could be counted on not only to bite, but to bite speedily. To begin with, Kaunda asked that Britain demonstrate its good faith by broadening and strengthening its own sanctions arsenal. One argument London had used in the past to excuse its failure to act more swiftly and decisively was that forceful British action might have triggered a premature Zambian cut-off. With that risk eliminated, Wilson now undertook to institute a comprehensive ban on Rhodesian imports by the end of January. At the same time, however, he continued to resist (for another year) Zambian suggestions that the UN Security Council impose even selective mandatory sanctions. He was even more adamant in dismissing Kaunda's call for a severing of postal, telecommunication, and banking ties.[181]

The second Zambian request was for adequate contingency support to prepare the country to dispense with Rhodesian imports and routes safely and to withstand the retribution Salisbury would inevitably visit upon it. This too was conceded – in principle.

Wilson agreed to consider sympathetically any new aid submission designed to arm Zambia for the ordeal. Zambians would be entitled to the minimum supplies needed to keep the country ticking over and to prevent the mines from flooding. With respect to compensation, however, they would have to accept that there would be an interruption in the export of copper and probably in its production too. Moreover, Wilson warned, and British officials subsequently reiterated, that Britain could not accept responsibility for the consequences of any imprudent Zambian behaviour not previously sanctioned by London. Nor would it entertain any claims for general economic injury, such as the loss of export earnings arising out of mine closures, let alone assume any commitment to restore the Zambian economy to its pre-UDI state, as Kaunda urged. Wilson's limited liability approach to burden-sharing was neither new nor unexpected. Nevertheless, it was bitterly disappointing.[182]

Kaunda's overriding fear, and one Kapwepwe shared even more strongly, was that the Zambian economy would collapse before Rhodesia's did. This was a distinct possibility. "Even a limited moratorium on economic activity in Zambia," Kaunda argued, "would be catastrophic."[183] Wilson's perverse refusal to take seriously the spectre that Zambia had repeatedly raised, most recently at Lagos, of massive South African and Portuguese sanction-breaking, was scarcely encouraging. Accordingly, the Zambians felt compelled to press for some fail-safe guarantee that, in the event the quick-kill strategy failed to kill quickly enough, Britain would not only rush to Zambia's rescue, but also, after an agreed period of time, resort to force to crush the rebellion. Once again Wilson balked at the prospect. He was quite prepared to ask Zambia to assume open-ended economic obligations but not Britain.[184] He did, however, confide to Kaunda in the privacy of the garden at State House that he intended to call a snap election and hinted that, if he won a secure majority, it would then be politically possible to adopt a much tougher stance – conceivably even military action – against Rhodesia.[185] This vague and disingenuous assurance did the trick with Kaunda. Wilson even managed to extract a promise that Kaunda would restrain his ministers from intemperate actions that might prejudice Labour's prospects at the polls.[186]

The one concession Wilson failed to secure from Kaunda in the course of their private conversations was a withdrawal of his opposition to the posting of a British battalion to Zambia. Wilson was anxious to have troops in place in Zambia as a precaution in case the anticipated collapse of the Smith regime led to a breakdown of law and order (and a threat to white lives).[187] Kaunda, on the other hand, continued to insist that this was acceptable only if there was a firm British undertaking to invade Rhodesia if the rebellion had *not* ended by a specified date. In the circumstances, the most Kaunda would agree to was to receive a British military mission.[188] Wilson hoped thereby to educate the Zambians on the realities of mounting an assault across the Zambezi.[189]

Choice

Despite the immensity of the issues confronting them, Zambian leaders had little real scope for manoeuvre. Dependence on the British for contingency aid and apprehension at their evident predilection to resume negotiations with the rebels, combined with severe time constraints and Wilson's mastery at manipulation, effectively reduced the options to one. The most Kaunda and his colleagues could aspire to was some marginal influence on the preconditions for a safe and successful implementation of a quick-kill strategy in return for significant Zambian concessions. By midday, when Wilson flew out to Nairobi, the cumulative commitments Kaunda had made on his own authority, or in association with his senior ministers, were substantial. These decisions were:

1 To allow Britain a reasonable opportunity, without imposing a specific time limit, to demonstrate that sanctions could work swiftly and effectively;
2 to take all possible and appropriate measures to mobilize the nation to cope with a sudden closing of the Rhodesian border (except to Wankie coal, Kariba power, and re-exports to Zaire) by 15 February;
3 to submit a comprehensive shopping list of essential requirements to the forthcoming meeting of the Commonwealth Sanctions Committee in London;
4 to receive a British military mission to advise on the possibilities and implications of undertaking military operations in Rhodesia; and
5 to avoid embarrassing the Labour government in the weeks leading up to the British general elections.

Collectively, these decisions put the seal on Zambian acceptance of British policy.

The British prime minister's brief sojourn in Lusaka proved a personal triumph in breaking down much of the barrier of Zambian suspicion of British intentions.[190] President Kaunda emerged from the encounter captivated by Wilson's reckless but infectious self-confidence, and with his faith in British determination and sincerity fully restored. At last, Wilson really seemed to mean business. The views of the two countries, Kaunda professed, were now "nearer to each other than ever before." As Colin Legum observed, "Probably for the first time since the crisis began, the Zambian government believes sanctions will do the job, more slowly but equally as well as British military intervention." Asked if he would attend the Commonwealth conference scheduled for July, Kaunda responded that, "I don't for one moment believe that Smith will still be in power then."[191] Certain members of the cabinet who had not experienced the full impact of Wilson's slick salesmanship appeared less than completely persuaded that a "quick kill" was either wise or workable, especially within the time frame proposed. Nevertheless, any misgivings – even Kapwepwe's – were silenced, at least for a time, when Kaunda met his ministers on 18 January, and assured them that, on the basis of confidential disclosures, "Harold will do the right thing at the right time."[192]

Although Zambia appeared destined to experience in the next few weeks one of the most traumatic trials any young nation was ever called upon to endure, the mood of Zambian leaders, and especially of the president, was surprisingly confident, almost complacent. A distinct shift in Zambian crisis perceptions had taken place, with the prevailing view that the threat to national economic survival had now peaked and passed. Salvation lay in trusting Britain and accepting its leadership. In terms of actor stress, the post-crisis period had arrived.

VII Post-Crisis Planning – Trusting Britain: 14 January–27 April 1966

The failure and subsequent suspension of Lusaka's sustained campaign to persuade the British that force offered the swiftest and surest solution to the Rhodesian rebellion paradoxically did not leave any great legacy of bitterness and discord. Rather it ushered in an era of comparative harmony in Zambian relations with Britain. This proved only an interlude between crises, a false dawn based on misplaced trust in Prime Minister Wilson's good faith. Nevertheless, for the next three months or more, Zambian behaviour towards Britain was characterized by conscious cooperation and constraint. At last London and, somewhat less confidently, Lusaka were broadly agreed on a common strategy. Even the very real differences in the goals of Rhodesian policy were temporarily blurred.

Once the commitment to an early "quick kill" had been made, the Zambian government set about preparing the country to survive the shock of the coming crunch by the target date of 15 February. Three tasks preoccupied the contingency planners. The first was the compelling need to develop alternative outlets to the sea capable of carrying the country's essential imports and, if possible, a proportion of its copper exports. Secondly, it was necessary to anticipate Rhodesian counter-moves. These could conceivably take the form of cutting off the supply of Wankie coal or Kariba power, expelling Zambian migrant workers, or intensified sabotage activities.[1] Finally, the domestic implications of a sudden severance of relations with Rhodesia had to be carefully assessed, especially the prospect of mass unemployment, of an exodus of skilled white miners and railwaymen, and of rising racial tensions.[2]

By the end of January 1966 the full import of the Zambian undertaking had begun to sink in – in Lusaka even more than in London. For Zambians, the dawning realization of what was involved gave rise to a renewed debate on a broad range of policy choices. Principal among the options the Zambian government canvassed over the succeeding weeks were implementation of the quick kill on schedule (Decision No. 30); postponement of the *coup de grâce*, at least until the end of the rainy season (Decision No. 32); gradual disengagement over the "long haul" (Decision No. 34); and, on occasion, abandonment of any serious resolve to work towards an eventual break with Rhodesia. In Britain, too, questions were beginning to be asked. Officials were no longer as certain as they had once been that their sanctions strategy was operationally sound, or as sanguine that it could succeed in toppling Smith in a matter of months, let alone weeks. Consequently, there was relief in London when Lusaka quietly allowed the deadline to pass uneventfully.

Later, as evidence mounted of massive South African and Portuguese breaches of oil sanctions, interest in both capitals in a sudden and complete rupture in Zambia's remaining ties with Rhodesia flagged further. Zambian attention became increasingly focused on the outcome of the 31 March British general election. Despite the grave and growing doubts that were now prevalent in Lusaka concerning the feasibility of a "quick kill" strike, faith in the British Labour party remained surprisingly strong, especially with the president. Even if sanctions were to falter, Kaunda knew (or so he thought) that he could rely implicitly on Wilson's assurance that more forceful measures could be contemplated once he commanded a secure parliamentary majority. Tragically, this was not to be.

DECISION NO. 31: GIRDING FOR THE CRUNCH
(C. 24 JANUARY 1966)

Kaunda took advantage of his first weekly cabinet meeting following Wilson's whirlwind visit to brief his ministers on the decisions taken. For some, the instinctive reaction was less than enthusiastic though the president eventually managed to assuage most of the initial misgivings.[3] In the meanwhile, the process of girding Zambia for the projected crunch had begun. In particular, steps were taken:
1 to draft detailed lists of import requirements;
2 to explore further the prospects of sustaining partial production on the mines and at least a minimum level of copper exports;

3 to ensure the continuation and, if possible, the expansion of the Anglo-American-Canadian airlift;
4 to increase the capacity of alternative surface routes and procure the required rail equipment and road transport;
5 to mobilize the necessary material and financial support of neighbouring states, overseas partners, and international organizations; and
6 to minimize the disruptive effects, economically and socially, that could result from profiteering from temporary shortages and enforced unemployment as a consequence of production cutbacks.

Coping

The task of cataloguing Zambia's precise requirements was largely left to the Contingency Planning Organization (CPO) which, predictably, experienced considerable difficulty in assembling the basic statistical information quickly enough. For instance, collecting reliable data on existing inventories of essential goods in the country proved a laborious undertaking, in spite of the assistance of the government's Industrial Development Corporation (IDC) and a number of committees of businessmen.[4] As a result, the initial estimates, especially of foodstuffs, were later found to exaggerate the shortages. Nevertheless, despite the practical problems encountered, the memorandum the CPO prepared on the "Essential Requirements of Zambia" in the event of a quick kill was an impressive and persuasive document.

When ministers came to review progress at their next meeting on 24 January,[5] they relied heavily on the CPO submission. They also had the benefit of Kaunda's discussions with Malcolm MacDonald, who had arrived in Lusaka on his latest mission four days earlier. There were also consultations with President Nyerere and his minister of communications and works, whose arrival at Lusaka airport that morning led the cabinet to adjourn and resume its session later in the day.[6]

The cabinet appears to have given scant consideration to alternative approaches. Implicit in its discussions was continued acceptance of 15 February as the target date for the cut-off. Rather, the focus of concern was on strengthening the economy for the projected ordeal. Relatively little time seems to have been devoted to evaluating the specific proposals presented to it, in part as a consequence of competing claims on ministers' attention. In addition to the interruption occasioned by the Nyerere visit, the president was grappling with an incipient cabinet crisis that culminated in the sacking on 28 January of two ministers (one of whom was the minister of commerce and industry) for minor financial indiscretions. At the same time a scandal involving Vice-President Kamanga came to a head.[7] These distractions may help to account for some of the subsequent confusion concerning import control policy (Decision No. 32).

Choice

In addition to confirming by implication the mid-February deadline, the cabinet approved the substance of the CPO memorandum and authorized its formal presentation to the Commonwealth Sanctions Committee which was holding its first meeting in London the following day.[8] The Zambian document contained three basic requests:

1 *Oil airlift*. In view of the restricted capacities of the Tanzanian and Malawian surface routes during the current rains and the uncertain prospects concerning routes through Zaire, Zambia urged the British, American, and Canadian governments to maintain their airlifts "until the end of the wet season," normally mid-April and, if possible, augment them "to the maximum capacity that can be achieved." In the case of the Canadian airlift, Kaunda wrote personally to Prime Minister Pearson on 26 January to appeal for its continuance beyond the end of February. Ottawa promptly agreed to a two-month extension though, to Kaunda's great disappointment, with only half the number of aircraft. At the same time Lusaka pressed ahead with the politically delicate negotiations with the Portuguese for an RAF airlift based on Beira in Mozambique. As this project constituted a major pillar of Wilson's policy, Zambia readily agreed to join in technical talks in Beira on 27 January (see Decision No. 27).[9]

2 *Road transport*. The government's second requirement was the provision of a huge fleet of road vehicles, which it urged should reach Zambia by 15 April at the latest. The request specified a minimum of 100 large oil-tank trucks and trailers (with a further 150 if at all possible) as well as 150 to 250 general cargo carriers with trailers, all for use on the Great North Road to Tanzania and the Great East Road to Malawi. These numbers represented a significant increase on previous estimates of Zambian needs. Three factors account for this upward revision: more realistic assessments of the likely length of the siege period, ominous indications of restiveness among the independent-minded expatriate miners on

the Copperbelt at the prospect of restrictions on their continued enjoyment of the "good life,"[10] and growing confidence concerning the possibilities of salvaging some copper production. With the conversion of some mines from coal to oil firing, it was hoped to maintain output at as much as one-third the current level (provided import routes could handle the required additional 10,000 tons of heavy fuel oil a month). So encouraging were these reports that a special committee was constituted to explore the prospects of alternative air and ground routes for the continued export of copper in the event the Rhodesian rail route was closed – a consideration of great concern to the British.[11]

3 *Essential imports.* Finally, the Zambian memorandum detailed the country's minimum import requirements following the planned break with Rhodesia. These totalled nearly 30,000 tons a month (excluding coal, oil, medicines, mining equipment, and explosives) or a mere third of the normal level of imports. The Zambian appeal emphasized the vital necessity, in view of the "low level of stocks of many items," of placing orders early to ensure delivery by mid-April. Existing stocks would in most cases be exhausted by then, though it was hoped the alternative routes would be capable of coping with the anticipated volume of imports.

The whole elaborate scenario was based on four crucial assumptions, each of which was questionable to a greater or lesser degree. The first was that the Rhodesians would retaliate in the event of a quick kill by banning Wankie coal shipments and denying Zambia access to the Rhodesia Railways, but that they would not cut off power from the jointly owned Kariba dam complex. Secondly, Commonwealth countries would be both able and willing to meet Lusaka's pressing material demands. The meeting of the Commonwealth Sanctions Committee revealed an enormous reservoir of goodwill towards Zambia, though little in the way of concrete offers of assistance. In view of the limited opportunity members were given to study the document in advance, the British suggested it be referred to a Subcommittee on Cooperation with Zambia (which considered it twice in the course of the following month). Thirdly, it was envisaged that, with the end of the rains and the delivery of the vast fleet of vehicles requested, the country could meet its minimum needs without reliance on the southern rail route through Rhodesia. According to the American ambassador at the time, this projection was "wildly optimistic."[12] Finally, it was assumed that Zambia could survive for up to two months (from mid-February to mid-April) before the alternative routes were fully developed, provided adequate stocks were on hand prior to the cut-off date. In practice, this meant sharply increased purchases from Rhodesia – contrary to the declared policy of cutting back such imports to a minimum.

DECISION NO. 32: STOCKPILING ESSENTIAL SUPPLIES (5 FEBRUARY 1966)

UDI injected a powerful incentive and a fresh sense of urgency into efforts to give some substance to Zambia's long-articulated aspiration to lessen its economic dependence on white Southern Africa, and especially on Rhodesia. Its initial sanctions measures, except for oil, did little to disrupt the traditional cosy trading relationship; nevertheless, steps were taken that provided the groundwork for the country's subsequent defiant assertions of economic independence. The introduction of import and export controls, restrictions on foreign exchange transfers, and visa requirements for Rhodesian businessmen,[13] as well as the chronic congestion on the Rhodesia Railways, the opening up of new road and rail outlets to the sea, and the increasingly insistent appeals to diversify import sources and routes[14] – all these contributed to the process of disengagement. In addition, the implementation of the protectionist Pioneer Industries Act in conjunction with a national "Buy Zambian" campaign gave further impetus to the government's longer-term objective of import substitution.[15]

While the cumulative impact of these measures during the first two months after UDI was not imperceptible[16] (Figure 2), it was only in the aftermath of the Wilson visit that Lusaka attempted to give more explicit direction to its disengagement policy. Its first effort – the imposition of restrictions on non-essential imports – proved something of an administrative fiasco and was abandoned within a few weeks. Although the original intention of the exercise – to reserve the congested southern rail route for priority supplies – was admirable, in practice the Ministry of Commerce and Industry rejected import permit applications for non-essential goods indiscriminately, regardless of the country of origin or route of entry designated. This, and the delay in making the elusive list of restricted imports generally available, created such widespread confusion and concern within the (largely expatriate) commercial community during the course of the second half of January that the cabinet was forced to intervene on 1 February to end the system.[17] To redeem the situation, Kamanga explained somewhat disingenuously that there was "no restricted import list. There is an arrangement for the allocation of priorities in view of the present restricted transport capacity, especially applying to our imports coming through the South. The importer may import any items ... provided he can arrange suitable import routes."[18] Finally, on 5 February the cabinet clarified the matter further by deciding definitively to urge importers to "bring their stocks up to a minimum of three months' supply of essential commodities" as rapidly as possible.[19]

Coping

In reaching its conclusion, the cabinet appears to have felt little need to undertake an extensive search for additional information. The issues at stake were more matters of political judgment and economic interest than questions of fact. Nevertheless, fresh feedback on the impact and implications of emergency measures continued to emerge almost daily, principally from the CPO and business lobbies. When fed to ministers, it helped fuel their discussions. A considerable amount of systematic consultation also took place with interested parties inside and outside the government. One significant forum was a major government-sponsored conference with commerce and industry on 26 January. Initially convened to consider the developmental role of the private sector in the forthcoming First National Development Plan 1966–70, it did in fact provide an occasion to consider some of the more immediate "problems raised by the national emergency brought about by UDI in Rhodesia."[20] The British, too, consistently urged Zambia to embark on a concerted stockpiling exercise as a precondition for a cut-off. Their viewpoint was given ample expression both at the meeting of the Commonwealth Sanctions Committee on 25 January (and that of the Zambia subcommittee on 3 February) and in the course of regular diplomatic exchanges. The presence in Lusaka at that time of a strong British National Export Council mission also served to reinforce London's arguments. The final proposal considered by cabinet, however, originated from within the CPO.[21]

The cabinet's consideration of policy options reopened the recurring controversy over Zambian sanctions strategy. Ministers were called upon to weigh up a complex series of cross-cutting interests and objectives. Principal among these were the current capacity and state of congestion of alternative routes, the trade-off between acceptable sources of supplies and delivery time, the priority to be accorded essential imports at the expense of luxury goods for expatriates and the emerging elites, the risks of an early cut-off date compared to the advantages of delay, the foreign exchange and inflationary implications of alternative initiatives, and the

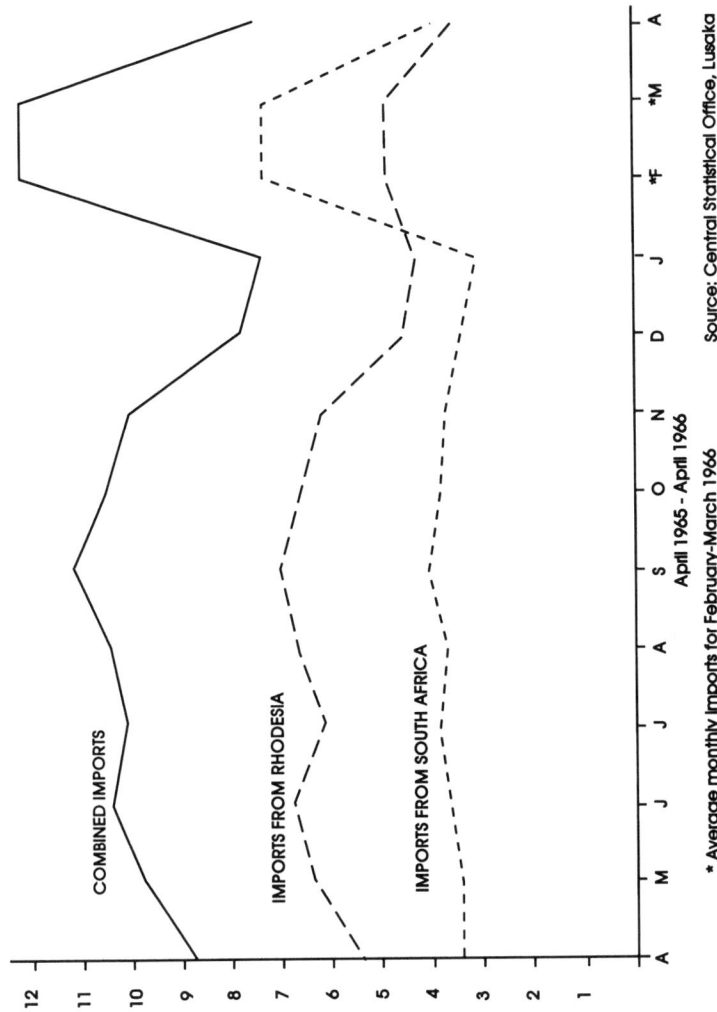

Figure 2: Zambian Imports from Rhodesia and South Africa, April 1965–April 1966

developmental costs of enforced disengagement. Yet underlying all these factors was a basic conflict over incompatible priorities: whether to press ahead quietly with a progressive but gradual phasing out of Rhodesian imports, or to increase imports sharply in the short run as part of a deliberate policy of building up reserves of essential goods to equip the country to withstand the planned cataclysmic confrontation.[22] In attempting to resolve this dilemma, the cabinet also sought to respect its commitment to Wilson's quick-kill doctrine.

Choice

The principal outcome of the cabinet's deliberations was the decision to stockpile three months' normal supplies of essential dry cargo imports as a matter of some urgency. As corollaries of this basic directive, it was also resolved to provide the necessary foreign exchange for the exercise, encourage diversification of import routes and sources through licensing incentives and trade missions, and implicitly delay the cut-off date.

The stockpiling operation was a huge success. The minister of commerce and industry addressed a circular letter to 350 leading importers in the country appealing to them to ensure that they maintained inventories of essential goods adequate to meet three months' normal demand. No deadline was indicated for achieving this target, but the obvious implication was the sooner the better.[23] In drawing up its list of priority imports, the government interpreted the term "essential" liberally to include not only everything needed for "maintaining the life of the people" and "keeping the economy going," but also critical morale-boosting items. As Kamanga was careful to highlight, the list covered "the cosmetic requirements of the ladies as well as the spirituous requirements of the gentlemen." Six weeks later, he could proudly declare that the results were "most encouraging," with the position improving "every day."[24]

Kamanga was considerably less impressed with the progress in diverting purchases away from traditional Rhodesian suppliers. Disengagement had been seen both as a sanction to deny Rhodesia vital foreign exchange earnings and as a security measure in the event the rebels unilaterally closed the border. Accordingly, action was taken to place "imports of all kinds" from neighbouring African states under open general licence[25] and to despatch a number of trade missions – largely composed of "hard-headed" (expatriate) businessmen – to selected African, East Asian, and East and West

European countries to awaken them to the opportunities opening up in the Zambian market.[26] The results were disappointing. Although during the first two months of 1966 imports from Rhodesia had been cut back by a further one-quarter, the principal beneficiary had been South Africa (Figure 2). Now, with the pressure to stockpile, importers once again turned first to Rhodesia. Ironically, it was the flood of Zambian orders that provided many hard-pressed Rhodesian manufacturers with the desperately needed breathing space that enabled them to survive while they adapted to the exigencies of sanctions.[27]

The de facto abandonment of 15 February as the target date for the execution of the Zambian *coup de grâce* was intended merely as a temporary postponement to allow time for inventories to reach safe levels; formally, the commitment to a quick-kill strategy remained undiminished.[28] Although no new date was set, March was the earliest possibility, with April preferred. This suited the British admirably. Far from being dismayed at the delay, they had been "fearful lest Zambia act too soon and commit economic suicide without dislodging Mr. Smith." With this in mind, Malcolm MacDonald had been ordered to Lusaka once more to ascertain discreetly the likelihood of Zambia indulging in some foolish gesture of defiance. He reported back that Kaunda and his cabinet were only too conscious that the country was ill-prepared to withstand a crunch.[29] No doubt he also noted that every minister would be out of Lusaka or out of the country on 15 February.[30] Despite this reassurance, London was visibly relieved when the designated deadline passed uneventfully. So was Salisbury, which had become needlessly alarmed and reacted with a shrewd campaign designed to deter Zambia from taking the plunge.[31]

DECISION NO. 33: RESTRAINING OAU MILITANCY (26 FEBRUARY 1966)

The major factor in Zambia's acquiescence in Britain's quick-kill policy was Kaunda's readiness to accept at face value assurances by Wilson that were subsequently found to be worthless. These were, first, that sanctions could be relied upon to work quickly and effectively but, secondly, that if they did not Wilson would undertake to implement other appropriate measures as soon as he was in a parliamentary position to do so. With respect to the first, Wilson's passionate appeals in Lagos and Lusaka in January to allow him the time to prove that sanctions could topple Smith persuaded Kaunda to give him the benefit of the doubt. Moreover, for the first few weeks Zambia seemed satisfied with their performance record. Initial Zambian judgments, particularly those intended for public consumption, were surprisingly positive.[32] The tone changed perceptibly as the evidence accumulated that, while sanctions were pinching, they were certainly not biting. Concern rapidly escalated into alarm as indubitable reports began to filter in of serious South African and Portuguese oil sanction infractions.[33] By mid-February confidence in Lusaka in the sanctions weapon had seriously eroded. Thereafter Zambian spokesmen reverted increasingly to their earlier refrain that sanctions alone would not suffice to compel a rebel surrender.[34]

Despite the restlessness in Lusaka over the meagre impact of British policy, there was no open revolt against it. Kaunda continued to act as if sanctions still represented a viable strategy. The explanation for his conscious deference to Britain lay in the high hopes that he held of a dramatic new direction to policy if Labour triumphed at the polls – and, conversely, his profound (and justifiable) fear of a sellout to Smith if the Conservatives came to power.[35] So vital was the perceived Zambian interest in a Labour victory that Kaunda took every precaution to avoid prejudicing Wilson's prospects. The critical test of Zambian loyalty to Labour came at the end of February when the OAU Council of Ministers met in Addis Ababa to construct a new consensus on Rhodesia. To the surprise of many, Zambian delegates preached a policy of patience pending the outcome of the British election. Their action succeeded in averting a repetition of previous bitter confrontations with Britain, though at the cost of exacerbating the divisions within the organization.

Coping

Although Lusaka had a clear perception of its own policy objectives at the forthcoming meeting of African foreign ministers, it was anxious to ascertain the views of other OAU states before formulating its final position and tactical plan. As this was the first session of the Council of Ministers since the débâcle of December when three-quarters of the member governments had failed to comply with the resolution on severing diplomatic relations with Britain (see Decision No. 22), Zambia was acutely conscious of the importance for the future of the OAU of seeking solutions that would serve to heal wounds and restore unity. Moreover, as one of the most respected "defectors," it felt particularly sensitive and vulnerable. Despite, or perhaps because of, its proud record of commitment to the organization, Zambia had been singled out by certain radical states for some pointed criticism.

In canvassing the opinions of member states, Lusaka made use of its resident representatives in six major capitals – Accra, Addis Ababa, Cairo, Dar es Salaam, Kinshasa, and Lagos. In mid-February the Zambian high commissioner in Ghana was sent on a mission to Guinea (which had been especially outspoken) and Mali, and two senior cabinet ministers headed a trade delegation to Egypt, in each case principally to smooth out political relations and prepare the ground for the forthcoming OAU meeting.[36] The Commonwealth Sanctions Committee (which met on 23 February) and contacts at the United Nations also afforded opportunities to test the pulse of African opinion. Finally, there was evidently some limited feedback from the advance party of Zambian delegates which arrived in Addis Ababa a week early for the preparatory meeting of the Defence Committee (Committee of Five) and particularly its discussion of the report of the OAU military reconnaissance group to Zambia.[37]

During the weeks leading up to the foreign ministers' meeting, the Zambian government was buffeted by strong but contrary pressures from African states and from Britain. London become overly alarmed at the prospect that OAU members might seek to resolve their internal differences by uniting behind a peremptory demand for an immediate resort to force in Rhodesia. To forestall this threat, the British requested a meeting of the Commonwealth Sanctions Committee (on 23 February) in the hope of persuading sceptics that the well-advertised breaches in the oil sanctions were greatly exaggerated and could safely be ignored. They also embarked upon a diplomatic offensive throughout Africa, with Zambia the prime target. Malcolm MacDonald arrived in Lusaka on 17 February with instructions to impress on Kaunda the importance of observing caution, to bolster his resistance to pressures for militant measures, and to reassure him that the sanctions program was proceeding as planned, even if a little behind schedule. His arguments were not fully successful in assuaging Zambian misgivings. Six days later he returned for the third time that month, armed with a personal and confidential message from Wilson revealing the date of the forthcoming British elections – five days in advance of the official announcement. This heartening news, with its implied promise of tough new British initiatives early in April, restored Kaunda's confidence, not in sanctions, but in the worth of continuing to exercise restraint a little longer.[38] In his reply to Wilson the next day, acknowledging the election tip-off, Kaunda reiterated his undertaking to advise his ministers to "hold their fire" during the campaign, but he warned that, once the election was out of the way, Zambia would use "all possible pressures to gain the swiftest action against Rhodesia." Any failure then by London to live up to its Rhodesian responsibilities (and he promised to spell these out) would "finish" Britain as far as Africa was concerned.[39]

Although agreement in Lusaka on the broad lines of policy was reached early, apparently at the weekly cabinet session of 22 February, the government's position was not finalized until 26 February, on the eve of Kapwepwe's departure for Addis Ababa. The issue Kaunda and his senior ministers faced when they met at State House late that Saturday evening[40] was essentially how vigorously to press the case for allowing Britain a few more weeks' breathing space. It was a matter of balancing the short-term rewards hoped for from a strong Labour government against the longer-term risk of perpetuating OAU disunity and prejudicing Zambian influence in progressive African circles. The spectrum of options open to the ministers ranged from meek acquiescence in an uncompromising OAU reaffirmation of previous militant demands to passive support for a deferment of a decision, to determined lobbying in support of a temporary reprieve for the British.

Choice

Although the Zambian government was fully persuaded that the experiment with voluntary sanctions had now failed and that force remained the only sure way to end UDI, it recognized that the pre-election period was not an appropriate time to press these claims.[41] Instead, ministers concluded at their nocturnal conclave that the Zambian delegation should:
1 be outspoken in its opposition to any ultimatum on force or other extreme measures at this juncture;
2 urge that sanctions be tightened up and made mandatory; and, as a corollary,
3 insist that OAU members accept a collective responsibility to assist Zambia to participate fully in sanctions.

In Addis Ababa, Kapwepwe's firm advocacy of patience with Britain paid off. While "we still think force would be the quickest answer," he argued, "we have to throw the ball to Britain now," and await the "new decisive action" anticipated after a Labour victory.[42] He experienced little difficulty in getting his proposals adopted, as the moderates in the Council were now in a majority. What he failed to achieve was a broad consensus including the radical states.

The Tunisian motion, co-sponsored by Zambia and others, merely noted that "economic sanctions have not been sufficiently applied to overthrow the illegal minority regime," called on Britain to "apply such effective measures, including the use of force, that would bring about the immediate downfall of the Ian Smith regime," and recommended that the UN Security Council "examine" the possibilities of enforcement action under chapter 7 of the UN charter.[43] Adoption of this mild resolution, following the rejection of the rival Algerian proposal, so enraged a minority of militant members that they ended up storming out of the meeting. For Kapwepwe it was an embarrassing victory, for it was won with the support of the colonial "stooges" and opposed by the "progressive" OAU members with whom he identified.[44] On the other hand the British, who had been observing events from the sidelines, were naturally pleased and relieved. They had good reason to be grateful to Zambia for fighting their battle for them.

In contrast to the dissension the debate over the advisability of delay generated, Zambia's appeal for all possible assistance to lessen the hardships experienced as a result of sanctions was non-contentious. In response to Kapwepwe's recital of his country's tribulations, a "Committee of Solidarity for Zambia," composed of Egypt, Ethiopia, Kenya, Tanzania and the Sudan, was established with the task of seeking "appropriate measures of technical and economic assistance by member states to Zambia." While Lusaka welcomed this expression of concern, it was sufficiently realistic not to expect too much to come of it; after all, only four OAU members (including Zambia) were up to date with their dues. Indeed, so completely unproductive did the committee prove in practice that at one stage Kaunda seriously considered boycotting the next OAU summit in protest.[45]

With the OAU hurdle more or less successfully surmounted, Zambian attention now turned to a consideration of possible post-election scenarios and, in particular, the implications for Zambia of the collapse of the oil embargo.

DECISION NO. 34: THE "LONG HAUL"
(C. 8 MARCH 1966)

Pending the outcome of the British general elections on 31 March (and the South African elections for whites a day earlier) and in anticipation of resolute action on Rhodesia shortly thereafter, the Zambian government continued to ponder what its own further response to the Smith rebellion ought to be. The answer was no longer as simple and self-evident as it had seemed at the time of Wilson's visit in mid-January. Much had happened in the intervening weeks to cause Zambians to begin to question the dubious assumptions on which the quick-kill strategy had been based.

One concern prompting Zambians to reconsider their commitment was a dawning recognition of the awesome consequences of a sudden and complete cut-off of trade and communications for both the development of the country as a whole and the welfare of ordinary citizens. Related to this were the difficulties encountered in opening up alternative routes, especially their costs, capacities, and turn-around times. Maintaining the flow of traffic along the Great North Road "hell run" during the rainy season was posing a constant challenge, while the inadequate facilities of Dar es Salaam harbour were already creating congestion problems. The collapse of negotiations for a Beira airlift, and the prospective winding up of the American and Canadian airlifts at the end of April, also affected contingency calculations.

Zambians were now beginning to appreciate more fully how formidable a foe they faced. Smith's surprising New Year's climb-down over coal royalties (Decision No. 26) had encouraged the belief that Rhodesia was something of a paper tiger. Subsequent events modified this perception and led Lusaka gradually to acquire a grudging respect for the resilience of the Rhodesian economy, the resourcefulness of the settler minority, and the ruthlessness of the rebel regime, all of which cast doubt on Zambia's ability to survive, let alone win, a war of attrition with its powerful southern neighbour. As Good comments, a contest to see whether Kaunda or Smith "could hold his breath the longer" was "rather one-sided."[46]

What residual faith Lusaka retained in the efficacy of sanctions was finally shattered by the shocking revelations concerning massive oil leaks through Mozambique and South Africa. Sanctions were not only not working; there were few grounds for optimism that they could or would ever be made to work, and none that they would do so quickly and decisively, at least as long as Britain continued to block mandatory sanctions. For Zambia to attempt a quick kill while the rebel regime (to quote one disillusioned Zambian official) was "hardly even groggy" might be an heroic act, but it would not deliver the intended *coup de grâce*. The scenario that many Zambians foresaw and feared most now loomed up as a distinct possibility. This was a situation in which, three months into the crunch, the country would find its stockpile exhausted, its copper mines crippled, and its supply routes choked, while Rhodesia escaped largely unscathed. In the circumstances, Zambians were understandably reluctant to ruin their economy in a vain gesture of solidarity and defiance.

As the weeks passed and the prospects worsened, opposition within the government, led by Kapwepwe, mounted and became more vocal. Early indications of this surfaced at the beginning of February at the time the stockpiling proposal was under consideration. However, it was not until the passing of Wilson's 15 February deadline that observers began to note a pronounced decline in Zambian political will and an absence of the earlier sense of urgency.[47] Part of the explanation was, no doubt, a diversion of government energies into attending to neglected domestic affairs: industrial strife, regional strains, and development planning as well as rumoured power struggles within the ruling party. Ministers also exhibited a marked reluctance to commit funds for contingency planning purposes. In one case, the decision to renew an order for the supply of oil through Zaire was deferred for nearly a month, a delay that cost the country 4,000 tons of fuel it could ill afford to lose at a time of stringent petrol rationing and costly airlifts. There was also a revival of interest in longer-term disengagement projects: an oil pipeline from Dar es Salaam, paving the Great North Road, the joint Zambia-Tanzania Road Service (ZTRS), and the long-sought TanZam railway.[48] Finally, government spokesmen, in their public pronouncements, once again began to emphasize an earlier Zambian theme – namely, that Rhodesia was primarily a British responsibility and, by implication, not a direct Zambian one.[49]

Coping

There appears to have been no formal decision to abandon efforts to mobilize the country for a quick kill; certainly none was announced. Rather, Zambia simply drifted away from it through a series of incremental steps and mental adjustments until it arrived at a point where the decision makers recognized that they were no longer actively organizing for the crunch. That point was reached early in March (Decision No. 34).

In the process of coming to this conclusion, Zambian leaders appear not to have suffered from inadequate intelligence on the deteriorating sanctions situation in Southern Africa. On the contrary, they were amply served by a steady flow of published reports and private briefings. Depressing accounts flowed in, largely unsolicited, from a variety of quarters, among them enterprising journalists, Rhodesian businessmen resident in Zambia, diplomatic contacts, and overseas visitors as well as normal media sources.[50] The mounting evidence of major oil leaks was deeply disturbing, anxiously analysed, and eagerly ingested, especially by those ministers and officials already sceptical of the feasibility of a quick kill. Despite the pathetic efforts of the Commonwealth Relations Office in London to dismiss as "grossly exaggerated" the documented evidence of significant supplies of oil reaching Rhodesia,[51] the avalanche of information received from reliable sources convinced Zambians otherwise, and compelled them to reconsider and eventually reverse their policy.

The one area where Lusaka seems to have felt a need to seek additional data concerned the precise content and extent of external assistance it could expect in a crunch. Here consultations with the Commonwealth and the OAU proved instructive, if not altogether reassuring. Regular exchanges of opinion also took place with interested groups inside the country and overseas in an almost continuous process of reassessing Zambia's changing situation. The CPO in particular was in constant communication with the mining companies and the various commercial bodies in the country.[52]

In the light of the new realities, the Zambian government faced three broad policy options: to persevere with contingency plans for a quick kill, at least until after the British elections; to suspend preparations indefinitely, and instead opt for gradual disengagement over the long haul along with mandatory sanctions and other effective measures to plug the oil leaks; or to abandon sanctions altogether and concentrate once more on persuading Britain to resort to force. Although these alternatives were essentially reformulations of courses of action under almost continuous debate since mid-January if not earlier, the circumstances now were different and the emphasis therefore altered.

While the predisposition among Zambian leaders in favour of a quick kill waned rapidly, there was some hesitation to acknowledge openly that it was no longer perceived as a viable strategy, principally for fear of prejudicing the provision of contingency aid to the country. By early March, however, it seemed pointless to maintain the pretence any longer. Even a delay until after the British elections offered few advantages. Of the other alternatives, the third carried considerable appeal. Kaunda continued to believe, on the basis of hints from Wilson, that force had not been completely ruled out for the future. Moreover, it could be argued that to continue to accord any credibility to sanctions reduced the likelihood of military measures ever being seriously explored. Although the force option remained open for later consideration,[53] the consensus that eventually emerged within the senior Zambian leadership – in practice, it was never fully articulated – envisaged a gradual tightening of the Zambian sanctions screws as part of a greatly strengthened program of global economic measures. There was little confidence that mandatory UN sanctions would prove a panacea; their purpose was purely political, rather than economic. By opening the door to enforcement action under chapter 7 of the Charter, it was hoped to attain "a half-way stop on the route towards the use of force, internationalizing the issue and focusing the spotlight on South African and Portuguese connivance in the obstruction of the sanctions campaign."[54]

Choice

The shift in Zambian policy took place progressively over a period of weeks, but certain developments, notably the meeting of the OAU Council of Ministers from 28 February to 6 March, helped to accelerate the process and clarify the issues. By the time President Kaunda opened Parliament on 8 March, the views of the principal Zambian decision makers had achieved a substantial measure of convergence. In his address, Kaunda's remarks on Rhodesia were surprisingly brief. He confined himself to declaring that the government had "no confidence whatsoever in the use of economic sanctions as the best means of bringing down the illegal regime."[55] In operational terms, the new thrust of policy could be defined as:
1 force remained the quickest and most reliable way to end UDI, but since there was no assurance that it would be adopted, Zambia was prepared to give British policies a fair chance to prove they could bring down the Smith regime within a reasonable period of time;
2 contingency planning for a quick kill should be suspended indefinitely, and possibly permanently;
3 economic disengagement from Rhodesia should continue to be pursued, but cautiously so as to create a minimum of domestic disruption;
4 the pace and extent of Zambian participation in sanctions should take into account the cost, capacity, and convenience of alternative routes and supplies as well as the level of external support actually received; and
5 comprehensive mandatory UN sanctions should be adopted and enforced, though with provision for the partial exemption of Zambia.[56]

Zambia was clearly no longer prepared to accept sacrifices for the sake of Rhodesia unless there was a guarantee of swift success and equitable burden-sharing. The political will to engage in unconditional economic warfare no longer existed. The next move was up to the British.

WAITING FOR WILSON

Lusaka greeted the Labour party's triumph at the polls on 31 March with unrestrained relief. The increase in its parliamentary majority from four to ninety-six seemed, in Kapwepwe's words, "an answer to a prayer," and prompted a swift congratulatory cable from Kaunda. Expectations of an early bold new initiative on Rhodesia soared. "Now you will see," Kaunda declared in cabinet, "Harold will do the right thing."[57]

Prior to the election, Kaunda had persuaded his ministers to exercise uncommon patience during the campaign and, with characteristic consideration, he now indicated his willingness to wait a little longer to enable Wilson to form his new government and refine his strategy. But as the weeks passed and the eagerly-awaited message failed to arrive there was growing unease in Lusaka.[58] On 15 April Kapwepwe summoned the British high commissioner to request an explanation for the delay and to suggest that Malcolm MacDonald, then in London, should fly to Lusaka that weekend to bring Kaunda up to date on current British thinking. Sir Leslie Monson, who had been kept equally in the dark, could only undertake to report the conversation to London.

The appeal evoked no response. Nor did subsequent discreet inquiries. Asked if he was expecting an early visit from Malcolm MacDonald, Kaunda replied somewhat impatiently, "I have been waiting to see him for three weeks."[59] Yet before MacDonald finally did appear, the political climate had been transformed.[60] On 27 April Wilson rose in the House of Commons to announce, not the tough new stance Lusaka anticipated, but his intention to seek "talks about talks" with Smith. Labour had won the election, but the Conservatives, who were equally incredulous at Wilson's turnabout, had won the debate over Rhodesian policy.[61] To add insult to injury, Kaunda first heard the shattering news from the BBC.[62] With it, the bottom fell out of his world. He felt understandably bitter, betrayed, and abused as well as humiliated in the eyes of his cabinet and the OAU. Kaunda's sense of moral outrage was further heightened the next day when seven ZANU freedom fighters, who had crossed the Zambezi into Rhodesia, were massacred by security forces in a fierce battle at Sinoia – and the British failed to react.[63] Both personally and politically, the long honeymoon with Wilson was over.[64] The next phase in the protracted UDI conflict had begun.[65]

PART THREE

Crisis Behaviour Patterns

VIII Crisis Components

The preceding chapters have analysed the course and content of decision making during successive stages of the UDI crisis of 1965–66. The second major purpose of this study is to assess the impact on Zambian crisis behaviour of the four components in the crisis model.

As indicated in chapter 1, an international crisis constitutes a significant discontinuity in the foreign relations of an international actor. Its essential precondition is a situational change in the external or internal environment which induces changes in levels of stress within the decision-making elite arising from perceptions of:
1 grave threats to basic values,
2 the likelihood of military hostilities (or, in time of war, a shift in the military balance), and
3 time constraints on the decisional response.

The levels and directions of change in stress experienced between and within crisis periods will be probed in this chapter. Secondly, their consequences for the coping mechanisms of Zambian decision makers – namely, information-processing, consultative procedures, decisional forums utilized, and the search for and evaluation of policy alternatives – will be explored in the next chapter, particularly in the light of the nine research questions identified in chapter 1 and Table 1. Finally, the attempt will be made in chapter 10 to relate stress to the differing dimensions of the decisional outcomes. The statistical evidence on which this assessment is made will be found on pp. 261–90.

ENVIRONMENTAL CHANGES

Each of the five phases of the crisis analysed in the previous chapters was triggered by an external event, the first three of Rhodesian origin and the latter two British (Table A1). The inception of the pre-crisis period can be traced back six months prior to UDI to the publication on 26 April 1965 of a Rhodesian white paper minimizing the adverse economic and political consequences of an act of rebellion against Britain. Apart from confirming Ian Smith's clear intention of seeking a mandate in the elections of 7 May to seize independence illegally if necessary, this provocative document contained specific economic threats directed at Zambia.[1] Salisbury's headlong rush towards independence received added impetus in early August following Britain's blunder in rashly reassuring Rhodesians that they need not fear military reprisals in the event of UDI. The subsequent escalation in Rhodesian abuse heaped on the British Labour government, as well as the fresh outburst of rhetoric threatening hostile action against Zambia, signalled the onset of the second phase of the pre-crisis period.

For most of the outside world the UDI crisis began with the formal proclamation of independence on 11 November. North of the Zambezi, however, the event that triggered the crisis period proper was the Rhodesian institution of a state of emergency six days earlier. Zambia's immediate reaction was to demand a British military response against Rhodesia. Eventually, after some three weeks of futile personal pleading, President Kaunda came to recognize that Prime Minister Wilson's refusal to countenance the use of force was firm, thus ushering in the second, primarily economic, phase of the crisis period. Similarly, it was Wilson who succeeded in mid-January in easing the mood of crisis prevailing in Lusaka. His extravagant claims in defence of his daring quick-kill strategy and his private intimations to the president hinting at bold new initiatives once parliamentary elections were out of the way restored Kaunda's confidence and convinced him of Wilson's determination and sincerity. The road ahead promised to be rough, but there now appeared to be credible grounds for believing that the ordeal would be brief and the outcome assured.

An analysis of the stimuli that precipitated each individual decisional response reveals similar patterns and trends. In terms of source, Rhodesia was responsible in half the cases, though more so in the earlier phases than the later ones; by comparison, there were few consequential Zambian initiatives (Table A2). Nearly half of the trigger mechanisms were in the economic sphere. Economic impulses predominated during the pre-crisis and post-crisis periods, with political and military actions more in evidence at the height of the crisis and especially during its first phase (Table A3). This is consistent with the ICB definition of a crisis.

Brecher has observed that the source of an international crisis need not be external to the country concerned.

> In many Third World states, the situational change that triggers an international crisis for decision makers often occurs within the domestic environment, usually through physical challenges to the regime by strikes, demonstrations, riots, assassination, sabotage and/or attempted coups d'état ... The phenomenon of internal situational change triggering a crisis in the international realm is ubiquitous in Africa and Latin America.[2]

This was not the situation that faced Zambia in the UDI crisis; the stimuli at each stage were essentially external. The Rhodesian rebellion did create domestic difficulties for the Zambian government by, for instance, dangerously inflaming racial passions within the country; a strike by Rhodesian railway workers was at least partially politically inspired, and isolated incidents occurred of molestations of whites.[3] Nevertheless, the crisis was in no sense a conflict which originated within Zambia and then escalated to the point where it assumed international proportions.

CRISIS-INDUCED STRESS

The concept of stress is the crucial independent variable in the ICB equation which seeks to relate changes in anxiety or fear experienced by decision makers in the course of a crisis to both the strategies employed to cope with the threats and the policy outcomes that ultimately emerge. As Holsti and George note, there is a widespread assumption in the literature, not only that stress is dysfunctional for decision making, but that "the magnitude and adverse effects of stress on performance is likely to be appreciably greater in 'crisis situations'" than in less stress-producing circumstances.[4] As a consequence, intensity of stress has become the defining characteristic of a crisis and the basis for delimiting the parameters of the successive periods (pre-crisis, crisis, and post-crisis) in its evolution and dénouement. Yet stress is not an easy emotion to deal with analytically. It poses formidable methodological and conceptual problems, not all of which have been resolved completely satisfactorily here or elsewhere.

To begin with, the concern of this study is with the psychological aspects of stress rather than with its physiological manifestations. Moreover, stress as understood here is not an attribute of the environmental change creating the crisis but rather the product of the decision makers' perceptions of the significance of that source. In the UDI case, the operationalization of stress has involved the measurement of the perceptual responses of Zambian decision makers to the diverse threats generated directly or indirectly by the Rhodesian rebellion. Stress occasioned by other causes is disregarded on the not unreasonable assumption that preoccupation with the implications of UDI eclipsed all other personal, political, or organizational concerns, particularly during the peak period of the crisis.

The basic methodology employed has been a content analysis of major official statements by Zambian leaders at the time. The scope and adequacy of these procedures are explored in Appendix 1. Although the indices of stress derived in this way clearly need to be treated with suitable caution, they can legitimately claim a considerable degree of validity. The trends they reveal are undoubtedly significant, even if the detailed data on which they are based may inspire somewhat less confidence. Moreover, an attempt has been made to compensate for some of the inherent limitations of the quantitative indicators by drawing upon the qualitative judgments of informed academic, diplomatic, and journalistic observers as well as additional evidence, where available, from the decision makers themselves.

Evidence of the stress President Kaunda experienced as a result of UDI is overwhelming. Although this was rarely apparent to the public, it was commented upon by virtually every journalist or other visitor who came in contact with him at the time.[5] As the correspondent of the London *Sunday Times* reported at the peak of the crisis in early December, "Dr. Kaunda is at this moment in as unpleasant a spot as any national leader in the world. Upon his personal reaction to the enormous pressures on him from other black African states, from his own people and from the rebellious whites of Rhodesia, peace in Africa probably depends." Wilson, too, remarked publicly on "the most tremendous pressure" Kaunda was subject to – not least from Wilson himself.[6] On the other hand, with the onset of the post-crisis period, Kaunda began to appear much more relaxed.

A more fundamental concern is whether it is possible to secure a meaningful measure of the stress felt collectively by members of a decisional group. The perceptual reactions as manifested in the stress experienced by individuals confronted with a threat situation are highly idiosyncratic, as is the impact on subsequent behaviour. Some prominent individuals with high thresholds of tolerance to stress may positively thrive under conditions of acute pressure, though perhaps not as much as they would like others to believe. This renders suspect any attempt to devise a composite index of group stress. In the case of Zambia, however, the problem is made manageable by the fact that the stress that has been quantified was principally that experienced by the dominant decision maker, President Kaunda. A substantial majority of the speeches that were analysed for content were his, and most of the remainder would have been deliberately drafted with a view to ensuring that they accurately mirrored presidential perceptions and policies. Moreover, the relevant measure is not the absolute intensity of stress but rather the trend of changes in levels – that is, whether stress is rising or receding. The data demonstrate this convincingly. As indicated in Table A4 and Figure 3 below, stress intensities as reflected in threat perceptions increased dramatically with the onset of UDI in early November 1965 and declined sharply in mid-January, thus clearly delineating the span of the crisis proper.

While the validity of indices of stress by crisis period and phase can be accepted with reasonable confidence, any attempt to draw firm conclusions based on fluctuations in stress recorded within periods, or levels associated with specific decisions would constitute a more hazardous undertaking, and not particularly instructive. The most that can be asserted on the basis of the linear regression lines portrayed in Figure 3 is that the stress level did not rise steadily throughout the pre-crisis period nor decline evenly during the post-crisis period. Also, stress intensity during the crisis period was not uniformly high, and appears to have peaked in early December. These findings are scarcely startling; it would be surprising if threat perceptions within periods did not vary. The fluctuations revealed no doubt partially reflect deficiencies in the data, if only because speeches were frequently designed to calm nervous public opinion rather than accurately reflect the real sense of anxiety felt (see Appendix 1). They can also plausibly be explained by the eruption of "crises within crises." Within as well as between periods, the course of a crisis is typically characterized by discontinuities. In the case of the UDI crisis, the stress profile portrayed is a somewhat distorted, if nevertheless recognizable version of a classic bell curve.

STRESS CONDITIONS

An analysis of the three stress conditions which define an ICB crisis further illuminates the commencement, culmination, and conclusion of the UDI crisis. In each of the three cases, the intensity of

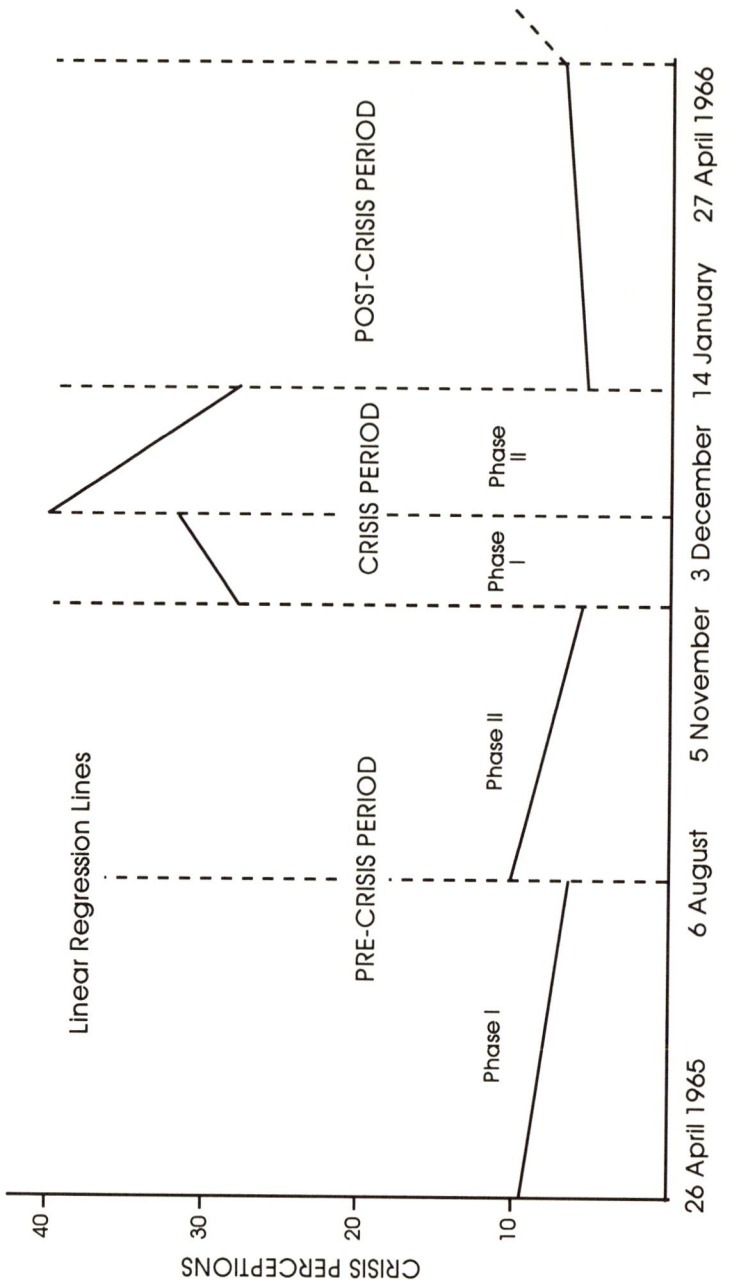

Figure 3: Level of Crisis-Induced Stress

the stressful perceptions increased sharply with the onset of the crisis proper and subsequently receded rapidly towards its termination. Throughout the crisis the threat to basic Zambian values was overwhelmingly the predominant component and, during the pre- and post-crisis periods, the only significant one (Table A5). This pattern conforms to expectations derived from the model which posits that an awareness of time pressure and of the likelihood of military conflict are characteristics essentially confined to the crisis period proper.[7]

Threats to Basic Values

When the analysis is taken a step further and Zambian core values disaggregated into their four principal constituents and rank-ordered (Table A6), the threat to economic interests is revealed as the primary concern of decision makers, both overall and at each stage other than the pre-crisis period, when challenges to Zambian ideological beliefs assumed greater prominence. A further conclusion revealed by the data is that, at the apex of the crisis, threats to national security and to external influence and support emerge as of almost equal salience with the other two.[8]

Time Constraints

Although the awareness of threats to basic values was, in quantitative terms, overwhelmingly the preponderant source of stress, Zambian decision makers also experienced pressures emanating from the other two prerequisites of an ICB crisis: time constraints, and an increased likelihood of military hostilities. The conviction that there was only a finite time for response was particularly keenly felt in the immediate aftermath of the Rhodesian declaration of independence, though the required response – a resort to force – was one which only Britain was in a position to undertake.[9]

An emphasis on the importance of the time factor constituted a major thrust of President Kaunda's initial appeal to Prime Minister Wilson on 14 November 1965. His concerns were twofold. The first was to challenge British confidence in sanctions as the sole mechanism for crushing the rebellion. "They'll never work immediately," he complained to an aide. "By the time they do begin to take effect, Smith will be too entrenched for them to make any difference. I'm certain that if Smith can last out for more than three months it will be too late to do anything."[10] That this was no impulsive outburst in a moment of despair is confirmed by the American ambassador who credits the president with the same perceptive prophecy: "If Smith were not down within three months, ... he would not be downed at all." Such a prospect was particularly appalling for Zambia for, as "Kaunda reasoned, the longer the rebellion continued, the greater the risk of racial strife at home and the danger of economic strangulation by a racist and rebellious regime deeply antithetical to everything Zambia stood for."[11]

If Kaunda strove to avoid the Scylla of a pathetically inadequate British response, he was also anxious to shun the Charybdis of an ill-considered African crusade to liberate Rhodesia. Once the OAU had decided to meet in emergency session, "Kaunda knew that he must act quickly to prevent a racial conflagration in Central Africa."[12] His initiative in demanding direct British military intervention precipitated the gravest and most intense personal and political confrontation between London and Lusaka of any throughout the course of the crisis. The immediate conflict was partially resolved on the very eve of the OAU ministerial meeting when Zambia agreed to accept the protection of an RAF fighter squadron. Although Kaunda insisted that in the timing of the decision there was "no question of beating the OAU conference," it seems likely that that looming deadline was not entirely irrelevant.[13]

This same consciousness of time constraints was also evident to a greater or lesser extent in many of the other crisis decisions. It was apparent in the president's swift reaction to the Rhodesian coal surcharge (Decision No. 26) and in the desperate search for alternative routes to the sea. "We can be squeezed very badly," Foreign Minister Kapwepwe declaimed at the OAU, "and will be completely paralysed if no arrangements are made. Time is against us in Zambia."[14] The Zambian sense of urgency frequently found expression in a call for a "time of action" rather than more meetings or, as Zambian frustrations mounted, in an insistence on firm time limits. However, where the implementation of decisions was dependent on British cooperation, such appeals typically fell on deaf ears.

In addition to the quantitative data on time pressures generated by the content analysis of official texts (Table A5), an analysis of the time frames within which Zambian leaders reached their decisions provides further confirmation of variations in the salience of time concerns during the course of a crisis. Whereas prior to and following the crisis period proper, tight time constraints characterized less than 30 per cent of the decisions, at the peak of the crisis severe limitations on decision time were experienced in over 80 per cent of the cases (Table A7).

Likelihood of Military Hostilities

"What is crucial to the existence of an international crisis," according to the ICB model, is a "high – or substantial rise in – perceived war likelihood," with war interpreted broadly to embrace any kind or degree of involvement in military hostilities.[15] Even prior to UDI, Zambian leaders were acutely conscious of the marked imbalance in the size and capabilities of the military forces north and south of the Zambezi. With the breakup of the Federation of Rhodesia and Nyasaland, Rhodesia had inherited the core of the federal armed services, including the white army units (the Rhodesian Light Infantry and the Special Air Service) and the Royal Rhodesian Air Force virtually intact. The handover of the RRAF to the Smith regime provided it with a powerful strike weapon to which there was no Zambian counterpart (Table A8). Rhodesia's initial material superiority was further enhanced by subsequent substantial arms purchases,[16] and the seizure, first by the Portuguese and then by the Salisbury authorities, of arms in transit to Zambia (Decisions No. 7 and 10). In addition, several related developments increased uncertainty in Zambia concerning its security situation. Kaunda was "greatly disturbed" to discover that South Africa was constructing a major air base in the Caprivi Strip in South West Africa (Namibia) a few miles from the Zambian border, an action he regarded as a "direct threat to Zambia's integrity."[17] Even more disconcerting was Britain's gratuitous assurance to Smith that it would not respond with force in the event of rebellion. There were also doubts concerning the political reliability of some Zambian army officers, as a majority were white Rhodesians or South Africans with personal ties and often political sympathies with the south.[18] Finally, in October, the first reports began to filter through of the movement of Rhodesian troops into the border area.[19] Nevertheless, prior to UDI, there was no real fear in Lusaka that conflict with Rhodesia might escalate into military hostilities.[20] That military appreciation quickly changed with the outbreak of the Rhodesian rebellion, Smith's solemn assurances of immunity notwithstanding.

In surveying the range of military options open to Rhodesia, Lusaka envisaged several possible scenarios, but a full-scale invasion was not one of them. While Kaunda contended that a rebel regime could not be trusted to act rationally,[21] and he remained fully convinced that Smith was determined to ensure that Zambia's fragile experiment in multi-racialism failed, the danger of outright occupation was discounted. More credible was the threat of commando-style incursions against border towns or suspected guerilla camps. Rhodesia's positioning of two battalions of specially equipped white troops along the border and stepped-up aerial surveillance flights on the eve of the rebellion added credence to Zambian fears. Yet, after detailing these and other menacing measures in his post-UDI broadcast to the nation, Kaunda concluded on a note of defiance: "Let me now warn Smith and his fellow traitors that, if Zambia is invaded or if our territory is violated in any way, we will not hesitate to meet force with force."[22] One cause for confidence was Kaunda's assumption that Rhodesia's dependence on Zambia for more than a quarter of its exports offered some guarantee against immediate attack. "My own conviction," he declared a few days earlier, "is that as long as our economic relationship continues to suit Mr. Smith, we will be all right. But, when he feels strong enough to do without our market, then he will strike at us."[23] In any case, the government claimed – somewhat rashly as events in the 1970s showed – that it was capable of containing any conceivable incursion with its existing resources. "Zambia does not need defence by other troops," Kaunda asserted in justification of his rejection of the offer of a British battalion. "We are quite satisfied and confident that our own troops can cope with any offensive attacks from Rhodesia."[24]

There was less confidence in Lusaka that it could repel a Rhodesian air assault, and greater anxiety that the wild men in Salisbury might attempt it. When Kaunda was asked if he feared an attack on Zambia, he replied unequivocally: "From the air, yes. Not on the ground."[25] Not only were many Zambians mesmerized by the spectre of RRAF power,[26] they were also mindful of the unhappy precedent provided by the rescue mission by Western paratroopers in Stanleyville (Kisangani) in Zaire a year earlier.[27] Moreover, the country was so "thin on air defence" as to be effectively defenceless, which is why the government turned to Britain for assistance in the form of a squadron of Javelin jet fighters and early warning radar equipment (Decision No. 21). Although the British considered Zambian fears unjustified, Kaunda insisted that without such support the country would be "subject to probable and serious damage from the air by the rebellious regime in the event of an economic squeeze leading them to desperation."[28]

Of all the potential targets of Rhodesian military adventurism, the one that occasioned the greatest foreboding in Lusaka was the Kariba power station which, though jointly owned, was physically located on the south bank of the Zambezi. As Colin Legum reported after a private interview with the president, "Kaunda is firmly convinced that Smith is capable of either throwing the switch or even, in desperation, of blowing up the Kariba power-house as his deterrent against action to bring down his regime. Kaunda thinks the danger of this happening will increase as the rebels feel pressures mounting against them."[29] Without Kariba power the copper mines would quickly grind to a standstill (and flood) and the economy of the country would collapse. That Zambian concerns for the security of supply of hydro-power were legitimate was confirmed dramatically within two weeks of UDI when a giant pylon carrying electricity to the Copperbelt was sabotaged.[30] This belligerent action reinforced Zambian determination to press for swift British military neutralization of the dam site (Decision No. 20). Although London firmly rejected this demand, the threat to Zambia's vital power source continued to agitate Lusaka. "Any interference with these installations," Kaunda warned, "will be a declaration of war on Zambia and I will not hesitate to order my country into action."[31]

With the exception of sabotage and subversion, none of the Zambian scenarios anticipating military conflict with Rhodesia materialized. This does not mean that the grave threats of Rhodesian aggression that Zambians perceived were merely figments of their imagination. There were ample grounds for genuine concern, and the cumulative effect of these fears had profound implications for the intensity of stress Zambian decision makers experienced. As Colin Legum observed, Kaunda felt "trapped."

The nightmare of what Zambia's fate would be if power stopped flowing from Kariba haunts Kaunda and his colleagues. Over and over again one hears them saying: "We are living on our nerves." This is a fair description of the atmosphere within which President Kaunda is operating. Added to the fears of the consequences of even a temporary disruption of Zambia's economy is the knowledge that relations between Africans and whites in Zambia are balanced on a razor's edge as a result of the Rhodesian rebellion ... These white attitudes contribute enormously to Zambia's nervousness.[32]

IX Crisis and Coping

The principal theoretical focus of this study is on the linkages between changes in the levels of decision-maker stress over the course of a crisis and, first, the processes and mechanisms employed by the Zambian leadership to cope with the consequences of UDI, and secondly, the decisional choices reached as a result. In operational terms, this involves attempting to determine qualitatively, and to some extent quantitatively, the relationship between the broad measures of crisis-induced stress derived from the three components of a crisis and Zambian reactive behaviour both in its procedural aspects and as expressed in policy outcomes as recorded in the analysis in Part Two.

In the case of coping activities, their association with stress intensity is explored on the basis of the nine research questions posed in chapter 1 as well as sets of hypotheses abstracted from the literature on crises, especially Brecher's Israeli case study.[1] A framework of analysis for this exercise is provided by the model's four dimensions of decision-making: information processing, consultative patterns, choice of decisional forums, and the search for and evaluation of policy alternatives (Table 1). The available data on coping behaviour are summarized in tables A9 to A13.

INFORMATION PROCESSING

The stress-information nexus provides the common theme for the first three research questions. These are: What are the effects of escalating and de-escalating crisis-induced stress on

1 cognitive performance (to be discussed later);
2 the perceived need and consequent quest for information; and
3 the receptivity and size of the information-processing group.[2]

The Zambian case offers some support for the claim that, under conditions of increasing stress, decision makers exhibit greater interest and energy in probing all possible sources of relevant information on the nature of the conflict, the specific values threatened, the costs and consequences of alternative courses of action, and other pertinent aspects of the crisis.[3] This is not to suggest that there was little felt need for factual inquiry during the pre-crisis period. In the information sphere, as in others, Zambia was heavily dependent on external inputs. Throughout the six months leading up to UDI its imminence and impact constituted major elements of uncertainty. Moreover, in the course of contingency planning (notably Decisions No. 2, 4, and 6 and the successive searches for alternative routes), enormous informational gaps came to light, prompting systematic and careful explorations for reliable data. In the case of the mission to London in late September (Decision No. 8), the whole purpose was fact-finding. Nevertheless, it was only with the onset of the Rhodesian rebellion that a new sense of urgency was injected into Zambian inquiries, and complaints of inadequate information, principally with respect to British intentions or sincerity, became an almost constant ingredient of crisis behaviour in Lusaka.

Within hours of the proclamation of UDI, Kaunda summoned the British high commissioner to inquire anxiously what London proposed to do to end the uprising in its colony. Neither on that occasion nor subsequently did he succeed in receiving a satisfactory reply, though he persisted in pressing the British. In numerous statements over the following weeks, the president revealed his growing frustrations. "We are anxiously waiting," "I am waiting for replies," "No replies have come through," were his regular refrains in public and in private.[4] Ambassador Good alludes to the appalling uncertainties under which the Zambian cabinet was compelled to operate and reports the bitter comment of one exasperated senior minister on Zambia's inability to elicit adequate and authoritative information on contingency plans: "Our queries are met with a conspiracy of silence."[5] Kaunda was equally frank. "It is a terrible problem," he confessed, "for the Zambian cabinet and me to decide whether Mr. Wilson is determined with sufficient single-mindedness to carry this opposition to Smith through to the end."[6] Thus the inadequacies of Zambia's sources of information were themselves causes of decision-maker stress.

Quantitative evidence provides further substantial support for the hypothesis that the greater the stress, the more thorough the information search (Table A14).[7] The reverse relationship, however, is not confirmed. As stress receded, the preoccupation of Zambian decision makers with fact-finding appears not to have diminished, though the data base is too slender to assert this conclusion with complete confidence. The grim prospect of girding the country to survive a quick kill led Lusaka to raise numerous tough questions, especially in London, for which it eventually transpired there were no satisfactory answers.

When the probing procedures are disaggregated, a number of indicators emerge that lend added credence to the hypothesis. In the first place, the crisis period witnessed increased reliance on the resources of Zambian diplomatic posts elsewhere on the continent and overseas, notably in formulating a response to the OAU call for a break in relations with Britain. Prior to that decision (No. 22), six heads of mission were recalled to Lusaka.[8] Similarly, the four occasions on which ministerial delegations were dispatched abroad on fact-finding missions all occurred during the crisis period proper.[9] UDI also opened an era of intense and frequently forthright exchanges of personal letters and messages between the Zambian president and the British prime minister, with the quest for fuller and more precise information a recurring theme in Kaunda's correspondence.[10] These patterns of search behaviour reinforce Hermann's hypothesis that "in crises, the rate of communication by a nation's decision makers to international actors outside their country will increase."[11]

It is less clear how strong a relationship exists between decision makers' perceived levels of stress and the objectivity with which they assimilate and evaluate information flows as opposed to screening them on the basis of ideological beliefs, expectations derived from previous experiences, or emotional idiosyncrasies. Brecher's findings indicate that, "as crisis-induced stress rises, decision makers' receptivity to new information tends to become more open," and as it declines, "receptivity becomes permeated by more bias."[12] In the present study, the quantitative evidence suggests only a moderately positive relationship with increases in decision-maker stress (and a weaker, but still positive one as stress declines) (Table A15). Nevertheless, in each period, receptivity in information-processing characterizes at least half of the decisions.[13]

A more critical determinant would appear to be the source of the information. In 64 per cent of the decisions most closely associated with Rhodesian trigger events or circumstances, Zambian decision makers were "unreceptive" to the information they received; in other cases, the rate of "unreceptivity" was only 20 per cent. The Zambian government prided itself on its unique understanding of the mentality of the white Rhodesian settlers, having been compelled to cohabit with them during the ten long years of the Federation. As Kaunda explained, UDI "was such an irresponsible threat that perhaps only a few outsiders really thought it could materialize, but we in Zambia, who know the mental contortions of racialists, had every reason to expect it to happen unless Britain stemmed it."[14]

Zambia's psychological insights into the rebel regime were generally much sounder than the wishful thinking that often characterized British judgments (and, from a different perspective, those of many OAU members). In practice, and most notably during the crisis period proper, Lusaka was typically more willing than London was to attribute malevolence, guile, and irrationality to Salisbury's actions and arguments. At the same time Zambian leaders, and especially the president, were prepared to credit the British (and the Labour party) with more intelligence and integrity than subsequent events justified. This was most apparent during the pre- and post-crisis periods. Accordingly, there is some support for an hypothesis that the greater the stress decision makers experience, the more inclined they are to distrust their sources of information.[15] Kaunda certainly seemed to conform to this pattern.

CONSULTATIVE PATTERN

The consultative process has given rise to two ICB research questions. These concern the effects of escalating and de-escalating crisis-induced stress on
4 the type and size of consultative units; and
5 group participation in them.
In addition, two other areas of inquiry suggest themselves: the relationships between stress and intensity of consultations, and between stress and motivation.

In the Zambian case, little hard data exist on the precise types and sizes of units involved in successive consultative exercises or on the nature and relative importance of such contacts. What limited evidence does exist suggests that their frequency and variety increased significantly with the intensification of crisis-induced stress, and that this pattern was even more pronounced in the post-crisis period. On the other hand, contrary to Brecher's findings on Israeli behaviour in the 1967 and 1973 crises, stress seems to have had little or no effect on the extent of reliance on ad hoc forums as opposed to institutional structures – which effectively meant formal sessions of the cabinet (Table A16).[16] Moreover, despite the hurriedly convened late-night strategy sessions of senior ministers and officials at State House that became such a familiar feature of Zambian crisis management behaviour,[17] the frequency of ministerial consultations steadily declined over the course of the crisis. Some increase in the proportion of non-ministerial consultations was evident during the crisis period proper, while in the post-crisis period the cabinet came to assume greater prominence, though its role was still limited.

Brecher has also hypothesized that "as crisis-induced stress rises, the scope of consultations by senior decision makers broadens steadily" and with its decline, "the consultative circle becomes narrower."[18] The quantitative evidence available on the range and character of interests drawn into the Zambian consultative network is strongly supportive of the first proposition, but not the second. For the crisis period the proportion of decisions involving "minimal" prior consultation was only half that for the pre-crisis period, while instances of moderately broad or extensive consultations are substantially greater. However, the decline of stress during the post-crisis period is not reflected in any significant change in the pattern of consultations (Table A17).[19]

The strength of the felt need to widen the consultative circle as the crisis deepened is slightly surprising since the decision times during the peak period of stress were typically more restricted than at other stages in the crisis (Table A17). Moreover, a correlation between the severity of time constraints and the scope of consultations reveals that the coincidence of significant pressures of time on decision makers combined with a comparatively extensive process of consultation was proportionately greater following the onset of the crisis period than prior to it. The position with respect to the post-crisis period of declining stress is less clear, as the data available are too meagre.[20]

When the participants in the consultative processes are disaggregated into functional categories – political, bureaucratic, corporate, and external – several significant distinctions emerge, especially when the data are analysed by period and by principal actor for each consultative operation (Table A18). Throughout the crisis the Zambian political leadership remained the single most salient consultative group, with a level of participation that was uniformly high. At the other extreme, the role of the corporate sector was consistently modest, though by no means minor, and was least when crisis tension was greatest. This finding is somewhat unexpected in view of the penetrated character of Zambia's political economy. Nevertheless, it is indicative of decision-maker priorities. With respect to the bureaucratic elite (which embraced the nascent diplomatic service, the military leadership, and expatriate policy advisers, as well as senior Zambian civil servants), its prominence in the consultative process grew steadily over the course of the crisis. The same was true of external actors, principally foreign governments (notably the British and the Tanzanians)[21] and international organizations (the OAU and the Commonwealth). As crisis-induced stress increased, in both cases participation rates rose dramatically, from 57 to 75 per cent for the bureaucracy and from 50 to 87 per cent for external interests. But as the crisis receded, there was no corresponding decline in activity; rather, the evidence points to even greater involvement in the post-crisis period (Table A18).

One hypothesis in the literature that the Zambian data do not fully support is Paige's common-sense claim that "the longer the decision time, the greater the consultation with persons outside the decisional unit."[22] The opposite is closer to reality, at least as far as the inputs of external actors and Zambian officialdom were concerned. (Corporate contacts remain something of an exception, which is curious since, as already noted, in the Zambian context most businessmen were essentially externally oriented and most companies were foreign-owned.) Not only was the profile of the political elite higher than that of any other consultative group when decision times were not restricted, but also the greater the pressures of time, the greater the involvement of external and bureaucratic interests in the consultative process (Table A19). This pattern of consultation was even more pronounced during the peak crisis period.[23]

The Zambian case study also suggests that the consultative process was not only more extensive under conditions of rising stress levels, but more intensive, in the sense of involving a more searching and sustained exploration of views, at least with respect to political elites and external contacts (Table A20). The data also underscore the sharp decline in the intensity of consultations in the post-crisis period.[24]

The consultative process involved more than mere fact-finding. It was essentially an exercise in sounding out the opinions of other interested and informed individuals and groups on how Zambia might best cope with the awesome challenges it confronted. While eliciting advice on the appropriateness and practicality of specific policy responses remained the primary purpose, three additional incentives for Zambian decision makers to initiate consultations can also be detected: the need for support, for reassurance, and for legitimation.[25] Though analytically distinct, these motives were interrelated and sometimes mutually reinforcing. Moreover, their frequency correlated closely with changes in the intensity of stress that decision makers experienced (Table A21).

The most frequent explanation for the prevalence of consultations (other than as a quest for advice) was the need to solicit support for a preferred policy option, or in opposition to one that was viewed with disfavour. This typically took the form of active lobbying where, as in the case of Tanzanian participation in the airfield survey or the oil airlift (Decisions No. 9 and 24), prior endorsement or commitment was a *sine qua non* for viability. The operation at times proved far from routine, and called for determined salesmanship on Zambia's part. The clearest example of this was Lusaka's sustained campaign to persuade Britain to commit troops to the south bank of the Zambezi, or at least to impose punitive sanctions. Similarly, Zambia repeatedly felt the need to educate OAU members on the risks involved in seeking an African military solution to the Rhodesian crisis (Decisions No. 12, 19, and 33). On several occasions, notably over the issue of continued diplomatic relations with Britain (Decision No. 22), Kaunda found himself compelled to tutor President Nyerere (not always fully successfully) on the realities of survival in a landlocked state dangerously dependent on the caprice of its rogue neighbour.

Winning Nyerere's approval, or at least his acquiesence, was personally as well as politically important to Kaunda as a means of coping with mounting stress. Although he was normally fairly confident of the rightness of his judgments and the righteousness of his cause, at times and especially under conditions of imperfect information and value complexity, he felt a keen inner need for the additional emotional and psychological reassurance that the approbation of Mwalimu Nyerere alone could provide. Again, as with respect to diplomatic sanctions, the desired support was not invariably forthcoming in full measure.

A final objective of consultation was to ensure greater legitimacy for the decision that eventually emerged. The more crucial and controversial the issue under consideration, the more essential it was for Kaunda to carry his cabinet colleagues and ultimately his party with him. The more ministers came to feel a sense of participation, the broader was the consensus likely to be achieved. Widening the political consultative net was also a means of deepening the degree of commitment of individual members of the cabinet, of containing any residual dissatisfaction, and of providing reinsurance against the possibility of subsequent unexpected political costs.

To the extent that crisis-induced stress influenced the motives for undertaking consultations and, therefore, the volume and intensity of such interactions — and these seem to have been considerable (Table A21) — it also transformed the consultative process into something that went beyond simply a search for information and ideas.

DECISIONAL FORUM

The research questions associated with the activation of the ultimate decision-making body concern the impact of changes in the intensity of crisis-induced stress on
6 the size and structure of decisional forums; and
7 the authority patterns within the decisional unit.
While decisional groups frequently serve in a consultative capacity, their responsibilities in their decisional roles extend beyond the mere quest for advice to the evaluation of alternative courses of action and the selection of final choices.

Zambian decisional forums differed in size and composition. Typically, they were of three types: the president acting essentially on his own, a medium-sized ad hoc group of senior ministers (three to six persons), and a large meeting comprising the full cabinet (twelve to sixteen persons). The distinction that Paige draws between ad hoc groups (of ministers) and institutional structures (the president and the cabinet) is not particularly instructive in the Zambian case. In common with many newly independent countries, where the process of political development was still in its early stages, Zambia's inherited political institutions had not yet struck deep indigenous roots. To the extent that the distinction has any relevance, the proposition that "crisis decisions tend to be reached by ad hoc decisional units" appears, as Brecher also found, not to be confirmed (Table A22).[26]

During the pre-crisis period ministerial groups accounted for fully half the decisions, but with the onset of the crisis period proper, their predominance declined slightly (though they remained the most frequently utilized forum) while cabinet participation increased (Table A22). The trend to broadening the decisional base was particularly apparent at the climax of the crisis in the many exhausting meetings devoted to the troublesome issue of stationing British troops in Zambia (Decision No. 20). This conclusion contradicts the widely reported observation of Holsti and

George that "in high stress situations, decision groups tend to become smaller," but substantially confirms Brecher's similarly deviant finding on Israel's decisional forums. The Zambian case also provides support for his hypothesis that in the post-crisis period the preference for large decisional bodies is even more pronounced.[27]

The explanation for Zambia's mildly unorthodox crisis behaviour can be traced in part to President Kaunda's firmly held belief in consensus-style politics. Constitutionally, plenary executive authority resided in the presidency, and he felt no hesitancy in exercising it if the need arose. Nevertheless he was anxious, for a variety of personal and political reasons, to involve his cabinet colleagues in decision making as fully as circumstances permitted, and especially to have them share responsibility for the more difficult and divisive decisions.[28] Although ministers often participated fully and freely in the hammering out of policies, at other times cabinet ratification amounted to little more than the rubber-stamping of actions already agreed upon by the president alone or in communication with his senior ministers. For this reason, it is useful to draw a distinction between the formal decision-taking authority and the effective locus of decision-making power – with the latter the relevant forum for the analysis here.[29] The difference was most marked in the pre-crisis period when the cabinet was formally responsible for nearly three-quarters of the decisions, but was the actual decisional body in less than one-quarter of them. During the crisis period the gap narrowed dramatically, and in the post-crisis period it disappeared entirely (Table A22).

The trend in favour of enlarged decisional forums over the course of the crisis coincided with an apparently contrary tendency towards enhanced presidential influence in the deliberative process (and a decline in the exercise of his persuasive powers as the crisis receded). Whereas Kaunda's personality and opinions appear to have been decisive in ministerial and cabinet discussions in only one-fifth of the pre-crisis and one-quarter of the post-crisis decisions, at the peak of the crisis he dominated the decisional debates nearly two-thirds of the time (Table A23, section a). Presidential predominance in decision making was particularly evident on questions within the political-security issue-area, and not least during the prolonged agonizing over the British troop proposal.[30]

This is not to suggest that Kaunda's views went entirely unchallenged – quite the contrary on a number of vital issues. The evidence suggests that, as crisis-induced stress increased, ministerial and cabinet sessions became more prolonged and disputatious, and that this pattern persisted into the post-crisis period (when Kaunda's influence on decisions was less clearly exercised or felt). While intra-group argumentation never reached unmanageable proportions, it did increase in frequency and vigour as the crisis deepened and differences in perceptions and approaches emerged more starkly. Initially, in over two-thirds of the cases, debates were characterized by little or no tension among participants. However, during the period of greatest stress, less than half of the decisional sessions could be so categorized, a situation which in itself served as an additional source of stress (Table A23, section b).

Similarly, the search for a consensus was significantly more protracted under conditions of mounting stress (Table A23, section c). During the pre-crisis period, there was only one marathon ministerial or cabinet meeting (Decision No. 4) compared with five over the crisis period. Nevertheless, however difficult and delicate the process of decision-making, a consensus always managed to emerge in the end. Intra-group harmony was severely strained on occasion by disagreements over how to cope with perceived increases in threats to basic values, especially when aggravated by time constraints. Yet the capacity of decisional forums to reconcile their differences, if not always to resolve them once and for all, contributed immeasurably to a sense of solidarity among their members. It might be an exaggeration to suggest that "the greater the group conflict aroused by the crisis, the greater the consensus once a decision is reached."[31] But there was no decision that Kaunda found fundamentally disagreeable – certainly not the rejection of the British troop offer (Decision 20) – and none that Kapwepwe felt he could not live with, though clearly in some cases (notably on Decisions No. 19, 21 and 22), he continued to retain mental reservations concerning the wisdom of certain aspects. Dissension among Zambian decision makers was never so great as to threaten the prospect of ultimate agreement. Nor did the pressures for conformity at all costs appear to have been so powerful as to stifle frank and open discussion or impair critical judgment, and thus cognitive performance.[32]

ALTERNATIVES: SEARCH AND EVALUATION

The exploration by decision makers of alternative policy options raises two further questions related to the mechanisms for coping with crises – in particular, the effects of changing decision-maker stress on
8 the search for and evaluation of alternatives; and
9 the perceived range of available alternatives.

Much of the empirical literature on the subject highlights the generally deleterious effects that crisis-induced stress is reputed to have on the search and evaluation processes as well as on the other decision-making tasks. According to this critique, elsewhere designated the law of diminishing options,

> stress is liable to reduce the breadth and quality of the search for alternative courses of action ... the evaluation of alternatives and their consequences tend to be less constructive, the costs and benefits receive less critical scrutiny and the analysis is curtailed by the pressure for rapid closure.

The Zambian case study provides only limited confirmation of this prognosis.[33]

One finding that is substantiated is the claim that, as tension mounts and as a consequence of it, decision makers devote less time and energy to seeking out and identifying the full range of policy options (Table A24, section a).[34] Whether the alleged debilitating effect of stress on innovation and creativity can fully account for this decline is unclear. There is evidence that short decision times (and the intensified stress they engender) led to less exhaustive searches for alternatives; moreover, this tendency towards greater selectivity under pressures of time was more pronounced during the crisis period than earlier (Table A25, section a). However, a further factor contributing to this behaviour is undoubtedly the fact that, as the crisis developed, the same unresolved issues kept recurring, though in different contexts. In the later stages of the crisis, therefore, the Zambian government was in the position of having already done much of its homework; often all possible policy responses had been fully probed previously, and it remained only to reassess them in light of the prevailing circumstances. Among the critical issues that resurfaced on more than one occasion were the troublesome question of OAU military intervention (Decisions No. 12, 19, and 33), appeals for adequate British contingency aid (Decisions No. 8, 25, and 30), the development of alternative outlets to the sea (Decisions No. 2, 6, 7, 9, 11, 14, 24, 27, and 28), and insistent demands for British military retaliation against Rhodesia (Decisions No. 3, 18, and 20). Whether, without the intrusion of this intervening variable, the evidence would have supported the contrary Brecher proposition that under conditions of rising stress "the search for options tends to increase" cannot be established. The modest trend already observed towards a greater reliance on larger decisional groups provides some minimal encouragement for this belief, as elsewhere this pattern has been considered conducive to a more systematic and sustained search for alternatives.[35]

One point to emerge from the Zambian experience is the comparative consistency with which decision makers perceived that their options were severely constricted (Table A24, section b). In this, their situation differed somewhat from that detailed by Brecher.[36] While the increase in stress during the peak crisis period further accentuated this feeling, the predominant perception among Zambia's leaders throughout the course of the crisis was that, in their efforts to live up to their ideological commitment to the liberation struggle in Southern Africa, they were gravely and habitually constrained geographically, economically, and militarily by the country's landlocked condition, its dependence on British goodwill, and its vulnerability to Rhodesian retribution. Despite determined initiatives to broaden its options (notably by pressing London to employ force to end the Rhodesian rebellion), Lusaka found itself frustrated at every turn, and compelled to fall back on a strategy of sanctions in which it had little confidence. For a newly independent state, UDI was a painful introduction to international *realpolitik*.

The limited options available to Zambia reinforced pressures on Lusaka to accord greater priority to the short-term requirements for national survival than the government would have wished. As a result, it found itself diverting energy and resources designated for development to emergency measures, including defence, pleading in desperation to otherwise politically repugnant regimes in neighbouring states for access to alternative transit routes, and restricting the operational activities of liberation movements hosted on its territory. This shortened time perspective on the part of decision makers is consistent with the proposition that, "as stress increases, decision makers become more concerned with the immediate than the long-run future."[37] Admittedly, there is nothing remarkable in this reaction. What is notable in the behaviour of the Zambian leadership is the extent to which it successfully resisted the temptation to pursue the narrow path of national self-interest. The carrot of a comfortable and profitable accommodation with Rhodesia which the rebel regime repeatedly dangled before the Zambians was invariably spurned. In the months following UDI, as in the long years that lay ahead, Zambia paid a high price for its principles – in striking contrast to the self-interest and shame that characterized the attitude and activities of Britain and other actors in the drama.

Brecher's hypothesis that, "as crisis-induced stress rises, the evaluation of alternatives becomes less careful," finds scant support in the Zambian case. There is little to suggest that the process of assessing the relative merits and consequences of perceived alternative courses of action was adversely affected. On the contrary, what evidence does exist indicates that overall the evaluative process was more thorough during the crisis period than in either earlier or later periods (Table A24, section c). What the data do reveal is that time constraints, which contributed to stress, did have a modest impact on the extent to which policy options were scrutinized. This accords with Holsti's hypothesis that "selective perception is most acute when time is shortest."[38] The briefer the decision time, the less thorough was the evaluation of alternatives. However, contrary to the situation with respect to the search process (Table A25, section a), the reduction in evaluative rigour was less marked during the crisis period of high stress than during the pre-crisis period (Table A25, section b). There was only one instance of possible overhasty evaluation, or "premature closure"; this was Kaunda's capitulation to Wilson's fast sell of his quick-kill strategy (Decision No. 30). Yet even here the president's swift acquiescence was not the more typical case of succumbing to intra-group pressures for early decisive action.[39] On balance, in terms of assiduity and adequacy, the evaluative endeavours of Zambian decision makers were both acceptably high and creditably consistent.

COGNITIVE PERFORMANCE

As noted earlier, the initial question posed on the ICB project's research agenda concerns the overall impact of escalating and de-escalating crisis-induced stress on certain aspects of cognitive performance. This relationship provides a useful focus and framework for assessing the quality of the Zambian decisional process in general and the effectiveness under conditions of crisis of the four coping mechanisms in particular.

In this connection, the conventional wisdom, as reflected in the literature, is scarcely encouraging. "A vast body of theory and evidence," Ole Holsti asserts, "suggests that intense and protracted crises tend to erode rather than enhance ... cognitive abilities." He adds that

among the more probable casualties of crises and the accompanying high stress are the very abilities that distinguish men from other species: to establish logical links between present actions and future goals; to search effectively for relevant policy options; to create appropriate responses to unexpected events; to communicate complex ideas; to deal effectively with abstractions; to perceive not only blacks and whites, but also to distinguish them from the many subtle shades of gray that fall in between; to distinguish valid analogies from false ones, and sense from nonsense; and, perhaps, most important of all, to enter into the frame of reference of others.

He concludes the recital of his formidable list of requirements with a warning: "With respect to these precious cognitive abilities, the law of supply and demand seem to operate in a perverse manner; as crisis increases the need for them, it also appears to diminish the supply."[40]

Fortunately, Zambian experience does not point to such a pessimistic conclusion,[41] although it might be contended that the level of anxiety among Zambian decision makers was insufficiently high for impairment of faculties to occur. Elsewhere Holsti has employed an "inverted U" model to describe the relationship between cognitive performance and stress. "Low-to-moderate stress," he has argued, "may facilitate better performance, but high stress degrades it." However, he gives no guidance on how to determine empirically the precise threshold (for each decision maker) above which a deterioration in the quality of performance sets in, and the task would appear to be formidable. It seems implausible that the level of stress generated by the UDI crisis would not qualify as "intense" under any reasonable criteria.[42] On this assumption, the cognitive quality of Zambian decision making is explored in terms of four interrelated variables that impinge on the process.[43]

Impaired attention and perception. Both experimental and historical evidence suggest that, as a consequence of high decision-maker stress,

> aspects of the crisis situation may well escape scrutiny; conflicting values are likely to be overlooked; the range of perceived alternatives is apt to narrow, but not necessarily to the best alternatives; and the search for relevant information and options tends to be dominated by past experience with a tendency to fall back on familiar past solutions.[44]

Moreover, East suggests that

> small states are likely to be slower in perceiving events and developments in the international system. Because they have a smaller capacity to monitor the system, it is less likely that they will perceive various earlier warning signals indicating new developments and important policy shifts by other international actors.[45]

In the case of Zambia, East's assumption is scarcely sustainable. On the contrary, Lusaka was consistently ahead of London in recognizing the storm signals emanating from Salisbury. In fact, so preoccupied were Zambian decision makers with national survival that, during the peak period of the crisis, few other issues managed to compete for their attention; the impact of UDI was so pervasive that it involved virtually every aspect of national life and external relations. In the circumstances, the normal device of ruthlessly selecting and defining priorities was inadequate to relieve the burden on government. Continued agenda overload added to the stress that decision makers were already experiencing, but the check on any excessive narrowing of the span of attention of decision makers had the merit of reducing the risk of inadvertently suppressing relevant information or overlooking promising options.

A review of the Zambian data confirms that, as stress intensified, the search for and evaluation of information and options were more, not less thorough (tables A14, A20, and A24). Only when decision time is introduced as an intervening variable is there some suggestion of lessened rigour and creativity, especially in the identification of alternatives but also in assessing their acceptability (Table A25). A related danger presaged in the literature is a tendency, as tension mounts, for the range of perceived policy options to narrow. This phenomenon was certainly evident in the Zambian crisis situation, though it is difficult to characterize it as a misperception. It represented an all-too-realistic appreciation of the unenviable condition of multi-dependency that Zambia found itself in (Table 24, section b).

Another dimension of decision-maker deterioration related to stress that is highlighted by the research findings is an enhanced dependence on the "lessons of history." In the Zambian case, the salience of legacies of the past are powerfully apparent over the whole course of the crisis. Two perceptions in particular influenced the outlook and actions of Lusaka, and above all of the president. The first was a deep distrust of Rhodesian racists, based on long and bitter experience and intimate knowledge of their "mental contortions."[46] Yet far from warping the judgment of Zambians, familiarity equipped them with unique insights into the rebel mind that the British, in particular, proved incapable of fathoming – with consequences that were tragic, not least for Zambia. In one notable encounter (the confrontation over coal royalties) Kaunda's profound understanding of settler psychology enabled him to pull off a remarkable coup. Although his bold brinkmanship terrified the British and Americans, he succeeded brilliantly in calling Ian

Smith's bluff and compelling the rebel leader to climb down completely.

Secondly, Kaunda retained a surprising faith, which few of his ministers fully shared, in British integrity and fair play. Despite repeated disappointments which strained his feelings of Christian charity, he remained persuaded that his friend Harold Wilson and other British Labour party comrades from the early days of the nationalist struggle in the 1950s would "do the right thing" in the end.[47] Privately, disturbing doubts began to creep in; nevertheless, Kaunda persisted in giving Wilson the benefit of the doubt, bending over backwards to make allowance for Wilson's precarious parliamentary majority and respecting his appeals for caution. Whether a more cynical view of British motives and machinations would have affected the course of events is doubtful. The only difference that more realistic expectations concerning British intentions might have made is to have rendered the trauma that Zambia leaders experienced somewhat less stressful.

Increased cognitive rigidity. Research findings also postulate that the stress associated with crisis conditions impacts adversely on the cognitive capacities of decision makers. In particular, it contributes to

> impaired ability to improvise and reduced creativity; less receptivity to information that challenges existing beliefs; increased stereotypic thinking; and decreased tolerance for ambiguity, which results in a tendency to cut off information search and evaluation and to make decisions prematurely.[48]

Kaunda's reluctance to abandon all credence in the ultimate good faith of Harold Wilson revealed a certain unwillingness to credit evidence that did not conform to some of his cherished hopes and beliefs. Zambians exhibited a similar disinclination to face up realistically to the implications of a full-scale British invasion of Rhodesia. Their instincts in arguing for the strategic use of force to crush the Smith regime were undoubtedly sound, but they undermined the credibility of their case by discounting the very real problems associated with mounting and supplying a military operation across the Zambezi on the scale required.[49] The limited expertise of Zambian leaders in this area is scarcely surprising, as military matters had never formed a significant part of their political education.

Apart from the evidence of impaired cognitive abilities in these two respects, Kaunda and his colleagues maintained a generally high level of openness and objectivity towards new information and ideas. Moreover, receptivity was most evident when stress was greatest (Table A25). One indication of the willingness of Zambian decision makers to view developments objectively was their progressive acceptance of the need for greater pragmatism in policy, particularly with respect to transit routes through neighbouring countries with regimes of varied ideological hues (Decisions No. 7, 11, 14, and 27).

The corpus of literature on foreign policy decision making under conditions of crisis-induced stress identifies two further psychobiological effects. The first is a *shortened and narrowed perspective* which results in "less attention both to longer-range consequences of options and to side effects of options."[50] As already noted, time pressure did adversely affect the process of searching for and evaluating alternatives, and in one case appears to have occasioned premature closure (Decision No. 26). Nevertheless, despite the almost total absorption of Zambian decision makers in immediate concerns of pressing national importance, they never lost sight of their ultimate objective of a liberated Southern Africa. Indeed, it is the strength of this conviction which explains their willingness to bear the brunt of the burden of resistance to racism and rebellion in Rhodesia.

As for the sensitivity of the government to the side effects of its decisions, it was acutely aware of the constant dilemmas it faced. For instance, how much in the way of sacrifices would white South African miners and Rhodesian railwaymen be prepared to countenance before crippling the Zambian economy with thinly disguised political strikes? Could Zambia afford to allow exiled liberation movements freedom of action when it was dependent on their home countries for access routes to the sea? There were no easy answers to these questions, but there was never any possibility of them being inadvertently overlooked.

A final anticipated consequence of crisis stress is a predisposition among decision makers to *shift the burden of responsibility to the opponent*. According to the argument, this distinctive behaviour reflects a "belief that one's own options are quite limited and that only the other side has it within its power to prevent an impending disaster."[51] There is little doubt that Lusaka looked expectantly to London, though not to Salisbury or the OAU, for salvation. For a country as vulnerable and dependent as Zambia, this was inevitable and justified. After all, Britain was adamant in insisting on its exclusive responsibility for its wayward colony, whereas Zambia was in a very real sense an innocent bystander, even if a keenly interested one.[52] In no way can this reasonable response be interpreted as a negative reaction reflecting on the quality of the cognitive performance of Zambian decision makers.

In conclusion, the evidence does suggest that crisis-induced stress accounted for some impairment in the cognitive abilities of decision makers in Zambia. Nevertheless, the degree of deterioration was nothing like as catastrophic as implied in Ole Holsti's catalogue of "the more probable casualties of crisis" cited at the outset of this section. On the contrary, the level of cognitive performance of Kaunda and his colleagues, despite their limited means and comparative inexperience in the world of high politics, was commendably high.[53] In most respects, as is now widely acknowledged, Lusaka had a far better grasp of the realities of the Rhodesian situation than London.[54]

HYPOTHESES

It remains only to summarize the findings of this chapter concerning the impact of changing levels of crisis-induced stress on the mechanisms that Zambian decision makers employed in their efforts to cope with the UDI crisis. This is done in Table A26. While the strength of support for the different hypotheses (and therefore the credibility to be accorded them) varies considerably, fully half of them are confirmed (or disconfirmed) strongly.[55]

Another observation of interest is that barely half the hypotheses are symmetrical - that is, they register positive (or negative) changes with *both* increases in stress and decreases. This is intriguing. Admittedly, the limited number of decisions during the post-crisis period undermines confidence in the complete reliability of the data for that period. Nevertheless, the frequency with which the post-crisis pattern of behaviour represents a continuation rather than a reversal of the trend established during the crisis period raises the question whether the post-crisis period is in all respects simply a mirror image of the pre-crisis period. As it happened, the post-crisis period did not mark the end of UDI; it was soon followed by a fresh crisis in Zambia's relations with Rhodesia. Further investigation of this phenomenon could well prove instructive.

While many of the hypotheses drawn from Zambian experience confirm the prevailing academic consensus, a few of them challenge widely accepted propositions, including some of Brecher's findings. Two are of special interest and importance. As already observed, contrary to Brecher but consistent with much conventional wisdom, the Zambian data indicate that the search for options became more restricted under conditions of stress, and less so as stress receded.⁵⁶ On the other hand, with respect to the evaluation of alternatives, the positions were reversed. In the Zambian case, the process was more thorough during the peak crisis period than either earlier or later (except when decision times were short), whereas Brecher contended that decision-maker anxiety led to "less careful" evaluative efforts.⁵⁷

X Stress and Choice

The ICB model postulates a relationship between
1 decision-maker perceptions of crisis (the independent variable);
2 the four mechanisms for coping with crisis (the intervening variables); and
3 foreign policy choices (the dependent variable).

The bulk of the literature on crisis decision making focuses on the first and second sets of variables: the extent to which decisional procedures are conditioned by the intensity of crisis-induced stress. However, any systematic assessment of the impact of stress on the decision making process must also consider the character of the final foreign policy product. As Holsti and George contend, "We must find ways of evaluating the effects of stress not merely on the *process* of decision making, but also on the *content and quality* of the decisions or choices that emerge from that process."[1] Accordingly, the attempt will be made to analyse the pattern of Zambian decisional choices, qualitatively and quantitatively, under changing conditions of stress in terms of both the perceptions of their authors and the operational results.

DIMENSIONS OF CHOICE

To explore the relationship between levels of stress experienced and foreign policy outcomes the thirty-four Zambian decisions have been coded on the basis of the eight ICB dimensions of choice. The data for each crisis period are recorded in tables A27 to A29.

Core Inputs

The events triggering each decisional process were analysed in an earlier chapter in terms of period, source, and issue area. The focus of concern here is somewhat different – namely, the identification of the stimuli which, in the perceptions of decision makers, contributed crucially to the final policy choices. The evidence indicates that multiple stimuli were the norm, with instances of only a single input a rarity (and mainly confined to the pre-crisis period). The explanation for this is no doubt that Zambia was caught in the midst of a triangle of contending forces comprising the nominal colonial power Britain, the rebel regime in *de facto* control of Rhodesia, and a vocal OAU lobby committed to the liberation of Zimbabwe. Lusaka thus found itself the object of conflicting pressures from diverse quarters.

Contrary to Brecher's findings,[2] neither the number of inputs per decision nor the range of influences experienced altered greatly over the course of the crisis, though the salience of specific stimuli did vary with changing crisis stress (Table A30). In aggregate terms, Southern Africa (essentially Rhodesia) predictably served as the single most important source of inputs. Nevertheless, its dominance declined as the crisis unfolded, while domestic Zambian concerns acquired increasing prominence over time. During the peak crisis period, Britain and the OAU also emerged as significant, if sometimes secondary, sources of core inputs to choice, as each sought to manipulate and manage the response of the world community to the challenge that UDI posed.

Costs and Importance

The exercise of balancing the perceived importance (or benefits) of a course of action against estimates of losses likely to be incurred is critical to the decision-making calculus. With respect to Zambia, the relevant costs at this stage in the protracted Rhodesian crisis were essentially political and material rather than human – that is, casualties of war. Nevertheless, the human element in the equation was far from absent from the minds of decision makers in Lusaka. Not only did they have to face the ever-present prospect of a mass exodus of skilled whites from the mines and the railway, they also had to contend with the nightmare in terms of human misery of a vindictive Rhodesia determined to punish landlocked Zambia for the action of the international community in imposing sanctions.

In the case of both costs and importance, decision-maker assessments co-varied moderately but positively with the level of crisis-experienced stress. Policy choices were perceived as more costly and their value greater at the height of the crisis than during the pre- or post-crisis period (Table A31). This conclusion confirms Brecher's findings, though the magnitude of the perceptual changes was less pronounced in the Zambian situation, presumably because the UDI crisis erupted less suddenly and with less element of surprise than in the case of the Middle East crisis.[3]

Complexity

In contrast to Israeli experience, where the complexity of decisions, as gauged by the median number of issue areas reflected in the final policy choices, increased steadily over the course of the crisis, in the Zambian case, complexity decreased steadily (Table A32, section a).[4] At the same time, the scope of Zambian decisions was consistently broader; the median number of issue areas per decision was two compared with only one in the Brecher study. Part of the explanation is the intense preoccupation in Israel with military operations at the expense of economic concerns. Although Kaunda repeatedly called for military intervention to crush the Rhodesian rebellion, Zambia lacked the capability to undertake the task on its own. Nor was military aggression the principal threat that confronted it at that time. On the contrary, the military-security issue area ranked lowest, while the economic-developmental content of decisions was second only to political-diplomatic considerations in salience. As a newly independent state as well as a landlocked country, issues of status and legal rights, especially as they related to its jointly owned common services with Rhodesia, featured prominently at times (Table A32, section b).[5] On one occasion Kaunda even went so far as to warn that "any interference with these installations" would be regarded as "a declaration of war on Zambia."[6]

Systemic Domain

As with their perceptions of issue areas, Zambian decision makers did not view the repercussions of their choices as narrowly constricted in scope. UDI was no parochial issue of mere local or regional concern. Its effects, it was feared, would reverberate around the world. Racism and repression in Rhodesia represented in microcosm some of the greatest global challenges of the time, and failure to come to grips with them there would imperil world peace. "I do not know," Kaunda announced rather over-dramatically to a startled press conference two weeks after Salisbury's proclamation of independence,

how many of you gentlemen realize how close we are here to the third world war. I personally realize this, and only the British can stop this ... It is something I would not like to explain at the moment ... But we are certainly very close to a third world war and, in all this, I realize sadly enough how much depends on the Zambian government.[7]

The median number of domains that Zambian decisions were viewed as embracing was three; no decision was perceived as of purely bilateral significance,[8] though clearly relations with both Britain and Rhodesia could frequently be characterized as "dominant bilateral." Moreover, their ramifications broadened significantly as the crisis peaked, and declined moderately with the advent of the post-crisis period (Table A33).[9] Not that the pattern of interaction over time was uniform at all systemic levels. On the one hand, increased crisis-induced stress coincided with expectations of a more potent decisional impact both domestically and within the wider international community, including Britain and the OAU. On the other hand, Zambia appears to have anticipated a decline in the extent to which decisions would impinge upon its immediate neighbours, black and white, when the crisis was at its height (Table A33, section b).

The preoccupation of Zambian decision makers with the regional and global implications of their actions did not blind them to the gravity of the threat that the racial conflict south of the Zambezi posed domestically for Zambia's fragile multi-racial experiment and the economic welfare of its people. Although it was not always possible for the government to take the public fully into its confidence, there were sufficient warnings to leave no one in any real doubt as to the dangers that lay ahead for the nation. In his initial broadcast in May 1965 at the outset of the crisis, President Kaunda appealed to his countrymen "at this critical hour" not "to take a racial approach to the troubles ahead ... We must not allow outside actions by racialists to divert us from our noble goals ... in the dark days that might lie ahead. Do nothing that might make the situation more complicated."

Similarly, on the eve of UDI he repeated his appeal, and again warned the nation "I cannot promise you an easy passage and, should the need arise, I shall call on you to tighten your belts. No matter what confronts us, we shall continue to remain calm and face events with the dignity and discipline which we have already demonstrated."[10] Apprehension concerning the explosive potential of the Rhodesian rebellion was a spectre that Zambian decision makers could rarely afford to ignore.

Mental Process

The task of assessing the mental processes by which an individual decision maker selects a policy choice from among the range of available options is formidable enough. To attempt the same undertaking with respect to collective decision making is even more daunting. In the Zambian case, the frequent resort to more than one operative procedure introduced a further complication. Fortunately, some evidence on which to base cautious judgments concerning the effective processes used to reach decisions can be deduced from the arguments of the relevant participants. Nevertheless, the data thus derived must perforce be treated as more indicative than definitive.

The computations recorded in Table A34, section a, suggest that, in nearly two-thirds of the cases, Zambian decision makers employed a rational calculus process, based on the weighing of costs and benefits. This conclusion differs from Korany's contention that "a rationalistic conception of decision making" is not "common practice in Third World countries."[11] For most of the remaining decisions, an affective procedure, defined as "reliance on past experience, ideology, rooted beliefs, emotional preferences, etc.," appeared to operate. This accounted for one-third of the cases – a relatively high proportion in comparison with experience elsewhere. The partiality for rational processes varied inversely with the level of decision-maker stress, whereas affective influences exhibited a positive relationship.[12] As for routine decision-making procedures, in only one instance (the deployment of troops along the southern border in the immediate aftermath of UDI) can the decisional process be so characterized. This is scarcely surprising in view of the limited opportunities that Zambia, as a young state, had had to develop standard operating procedures for coping with crises.

Activity and Novelty

Virtually all Zambian decisions were action-oriented. Even the two instances of delay (Decision No. 17 introducing only an interim program of sanctions and Decision No. 19 parrying an OAU military initiative) involved active elements. The same was true of the two decisions not to act (Decision No. 20, not to host a British battalion and Decision No. 22, not to break diplomatic relations with Britain). In the great majority of cases in all periods, the thrust of activity was verbal rather than physical in nature (Table A34, section b).[13] The explanation for this apparent passivity is once again the dependent condition of the Zambian state. With respect to at least half the decisions, implementation required action by one or more external actors, most commonly Britain.

With limited experience of high international politics and few policy precedents to draw upon, it was inevitable that a substantial proportion of the decisions could be characterized as innovative. Moreover, as has been evidenced in other studies, the predisposition to resort to unprecedented behaviour increased over the course of the crisis (Table A34, section c).[14]

QUALITY OF DECISIONS

In addition to evaluating decisions on the basis of the eight principally perceptual dimensions embodied in the ICB model, policy outcomes can be assessed in terms of their objective content and consequences. As far as President Kaunda was concerned, there was no doubt in his mind concerning the rightness of his policy prescriptions, especially in relation to Rhodesia. "We in Zambia," he declared following his failure to persuade the British to end UDI through military action,

are on record as being right on more than one occasion in our advice to the British government in the past ... the British government impliedly claimed better knowledge of their kith and kin. But we, who have lived together so long with the Rhodesians, know only too well how unkith and unkin they are to their kith and kin in London.[15]

Kaunda's confidence in the soundness of his judgments was abundantly justified. On the central issues of strategy – sanctions and the use of force – his consistent contentions have been largely vindicated. Certainly, the validity of Zambian scepticism concerning the efficacy of sanctions, at least as conceived and executed by the British government, has now been widely acknowledged. The American ambassador characterized Kaunda as "prophetic," and praised him for "astutely" predicting that treason would triumph if the rebellion were not crushed within three months.[16] Kaunda rightly insisted that full and immediate implementation as well as effective enforcement action to counter South African and Portuguese sanction-busting were essential if sanctions were to have any chance of success. The incredible naïveté of London in assuming that Pretoria would respect sanctions as well as its blind refusal to credit reports of massive breaches in the oil embargo, must count among the classic instances in history of cognitive dissonance.[17]

Kaunda's persistence in pressing for military sanctions on every conceivable occasion is perhaps more controversial. Nevertheless, there is mounting evidence to suggest, not only that the scheme was inherently feasible, but that it would have offered the quickest and cheapest resolution of the crisis. Even at the time there were responsible voices in London, especially in the immediate aftermath of UDI, promoting a British military initiative and fully persuaded of its wisdom, justice, and practicality. The constraints on intervention were essentially political rather than military.[18] Perhaps the most balanced judgment on the failure of British political will – and testimony to the validity of Zambian demands – is the confession, written in the perspective of history, of James Callaghan, chancellor of the exchequer at the time:

I now regret that my preoccupation with [the problems of sterling and the balance of payments] prevented me from urging forceful action by Britain to compel Rhodesia's return to legality. We should have used whatever means were necessary to apprehend and arrest Mr. Smith and his followers ... I must accept my full share of collective responsibility for our decision to limit our action to taking trade and financial sanctions – and there were arguably good reasons for going no further – but I do not disguise my regrets nor my belief that more forceful action by us at the time might have saved Britain from many uncomfortable moments in later years."[19]

As well, he might have added, as sparing Zambians the high price they were called upon to pay for Britain's excessive caution.

Success

Being right in one's foreign policy choices is not the same as being successful, especially for a small, weak, dependent power. The ultimate measure of the merits of decisional choices is whether their goals are realizable in terms of both the resources available and their relevance to reality. This means, in the first place, "the ability of foreign policy makers to pursue objectives within the realm of their country's capabilities." Secondly, in the familiar terminology of the Sprouts, success in foreign policy depends on a coincidence between the psychological environment of the decision makers and the operational environment in which decisions are executed.[20] The narrower the gap, the more likely that the intended consequences can be realized, although in some circumstances even the most apposite choice may not be adequate to ensure success. For some disadvantaged actors there may be no policy option that offers benefits to match the costs. Nevertheless, it is legitimate to inquire whether Zambian decision makers maximized their opportunities, or at least minimized their net losses, or whether alternative courses of action existed which might have been more productive in preserving and promoting national values.

In conceptualizing success, it is material to go beyond the immediate action required of the decision to assess its subsequent impact on the course of events. This perspective is particularly pertinent in Zambia's case as many of its foreign policy initiatives exceeded its competence to execute unilaterally. It would not be sufficient, for example, merely to inquire how forcefully Lusaka pressed its demands on London. The substance and significance of the British response also have to be ascertained.

Analysis of the fate of Zambian decisions reveals that over 60 per cent succeeded in realizing their objectives, and that the rate of success rose steadily over the course of the crisis (Table A35, section a). Several of the successes represented signal achievements, notably Kaunda's coup in compelling Ian Smith to withdraw his punitive coal surcharges. Also, in few if any of the thirteen cases categorized as unsuccessful is it possible, even with the benefit of hindsight, to conceive of any alternative policy choice which might have resulted in a more favourable outcome.

The one significant exception concerns the use of force in Rhodesia. Could Zambia have done anything differently to cajole or coerce Britain into intervening militarily? The answer is almost certainly no. Nevertheless, several intriguing, if ultimately unconvincing scenarios can be envisaged. The first questions the wisdom of Zambia's rejection of the conditional British troop offer. Apart from the fact that this action relieved Wilson of an obligation he was reluctant to undertake, analysts are left to speculate what might have eventuated if Lusaka had decided to swallow its pride, gamble on the "law of unexpected consequences," and permit the positioning of a battalion of the Scots Guards along the north bank of the Zambezi. Once the troops were conveniently entrenched on the border, it is at least conceivable that London might have found it politically less difficult to take advantage of some subsequent development in the Rhodesian situation to lift its offending operational restrictions. At a minimum, the physical presence of the force might have injected a salutary element of uncertainty into Salisbury's strategic calculations. However seductive this scenario might seem, it suffers from one fatal flaw: no new circumstance ever arose to accord the slightest encouragement to the belief that Wilson would ever have been prepared to confront the Smith regime militarily.[21] Some of Wilson's ministers came to doubt his judgment, but they represented a small and ineffectual minority.

A second conceivable strategy would have been to attempt to force Wilson's hand by actually implementing his quick-kill brainchild. By deliberately setting out to threaten national suicide, Lusaka might have compelled London to intervene decisively in Rhodesia to rescue Zambia (or, at least, its copper) from inevitable disaster. Wilson may have felt no great commitment to Zambia's survival, but he did have an exaggerated perception of the risk to millions of British jobs of an interruption in supplies of Zambian copper.[22] In December 1965 Zambian ministers briefly entertained the idea of precipitating a total break with Rhodesia,[23] and the following month Kaunda succumbed to Wilson's infectious optimism and committed the country to an early deadline. Nevertheless, despite the obvious appeal of a short, sharp confrontation over the slow agony of inadequate sanctions, Lusaka rightly reasoned that the sacrifice would in the end prove futile.[24] Faced with a crunch of its own creation, Britain would have had few qualms over abandoning Zambia to its certain fate, or at best pressuring it to back down as, in fact, happened in late April 1966 when Lusaka suddenly blocked all payments to the headquarters of Rhodesia Railways in Bulawayo.[25]

Finally, it might be contended that Zambia did not adequately capitalize on its tactical opportunities. In particular, by consistently ruling out any non-British force and by not insisting more firmly on the linkage between the requests for British ground troops and air support, Lusaka weakened its bargaining power crucially and needlessly. Appealing as these prospects might appear, it is entirely illusory to suggest that Britain could have been budged by arguments of this kind. Frustrating as it was for Lusaka to witness London's inaction, Zambian decision makers were helpless to do anything effective about remedying the situation. The tedious reiteration of their demands may even, in later years, have proven counter-productive.

Rationality in decision making has conventionally been conceived of as an essential ingredient in a sound and successful foreign policy. In challenging this belief, Holsti and George conceded that

> while this is often the case, it is by no means uniformly so ... A "rational" process of decision making is neither a sufficient nor ... a necessary condition for achieving decisions of high substantive merit and quality. Good decisions can and often do emerge from decision processes that do not meet the formal procedural requirements for "rational," orderly, and systematic consideration of alternatives."[6]

Zambian experience confirms this judgment; six "rational" decisions proved unsuccessful, while an equal number of "affective" choices fulfilled expectations. Nevertheless, the proportion of successes among "rational" decisions was consistently above average and for "affective" decisions correspondingly below average (Table A35, section b). In both cases, however, the success rate improved as decision-maker stress intensified.

HYPOTHESES

The qualitative and quantitative data generated by the universe of Zambian decisions project a clear relationship between changing crisis-induced stress and choice along six of the eight ICB dimensions of decision. However, in half of these cases the relationship is negative, although only with respect to the propensity to rational decision making is it negative for both increasing and diminishing stress. On three dimensions – costs, importance, and novelty – the hypotheses derived confirm those formulated by Brecher and Dowty on the basis of their Middle East studies (Table A36). Finally, nearly half the hypotheses are asymmetrical, again suggesting that the post-crisis period must be viewed as distinctive in a number of respects, and not merely a replication in reverse of the pre-crisis period.

XI Significance

The present inquiry has combined two approaches: first, the concerns of the area specialist with the course and conduct of Zambian policy as Lusaka confronted the consequences of a settler rebellion on its doorstep; and, secondly, the insights of the social scientist preoccupied with general patterns of crisis behaviour. Using the empirical base derived from a quantitative and qualitative analysis of a series of case studies of Zambian decision making in practice, the study has sought to probe and profile the characteristics of both the coping processes employed and the final policy product, under changing perceived intensities of crisis tension. In retrospect, the exercise has proved more productive than appeared probable at the outset, in view of the daunting conceptual, methodological and informational constraints inherent in the undertaking. It remains only to assess its significance. This will be explored within three domains: its relevance for the ICB research project, for Zambian crisis decision making, and for African foreign policy studies generally.

IMPLICATIONS FOR THE STUDY OF INTERNATIONAL CRISIS BEHAVIOUR

The Rhodesian rebellion differed in a number of important respects from other international crises chronicled in the ICB research studies.[1] Zambia was in a very real sense an innocent bystander caught up in a colonial quarrel between Britain and

Rhodesia, though it was not content to remain on the sidelines but instead took a deliberate decision to intervene actively in the dispute. As a result, Lusaka quickly found itself pitted against not only Salisbury but London as well. Zambia contested both the declared ends of British policy towards Rhodesia and the means chosen to attain them. It argued vociferously that economic sanctions were inadequate and that military measures were indispensable. It also insisted that the objective of international action against Rhodesia should be the liberation of Zimbabwe – subsequently popularized as NIBMAR[2] – and not merely the restoration of the *status quo ante* and the legalization of the rebel regime.

Thirdly, the security threat that Rhodesia posed was primarily economic rather than military, thus reinforcing the argument for qualifying any strictly "military" assumptions underlying the definition of an international crisis. The conventional military challenge which Zambia faced in the immediate aftermath of UDI was, in a sense, quickly swallowed up in a larger and more fundamental concern for survival. The possibility that its vital lifeline to the sea and its power supply might at any moment be suddenly severed clearly placed the security of the nation in grave jeopardy.

A fourth distinctive feature was the minimal extent to which superpower rivalry intruded into the conflict. UDI was not a crisis that erupted within the context of the Cold War. The Russians stood studiously aloof, and the Americans, increasingly bogged down in Vietnam, were content to tag along behind the British. Finally, the Rhodesian rebellion can be characterized as a protracted crisis, with the period of the present study only the opening chapter in a long and bitter struggle. Before the emergence of Zimbabwe as a nation in 1980, Zambia was to experience even more emphatically the military costs of conflict spilling across its frontiers and the crippling impact on its economy of both sanctions and the collapse of world copper prices.

Not only was UDI atypical when compared with other ICB crises, but Zambia as an actor was also an exception to the general pattern in other studies. Even India, although a Third World state, is not completely comparable. In terms of size, economic resources, and military power, it vastly outranked Zambia. Neither was it equally dependent, regionally or globally. Moreover, the threat that Chinese border incursions posed, though traumatic for Nehru and the nation, was not as fundamental a challenge to the basic structures of the country as that faced by Zambia. Israel, as a small beleaguered developing state, provides a closer parallel, although there are legitimate doubts concerning its Third World credentials. Certainly, Israel was also neither economically as underdeveloped, militarily as weak, nor physically as dependent on its neighbours as Zambia clearly was. In thus offering an alternative perspective on crisis decision making, the Zambian case is particularly instructive.

Despite these undoubted differences, the Zambian experience was found not to be so deviant that it could not fit comfortably within the ICB framework. In part, this reflected the inherent flexibility of the model itself, which enabled it to accommodate quite disparate demands imposed on it.[3] More significant was the fact that the UDI crisis in essential respects did conform closely to the model. This was most apparent in the sharp inter-period discontinuities evident in the perceived levels of decision-maker stress, even when disaggregated into its constituent components. When tested in practice, the ICB model proved readily capable of being adapted to the Zambian context. While it is necessary to recognize the dangers of generalizing too broadly, the Zambian case does provide grounds for confidence in the comparability of behavioural characteristics across a mix of "old" and "new" state actors.

A decision-making focus for the study of crisis-induced stress in developing states illuminates a number of promising areas for advancing comparative crisis research. Four such areas in particular emerge from the Zambian case study:

1 the role of domestic capabilities and constraints where conditions of dependency intensify threat perceptions and affect responses to crises in structural and temporal ways;
2 the impact of transnational associations: corporate, racial, military, and infrastructural;
3 contrasting orientations to crisis situations: conflict avoidance, conflict management, and conflict resolution; peacekeeping, peacemaking, and peacebreaking (through armed struggle); and preservation of the status quo and promotion of fundamental change; and
4 the structure and salience of the regional subsystem, global dependencies, and crisis levels.

One specific issue meriting further exploration, one without a clear conclusion, concerns the symmetry of decision-maker behaviour over the course of the crisis. As observed in an earlier study,[4] one intriguing, if tentative, conclusion to emerge on the basis of these sketchy data is that the post-crisis pattern of behaviour is not necessarily a mirror image of that during the pre-crisis period.

IMPLICATIONS FOR THE ANALYSIS OF ZAMBIAN FOREIGN POLICY

Maurice East has identified two models of small-state foreign policy behaviour. The traditional one assumes that, while small developing states perforce operate internationally on a more modest scale than large developed states, their decision-making processes are essentially the same, basically reflecting a rational actor model. East's own communications model, on the other hand, postulates that the policies and procedures of small states are fundamentally different from those of the major powers. In operational terms,

> the major difference between the two models of foreign policy behaviour ... concerns the degree to which small states engage in what can be considered high-risk behaviour. The alternative model predicts more high-risk behaviour for small states, while the conventional model predicts a more cautious, low-risk behaviour pattern.[5]

Zambian behaviour conformed to that anticipated under the alternative model only partially. Lusaka was clearly prepared to pay a substantial price for its liberationist ideals and on occasion even toyed with the idea of threatening economic suicide in a desperate bid to force Britain to intervene decisively. Nevertheless, it was notably cautious in initiating actions involving commitments clearly beyond its ability to deliver. Even Kaunda's vigorous riposte to the Rhodesian coal royalty challenge was not without an element of calculation, and was in any case a purely verbal response. The one truly madcap scheme he was stampeded into agreeing to – the quick-kill strategy – was not his brainchild, but Wilson's. Zambian decision makers, Kapwepwe included, cannot justly be accused of letting their hearts overrule their heads unduly, despite the periodic temptation they felt to give vent to their intense frustrations by some dramatic sacrificial act. Although Kaunda has claimed that Africans "allow both rational and non-rational elements" scope in African problem-solving,[6] the available evidence, even if somewhat speculative, suggests that Zambia's record of rationality in decision-making was quite striking. Throughout the UDI crisis, a rational calculus mode appears to have been the dominant mental process employed in nearly two-thirds of the decisions taken (Table A34, section a).

East attributed the alleged propensity of small developing polities to indulge in "high-risk, high-commitment action" to the "limitations on their organizational capacity and ability to monitor international affairs adequately."

Because they have a smaller capacity to monitor the system, it is less likely that they will perceive various early warning signals indicating new developments and important policy shifts by other international actors ... By the time a small state perceives the signals regarding a situation, that situation has frequently reached a stage where only definite "high-commitment" action will be effective.

Robert Rothstein, from a somewhat different perspective, has highlighted the same systemic shortcomings as critical intervening variables affecting the capabilities of Third World states to perform effectively in the sphere of foreign policy. Developing countries, he argues, "abound with organizational and informational deficiencies" which "may be even more profound in foreign affairs, for the skills and knowledge to deal with the external world may be particularly hard to come by." Similarly, Rothchild and Curry assert that "the quality of policy-making in the LDCs tends to be lower than that in the developed countries primarily because of the lack of resources," human and material.[7]

Again, Zambian experience affords only limited support for this contention. It was Britain rather than Zambia that was insensitive and unresponsive in face of the clear signs of the gathering Rhodesian storm. Both prior to UDI and subsequently, Kaunda proved to be a prophet crying in the wilderness, warning leaders elsewhere in Africa and overseas to wake up to the realities of the escalating conflict in Southern Africa. Moreover, as previously intimated, the quality of Zambia's decisional performance was impressive, and its policy prescriptions usually eminently sound, even in the light of hindsight.[8] The supposed impediment of inadequate infrastructural support combined with limited experience in foreign affairs would appear, at least in Zambia's case, to have been less grave than commonly assumed.

Yet inspired generalship on the battlefield offers no assurance of ultimate victory in the war. Although Zambia was generally astute in maximizing its foreign policy opportunities, Lusaka was never in a position to impose its own solution to the UDI crisis. Zambia remained critically constrained by its historically conditioned dependence on its immediate neighbours, notably, but not exclusively, Rhodesia. At the same time, economically and ultimately militarily, it continued dependent on the willingness of the British to recognize their responsibility, as the nominal colonial power, to end the rebellion and to sustain Zambia in the process. As Lusaka quickly discovered, on most issues it could proceed no faster or further than London was prepared to countenance. This fundamental fact of international life proved to be perhaps the most painful lesson in *realpolitik* Zambia was forced to learn in the course of the crisis. It also underscored how crucial to any real understanding of Zambia as a foreign policy actor was an appreciation of the potency of the systemic constraints within which it was compelled to operate, especially in limiting its policy options. External dependency compounded the threat which UDI posed for Zambia, nationally and regionally, and constituted a major contributing factor to the stress Zambian decision makers experienced.

Among the hypotheses generated by the study (tables A26 and A36), that concerning the role of the president merits special attention. Conventional wisdom contends that the institutional underdevelopment characteristic of Third World states inevitably gives rise to highly personalized presidential foreign policy decision making. As Rothstein explains,

With few experts at home and few embassies abroad, with few interest groups and little public interest, and with few sources of knowledge, foreign policy tends to be the unfettered preserve of the leader and his friends ... When the dominant leader is particularly popular and his rule unchallenged, the distinction between personal views and state policies may disappear.[9]

This portrayal finds partial confirmation in the Zambia of the mid-1960s. At that time, Kaunda and his colleagues lacked the professional support routinely available in more established states. As the fathers of their country, they enjoyed immense personal and political prestige; no one was disposed to challenge the legitimacy of their leadership. Their forthright reaction to the UDI challenge highlighted the role of individuals, particularly that of President Kaunda, in the Zambian decision-making process. While Kaunda preferred to govern by consensus, it was a consensus which he actively sought to shape rather than one he passively acquiesced in. The passion with which he pursued his commitment to the eradication of Rhodesian racism and colonialism – which he saw as an extension of Zambia's own independence struggle – proved a crucial ingredient in determining the orientation of the country's foreign policy.

Yet despite the widespread conviction that the personalization of foreign policy is characteristic of Third World countries, the concept is applicable to the Zambian situation only with qualifications. It is scarcely possible to ascribe Zambian foreign policy solely to Kaunda in the same sense that it is common to refer to Nasser's foreign policy, or Nkrumah's, or even Nyerere's. Under a different Zambian president the policies pursued would undoubtedly have differed in some respects. Kapwepwe would not have responded to UDI in quite the same way as Kaunda did. Nevertheless, the divergences would have been more a matter of style than of substance: the exigencies of Zambia's geopolitical state of dependence would have ensured this. Moreover, whatever the validity of the proposition, it is not unique to developing countries. British policy on Rhodesia, for example, clearly bore Prime Minister Wilson's personal stamp, and was at least as idiosyncratic as Zambian policy. As for Kaunda's command of foreign policy decision making, it was far from "unfettered." His powers of persuasion were not unlimited. He could not and did not dictate policy. Debates within the decisional forums were real. Great as his prestige and influence were throughout the course of the crisis, only at its peak did they appear decisive, or nearly so (Table A23, section a).

In assessing the restraints on Zambian foreign policy formulation, the role of public opinion is instructive. Civil society in the early years of independence was seriously underdeveloped. Few domestic interest groups existed, and hardly any of them evinced any active interest in the implications of the UDI issue for the country. Even Zambian trade unions were uncharacteristically quiescent. Only the expatriate business community, and especially the mining companies, were actively involved in the policy process. Nevertheless, among the Zambian population in general, there existed a broad popular understanding of the issues at stake in the conflict. Evidence emerged periodically of public unease at the evolution of events, especially the primacy accorded foreign policy imperatives at the expense of developmental needs. As a result, the government felt compelled to mount a series of "meet the people" campaigns throughout the country to "explain to the people what the government has been doing about development and the Rhodesian situation."[10] Compared to the country's external regional and global dependencies, public opinion constituted only a minor constraint on presidential autonomy in foreign policy decision making. At the same time, it was never a factor that could be ignored.

The initiation of Zambian policy makers into the intricacies of international politics left them under no illusions concerning Zambia's future diplomatic prospects. They quickly came to appreciate that independence for a small, weak, dependent state inevitably posed difficult and dangerous challenges and choices. Four lessons in particular, each with important policy implications, emerged from Zambia's baptismal experience:

1 The perfidy of states and statesmen is pervasive. International goodwill and personal friendships go only so far in tempering national interests, as Kaunda's experiences with British Labour party leaders (and, to some extent, with Nyerere) confirmed.
2 The pan-African spirit, too, has its limits. In the case of the great majority of OAU members, no credence could be placed in their fervent assurances of support. Even Zambia's immediate neighbours had their own national priorities.
3 Dependence on routes through and resources of other states can have a crippling effect on a landlocked country's freedom of action internationally.
4 It is crucial to rank foreign policy objectives realistically. The higher the ranking, the more principled a state can afford to be. The lower the ranking, the more pragmatic it may need to be.

Lusaka also came to realize that the country's copper wealth was a mixed blessing. As a source of foreign exchange and government finance it was a tremendous asset. Its strategic importance also enabled Zambia to exercise some leverage internationally, especially with its customers. On the other hand, copper greatly complicated its external relations. Without copper, Zambia would have been much less dependent on imports of coal, oil, and electricity and on road and rail routes through neighbouring countries. Moreover, fully half the decisions analysed in this study would not have had to be taken.

The lessons Zambian decision makers ingested, in the course of coping with the traumatic events arising out of the first UDI crisis, stood them in good stead in subsequent years as they confronted a succession of new conflict situations. While the specific issues that preoccupied policy makers changed as the tide of independence swept south, the principal determinants of Zambian foreign policy remained remarkably constant. The country's dependent condition was as great a constraint as ever, at least until the 1980s. Political leadership was characterized by exceptional continuity until the electoral upheaval of 1991. The regional military imbalance persisted, and assumed greater prominence as Zambia became increasingly the target of destabilization by hostile Portuguese, Rhodesian, and South African regimes. The one change in Zambian circumstances to have a significant impact on foreign policy practice was the drastic deterioration in the country's economy. In part, this represented the price Zambians paid for their exemplary support of the liberation struggles in Southern Africa. Even more important as influences on policy were the catastrophic collapse of the world price of copper, the plummeting in value of the kwacha,[11] and the mounting debt burden.

In the process, a further concentration of power in the presidency occurred, and the influence of international donors was greatly enhanced. The role that the International Monetary Fund came to play in the 1980s was, in many respects, comparable to that the British performed in the 1960s. None of these developments appears to have occasioned any fundamental change in the process by which Zambian foreign policy decision makers sought to cope with and contain the myriad and multi-level pressures and perils they constantly confronted. While this conclusion has yet to be properly tested empirically, what evidence does exist suggests that the seminal experiences of the sixties set a pattern for foreign policy decision making that continued substantially unchanged throughout the seventies and eighties.[12]

IMPLICATIONS FOR AFRICAN FOREIGN POLICY RESEARCH

The primary contribution of this study to the systematic analysis of African foreign policy generally is in demonstrating the essential viability, as well as the inherent limitations, of a decision-making approach in the research climate currently prevailing on the continent. While it is not contended that the judgments expressed and the data generated are necessarily definitive, there are grounds for regarding them as meaningful and instructive. Despite Korany's continued scepticism concerning the utility of content analyses of official statements as a reliable source of candid insights into decision makers' perceptions, stress, and coping efforts, the exercise has provided empirical data which, on a judgmental basis, appear credible as well as suggestive. Government spokesmen may in certain circumstances be less than completely frank and open in their public pronouncements, yet to reject all such primary source material out of hand because some of it may be suspect is to toss the baby out with the bath water.[13] If the present pioneering endeavour succeeds in encouraging others tempted to undertake similar inquiries to feel less intimidated by the undoubted difficulties and deficiencies in the approach, it will have served one of its purposes. Stress is obviously not the sole factor affecting foreign policy decision making but, in crisis situations, it is a significant ingredient that logically cannot be disregarded simply because of the problems associated with assessing its intensity.

Finally, the study points to a number of potential areas for further research into aspects of African foreign policy decision making. These include, in addition to those already enumerated:

1 the relative salience for decision makers of domestic and external variables, and especially the priority accorded security concerns as opposed to developmental goals;
2 the relative potency of objective and psychological environmental factors in the formulation of foreign policy under differing crisis conditions and degrees of dependency;
3 the role of individuals in comparison with institutions, especially under different political regimes and political economies; and
4 changes in the quality and character of decisional processes and outcomes over time as state-building proceeds and leaders acquire greater experience in world affairs.[14]

Zambia is one of the few countries in Africa to have survived from independence to the early 1990s under the leadership of the same party and president. It is also the only one to have been in the frontline of the struggle for human dignity in Southern Africa continuously throughout those years, despite the cost in sacrifice and suffering. It remains to be seen how Zambia will adapt to the emerging post-apartheid South Africa. In the meantime, it is instructive as well as inspiring to look back and reflect on the opening chapter of Zambia's arrival onto the world stage, and recall how Kaunda and the country first rose to the challenge that has continued to absorb the energies of the nation for most of the years since then.

Appendices

APPENDIX 1
Content Analysis

The content analysis of Zambian official statements was undertaken in an attempt to establish approximate measures of relative levels of decision-maker stress over the course of the UDI crisis. Despite the intimidating conceptual complexities and methodological pitfalls associated with operationalizing personal anxiety, the outcome proved reasonably reassuring. When checked against primary and secondary sources on a judgmental basis, the aggregate data appear sufficiently reliable and revealing to serve as useful indicators of changing levels of crisis-induced stress.

The compilation of the speech set required certain decisions concerning the selection process and the coding of the texts which had important implications for operationalizing crisis variables and the subsequent findings.[1] Lack of uniformity in the Zambian foreign policy speech population ruled out a resort to standard sampling procedures to produce a representative selection. To ensure that all aspects of official policy and different documentary formats were included in the file, it proved necessary to fall back on qualitative judgments. In the end, a comprehensive collection of forty-nine significant and relevant public statements issued between May 1965 and April 1966 by official spokesmen of the Zambian government was assembled and analysed. Although the distribution of statements by period was relatively even, their frequency at the height of the crisis was considerably greater than during the lengthier periods that preceded and followed it. With respect to sources, presidential pronouncements accounted for well over half the total, with the proportion even higher during the period leading up to the crisis and especially at its peak; in the post-crisis period, the vice-president's weekly radio reports to the nation predominated. In terms of the forums addressed, the vast majority were domestic, with national broadcasts and presidential press conferences the most common media (Table A37).

The disparate nature of the speech file posed certain problems for coding and coder reliability[2] which, for the most part, are not encountered in the content analysis of documents of Western political systems. In the first place, in the coding of threat perceptions, the diversity of statements in terms of targets and textual structure significantly influenced procedures for identifying theme changes. Normally, in coding perceptual data the standard context unit is the paragraph; a new paragraph provides a reliable indicator signalling a change in subject matter. In the case of Zambian transcripts, application of this rule was not always feasible. In particular, unscripted addresses at "national rallies" were typically characterized by arbitrary paragraphing as well as a discursive delivery style. Yet this medium of expression could not be ignored, as it reflected the vitality of the oral tradition in African societies, and might well provide a more authentic projection of the emotional state of government leaders than the carefully constructed phraseology employed on more formal occasions.[3]

Secondly, the problem was compounded by overlapping and interrelated thematic categories. It was by no means easy in many cases to classify basic values embedded in statements of perceived threat; literal meanings often proved misleading. It was not always immediately obvious whether, for example, the prospect of a deliberate Rhodesian decision to cut off Zambia's major source of power, with a consequent closure of the copper mines, should properly be regarded as posing a threat to "economic independence" or "national security." Here, the complex interdependence of crisis issues rendered sole reliance on case indicators – that is, references to specific threats such as the interruption of supply routes – an inadequate basis of classification for coding purposes. In these circumstances, changes in the affect dimension (the extent to which the action was central or peripheral) offered a generally satisfactory guideline for coder sensitivity to thematic shifts within a coding statement. The perceived centrality of the anticipated harm was employed operationally to ascertain whether, for example, a strike among white (principally South African) miners represented a threat to "social harmony," "internal security," or even "influence within Southern Africa."

The analysis sought to identify by period and phase indicators of decision-maker stress within the three spheres comprising the crisis definition: perceived threats to basic Zambian values, the likelihood of military hostilities, and time constraints on the decisional response (tables A5 and A38 and Figure 3).[4] In addition, challenges to basic values were disaggregated in terms of four composite values – economic interests, belief systems and ideology, national security, and external influence and support – and sixteen subsidiary values (tables A6 and A39). The definitions of the threat categories as well as their rank-order differ somewhat from those employed in the original ICB model which, as Brecher concedes, reflect a Western bias. As he suggests, the categorization and ordering of values may "vary among cultures, belief systems, regime types, and the age of states as independent actors."[5] In the case of

Zambia, modifications were needed to take into account system-level interdependencies in its operational environments. These arose primarily from the salience of economic issues (a direct Zambian value threat) and the pervasive presence of the anti-status quo goal of majority rule for Rhodesia (a Southern African subsystem value) as well as the bilateral "love-hate" relationship of dependence on Britain and Zambia's status as a small, weak, developing landlocked state.

In addition to the technical problems associated with the methodology of selection and coding, there is the legitimate question whether the public pronouncements of official spokesmen fully reflect their true inner feelings. In some instances they obviously and deliberately do not. Political leaders sometimes consciously choose to appear alarmist in order to arouse public opinion, or even international opinion, as when Kapwepwe warned the UN General Assembly that, if Kariba power were cut off, "we could be dead in a few hours."[6] On the other hand, President Kaunda not infrequently sought to cool a potentially explosive situation by underplaying his real sense of unease. Thus, on 7 November 1965 in his broadcast to the nation on the "grave situation" created by Rhodesia's declaration of a state of emergency, he calmly assured his anxious listeners that "very little can go wrong." A week later, following the formal proclamation of UDI, he confidently told a mass rally that there was "no question" but that "Zambia is going to survive."[7] Similar motives led Kaunda to seek to restrain his more ebullient ministerial colleagues and to discourage inflammatory press reports. "Dick," he pleaded with the sympathetic expatriate editor of the country's sole national daily, "please refrain from printing stories which might cause anti-white riots."[8] Although the attempt to mould public opinion is widely practised, there is little that the content analyst can do to correct for it, other than to recognize that it may introduce a further distortion of uncertain magnitude into the data.[9]

Finally, there is the difficulty of operationalizing the concept of collective stress. Clearly, stress levels and their behavioural consequences vary with individuals. The most that can realistically be aspired to is a reasonably valid measure of the changing levels of stress experienced by the principal decision maker, in this case, President Kaunda.

This critique of the inexact science of content analysis undertaken here has highlighted its conceptual and methodological limitations.[10] An appreciation of these is essential to an understanding of the utility of the technique. Yet, real as its deficiencies are, they by no means discredit the data derived, especially when used as comparative measures. Even relatively crude indicators can prove surprisingly instructive, particularly when checked against and supplemented by qualitative evidence.

APPENDIX 2
Statistical Analysis

Table A1
Trigger Actions by Period

Trigger Actions	Period
	Pre-Crisis: Contingency Planning
26 April: Rhodesian white paper threatening economic retaliation	I Initial response 26 April–6 August 1965
7 August: Smith speech to party congress	II Securing the lifelines to the sea 7 August–4 November 1965
	Crisis: Confrontation on Two Fronts
5 November: Rhodesian declaration of state of emergency	I Military response 5 November–2 December 1965
2 December: Zambian failure to persuade British to use force	II Economic survival 3 December 1965–13 January 1966
	Post-Crisis: Trusting Britain
13 January: Wilson's new sense of commitment to crushing the Rhodesian rebellion	14 January–27 April 1966

Table A2
Soures of Decisional Trigger Actions by Period

	Source of Trigger Actions				
Period/ Phase	Rhodesian Government	Zambian Government	British Government	OAU and African Governments	Decisions
Pre-Crisis					
I	3	–	1	–	4
II	6	–	1	3	10
Crisis					
I	6	–	–	1	7
II	2	2	2	3	9
Post-Crisis	1	–	2	1	4
Total	18	2	6	8	34

Table A3
Issue Areas of Decisional Trigger Actions by Period

	Trigger Action Issue Areas			
Period/Phase	Economic	Political	Military	Decisions
Pre-Crisis				
I	3	–	1	4
II	6	3	1	10
Crisis				
I	–	2	5	7
II	4	5	–	9
Post-Crisis	3	1	–	4
Total	16	11	7	34

Table A4
Crisis Perceptions as Indicators of Stress by Period

	Crisis Perceptions		
Crisis Period	No.	Average No. (per statement)	Average No. (per week)
Pre-Crisis	129	8.1	4.7
Phase I	75	8.3	5.1
Phase II	54	7.7	4.2
Crisis	477	31.8	47.7
Phase I	181	31.7	46.9
Phase II	296	32.9	48.2
Post-Crisis	109	6.1	7.3
Total	715	14.6	13.6

Table A5
Crisis Perceptions as Indicators of Stress by Period and Crisis Component

	Crisis Components			
Crisis Period	Threats to Basic Values	Probability of Military Hostilities	Time Constraints	Total
Pre-Crisis	123 (95%)	4 (3%)	2 (2%)	129
Phase I	71	2	2	75
Phase II	52	2	–	54
Crisis	391 (82%)	42 (9%)	44 (9%)	477
Phase I	152	15	14	181
Phase II	239	27	30	296
Post-Crisis	99 (91%)	1 (1%)	9 (8%)	109
Total	613 (85%)	47 (7%)	55 (8%)	715

Table A6
Crisis Perceptions of Threats to Basic Zambian Values by Period and Dimension

	Basic Zambian Values Threatened				
Crisis Period	Economic Interests	Belief Systems/ Ideology	National Security	External Influence/ Support	Total
Pre-Crisis	47 (38%)	54 (44%)	20 (16%)	2 (2%)	123
Phase I	30	33	8	0	71
Phase II	17	21	12	2	52
Crisis	111 (28%)	90 (23%)	97 (25%)	93 (24%)	391
Phase I	40	35	38	39	152
Phase II	71	55	59	54	239
Post-Crisis	54 (55%)	19 (19%)	14 (14%)	12 (12%)	99
Total	212 (35%)	163 (27%)	131 (21%)	107 (17%)	613

Table A7
Time Constraints on Zambian Decision Making by Period

	Period							
Decision Time*	Pre-Crisis		Crisis		Post-Crisis		Total	
Extended	4	29%	0	0%	0	0%	4	12%
Moderate	6	43%	3	19%	3	75%	12	35%
Brief	4	29%	13	81%	1	25%	18	53%
Decisions	14		16		4		34	
Median polish†	1.50		2.38		1.67		2.00	
Deviation from median	−0.50		+0.38		−0.33		0.00	

* *Brief*: within a day or days; *moderate*: within a week or weeks; *extended*: within a month or months
† Assumes a uniform distribution of cases within categories

Table A8
Armed Forces of Zambia and Rhodesia, August 1964

	Strength	Defence Budget	Combat Aircraft
Zambia	2,250	$ 7 m.	—
Rhodesia	4,300	$16 m.	27 fighters
			12 bombers

Source: Neville Brown and W.F. Gutteridge, "The African Military Balance," *Adelphi Papers* 12 (August 1964): 8, 10.

Table A9
Pre-Crisis Decision-Making Processes and Mechanisms – Contingency Planning I: Initial Response, 26 April–6 August 1965

Coping Processes and Mechanisms	Decisions			
	1 Defiance c. 27 April	2 Copper Airlift c. 25 May	3 Military Base Offer c. 18 June	4 Coal Mining c. 14 July
Information Processing				
1 Extent of Probe: perceived need for information	minimal	thorough	minimal	thorough
2 Receptivity to Information	unreceptive	receptive	unreceptive	receptive
Consultative Patterns				
3 Breadth of Consultation	minimal	moderate	minimal	moderate
4 Participation (in rank order)	political, external	external, corporate, political	political, external	external, corporate, political
Decisional Forum				
5 Formal	ministerial	cabinet	ministerial	cabinet
6 Effective	ministerial	ministerial	presidential	cabinet
Alternatives: Search and Evaluation				
7 Extent of Search	minimal	extensive	minimal	extensive
8 Perceived Range of Available Options	limited	limited	limited	broad
9 Thoroughness of Evaluation	moderate	thorough	minimal	thorough

Table A10
Pre-Crisis Decisions-Making Processes and Mechanisms – Contingency Planning II: Securing the Lifelines to the Sea, 7 August–4 November 1965

Coping Processes and Mechanisms	Decisions				
	5 Unifed Rhodesia Railways 10 August	6 Modernizing Mpulungu Harbor c. 17 August	7 Overtures to Portugal c. 7 September	8 British Financial Commitment c. 14 Sept.	9 Anglo-American Airfield Survey c. 1 October
Information Processing					
1 Extent of Probe: perceived need for information	moderate	thorough	moderate	moderate	minimal
2 Receptivity to Information	unreceptive	unreceptive	receptive	receptive	receptive
Consultative Patterns					
3 Breadth of Consultation	minimal	moderate	extensive	moderate	minimal
4 Participation (in rank order)	bureaucratic, political	corporate, bureacratic, political	external, political, corporate, bureaucratic	bureaucratic, political, external	external, political
Decisional Forum					
5 Formal	cabinet	cabinet	cabinet	cabinet	ministerial
6 Effective	ministerial	ministerial	ministerial	ministerial	presidential
Alternatives: Search and Evaluation					
7 Extent of Search	extensive	extensive	extensive	moderate	minimal
8 Perceived Range of Available Options	modest	broad	limited	limited	limited
9 Thoroughness of Evaluation	thorough	thorough	moderate	moderate	minimal

Table A10 (continued)

	Decisions				
Coping Processes and Mechanisms	10 Rhodesian Arms Seizure 5 October	11 Reconciliation with Zaire c. 16 October	12 Tempering OAU Militancy c. 16 October	13 Common Services Rights c. 26 October	14 Malawi Oil Route c. 26 October
Information Processing					
1 Extent of Probe: perceived need for information	minimal	moderate	thorough	minimal	minimal
2 Receptivity to Information	unreceptive	unreceptive	receptive	unreceptive	receptive
Consultative Patterns					
3 Breadth of Consultation	minimal	moderate	moderate	minimal	minimal
4 Participation (in rank order)	political, bureaucratic	corporate, bureaucratic, political	political, bureaucratic	political	political, bureaucratic, corporate
Decisional Forum					
5 Formal	presidential	cabinet	cabinet	cabinet	cabinet
6 Effective	presidential	ministerial	cabinet	cabinet	presidential
Alternatives: Search and Evaluation					
7 Extent of Search	minimal	moderate	moderate	minimal	minimal
8 Perceived Range of Available Options	modest	limited	modest	modest	limited
9 Thoroughness of Evaluation	minimal	moderate	moderate	moderate	moderate

Table A11
Crisis Decision-Making Processes and Mechanisms – Confrontation on Two Fronts I: Military Response, 5 November–2 December 1965

Coping Processes and Mechanisms	15 Final Warning c. 6 November	16 Troop Deployment 12 November	Decisions 17 Initial Sanctions 12 November	18 Kariba Security c. 17 November
Information Processing				
1 Extent of Probe: perceived need for information	minimal	thorough	thorough	thorough
2 Receptivity to Information	unreceptive	unreceptive	receptive	unreceptive
Consultative Patterns				
3 Breadth of Consultation	minimal	moderate	moderate	moderate
4 Participation (in rank order)	political, external	political, bureaucratic	political, bureaucratic	political, external, bureaucratic
Decisional Forum				
5 Formal	ministerial	cabinet	cabinet	ministerial
6 Effective	ministerial	presidential	cabinet	ministerial
Alternatives: Search and Evaluation				
7 Extent of Search	minimal	minimal	extensive	extensive
8 Perceived Range of Available Options	limited	limited	modest	broad
9 Thoroughness of Evaluation	moderate	moderate	thorough	thorough

Table A11 (continued)

Coping Processes and Mechanisms	Decisions		
	19 Opposition to OAU Military Intervention 21 November	*20 Rebuffing British Troop Offer 2 December*	*21 RAF Air Cover 2 December*
Information Processing			
1 Extent of Probe: perceived need for information	minimal	thorough	minimal
2 Receptivity to Information	unreceptive	unreceptive	receptive
Consultative Patterns			
3 Breadth of Consultation	moderate	extensive	moderate
4 Participation (in rank order)	political, external, bureaucratic	political, external, bureaucratic	external, political, bureaucratic
Decisional Forum			
5 Formal	ministerial	cabinet	cabinet
6 Effective	ministerial	cabinet	cabinet
Alternatives: Search and Evaluation			
7 Extent of Search	minimal	moderate	minimal
8 Perceived Range of Available Options	limited	modest	limited
9 Thoroughness of Evaluation	moderate	thorough	thorough

Table A12
Crisis Decisions-Making Processes and Mechanisms – Confrontation on Two Fronts II: Economic Survival, 3 December 1965–13 January 1966

Coping Processes and Mechanisms	Decisions					
	22 Shunning OAU Diplomatic Sanctions 6–12 December	23 Diversifying Diplomatic Sanctions c. 12 December	24 Oil Sanctions c. 17 December	25 Contingency Aid c. 18 December	26 Rhodesian Coal Royalty 22 December
Information Processing					
1 Extent of Probe: perceived need for information	thorough	minimal	thorough	thorough	moderate
2 Receptivity to Information	receptive	receptive	receptive	receptive	receptive
Consultative Patterns					
3 Breadth of Consultation	extensive	minimal	extensive	extensive	moderate
4 Participation (in rank order)	external, political, bureaucratic, corporate	political, bureaucratic, external	political, external, bureaucratic, corporate	external, bureaucratic, political, corporate	external, corporate, bureaucratic, political
Decisional Forum					
5 Formal	cabinet	cabinet	cabinet	ministerial	presidential
6 Effective	cabinet	ministerial	cabinet	ministerial	presidential
Alternatives: Search and Evaluation					
7 Extent of Search	minimal	moderate	minimal	minimal	extensive
8 Perceived Range of Available Options	limited	limited	limited	limited	broad
9 Thoroughness of Evaluation	thorough	moderate	moderate	moderate	thorough

Table A12 (continued)

Coping Processes and Mechanisms	27 Beira Airlift c. 23 December	28 Tanzanian Obstruction c. 27 December	Decisions 29 Commonwealth Conference c. 7 January 1966	30 "Quick Kill" c. 13 January 1966
Information Processing				
1 Extent of Probe: perceived need for information	moderate	moderate	minimal	minimal
2 Receptivity to Information	receptive	receptive	receptive	receptive
Consultative Patterns				
3 Breadth of Consultation	minimal	moderate	moderate	minimal
4 Participation (in rank order)	bureaucratic, external	external, political	external, political	external, political
Decisional Forum				
5 Formal	presidential	presidential	ministerial	ministerial
6 Effective	presidential	presidential	ministerial	presidential
Alternatives: Search and Evaluation				
7 Extent of Search	moderate	moderate	moderate	minimal
8 Perceived Range of Available Options	limited	limited	modest	limited
9 Thoroughness of Evaluation	thorough	minimal	moderate	moderate

Table A13
Post-Crisis Decision-Making Processes and Mechanisms – Trusting Britain: 14 January–27 April 1966

Coping Processes and Mechanisms	Decisions			
	31 Girding for the Crunch c. 24 January	32 Stockpiling Essential Supplies 5 February	33 Restraining OAU Militancy 26 February	34 The "Long Haul" c. 8 March
Information Processing				
1 Extent of Probe: perceived need for information	thorough	minimal	thorough	moderate
2 Receptivity to Information	receptive	receptive	unreceptive	receptive
Consultative Patterns				
3 Breadth of Consultation	moderate	extensive	moderate	moderate
4 Participation (in rank order)	bureaucratic, political, external	external, corporate, political, bureaucratic	external, political, bureaucratic	bureaucratic, political, corporate, external
Decisional Forum				
5 Formal	cabinet	cabinet	ministerial	ministerial
6 Effective	cabinet	cabinet	ministerial	ministerial
Alternatives: Search and Evaluation				
7 Extent of Search	minimal	moderate	moderate	moderate
8 Perceived Range of Available Options	limited	limited	modest	modest
9 Thoroughness of Evaluation	minimal	thorough	moderate	moderate

272 Statistical Analysis

Table A14
Information Probe

Extent of Information Probe	Period			Total
	Pre-Crisis	Crisis	Post-Crisis	
Minimal	6	6	1	13
Moderate	4	3	1	8
Thorough	4	7	2	13
Total	14	16	4	34
Median polish*	1.25	1.67	2.00	1.50
Deviation from median	−0.25	+0.17	+0.50	0.00

*Assumes a uniform distribution of cases within the "moderate" category.

Table A15
Receptivity to Information

Receptivity to Information	Period			Total
	Pre-Crisis	Crisis	Post-Crisis	
Unreceptive (biased)	7	5	1	13
Receptive (open-minded)	7	11	3	21
Total	14	16	4	34
Median polish*	1.00	1.27	1.33	1.19
Deviation from median	−0.19	+0.08	+0.14	0.00

*Assumes a uniform distribution of cases within the "receptive" category.

Table A16
Number, Frequency, and Type of Consultative Groups

Type of Consultative Group	Pre-Crisis Period			Crisis Period			Post-Crisis Period			Total		
	No.	%	No./Dec.*	No.	%	No./Dec.	No.	%	No./Dec.	No.	%	No./Dec.
Institutional (Cabinet)	4	9	0.3	6	9	0.4	3	14	0.8	13	10	0.4
Ad Hoc	41	91	2.9	62	91	3.9	18	86	4.5	121	90	3.5
Ministerial	12	27	0.9	11	16	0.7	2	10	0.5	25	19	0.7
Other	29	64	2.1	51	75	3.2	16	76	4.0	96	72	2.8
	45		3.2	68		4.2	21		5.3	134		3.9

*Dec. = Decision

273 Appendix 2

Table A17
Breadth of Consultations

Breadth of Consultation	Period			Total
	Pre-Crisis	Crisis	Post-Crisis	
Minimal	7	4	0	11
Moderate	6	8	3	17
Extensive	1	4	1	6
Total	14	16	4	34
Median polish*	1.00	1.50	1.75	1.35
Deviation from median	−0.35	0.15	0.40	0.00

*Assumes a uniform distribution of cases within the "moderate" category.

Table A18
Participation in Consultative Process by Category and Crisis Period (percentage of decisions)

Consultative Group	Period							
	Pre-Crisis		Crisis		Post-Crisis		Total	
	%	%	%	%	%	%	%	%
Political	100	(43)	94	(50)	100	(0)	97	(41)
External	50	(29)	87	(44)	100	(50)	74	(38)
Bureaucratic	57	(14)	75	(6)	100	(50)	71	(15)
Corporate	43	(14)	25	(0)	50	(0)	35	(6)

Figures in brackets are percentage participation rates as principal consultative group.

Table A19
Consultative Group and Decision Time (percentage of decisions)

Consultative Group	Decision Time*							
	Extended		Moderate		Brief		Total	
	%	%	%	%	%	%	%	%
Political	100	(0)	100	(100)	94	(92)	97	(94)
External	50	(0)	75	(67)	78	(92)	74	(87)
Bureaucratic	50	(0)	75	(67)	72	(77)	71	(75)
Corporate	75	(0)	50	(33)	17	(23)	35	(25)

Figures in brackets are for crisis period only.
*Brief: within a day or days; moderate: within a week or weeks; extended: within a month or months.

Table A20
Intensity of Consultations by Consultative Group and Crisis Period*

Consultative Group	Period			
	Pre-Crisis %	Crisis %	Post-Crisis %	Total %
Political	7	44	0	24
Cabinet	7	31	0	18
Senior Ministers	0	25	0	12
External	14	50	0	29
Bureaucratic/Corporate	4	3	0	3
Total	7	25	0	15

*Percentage of decisions involving "intense" as opposed to "moderate" or "limited" consultations.

Table A21
Consultations: Motivations and Stress (Percentage of Decisions)

Motivations (except advice)	Period			
	Pre-Crisis %	Crisis %	Post-Crisis %	Total %
Support	29	63	0	41
Reassurance	0	13	0	2
Legitimation	21	38	0	26
Total	50	75*	0	56*

*excludes duplication

Table A22
Size and Types of Decisional Forums

Decisional Forum	Period							
	Pre-Crisis		Crisis		Post-Crisis		Total	
Presidential	29%	(7)	31%	(19)	0%	(0)	27%	(12)
Ministerial	50%	(21)	38%	(38)	50%	(50)	44%	(32)
Cabinet	21%	(72)	31%	(44)	50%	(50)	29%	(56)
Median polish*	1.42		1.50		2.00		1.52	
Deviation from median	−0.10		−0.02		0.48		0.00	

Figures in brackets are percentages for formal, as opposed to effective decision-making forums.
*Assumes a uniform distribution of cases within the "ministerial" category.

Table A23
Decisional Authority Patterns (Percentages)

Authority Pattern	Period			Total
	Pre-Crisis	Crisis	Post-Crisis	
No. of cases	10	11	4	25
a. Presidential Role				
Subsidiary	20%	0%	0%	8%
Influential	60%	36%	75%	52%
Decisive	20%	64%	25%	40%
Median polish*	1.50	2.22	1.67	1.81
Deviation from median	−0.31	0.41	−0.14	0.00
b. Group Dissension				
Low	70%	45%	25%	52%
Moderate	30%	45%	75%	44%
High	0%	10%	0%	4%
Median polish*	0.71	1.11	1.67	0.96
Deviation from median	−0.25	0.15	0.71	0.00
c. Extent of Debate				
Limited	20%	0%	25%	12%
Moderate	70%	55%	75%	64%
Extensive	10%	45%	0%	24%
Median polish*	1.43	1.91	1.33	1.59
Deviation from median	−0.11	0.32	−0.26	0.00

*Assumes a uniform distribution of cases within categories.

Table A24
Alternatives: Search and Evaluation (Percentages)

Search and Evaluation	Period			Total
	Pre-Crisis	Crisis	Post-Crisis	
a. Extent of Search for Alternatives				
Extensive	36%	19%	0%	24%
Moderate	21%	31%	75%	32%
Minimal	43%	50%	25%	44%
Median polish*	1.67	2.00	1.33	1.81
Deviation from median	−0.14	0.19	−0.48	0.00
b. Perceived Range of Available Options				
Broad	14%	12%	0%	12%
Modest	29%	19%	50%	26%
Limited	57%	69%	50%	62%
Median polish*	2.14	2.28	2.00	2.19
Deviation from median	−0.05	0.09	−0.19	0.00
c. Thoroughness of Evaluation Process				
Minimal	21%	6%	25%	15%
Moderate	50%	50%	50%	50%
Thorough	29%	44%	25%	35%
Median polish*	1.58	1.88	1.50	1.70
Deviation from median	−0.12	0.18	−0.20	0.00

*Assumes uniform distribution of cases within categories.

Table A25
Search and Evaluation of Alternatives: Decision Time

Search and Evaluation	Decision Time			Total
	Extended	Moderate	Brief	
a. Extent of Search for Alternatives				
Pre-Crisis Period				
Extensive	4	1	0	5
Moderate	0	2	1	3
Minimal	0	3	3	6
	4	6	4	14
Crisis Period				
Extensive	0	1	2	3
Moderate	0	1	4	5
Minimal	0	1	7	8
	0	3	13	16
b. Thoroughness of Evaluation				
Pre-Crisis Period				
Thorough	4	0	0	4
Moderate	0	5	2	7
Minimal	0	1	2	3
	4	6	4	14
Crisis Period				
Thorough	0	2	5	7
Moderate	0	1	7	8
Minimal	0	0	1	1
	0	3	13	16

Table A26
Zambian Hypotheses on Crisis and Coping

		Stress Level	
Hypotheses	Table	Increasing	Decreasing*
Relationship between increasing/decreasing levels of crisis-induced stress and:			
Information Processing			
1 thoroughness of the information probe	A14	strongly positive	strongly negative
2 rate of communication with external actors		strongly positive	strongly positive
3 receptivity (openness/bias) to new information	A15	moderately positive	weakly negative
4 distrust of information sources		weakly positive	weakly positive
Consultative Pattern			
5 frequency of consultation	A16	strongly positive	strongly negative
6 resort to *ad hoc* forms of consultation	A16	no relationship	weakly positive
7 breadth of consultations	A17	strongly positive	weakly negative
8 breadth of consultations under time pressure		moderately positive	–
9 frequency of consultations with the political elite	A18		
a. as principal consultative group	A18	weakly positive	strongly positive
b. consultations under time constraints	A19	weakly negative	weakly negative
c. intensity of consultations	A20	strongly positive	strongly positive
10 frequency of consultations with external actors			
a. as principl consultative group	A18	strongly positive	strongly positive
b. consultations under time constraints	A19	moderately positive	weakly negative
c. intensity of consultations	A20	strongly positive	strongly positive
11 frequency of consultations with bureaucratic elite	A18	moderately positive	moderately positive
a. as principal consultative group	A18	weakly negative	strongly negative
b. consultations under time constraints	A19	weakly positive	weakly negative
12 frequency of consultations with corporate elite	A19	strongly negative	strongly negative
a. as principal consultative group	A19	strongly negative	no relationship
b. consultations under time constraints	A19	weakly positive	weakly positive

Table A26 (continued)

Hypotheses	Table	Stress Level Increasing	Stress Level Decreasing*
Relationship between increasing/decreasing levels of crisis-induced stress and:			
13 intensity of consultations	A20	strongly positive	strongly positive
14 search for support, reassurance and legitimation	A21	strongly positive	strongly positive
Decisional Forums			
15 resort to *ad hoc* decisional forums	A22	moderately negative	moderately negative
16 size of decisional groups	A22	moderately positive	strongly negative
17 coincidence between the formal and effective decisional forums	A22	strongly positive	strongly negative
18 presidential influence in decision making	A23a	strongly positive	strongly positive
19 dissension among decision makers	A23b	strongly positive	strongly negative
20 extent of the debate over the decision	A23c	strongly positive	strongly positive
Alternatives: Search and Evaluation			
21 extent of the search for alternatives	A24a	strongly negative	strongly negative
a. under time constraints	A25a	moderately negative	–
22 perceived range of available options	A25b	moderately negative	moderately negative
23 concern for more immediate objectives		moderately positive	–
24 thoroughness of the evaluation process	A24c	strongly positive	strongly positive
a. under time constraints	A25b	weakly negative	–

*Less confidence can be placed in these conclusions because of the limited number of post-crisis decisions.

Table A27
Levels of Stress and Dimensions of Choice: Pre-Crisis Period

No. Decision	Core Inputs	Costs	Impor- tance*	Complex- ity†	Systemic Domain	Mental Process	Activity	Novelty
Pre-Crisis Period I								
1 Defiance	Rhodesian hostility & elections; national dignity	low	3	E-D, P-D, C-S	Southern Africa, domestic, global	afffective	verbal act	no
2 Copper airlift	UDI threat to trade & transit routes; external aid dependence	low	2	E-D, P-D	global, Southern Africa, black Africa	rational	verbal act	yes
3 Military base offer	British reject use of force; liberation commitment	medium	2	M-S, P-D, C-S	global, Southern Africa	affective	verbal act	no
4 Coal mining	UDI threat to coal supply	medium	3	E-D, P-D	domestic, Southern Africa	rational	physical act	yes
Pre-Crisis Period II								
5 Unified Rhodesia Railways	Rhodesian threat to divide railway; joint ownership	low	3	E-D, P-D, C-S	Southern Africa, domestic	rational/ affective	verbal act	no
6 Modernizing Mpulungu harbour	UDI threat to transit routes	medium	2	E-D	domestic, black Africa	rational	physical act	yes
7 Overtures to Portugal	UDI threat to transit routes; Benguela Ry report	medium	3	E-D, P-D, C-S	Southern Africa, global	rational	verbal act	yes
8 British financial commitment	UDI anticipated; contingency costs	medium	3	E-D, P-D	global, Southern Africa, black Africa	rational	verbal act	no

9	Anglo-American airfield survey	UDI anticipated; British initiative	low	2	E-D, P-D	global, Southern Africa, black Africa	rational	verbal/ physical act	no
10	Rhodesian arms seizure	Rhodesian threat to transit routes & seizure of arms	low	2	C-S, P-D, M-S	Southern Africa, global	affective	verbal act	no
11	Reconciliation with Zaire	UDI threat to transit routes; Tshombe dismissed	low	3	E-D, P-D	black Africa, Southern Africa	rational	verbal act	no
12	Tempering OAU militancy	anticipated OAU pressure; fear of racial war	medium	3	P-D, M-S, C-S	black Africa, Southern Africa	rational/ affective	verbal act	no
13	Common services rights	Smith's threat to legal rights; UDI imminent	low	3	E-D, P-D, C-S	Southern Africa, domestic, global	affective	verbal act	no
14	Malawi oil route	UDI imminent; surplus oil storage capacity	low	2	E-D, P-D	black Africa, Southern Africa	rational	verbal act	no

*1: marginal; 2: consequential; 3: important; 4: significant; 5: decisive
†E-D: economic-developmental; P-D: political-diplomatic; C-S: cultural-status; M-S: military-security

Table A28
Levels of Stress and Dimensions of Choice: Crisis Period

No.	Decision	Core Inputs	Costs	Importance*	Complexity†	Systemic Domain	Mental Process	Activity	Novelty
Crisis Period I									
15	Final warning	Rhodesian state of emergency	low	1	P-D, E-D	Southern Africa, domestic, global	affective	verbal act	no
16	Troop deployment	Rhodesian troop movements; UDI	medium	3	M-S, P-D	Southern Africa, domestic, global	routine	physical act	yes
17	Initial sanctions	economic protection; liberation commitment	medium	2	E-D, P-D	domestic, Southern Africa	rational/affective	verbal delay/act	yes
18	Kariba security	Rhodesian threat to Kariba power supply; liberation commitment	medium	4	M-S, E-D, P-D, C-S	global, Southern Africa, black Africa	affective/rational	verbal act	yes
19	Opposition to OAU military intervention	OAU pressure; fear of racial war; white exodus threat	medium	4	M-S, P-D	black Africa, domestic, Southern Africa, global	rational/affective	verbal delay	no
20	Rebuffing British troop offer	Rhodesian threat to Kariba; conditional British troop offer; OAU pressure	medium	4	M-S, P-D, C-S	global, Southern Africa, black Africa	affective/rational	verbal not to act	yes
21	RAF air cover	Rhodesian air strike threat; British & OAU pressures	medium	4	M-S, P-D, C-S	global, Southern Africa, black Africa	rational/affective	verbal/physical act	yes
Crisis Period II									
22	Shunning OAU diplomatic sanctions	OAU diplomatic break with Britain; dependence on Britain	medium	4	E-D, P-D, C-S	global, black Africa, domestic	rational	verbal not to act	yes

23	Diversifying dependence	OAU resolution rejected; assertion of independence	low	2	P-D, CS, E-D, M-S	global, Southern Africa	affective/ rational	verbal act	yes
24	Oil sanctions	Britain agrees to oil sanctions & airlift; liberation commitment	high	5	E-D, P-D	Southern Africa, global, domestic	rational/ affective	verbal/ physical act	yes
25	Contingency aid	British aid offer; contingency costs	medium	4	E-D, P-D	global, Southern Africa, domestic	rational/ affective	verbal act	no
26	Rhodesian coal royalty	Rhodesian retribution, national dignity; past experience	medium	4	CS, E-D, P-D	Southern Africa, domestic, global	rational/ affective	verbal act	no
27	Beira airlift	oil crisis; British pressure; Tanzanian ban on RAF	medium	3	E-D, P-D	Southern Africa, global, domestic	rational/ affective	verbal act	yes
28	Tanzanian obstruction	oil supply crisis; Tanzanian obstruction	low	4	E-D, P-D	black Africa, global, domestic, Southern Africa	rational/ affective	verbal act	no
29	Commonwealth conference	economic opportunity; OAU/Western pressures; Commonwealth loyalty	low	2	E-D, P-D	global, black Africa, Southern Africa	rational/ affective	verbal act	no
30	The Quick Kill	Wilson's salesmanship & intentions; liberation commitment	high	5	E-D, P-D	global, domestic, Southern Africa, black Africa	affective/ rational	verbal act	yes

*1: marginal; 2: consequential; 3: important; 4: significant; 5: decisive
†E-D: economic-developmental; P-D: political-diplomatic; C-S: cultural-status; M-S: military-security

Table A29
Levels of Stress and Dimensions of Choice: Post-Crisis Period

No.	Decision	Core Inputs	Costs	Importance*	Complexity†	Systemic Domain	Mental Process	Activity	Novelty
Post-Crisis Period									
31	Girding for the crunch	Quick-kill commitment; dependence on external aid	high	4	E-D, P-D	global, domestic, Southern Africa	rational	verbal act	yes
32	Stockpiling essential supplies	Quick-kill commitment; import control fiasco	low	3	E-D, P-D	domestic, global, Southern Africa	rational	verbal/physical act	yes
33	Restraining OAU militancy	British election; OAU pressure	medium	3	P-D, C-S	black Africa, global	affective/rational	verbal act	yes
34	The Long Haul	SA oil sanction-busting; import route crisis; domestic problems	low	3	E-D, P-D	Southern Africa, domestic, global	rational/affective	verbal act	no

*1: marginal; 2: consequential; 3: important; 4: significant; 5: decisive
†E-D: economic-developmental; P-D: political-diplomatic; C-S: cultural-status; M-S: military-security

Appendix 2

Table A30
Stress and Choice: Core Input Sources

	Perceived Source of Decisional Stimuli (percentages per period)			
	Period			
Source of Stimuli	Pre-Crisis	Crisis	Post-Crisis	Total
Domestic (Zambia)	22%	30%	45%	29%
Southern Africa	56%	25%	11%	34%
Black Africa	11%	20%	22%	17%
OAU	(4%)	(15%)	(11%)	(11%)
Global	11%	25%	22%	20%
Britain	(7%)	(22%)	(11%)	(16%)
No. of inputs per decision	1.9	2.2	2.2	2.1

Table A31
Stress and Choice: Costs and Importance

Dimensions of Choice	Period			Total
	Pre-Crisis	Crisis	Post-Crisis	
a. Costs:				
Magnitude of perceived losses from choice				
Low	8	6	2	16
Medium	6	8	1	15
High	0	2	1	3
Median polish*	0.87	1.25	1.00	1.07
Deviation from median	−0.20	0.18	−0.07	0.00
b. Importance:				
Perceived value of choice				
1 marginal	0	1	0	1
2 consequential	7	3	0	10
3 important	7	2	3	12
4 significant	0	8	1	9
5 decisive	0	2	0	2
Median polish*	2.00	3.25	2.67	2.50
Deviation from median	−0.50	0.75	0.17	0.00

*Assumes uniform distribution of cases within categories.

Table A32
Stress and Choice: Complexity

Complexity	Period			Total
	Pre-Crisis	Crisis	Post-Crisis	
a. No. of Issue-Areas per decision				
1	1	0	0	1
2	6	10	4	20
3	7	4	0	11
4	0	2	0	2
	14	16	4	34
Median polish*	2.00	1.80	1.50	1.80
Deviation from median	0.20	0.00	−0.30	0.00
b. Issue-Areas				
Political-Diplomatic	13	16	4	33
Economic-Developmental	11	12	3	26
Cultural-Status	7	6	1	14
Military-Security	3	6	0	9
	34	40	8	82

*Assumes uniform distribution of cases within categories.

Table A33
Stress and Choice: Systemic Domain (Perceived Scope of Reverberations of Decisions)

Systemic Domain	Period			Total
	Pre-Crisis	Crisis	Post-Crisis	
a. Number: per decision				
1	0	0	0	0
2	9	3	1	13
3	5	10	3	18
4	0	3	0	3
Median polish*	1.78	2.50	2.33	2.22
Deviation from median	−0.44	0.28	0.11	0.00
b. Level: percentages by period				
Domestic	15	22	27	21
Southern Africa	40	31	27	33
Black Africa	21	16	9	17
OAU	(3)	(12)	(9)	(9)
Global	24	31	37	29
Britain	(18)	(24)	(27)	(23)

*Assumes uniform distribution of cases within categories.

287 Appendix 2

Table A34
Stress and Choice: Process, Activity, Novelty

Dimensions of Choice	Period			Total
	Pre-Crisis	Crisis	Post-Crisis	
a. Mental Process				
Routine	0%	6%	0%	3%
Affective	29%	38%	25%	32%
Rational	71%	56%	75%	65%
b. Activity				
Physical action	2	1	0	3
Verbal/physical action	1	2	1	4
Verbal action	11	9	3	23
Delay	0	2	0	2
Inaction	0	2	0	2
	14	16	4	34
c. Novelty				
Innovative	4	10	3	17
Reliance on precedents	10	6	1	17
	14	16	4	34

Table A35
Crisis and Choice: Quality of Decisions

	Success Rate		No. of Decisions
	No.	Percentage	
a. Crisis Stress			
Pre-crisis period	8	57	14
Crisis period	10	63	16
Post-crisis period	3	75	4
	21	62	34
b. Mental Process			
Rational	14	70	20
Affective	6	46	13
Routine	1	100	1
	21	62	34

Table A36
Zambian Hypotheses on Crisis and Coping

		Stress Level	
Hypotheses	Table	Increasing	Decreasing*
Relationship between increasing/ decreasing levels of crisis-induced stress and:			
Core Inputs			
1 the number and variety of perceived core inputs	A30	no relationship	no relationship
Costs			
2 the magnitude of anticipated losses resulting from the decision	A31a	moderately positive	moderately positive
Importance			
3 the perceived benefits from the decision	A31b	strongly positive	moderately positive
Complexity			
4 the number of issue-areas involved in the choice	A32a	strongly negative	strongly positive
Systemic Domain			
5 the perceived scope of reverberations	A33a	strongly positive	strongly positive
a. domestically and internationally	A33b	strongly positive	strongly negative
b. regionally	A33b	strongly negative	strongly positive
Mental Process			
6 resort to a rational process of choice	A34a	strongly negative	strongly negative
7 reliance on an affective process of choice	A34a	strongly positive	strongly positive
Activity			
8 proportion of verbal acts	A34b	no relationship	no relationship
Novelty			
9 resort to choices without precedent	A34c	strongly positive	moderately negative
Success			
10 subsequent success in achieving decisional objectives	A35a	moderately positive	moderately negative
a. "rational" decisions	A35b	moderately positive	–
b. "affective" decisions	A35b	moderately positive	–

*Less confidence can be placed on these conclusions because of the limited number of post-crisis decisions.

Table A37
Analysis of Speech Sample by Source, Forum, and Period

Forum	Presidential	Ministerial	Total
Zambia	24	16	40
1 Press conference and statements	14	1	15
2 Broadcasts	5	12	17
3 Other	5	3	8
External	4	5	9
1 International organizations	2	5	7
2 Other	2	0	2
Total	28	21*	49
1 Pre-Crisis	11	5	16
2 Crisis	12	3	15
3 Post-crisis	5	13	18

*Vice-president: 13 (all but 2 in post-crisis period); Foreign Minister (including UN ambassador once): 5; other ministers: 3.

Table A38
Intensity of Crisis-Induced Stress (average number of statements by period and phase)

Period/Phase	Days	No. of Statements Coded	Crisis Components			Crisis-Induced Stress
			Threats to Basic Values	Probability of Military Hostilities	Time Pressure	
Pre-Crisis Period	193	16	7.7	0.25	0.12	8.1
Phase I	103	9	7.9	0.22	0.22	8.3
Phase II	90	7	7.4	0.29	–	7.7
Crisis Period	70	15	26.1	2.8	2.9	31.8
Phase I	28	6	25.3	2.5	2.3	30.2
Phase II	42	9	26.6	3.0	3.3	32.9
Post-Crisis Period	104	18	5.5	0.06	0.50	6.1
	367	49	12.5	0.96	1.12	14.6

Table A39
Frequency of Statements of Perceived Threats to Basic Zambian Values (by value, rank, and crisis period)

Basic Value Threatened	Total		Crisis Period		
			Pre-Crisis	Crisis	Post-Crisis
Economic Interests	212	(34.6%)	47(38.2%)	111(28.4%)	54(54.6%)
Economic development	61		13	30	18
Access to resources	59		8	34	17
Economic independence	41		16	20	5
External communications	30		6	12	12
Common services	21		4	15	2
Belief Systems Ideology	163	(26.6%)	54(43.4%)	90(23.0%)	19(19.2%)
Political freedom	77		32	34	11
Moral values	50		18	30	2
Social harmony	36		4	26	6
National Security	131	(21.4%)	20(16.3%)	97(24.8%)	14(14.1%)
Territorial integrity	49		12	35	2
Internal security	43		7	26	10
Military support and supplies	27		0	27	0
Survival	12		1	9	2
External Influence/Support	107	(17.4%)	2 (1.6%)	93(28.8%)	12(12.1%)
British support	57		1	49	7
Influence within Southern Africa	28		1	23	4
Influence within global system	15		0	14	1
Influence within African regional system	7		0	7	0
Total	613	(100%)	123 (100%)	391 (100%)	99 (100%)

Notes

PREFACE

1 Bahgat Korany, "Foreign Policy in the Third World: An Introduction," *International Political Science Review* 5:1 (January 1984), p. 7. Korany also claimed, in *How Foreign Policy Decisions Are Made in the Third World* (Boulder: Westview Press, 1986), that "not a single book exists on foreign policy decisions in the Third World" (p. xi).
2 Bahgat Korany, "The Take-off of Third World Studies?: The Case of Foreign Policy," *World Politics* 35:3 (April 1983), pp. 466–7.
3 Christopher Clapham, *Foreign Policy Making in Developing States* (Farnborough: Saxon House, 1977), p. 175. In Africa, "bureaucratic approaches to [foreign policy] decision making ... clearly fail to apply" (p. 88).
4 The closest contender is the late Robert C. Good's impressive "memoir," *UDI: The International Politics of the Rhodesian Rebellion* (Princeton: Princeton University Press, 1973). Good was the first US ambassador to Zambia, from 1964 to 1968.
5 Korany, *How Foreign Policy Decisions Are Made*, p. 39. Bahgat Korany and Ali E. Hillal Dessouki have sought to rectify this deficiency with their seminal study, *The Foreign Policies of Arab States: The Challenge of Change*, 2nd ed. (Boulder: Westview, 1991). Another important contribution is Steven A. Hoffman, *India and the Chinese Crisis* (Berkeley: University of California Press, 1990).
6 *The Times* (London), 7 March 1978, p. 17.
7 Korany and Dessouki, *Foreign Policies of Arab States*, p. 411.

8 Clapham, *Foreign Policy Making in Developing States*, pp. 9, 175.
9 Michael Brecher, *Decisions in Crisis: Israel, 1967 and 1973* (Berkeley: University of California Press, 1980), p. 361 n9. Richard C. Snyder, in his introduction to Glenn D. Paige's classic study, *The Korean Decision: June 24–30, 1950* (New York: Free Press, 1968), observes that, in the absence to access to national archives, "even this lengthy recounting will be just the tip of the iceberg" (p. xii).
10 Jacob Bercovitch, "A case study of mediation as a method of international conflict resolution: the Camp David experience," *Review of International Studies* 12:1 (January 1986), p. 43.
11 Michael Margolian, "The Rescue of Ethiopian Jewry: A Case Study of the Beliefs-Behaviour Relationship in Foreign Policy," (Ph.D. dissertation, Carleton University, 1989), p. 83.
12 The most important volume is Goodwin Mwangilwa's *The Kapwepwe Diaries* (Lusaka: Multimedia Publications, 1986), but even it is sketchy on details.

CHAPTER 1

1 Zimbabwe and its capital, Harare, are referred to throughout this study by their colonial names, Rhodesia and Salisbury, except where the context relates to the period after independence in April 1980.
2 The best histories of the period are: Robert C. Good, *UDI: The International Politics of the Rhodesian Rebellion* (Princeton: Princeton University Press, 1973); Richard Hall, *The High Price of Principles: Kaunda and the White South* (Harmondsworth: Penguin, 1973); Richard L. Sklar, "Zambia's Response to the Rhodesian Unilateral Declaration of Independence," in William Tordoff, ed., *Politics in Zambia* (Manchester: Manchester University Press, 1974), pp. 320–62. See also Douglas G. Anglin and Timothy M. Shaw, *Zambia's Foreign Policy: Studies in Diplomacy and Dependence* (Boulder: Westview Press, 1979).
3 For a preliminary report, see Douglas G. Anglin, "Zambian Crisis Behavior: Rhodesia's Unilateral Declaration of Independence," *International Studies Quarterly* 24:4 (December 1980), pp. 581–616.
4 Michael Brecher, *Decisions in Crisis: Israel, 1967 and 1973* (Berkeley: University of California Press, 1980), pp. 1–30; Michael Brecher and Jonathan Wilkenfeld, "Crisis in World Politics," *World Politics* 34:3 (April 1982), pp. 380–417.
5 Brecher, *Decisions in Crisis*, p. 1.
6 C.F. Hermann, *Crisis in Foreign Policy: A Simulation Analysis* (Indianapolis: Bobbs-Merrill, 1969), p. 14.
7 Brecher, *Decisions in Crisis*, pp. 5–6, 23, 232, 327. "In general, then, the change in probability perceived by the decision maker may be

just as salient as the absolute level of probability" (Michael Brecher, "Towards a Theory of International Crisis Behavior," *International Studies Quarterly* 21:1 [March 1977], p. 54).
8 Brecher, "Towards a Theory of International Crisis Behavior," p. 44, and "India's Devaluation of 1966: Linkage Politics and Crisis Decision-making," *British Journal of International Studies* 3:1 (April 1977), p. 1.
9 Brecher, *Decisions in Crisis*, pp. 15–30, and *The Foreign Policy System of Israel: Setting, Images, Process* (New Haven: Yale University Press, 1972), pp. 1–20.
10 Brecher, *Decisions in Crisis*, pp. 15–16.
11 Ibid., p. 19.
12 Adapted from ibid., pp. 21–2, 362.
13 Ibid., p. 27. Following Brecher's precedent, the nine dimensions of coping (Table 1) correspond closely but not exactly with the nine ICB research questions; in particular, no attempt is made to categorize cognitive performance in the case of each decision.
14 Ibid., pp. 29–30, 380–1.
15 Brecher, "Towards a Theory of International Crisis Behavior," p. 57.
16 Brecher, *Decisions in Crisis*, pp. 23, 25. The model (and the literature) reveals some ambivalence on whether the defining condition of the crisis period is rising stress or a high level. Brecher identifies three stress phases within his crisis period which he labels "rising," "higher," and "highest" respectively (ibid., p. 398). See also Avi Shlaim, *The United States and the Berlin Blockade, 1948–1949: A Study in Crisis Decision-Making* (Berkeley: University of California Press, 1983), pp. 403–4.
17 Brecher, *Decisions in Crisis*, p. 29.
18 On the delineation of the four issue areas, see Michael Brecher et al., "A Framework for Research on Foreign Policy Behavior," *Journal of Conflict Resolution* 13:1 (March 1969), p. 88.

CHAPTER 2

1 Richard Hall and Hugh Peyman, *The Great Uhuru Railway: China's Showpiece in Africa* (London: Victor Gollancz, 1976), p. 84.
2 Kenneth Young, *Rhodesia and Independence: A Study in British Colonial Policy* (London: Dent, 1967), pp. 166–7. On 24 October British Prime Minister Harold Wilson peremptorily demanded "a categorical assurance forthwith" from Rhodesian Prime Minister Ian Smith that there would be no UDI (*Southern Rhodesia: Documents relating to the negotiations between the United Kingdom and Southern*

Rhodesian Governments, November 1963 – November 1965 [London: HMSO 1965], Cmnd. 2807, p. 43).

3 The 420-ft. high Kariba Dam wall stretched across the Kariba Gorge from Rhodesia to Zambia for more than one-third of a mile, creating an artificial lake (Kariba Lake) 450 miles in length. For political reasons, the generating station was built on the South (Rhodesian) Bank. It was officially opened in 1960 with a capacity of 700MW. Zambia built its own North Bank power station in 1975.

4 Michael Brecher, *Decisions in Crisis: Israel, 1967 and 1973* (Berkeley: University of California Press, 1980), pp. 8–15.

5 The 1961 census recorded 74,549 Europeans; by 1969, their numbers had dwindled to 43,390, a decline of 42 per cent.

6 On the colonial history of Zambia, see Richard Hall, *Zambia* (London: Pall Mall Press, 1965); Robert I. Rotberg, *The Rise of Nationalism in Central Africa: The Making of Malawi and Zambia, 1873–1964* (Cambridge, Mass.: Harvard University Press, 1965); David C. Mulford, *Zambia: The Politics of Independence, 1957–1964* (London: Oxford University Press, 1967); Fergus Macpherson, *Kenneth Kaunda of Zambia: The Times and the Man* (Lusaka: Oxford University Press, 1974).

7 L.H. Gann and M. Gelfand, *Huggins of Rhodesia: The Man and His Country* (London: George Allen and Unwin, 1964), p. 270. As late as 1964 Ian Smith is alleged to have asked rhetorically, "Whoever heard of the horse sleeping in his master's house?"

8 Antony Martin, *Minding Their Own Business: Zambia's Struggle against Western Control* (London: Hutchinson, 1972), p. 36. On the eve of Zimbabwean independence, Kaunda observed that Zimbabweans were economically "much stronger than we are," adding: "They built their infrastructure at our expense" (*The Times* [London], 21 March 1980, p. 6).

9 *Copperbelt of Zambia Mining Industry Year Book, 1967* (Kitwe: Copper Industry Service Bureau, 1968), p. 33.

10 The London Metal Exchange mean annual cash price of copper wirebars rose steadily from $655 per long ton in 1963 to $1,540 in 1966, though the Zambian producer price was, beginning in January 1964, pegged at a lower level ($941 in 1966) in the interests of orderly marketing (ibid., p. 42).

11 The index of trade as a proportion of GDP for 1964 was 98.0 – 66.8 in the case of exports and 31.1 for imports. In 1965 the combined index declined to 90.9, but rose again to 94.5 in 1966 (Central Statistical Office, *Statistical Year-Book, 1970* [Lusaka: Government Printer, 1971], pp. 165, 183).

12 Colin Legum, ed., *Zambia: Independence and Beyond. The Speeches of Kenneth Kaunda* (London: Nelson, 1966), pp. 83–4.

13 *Constitution of Zambia*, sec. 48(2). Section 51(1) states that "the cabinet shall be responsible for advising the President with respect to the policy of the government." See also Ben O. Nwabueze, *Presidentialism in Commonwealth Africa* (London: Hurst, 1974), p. 41. Simbi Mubako conceded that the presidential power was "considerably less than in certain other African states" (cited in Ian Scott, "Middle Class Politics in Zambia," *African Affairs* 77:308 [July 1978], p. 330 n34).

14 *The Economist*, 5 February 1966, p. 561. On the other hand, in both January 1964 and January 1966, fierce lobbying preceded the final allocations of posts (ibid.; Mulford, *Zambia: The Politics of Independence*, pp. 329–31).

15 By 1969 the situation had changed. "President Kaunda as the years passed came to take upon himself – with every appearance of genuine reluctance – the initiative for deciding upon and announcing more and more of the major innovations of policy. The collective influence of cabinet must be judged to have correspondingly declined until ... his ministers were advised of the contents of the Matero address [to nationalize the mines] only upon the evening before it was made" (M.L.O. Faber and J.G. Potter, *Towards Economic Independence: Papers on the Nationalization of the Copper Industry in Zambia* [Cambridge: Cambridge University Press, 1971], p. 7). Richard Hall notes that, if there were squabbles in cabinet, Kaunda "sought the consensus and listened to all opinions; he was the fatherly chairman with a casting vote – although his authority far outweighed that of any other" member (*The High Price of Principles: Kaunda and the White South* [Harmondsworth: Penguin, 1973], p. 52). He adds that it took Kaunda "six years to accept that his dreams of being the inspiring chairman of a high-minded cabinet team were totally unrealistic" (*Africa Digest* [London] 21:5 [October 1974], p. 97).

16 While successive ministers of finance were committed to amending the royalty formula, successive ministers of mines were equally opposed, and "argued that the royalty was a mining matter not a revenue matter." According to one close observer, "the President's response to this situation ... was to replace the Minister of Mines [in January 1965] and then 'award' the responsibility for royalties to the new Minister. When this Minister [A.G. Zulu] too decided against advocating a change, that was effectively the end of the matter" until 1969 (Faber and Potter, *Towards Economic Independence*, p. 6). See Zambia Information Services (ZIS) *Press Release* no. 712/65, 7 May 1965.

17 For a critical assessment of the conduct of cabinet business, see Roy Christie, *For the President's Eyes Only: The Story of John Brumer Agent Extraordinary* (Johannesburg: Hugh Keartland, 1971), p. 140. See

also William Tordoff, ed., *Politics in Zambia* (Manchester: Manchester University Press, 1974), pp. 251–2.
18 ZIS *Press Release* no. 700/65, 6 May 1965 (amendment). Kaunda repeated his injunction on the eve of UDI (ibid., no. 1785/65, 7 November 1965, p. 1).
19 *Zambia Mail* (Lusaka), 24 December 1965, p. 1. The limited evidence available suggests that the cabinet met about twice as frequently as normal in November and December, and thereafter less often. There were seventy-four cabinet meetings in 1966, fifty-one in 1967, and only twenty-seven in 1968.
20 A summons to State House for these (often late-night) audiences was sometimes termed "going into the Deep Freezer," a reference to the practice of keeping the temperature of the cabinet room at an even 60°F. Kaunda allegedly justified this as necessary "to keep tempers cool" (Sikota Wina, "The Heart of the Nation," Lusaka, 1968, pp. 105–6, unpublished manuscript). Elsewhere, Wina noted in *The Night without a President* (Lusaka: Multimedia Publications, 1985), p. 75, that Kaunda himself had an "extremely short temper which he has, however, learnt to control."
21 Munakayumbwa Sipalo, as cited in Faber and Potter, *Towards Economic Independence*, pp. vii–viii.
22 Hall dismisses them as "idealistic liberals capable of wishful thinking" who contributed to the "confusion" in Zambian foreign policy (*High Price of Principles*, p. 23).
23 In April 1965 Valentine Musakanya (age thirty-two and a junior civil servant since 1955) was appointed secretary to the cabinet, Dominic Mulaisho (age thirty-one and a civil servant since 1953) became permanent secretary in the Office of the President, and Mark Chona (age twenty-nine) took over the Ministry of Foreign Affairs (ZIS *Press Release* no. 500, 1 April 1965). By the time of UDI, only two expatriate permanent secretaries remained – in Finance and in Transport and Works.
24 On the travails of a twenty-one-year-old appointed first Zambian ambassador to the Soviet Union, see Vernon J. Mwaanga, *An Extraordinary Life* (Lusaka: Multimedia Publications, 1982), pp. 105–17. See also Douglas G. Anglin and Timothy M. Shaw, *Zambia's Foreign Policy: Studies in Diplomacy and Dependence* (Boulder: Westview Press, 1979), pp. 94–106, and Benedict V. Mtshali, "The Zambian Foreign Service, 1964–1972," *African Review* 5:3 (1975), pp. 303–16.
25 One senior mining executive explained that, "At first the government did fear that we would come down on the side of Smith. We were pushed a lot and some of us felt that we should take a hard line in dealings with the government because of it. But ... we decided to

297 Notes to pages 26–7

disregard kicks in the teeth and make a genuine effort to cooperate fully with government in all matters" (Richard L. Sklar, *Corporate Power in an African State: The Political Impact of Multinational Mining Companies in Zambia* [Berkeley: University of California Press, 1975], p. 147).

26 Ibid., pp. 144, 146–7. Kaunda reported that the mining companies had been "very cooperative indeed" with respect to contingency planning (ZIS *Background* no. 56/65, p. 3, 30 December 1965). Their Rhodesian subsidiaries also found no difficulty in cooperating fully with the rebel regime in Salisbury.

27 Sklar, *Corporate Power in an African State*, p. 176. Charles Harvey also reported that "the top management in the companies had real sympathy with government and its aspirations" (*Economic Independence and Zambian Copper* [New York: Praeger, 1972], p. 141n). Marcia M. Burdette suggests that "the international mining companies seemed to play the major role in [global as opposed to regional] economic diplomacy and negotiations" ("Zambia" in Timothy M. Shaw and Olajide Aluko, *The Political Economy of African Foreign Policy: Comparative Analysis* [New York: St. Martin's Press, 1984], p. 323).

28 Faber and Potter, *Towards Economic Independence*, p. 7. See also Martin, *Minding Their Own Business*, p. 122 n1.

29 Richard Hall, *My Life with Tiny: A Biography of Tiny Rowland* (London: Faber and Faber, 1987), pp. 17–20. See also Suzanne Cronjé, Margaret Ling, and Gillian Cronjé, *LONRHO: Portrait of a Multinational* (London: Julian Friedmann, 1976), pp. 32–6, 40–1.

30 Tordoff, *Politics in Zambia*, p. 80. Molteno explains this phenomenon in terms of the salience of racial cleavages, rapid upward mobility, extended families, the absence of rural landlords and moneylenders, elite interests in obscuring class divisions, and the lack of national leaders articulating the class demands of peasants and workers (ibid., pp. 80–5).

31 Karen Eriksen [Carolyn L. Baylies], "Zambia: Class Formation and Detente," *Review of African Political Economy* 9 (May-August 1978), pp. 4–26; Tony Southall, "Zambia: Class Formation and Detente – A Comment," ibid., 12 (May-August 1979), pp. 114–19; Burdette, "Zambia," pp. 319–47; Ronald T. Libby, "Transnational Class Alliances in Zambia," *Comparative Politics* 15:4 (July 1983), pp. 379–400; Carolyn L. Baylies and Morris Szeftel, "The Rise of a Zambian Capitalist Class in the 1970s," *Journal of Southern African Studies* 8:2 (April 1982), pp. 187–213.

32 For example, in December 1965 INDECO's investments in its subsidiary companies amounted to less than $300,000, whereas by March 1969 they totalled over $50 million, and by March 1980, $435

million (Industrial Development Corporation of Zambia Ltd., *Annual Reports*).
33 Tordoff, *Politics in Zambia*, p. 241; Jan Pettman, *Zambia: Security and Conflict* (London: Julian Friedmann, 1974), p. 43. In December 1965 the National Assembly comprised sixty UNIP members (of whom five were nominated), ten ANC members and ten (white) NPP members (elected for the "reserved constituencies").
34 Kaunda wrote optimistically that a leader can "keep in touch with [the people's] mood and thinking through those highly sensitive reflectors of public opinion, party officials" who are "in daily contact with the masses" (*A Humanist in Africa: Letters to Colin Morris* [London: Longmans, 1966], p. 87).
35 *Guardian* (London), 7 December 1965, p. 1, and 11 December 1965, p. 9; Zambia *Nat. Ass. Deb.* no. 5, cols. 91–100, 9 December 1965; *Times of Zambia* (Ndola), 14 December 1965, p. 1. The convening of a special cabinet meeting kept Kaunda from addressing the "national rally" held on 12 December in conjunction with the National Council; instead, he reported to a hastily convened press conference. When he did address the Council the next day, his theme was party unity, not Rhodesia per se.
36 The meeting of 11–13 December 1965 was its only meeting between 9–11 April 1965 and 16–18 June 1966.
37 Pettman's claim that "the cabinet is a poor third to the President and UNIP's Central Committee as a policy-making instrument" is a misleading characterization of the relative importance of the cabinet and the Central Committee in 1965–66, especially with respect to foreign policy decision making (*Zambia*, p. 45).
38 Proclamation no. 33 under the (Rhodesian) Unlawful Organizations Act, 6 July 1965, promulgated 14 July 1965.
39 *Nat. Ass. Deb.* no. 5, cols. 223–36, 15 December 1965; Pettman, *Zambia*, pp. 66, 79.
40 *Guardian*, 5 December 1965, p. 2; *Zambia Mail*, 31 December 1965, p. 1, and 7 January 1966, pp. 1, 8; *Times of Zambia*, 21 January 1966, p. 8. The NPP warned Kaunda, at a time when there was talk of an OAU liberation army based in Zambia, that if Ethiopian troops landed at Ndola, whites would leave at Chingola (for Zaire). This was not a prospect that the Zambian government could contemplate with equanimity. In August 1966 the NPP finally decided to disband.
41 Tordoff, *Politics in Zambia*, p. 215.
42 N.J. Small, "Getting Ideas Across: Limitations to Social Engineering in a New State," *African Affairs* 77:309 (October 1978), p. 551.
43 *Guardian*, 7 January 1966, p. 18. In December 1965 there was some substance to government concerns regarding public morale. Earlier,

in September, Arthur Wina told his fellow Commonwealth finance ministers in Jamaica that "such is the mood and sentiments of our people on this issue [of sanctions] that we may have to go even further" than Britain in instituting them (*Times of Zambia*, 24 September 1965, p. 1).

44 Michael Brecher, *The Foreign Policy System of Israel: Setting, Images, Process* (New Haven: Yale University Press, 1972), pp. 11–12.

45 Bahgat Korany and Ali E. Hillal Dessouki, *The Foreign Policies of Arab States* (Boulder: Westview Press, 1984), pp. 324, 326.

46 Kaunda, Kapwepwe, and Kamanga were first appointed ministers in December 1962. Ten others attained ministerial office in January 1964 (though five of these had had previous experience as parliamentary secretaries), one more (Matoka) joined in October 1964, and the remaining two (Changufu and Nalilungwe) were added only in January 1965.

47 Kaunda, Kamanga, Chimba, Kalulu, Banda, and Kapwepwe had been professional politicians since the early 1950s. The participation of Changufu, Mundia, Sikota Wina, Zulu, and Chona as full-time officials dates from the late 1950s.

48 Macpherson, *Kenneth Kaunda of Zambia*, pp. 17–18, 147–51. See also Kenneth Kaunda, *Zambia Shall Be Free* (London: Heinemann Educational Books Ltd., 1962), pp. 31–6, 41–2, 73–7; Grace Keith, *Fading Colour Bar* (London: Robert Hale, 1966); Hall, *Zambia*, pp. 168–73.

49 Arthur Wina was told, "We do not have vacancies for Africans of your education" (Wina, *The Night without a President*, p. 26; *Sunday Times of Zambia* [Lusaka], 1 August 1971, p. 13). Chona, Matoka, Mundia, and Mwanakatwe, amongst other graduates, all encountered blatant discrimination in seeking employment (*Zambia News* [Ndola], 10 December 1967, p. 8; John J. Grotpeter, *Historical Dictionary of Zambia* [Metuchen, NJ: Scarecrow Press, 1979], pp. 57, 211; Hall, *Zambia*, p. 172).

50 Macpherson, *Kenneth Kaunda of Zambia*, p. 54.

51 Robert I. Rotberg, "Tribalism and Politics in Zambia," *Africa Report* 12:9 (December 1967), p. 32; *The Economist*, 5 February 1966, pp. 561–2.

52 *An Account of the Disturbances in Northern Rhodesia, July to October 1961* (Lusaka: Government Printer, 1961). The 1961 "cha-cha-cha" campaign was the only period during the liberation struggle that UNIP resorted to considerable violence.

53 *The British South Africa Company's Claims to Mineral Royalties in Northern Rhodesia* (Lusaka: Government Printer, 1964); Hall, *Zambia*, pp. 230–4, and *High Price of Principles*, pp. 80–6.

54 *Report of the Commission of Inquiry into the Former Lumpa Church* (Lusa-

ka: Government Printer, 1965); A.D. Roberts, "The Lumpa Church of Alice Lenshina," in Robert I. Rotberg and Ali A. Mazrui, eds., *Protest and Power in Black Africa* (New York: Oxford University Press, 1970), pp. 513–68.
55 See especially Stephen Chan, *Kaunda and Southern Africa: Image and Reality in Foreign Policy* (London: British Academic Press, 1992).
56 Lord Alport, last British high commissioner to the Federation of Rhodesia and Nyasaland, observed that in 1962 Kaunda's "political and personal aides did not feel any great awe in his presence." Since, in Africa, it was "necessary for political rulers to inspire a feeling of diffidence and apprehension in the breasts of their followers ... I was not convinced that he would last the full span of a political career in the cut-throat world of African nationalist politics" (*Sudden Assignment* [London: Hodder and Stoughton, 1965], pp. 213–14).
57 *High Price of Principles*, p. 41; Wina, *The Night without a President*, pp. 71–8.
58 "Kenneth Kaunda et le 'socialisme zambien'," *Esprit* 35:363 (septembre 1967), p. 249. Dumont was author of *False Start in Africa* (1966) and a similar devastating indictment of Zambian development strategy.
59 Quoted in Legum, *Zambia: Independence and Beyond*, pp. 219, 220. Hall claimed that Kaunda "interprets international affairs" in terms of "good and evil" (*High Price of Principles*, p. 41).
60 "This son of an African minister of religion had been formed in the struggle to gain dignity and rights for his own people and burned now with the desire to rid Southern Africa of racism; more than most leaders, he would do all he could to make the slender resources of his country serve this end." (Robert C. Good, *UDI: The International Politics of the Rhodesian Rebellion* [Princeton: Princeton University Press, 1973], p. 87.) Kaunda also testifies to the influence on his thinking of a South African master at Munali: "For the first time I understood the meaning of the word *apartheid*" (*Zambia Shall Be Free*, pp. 16–17).
61 Kaunda, *Zambia Shall Be Free*, pp. 80–3; Macpherson, *Kenneth Kaunda of Zambia*, pp. 229–45; Hall, *High Price of Principles*, pp. 44–5; Wina, *The Night without a President*, p. 56.
62 Good, *UDI*, pp. 154–6; Hall, *High Price of Principles*, pp. 139, 150–3.
63 Macpherson notes that "Gandhi and Jesus had a special magnetism" for the young Kaunda (*Kenneth Kaunda of Zambia*, pp. 105–6, also pp. 70, 308).
64 Address to Royal Commonwealth Society, London, 24 June 1965 (Legum, *Zambia: Independence and Beyond*, pp. 222).

65 ZIS *Press Release* no. 1710/65, pp. 22–3, 23 October 1965.
66 Colin M. Morris, ed., *Kaunda on Violence* (London: Collins, 1980), p. 7; Legum, *Zambia: Independence and Beyond*, p. 221.
67 *A Humanist in Africa*, pp. 28–30. Jan Kees van Donge observes that "Kaunda's mind seems to embrace the widest variety of political thinking without being particularly bothered by possible contradictions ... Also in politics he has a remarkable capacity to take contradictory positions ... However, the absorption of an enormous amount of ideas without being hindered by apparent contradictions can be found throughout Zambian society" ("Nadine Gordimer's 'A Guest of Honour': A Failure to Understand Zambian Society," *Journal of Southern African Studies* 9:1 [October 1982], pp. 85, 87).
68 Some Zambian officials were not averse to exploiting the alleged threat of a "left-wing" takeover to reinforce their appeals for overseas support (*The Cecil King Diaries, 1965–1970* [London: Jonathan Cape, 1972], p. 45, 8 December 1965; British *H.C. Deb.* vol. 721, col. 1435, 1 December 1965; *Guardian*, 5 January 1966, p. 11).
69 Good, *UDI*, p. 104. Arthur Bottomley, British secretary of state for Commonwealth relations, was particularly incensed at the militant tone of Kapwepwe's address to the UN General Assembly on 28 September 1965.
70 Macpherson, *Kenneth Kaunda of Zambia*, p. 46, interview of 8 November 1969. Kapwepwe claimed that Kaunda had inherited his quality of patience from his father (ibid., p. 47).
71 Legum characterized Kaunda as "first a humanist and secondarily a nationalist" (*Zambia: Independence and Beyond*, p. ix).
72 Hall, *High Price of Principles*, pp. 127, 130; *Guardian*, 4 December 1965, p. 9; *Times of Zambia*, 3 March 1966, p. 8.
73 OAU doc. ECM/PV.1:VI, 3 December 1965, p. 30. See also *Guardian*, 4 December 1965, p. 9. Kapwepwe was especially alarmed at the number of Rhodesians and South Africans in the mines and in the army.
74 Hall, *High Price of Principles*, pp. 136, 139, 153. "Mr Kapwepwe ... has accused Britain of trying to 'wash her hands' of Rhodesia. President Kaunda has repeated his belief that Britain will ultimately do what is expected of her" (*Times of Zambia*, 1 October 1965, p. 10). One source attributes Kapwepwe's apprehensions concerning the British to the fact that the Northern Rhodesia Regiment had helped to liberate Ethiopia from the Italians, "only to see Italians invited as immigrants into the Rhodesias to take African land" (Arnold Smith with Clyde Sanger, *Stitches in Time: The Commonwealth in World Politics* [London: André Deutsch, 1981], p. 62). A further explanation is Zambia's unhappy experience in the defederation exercise in 1963. See also *Nat. Ass. Deb.* no. 4, col. 931, 13 August 1965; Goodwin

Mwangilwa, *The Kapwepwe Diaries* (Lusaka: Multimedia Publications, 1986), pp. 56, 61, 64.

75 Following the first Commonwealth Conference Zambia attended, Kaunda exuded that his delegation would "go back to Zambia with a glowing faith in the Commonwealth," whereas Kapwepwe emphasized the dissatisfaction some countries felt with the outcome (*Times of Zambia*, 1 July 1965, p. 1, and 9 July 1965, p. 1). On the other hand, Kapwepwe succeeded in talking Kaunda out of announcing Zambia's withdrawal from the Commonwealth in a speech he gave on 12 July 1966.

76 Wina was approaching completion of his Ph.D. in political science at UCLA when he was summoned home to contest the 1962 general elections. His US connections made him an easy target for radicals who treated his "moderation" as evidence that he was under American influence.

77 ZIS *Press Release* no. 191/66, 29 January 1966; Hall, *High Price of Principles*, pp. 128, 175.

CHAPTER 3

1 President Kaunda, 5 May 1965, quoted in Colin Legum, ed., *Zambia: Independence and Beyond: The Speeches of Kenneth Kaunda* (London: Nelson, 1966), p. 218.

2 *Northern News* (Ndola), 4 May 1965, p. 1; *Daily Telegraph* (London), 28 April 1965, p. 23, and 29 April 1965, p. 26. See also Larry W. Bowman, *Politics in Rhodesia: White Power in an African State* (Cambridge, Mass.: Harvard University Press, 1973), pp. 75–81, where evidence is given that, despite Smith's denials, "UDI *was* an issue" (p. 80).

3 The Wilson statement was given on 27 October 1964. See Elaine Windrich, *The Rhodesian Problem: A Documentary Record, 1923–1973* (London: Routledge and Kegan Paul, 1975), p. 209; James Barber, *Rhodesia: The Road to Rebellion* (London: Oxford University Press, 1967), pp. 272–3; Kenneth Young, *Rhodesia and Independence: A Study in British Colonial Policy* (London: Dent, 1967), p. 199; Bowman, *Politics in Rhodesia*, pp. 78–80.

4 Prime Minister's Office, *Economic Aspects of a Declaration of Independence* (Salisbury: Government Printer, 1965), CSR 15–1965, pp. 3–4. The Rhodesian government estimated its Zambian population at forty thousand while a UNIP census set the number at sixty-nine thousand (*Northern News*, 19 May 1965, p. 8). The threat was repeated on several occasions during October (*Southern Rhodesia: Documents relating to the negotiations between the United Kingdom and Southern*

Rhodesian Governments, November 1963–November 1965 [London: HMSO, 1965], Cmnd. 2807, p. 85; *Rhodesia Herald* [Salisbury], 19 October 1965, p. 2; *US News and World Report*, 8 November 1965, p. 70).

5 Zambia Information Services (ZIS) *Background* no. 16/64, pp. 4–5, 28 August 1964. In July 1964 Portugal pledged its support to Rhodesia in the event of UDI. To cement the relationship, in September Smith visited Lisbon where President Salazar gave him "every encouragement to proceed with UDI" (Ken Flower, *Serving Secretly: An Intelligence Chief on Record: Rhodesia into Zimbabwe, 1964 to 1981* [Harare: Quest Publishing, 1987], pp. 32–5).

6 *Central African Mail* (Ndola), 12 February 1965, p. 1; *Northern News*, 19 February 1965, p. 1. On 27 January 1965, on the eve of his departure for London, Kaunda called in Kapwepwe, Kamanga, and Chona, and told them: "I have very bad news for you. The UDI is now a possibility" in June (Goodwin Mwangilwa, *The Kapwepwe Diaries* [Lusaka: Multimedia Publications, 1986], pp. 53–4).

7 *Central African Mail*, 30 April 1965, p. 3.

8 *Zambia News* (Ndola), 2 May 1965, p. 7.

9 On one occasion, Kaunda ordered a speech by the minister of education to the Zambia National Affairs Association (*Central African Mail*, 19 March 1965, p. 4) cancelled at the last moment. Misunderstandings concerning the president's motives in soft-pedalling ministerial statements on Rhodesia led to minor rumblings suggesting he was too deferential to whites.

10 Legum, ed., *Zambia*, p. 217.

11 *Central African Mail*, 30 April 1965, p. 3. Kaunda toured the Copperbelt from 30 April to 8 May, addressing eight national rallies and numerous lesser ones. His absence from the capital for much of this time was a further factor in slowing the decision-making process.

12 The US ambassador at the time noted that "Zambia had inherited from the colonial government a large cadre of white civil servants. Many of them had close ties with Rhodesia. So the whole planning operation was kept under wraps" (Robert C. Good, *UDI: The International Politics of the Rhodesian Rebellion* [Princeton: Princeton University Press, 1973], p. 95).

13 The top posts in the Zambian civil service were Zambianized only on 1 April, with the appointment (among others) of Valentine Musakanya as secretary to the cabinet, Dominic Mulaisho as permanent secretary, Office of the President, and Mark Chona as permanent secretary, Ministry of Foreign Affairs. This was the first presidential address these three were called upon to draft.

14 The next day Kaunda declared, with obvious reference to Smith, that he could not see "any person who is not mad discharging the

number of Zambians that we have who are in control in a number of important [Rhodesian] industries. Take the Wankie [coal] mines, for example – thousands of Zambians – and to dismiss all those and expect the Wankie Colliery to run is, as I say, really not realistic, if not actually stupid. To think that all the farm hands that come from Zambia that help to run the Rhodesian farms could be dismissed without affecting the tobacco industry of Rhodesia is to say the least madness" (ZIS *Background* no. 17/65, p. 2, 6 May 1965).

15 Legum, ed., *Zambia*, pp. 218–21. Vice-President Kamanga declared that, if the Rhodesian rail route were cut off, Zambia would still survive, "even if this means taking our copper on foot to the coast" (*Northern News*, 3 May 1965, p. 1). Finance Minister Wina warned that any interference with Kariba power or Rhodesia Railways (both jointly owned) would be "the same as Rhodesia occupying Lusaka" and Zambia "with or without her friends, would have to protect her interests" (*Zambia News*, 9 May, 1965, p. 1).

16 Rhodesia *Leg. Ass. Deb.* vol. 61, cols. 1460–2, 27 July 1965; *Central African Mail*, 23 May 1965, p. 1. The letter may have been timed to influence the (supposedly confidential) consultations on Zambian contingency planning held in Washington, 17–20 May. Kaunda's reply was a curt single sentence: "I thank you for your message of 14th May 1965."

17 It should be noted that "contingency planning is not, as is sometimes represented, the drawing up of firm plans to meet an infinite variety of hypotheses about the forms that the threat ... could take, which can then be pulled out of a card index when the adversary pushes a particular button, and immediately translated into action. It is much more a question of deciding what is the general scope of the reaction which it is realistic to contemplate, what are the limitations, what preparatory action is necessary, [and] what courses of action must be ruled out" (Alastair Buchan, *Crisis Management: The New Diplomacy* [Boulogne-sur-Seine: Atlantic Institute, 1966], p. 42).

18 "Britain was utterly dependent on [Zambian] copper supplies. Had they been cut off ... we would have had two million unemployed within a matter of months" (Harold Wilson, *Personal Record: The Labour Government, 1964–70* [Boston: Little Brown, 1971], pp. 182–3). Kaunda's estimate was more modest: "There would be about one million unemployed in Britain as a result of closing Zambia's mines" (ZIS *Background* no. 1/66, 2 January 1966, p. 2). Zambian negotiators capitalized on Wilson's concern by arguing that the airlift was needed principally to ensure the export of copper rather than to provide essential imports. One senior CRO official hotly denies that UDI caused Britain (unlike the United States) any

worry about its copper supply. See also Barbara Castle, *The Castle Diaries, 1964–70* (London: Weidenfeld and Nicolson, 1984), p. 73.

19 *Rhodesia-Zambia: A Study of the Feasibility of Mitigating the Disruption of the Zambian Economy and World Copper Supply following a Unilateral Declaration of Independence* (Washington: Department of State, 21 June 1965, mimeo). An airlift was first publicly alluded to shortly after Kaunda's broadcast of 5 May (*Northern News*, 8 May 1965, p. 1).

20 Even after UDI, the Americans did not prove "very forthcoming." As Barbara Castle noted, following a cabinet meeting on 30 November 1965: "They categorically refuse to release copper stocks as they are bothered by the effect of Vietnam on prices" (*Castle Diaries, 1964–70*, p. 73).

21 M.L.O. Faber and J.G. Potter, *Towards Economic Independence: Papers on the Nationalization of the Copper Industry in Zambia* (Cambridge: Cambridge University Press, 1971), p. 7; Antony Martin, *Minding Their Own Business: Zambia's Struggle against Western Control* (London: Hutchinson, 1972), p. 122 n1. When Zambian dissatisfaction with RST was made known to its chairman, Sir Ronald Prain, and to American Metal Climax, which had a controlling interest in RST, the company's president, Frank Buch (in Salisbury) was persuaded to "retire" for "personal and private reasons." His successor, James Reid, took up residence in Lusaka (*Times of Zambia* [Ndola], 30 July 1965, p. 1).

22 The Soviet government was not approached until late December of 1965; predictably, it proved disinterested in assisting the two multinational mining groups to export their copper (Vernon J. Mwaanga, *An Extraordinary Life* [Lusaka: Multimedia Publications, 1982], p. 110). The US aircraft operating out of Kinshasa did not in fact land in Zambia, but rather in Lubumbashi (from where the petrol, oil, and lubricants (POL) was railed or trucked to Zambia). The reason for this was technical, not political: Zambian airfields could not handle the giant Boeing 707s.

23 ZIS *Press Release* no. 1664/65, 15 October 1965.

24 The moderate tone of Nkrumah's speech caused Kapwepwe to comment, somewhat caustically, that that is what happens when a country gets into balance-of-payments difficulties.

25 Wilson, *Personal Record*, p. 116.

26 Douglas G. Anglin and Timothy M. Shaw, *Zambia's Foreign Policy: Studies in Diplomacy and Dependence* (Boulder: Westview Press, 1979), pp. 116, 123; *Guardian* (London), 22 June 1965, p. 1; Castle, *Castle Diaries*, p. 61. The first tentative invitation was extended at the time of the first UDI scare in February 1964 (*Rhodesia Herald*, 5 February 1964, p. 1).

27 It is not clear whether the issue was first raised by the president at a late-night briefing session (on 14 June) with his ministers and senior officials (*Northern News*, 16 June 1965, p. 1). Four ministers were present in London: Kapwepwe (Foreign Affairs), Wina (Finance), Mwiinga (Commonwealth Affairs), and Mundia (Labour and Social Development).
28 Arnold Smith with Clyde Sanger, *Stitches in Time: The Commonwealth in World Politics* (London: André Deutsch, 1981), p. 58.
29 *Northern News*, 23 June 1965, p. 1.
30 Wilson, *Personal Record*, p. 116.
31 Richard Hall, *The High Price of Principles: Kaunda and the White South* (Harmondsworth: Penguin, 1973), p. 114. This was not the last occasion on which Wilson's subsequent actions contradicted his confidential assurances.
32 The Anglo-American report (note 19) estimated that, with zero copper production, the demand for coal would drop from 100,000 tons a month to 65,000 tons, of which 45,000 tons would be required for thermal power generation.
33 David Livingstone had observed the outcroppings more than a century earlier (J.P.R. Wallis, ed., *The Zambezi Expedition of David Livingstone, 1858–1863* [London: Chatto and Windus, 1956], II:390), but no surveying was undertaken until after the Second World War.
34 Central Planning Office, *An Outline of the Transitional Development Plan* (Lusaka: Government Printer, 1965), p. 48. Formal cabinet approval of the survey was given on 23 December 1964 without significant debate.
35 Two surveys were undertaken. The first, by Kenneth Heath, AAC's assistant consulting engineer, was essentially an economic report, based on different sets of assumptions, rather than a detailed geological survey; it was completed on 8 July shortly before the cabinet decision. The second, by AAC's chief geologist and Zambia Exploration Ltd. (Zamex), traced the sub-outcrop of coal and assessed the thickness and quality of the seam on the basis of fieldwork undertaken between 12 April and 7 August (F.W. Cornwall, *Kandabwe Coal Report* [Lusaka: Anglo-American Corporation of Central Africa Ltd., 22 October 1965], mimeo). Zamex was chosen for this assignment rather than the Wankie Coal Company (which had more experience of coal mining but also an obvious interest in the outcome) at the suggestion of AAC chairman Harry Oppenheimer; both companies were AAC subsidiaries. See also *Economic Report, 1966* (Lusaka: Ministry of Finance, 1966), p. 20.
36 *Estimates of Revenue and Expenditure for the Year 1st July 1965 to 30th June 1966* (Lusaka: Government Printer, 1965), p. 87.

37 Ieuan L. Griffiths, "Zambian Coal: An Example of Strategic Resource Development," *Geographical Review* 58 (October 1968), pp. 545, 547. The first hint of the decision was contained in the budget address (Zambia *Nat. Ass. Deb.*, no. 4, cols. 31–2, 15 July 1965), with a fuller but still brief statement on 10 August (ibid., cols. 719–20).

38 Griffiths, "Zambian Coal," pp. 538, 549–51.

39 The decision was justified publicly as coming within the established policy of disengaging from dependence on Southern Africa (ZIS *Background* no. 28/65, p. 4, 4 August 1965) though, when the (white) Zambian opposition in Parliament pressed for details, the foreign minister hinted at the security aspect (*Nat. Ass. Deb.*, no. 4, col. 1396, 31 August 1965). It is doubtful if Rhodesian Intelligence was unaware of what was going on.

40 "Zambian Coal: Commitment to Error," *The Economist*, 15 October 1966, p. 284.

41 Good, *UDI*, p. 89. The report was prepared by John Thixton of AAC's Rhokana mine (*Times of Zambia*, 7 February 1967, p. 4).

42 *Financial Times* (London), 7 October 1965, p. 7; Francis Coleman, *The Northern Rhodesia Copperbelt 1899–1962* (Manchester: Manchester University Press, 1971), p. 141.

43 Shortly after UDI, at Kaunda's request, RST did experiment with oil-firing equipment flown in from Britain for the reverberatory furnaces at its Mufulira mine (*Times of Zambia*, 30 December 1965, p. 7, and 7 January 1966, p. 1; ZIS *Background* no. 56/65, p. 3, 30 December 1965).

44 Hall, *High Price of Principles*, pp. 117–18.

45 Despite their almost pathological preoccupation with secrecy, the British invited a number of South African firms to submit estimates of the cost. Among the firms contacted was a subsidiary of AAC, whose chairman Harry Oppenheimer was fortunately already closely involved in Zambian contingency planning. He attempted to redeem the situation by leaking a report that AAC was the source of the request.

46 ZIS *Press Release* no. 917/65, 18 June 1965; Wankie Colliery Company Limited, *42nd Annual Report*, 1965, p. 5.

47 *Times of Zambia*, 13 November 1965, p. 2.

48 Kapwepwe's diary for 10 February notes that "Grey Zulu, Minister of Mines, H. Banda, Minister of Transport and Works, and I met the Mining Company over the opening of the coal mine in [southern] Tanzania near Songea or near Tukuyu" (Mwangilwa, *Kapwepwe Diaries*, p. 54).

49 Interest in Tanzanian coal was revived after UDI following discus-

sions (on 28 December) with President Nyerere. Nothing came of these (ZIS *Background* no. 56/65, p. 3, 30 December 1965).
50 See note 41.
51 Good, *UDI*, p. 95.
52 Apparently, the "coal for stockpiling" idea persisted with its author, Minister of Mines Grey Zulu (*Financial Mail of Zambia* [Ndola], August 1965, p. 10).
53 The call in the Rhodesian legislature a few days earlier for a one-hundred-fold increase in the royalty on coal exports underlined Zambia's vulnerability but apparently did not determine the final decision (*Leg. Ass. Deb.* vol. 61, cols. 1060–2, 8 July 1965).
54 The Nkandabwe Coal Company set up in November 1965 to mine the deposit was owned 50 per cent by the government and 25 per cent by each of AAC and RST, with AAC holding the management contract (Gordon Gregor, "Developing Zambia's Coal Resources," *Horizon* 10:12 [December 1968], p. 7). The mines agreed to purchase the first 300,000 tons of coal at a price that would cover "all capital costs as well as the operating costs" (Richard L. Sklar, *Corporate Power in an African State: The Political Impact of Multinational Mining Companies in Zambia* [Berkeley: University of California Press, 1975], p. 145).
55 Good, *UDI*, p. 94.

CHAPTER 4

1 *African Research Bulletin: Political Social and Cultural (ARB:PSC)*, 1965, p. 337. The appointment of Harry Reedman was announced on 21 July. His arrival in Lisbon on 15 September, amid much controversy, added greatly to the UDI speculation. London's fierce protests seriously impaired its relations with Lisbon.
2 The statement on the non-use of force was first made by Arthur Bottomley, secretary of state for Commonwealth relations, in answer to a question at a press conference in Accra on 10 August, and repeated several times subsequently. *ARB:PSC*, 1965, p. 352; *The Times* (London) 18 August 1965, p. 6; Douglas G. Anglin and Timothy M. Shaw, *Zambia's Foreign Policy: Studies in Diplomacy and Dependence* (Boulder: Westview Press, 1979), pp. 117–18.
3 Rhodesia *Leg. Ass. Deb.* vol. 62, col. 998, 1 September 1965.
4 Kenneth Young, *Rhodesia and Independence: A Study in British Colonial Policy* (London: Dent, 1969), pp. 211–12.
5 Robert O. Matthews, "Talking without Negotiating: The Case of Rhodesia," *International Journal* 35:1 (Winter 1979–80), pp. 91–117; *Guardian* (London), 9 October 1965, p. 1.

6 Jorge Jardim, *Sanctions Double-Cross: Oil to Rhodesia* (Lisbon: Intervençao, 1978), pp. 19, 21, 24; *Sunday Times* (London), 12 June 1977, p. 63; *Times of Zambia* (Ndola), 13 November 1965, p. 2, and 16 November 1965, p. 1.

7 Proclamation No. 33 under the Unlawful Organizations Act, 6 July 1965, promulgated 14 July 1965; *Times of Zambia*, 14 July 1965, p. 1; *Leg. Ass. Deb.* vol. 61, cols. 1858–59, 1865–67, 5 August 1965.

8 *Times of Zambia*, 8 August 1965, p. 6; Roy Christie, *For the President's Eyes Only: The Story of John Brumer Agent Extraordinary* (Johannesburg: Hugh Keartland, 1971), pp. 119–20. As late as 1 October, Brumer relayed to Kaunda the claim that, "despite rumours circulated through the press, the Rhodesian Government does not want UDI if it can possibly be avoided."

9 Kasuka S. Mutukwa, *Politics of the Tanzania-Zambia Railproject: A Study of Tanzania-China-Zambia Relations* (Washington: University Press of America, 1977); Richard Hall and Hugh Peyman, *The Great Uhuru Railway: China's Showpiece in Africa* (London: Victor Gollancz, 1977); Bertha H. Zimba, "Zambian Decision-Making in Transportation: The Case of Tanzania-Zambia Railway," (Ph.D. dissertation, Brandeis University, 1987). Kaunda visited Dar es Salaam on 6–8 August and again on 27–8 September 1965 for discussions with Nyerere on the proposed railway.

10 Anglin and Shaw, *Zambia's Foreign Policy*, pp. 176–7.

11 Articles 1–3, "Agreement between the Government of Southern Rhodesia and the Government of Northern Rhodesia relating to the Rhodesia Railways," 10 December 1963, Northern Rhodesia *Government Gazette* LIII:72 (13 December 1963), p. 847.

12 *Times of Zambia*, 11 August 1965, p. 1; Richard Hall, *The High Price of Principles: Kaunda and the White South* (Harmondsworth: Penguin, 1973), p. 115.

13 Colin Legum, ed., *Zambia: Independence and Beyond: The Speeches of Kenneth Kaunda* (London: Nelson, 1966), p. 219; *Zambia News* (Ndola), 9 May 1965, p. 1; *Leg. Ass. Deb.* vol. 61, col. 1462, 27 July 1965.

14 *Rhodesia Herald* (Salisbury), 10 August 1965, pp. 1, 2; *Sunday Mail* (Salisbury), 5 September 1965, p. 12. Leon Dominion was a senior official of the governing Rhodesian Front party, and a notorious racist (Hall, *High Price of Principles*, p. 116).

15 *Leg. Ass. Deb.* vol. 62. cols. 1–3, 10 August 1965. He repeated the appeal on 27 August (ibid., cols. 819–22). The minister may also have intended his words to serve as a warning against proceeding with the Tanzania-Zambia Railway project, following the announcement on 7 August of its revival (Zambia Information Services [ZIS] *Background* no. 29/65, 10 August 1965).

16 *Guardian,* 14 August 1965, p. 7; *Zambia News,* 15 August 1965, p. 8; Zambia *Nat. Ass. Deb.* no. 4, cols. 748–52, 11 August 1965; *Sunday Mail,* 5 September 1965, p. 12; *The Economist,* 11 September 1965, pp. 976, 978. One independent study found that "Zambian traffic provides large 'excess profits' and Rhodesian traffic large 'losses'" (Edwin T. Haefele and Eleanor B. Steinberg, *Government Controls on Transport: An African Case* [Washington: Brookings Institution, 1965], p. 52).
17 Hall, *High Price of Principles,* p. 115.
18 See note 13.
19 *The Economist,* 11 September 1965, p. 976.
20 Throughout this period, the members were: A.D. McLean (deputy chairman); Kenneth J. Knaggs, permanent secretary of finance; and Robinson Puta, Zambian trade unionist, businessman, and politician.
21 Arthur R. Kemp, a businessman, mayor of Kabwe, 1957–60, and former United Federal Party politician.
22 H. Dingiswayo Banda (Transport and Works), Arthur N.L. Wina (Finance), and Nalumino Mundia (Labour and Social Development).
23 26 *August* 1965, ZIS *Background* no. 34/65, pp. 3–4, 30 August 1965.
24 Kaunda claimed that the British government had insisted in 1963 on joint operation of the rail system "despite the wish expressed by this country and Rhodesia that the railways should not be run on a unitary basis" (ZIS *Press Release* no. 2049/66, 14 November 1966, p. 2).
25 Ibid.
26 Articles 41–3.
27 ZIS *Press Release* no. 1373/65, 27 August 1965; see also *Leg. Ass. Deb.* vol. 62, col. 819, 27 August 1965; *Nat. Ass. Deb.* no. 4, cols. 748–52, 11 August 1965.
28 *Leg. Ass. Deb.* vol. 62, col. 821, 27 August 1965; *Rhodesia Herald,* 31 August 1965, p. 1. The Rhodesian transport minister attempted next day to soften the harshness of the threat by suggesting that "if we can solve these problems to everyone's satisfaction, I can see no reason why the railways should not continue as a unitary system" (*Financial Times* [London], 1 September 1965, p. 7, and 28 October 1965, p. 1).
29 ZIS *Press Release* no. 1614/65, 7 October 1965. Despite this, Salisbury inexplicably continued to appeal impatiently for a meeting (*Times of Zambia,* 7 October 1965, p. 1).
30 *Times of Zambia,* 10 November 1965, p. 1.
31 Central Planning Office, *An Outline of the Transitional Development Plan* (Lusaka: Government Printer, 1965), p. 56.

32 The distance between the Copperbelt and the sea was more than 1,700 miles: 590 miles of road from Ndola to Mpulungu, followed by 350 miles over water to Kigoma in Tanzania, and 780 miles down the East African Railways line to Dar es Salaam.
33 Kenneth Bradley, *Copper Venture: The Discovery and Development of Roan Antelope and Mufulira* (London: Mufulira Mines, 1952), p. 60n.
34 *An Outline of the Transitional Development Plan*, p. 56.
35 *Estimates of Revenue and Expenditure for the Year 1st July 1965 to 30th June 1966* (Lusaka: Government Printer, 1965), pp. 89–90; *Northern News* (Ndola), 11 June 1965, p. 8.
36 J. Eric Bright and George H. Hoganson reported their findings to the president on 23 July (*Times of Zambia*, 27 July 1965, p. 1).
37 The *Times of Zambia* (5 December 1965, p. 3) listed six different reports on alternative routes prior to UDI in 1965 alone. Even so, it overlooked the Bright-Hoganson report. Good notes that "each study, rather than spurring commitments, spawned yet more studies" (Robert C. Good, *UDI: The International Politics of the Rhodesian Rebellion* [Princeton: Princeton University Press, 1973], p. 92).
38 The oil terminal at Dar es Salaam, but not its dry-cargo handling facilities, had ample free capacity, as did the Dar to Kigoma railway. Following UDI, oil was transported from Kigoma to Mpulungu in large plastic balloon-type containers towed by lake boats, and then transferred to huge deflatable rubber and nylon storage tanks at Mpulungu (Good, *UDI*, p. 109).
39 ZIS *Background* no. 16/64, pp. 4–5, 28 August 1964; Legum, *Zambia*, p. 223; *Le Monde* (Paris), 14 September 1965, p. 7. Although Portugal at this time was actively supportive of UDI, South Africa sought to discourage it (Ken Flower, *Serving Secretly: An Intelligence Chief on Record: Rhodesia into Zimbabwe, 1964 to 1981* [Harare: Quest Publishing, 1987], pp. 31–5).
40 Ministério dos Negocios Estrangeiros, *Anuário Diplomático e Consular Português: referido a l de Julho de 1973* (Lisboa: Imprensa Nacional-Casa da Moede, 1974), p. 208; Anglin and Shaw, *Zambia's Foreign Policy*, p. 239. Similarly, but again unlike Malawi, Zambia invited nationalist leaders but not Portugal to its independence celebrations.
41 Luis B. Serapiao and Mohammed A. El-Khawas, *Mozambique in the Twentieth Century* (Washington: University Press of America, 1979), pp. 285–6.
42 *Daily Telegraph* (London), 17 April 1965, p. 13.
43 *Convention between the Government of the United Kingdom of Great Britain and Northern Ireland on their own behalf and on behalf of the Government of Southern Rhodesia and the Government of the Republic of Portugal*

relative to the Port of Beira and Connected Railways, Lisbon, 17th June 1950 (London: HMSO, 1950), Cmd. 8061, Article VI.

44 *Daily Telegraph*, 17 April 1965, p. 13, and 26 July 1965, p. 18; *Zambia News*, 5 July 1965, p. 1.

45 Col. S.F. Gauron, director of mechanical services, and Robert Oakshott, secretary of the Transport Sector Committee. The minister of commerce and industry called for greater use of the Benguela route as early as June (*Northern News*, 26 June 1965, p. 1). On pre-UDI efforts to increase Zambian traffic through Lobito, see *Financial Times*, 9 September 1965, p. 7, 23 September 1965, p. 1, and 1 October 1965, p. 14.

46 *Africa 1965* (London), no. 16, 13 August 1965, p. 3; *Le Monde*, 14 September 1965, p. 7.

47 *ARB: PSC*, 1965, p. 354.

48 ZIS *Background* no. 35/65, p. 3, 9 September 1965; *Daily Telegraph*, 8 October 1965, p. 32. The arms released by the Portuguese were promptly seized by the Rhodesians (Decision No. 10).

49 Good, *UDI*, p. 95.

50 It is not clear whether this provision was part of the original decision, or was added in early October.

51 ZIS *Background* no. 35/65, pp. 1, 4–5, 9 September 1965; *The Times*, 9 September 1965, p. 8. Kaunda's announcement on 9 September of the release by Portugal of the Zambian arms shipment coincided with the "clampdown" on liberation movements, but was not a *quid pro quo*. Kaunda had his own reasons for wishing to impose close supervision on arms in transit. FRELIMO cadres at this stage were not always well disciplined, and there was a danger that their arms might fall into the wrong hands. Accordingly, the procedure for handling arms in transit was completely changed to increase domestic security (and to avoid their interception by the Zambia Police).

52 *Times of Zambia*, 8 September 1965, p. 1; *Nat. Ass. Deb.* no. 4, col. 1747, 8 September 1965, and cols. 1761, 1769, 9 September 1965; WHO Regional Committee for Africa, fifteenth session, Lusaka, 6–16 September 1965, Minutes of the sixth meeting, 9 September 1965, AFR/RC15/Min/6, pp. 2–11. Kaunda defended the invitation to the Portuguese (ZIS *Background* no. 36/65, p. 4, 9 September 1965) and the divorce of health from politics (ZIS *Press Release* no. 1965/65, pp. 6–8, 21 October 1965).

53 *Foreign Report* (London), no. 933, 11 November 1965, pp. 1–2. See also Foreign Minister Franco Nogueira's address to the UN General Assembly, 11 October 1965 (A/PV. 1356, p. 23). It is not clear whether the Kapwepwe–Franco Nogueira meeting took place before or after this speech.

54 Good, *UDI*, p. 92.

55 Paul Gore-Booth, *With Great Truth and Respect* (London: Constable, 1974), p. 331; Good, *UDI*, p. 92. Gore-Booth adds that the Rhodesia story does "not make very happy remembering or reading."
56 See Ian Smith's letters of 14 May and 21 October 1965 to Kaunda (*Leg. Ass. Deb.* vol 61, cols. 1460–2, 27 July 1965 and *Times of Zambia* 23 October 1965, p. 1).
57 Good, *UDI*, p. 87.
58 *Financial Times*, 6 October 1965, p. 1. Mennen Williams (US assistant secretary of state for African affairs) announced on 1 October that the United States would assist Zambia in the event of Rhodesian "economic retaliation" (ibid., 2 October 1965, p. 1).
59 ZIS *Press Release* no. 1560/65, p. 8, 29 September 1965, and *Background* no. 37/65, p. 1, 30 September 1965. Publicly, Kaunda spoke only of "a good North/South road link" between East and Central Africa.
60 Good, *UDI*, p. 93. Asked at a press conference if the UDI situation had "hotted up," Kaunda replied: "I agree entirely. All the information I have is that that is how things are going" (ZIS *Background* no. 37/65, pp. 1–2, 30 September 1965).
61 Good, *UDI*, pp. 93–4; Hall, *High Price of Principles*, pp. 117–19; Richard Crossman, *Diaries of a Cabinet Minister* (London: Hamish Hamilton, 1975), I:378, 406.
62 Good, *UDI*, p. 92.
63 Ibid., pp. 89–90, 92.
64 *Times of Zambia*, 12 October 1965, p. 1; ZIS *Press Release* no. 1664/65, 15 October 1965. Prime Minister Wilson reportedly played his "last card" when, on 28 October, he warned Smith that "the world would lay on something equivalent to the Berlin airlift rather than allow Zambia to be strangled economically" (*Guardian*, 29 October 1965, p. 1).
65 *Zambia News*, 17 October 1965, p. 1, and 31 October 1965, p. 9; *Guardian*, 29 October 1965, p. 1, and 30 October 1965, p. 1; *Times of Zambia*, 3 November 1965, p. 1; *Rhodesia Herald*, 11 November 1965, p. 3. The British members argued that the only way to determine if an oil airlift was feasible was to make a plan and see if it was feasible; the American members initially resisted this approach until overruled by Washington.
66 "Background to Zambia's Case against the Oil Companies" (Lusaka: Ministry of Legal Affairs, 1977), p. 31, mimeo.; *Times of Zambia*, 28 October 1965, p. 1; ZIS *Press Release* no. 1742/65, 28 October 1965 and no. 1976/65, 6 December 1965; *Sunday Times*, 12 June 1977, p. 63. UDI was delayed a month to enable Rhodesia to build up her own stocks and run down Zambia's.
67 ZIS *Press Release* no. 1608/65, 6 October 1965.

68 Ibid.; UN doc. S/PV. 1260, p. 18, 13 November 1965. On the two agreements, see notes 11 and 43 above.
69 ZIS *Press Release* no. 1608/65, 6 October 1965; *Zambia News*, 10 October 1965, p. 1.
70 *Guardian*, 8 October 1965, p. 17.
71 *Times of Zambia*, 23 October 1965, p. 1, and 21 April 1966, p. 9; *Zambia News*, 10 October 1965, p. 1. See also Christie, *For the President's Eyes Only*, pp. 109–10.
72 Although Congo (Kinshasa) was not renamed Zaire until October 1971, it seems appropriate to refer to its present name even for the earlier period.
73 Good, *UDI*, p. 95.
74 Jan Pettman, *Zambia: Security and Conflict* (London: Julian Friedman, 1974), pp. 195–6; *ARB: PSC*, 1964, p. 165. Following the expiry in December 1964 of the agreement governing Zambian use of the Pedicle road, Kaunda announced a decision to build a bypass road (*Times of Zambia*, 12 July 1965, p. 1).
75 ZIS *Press Release* no. 1719/64, 22 October 1964; *Central African Mail* (Ndola), 12 March 1965, pp. 5, 12; *Zambia News*, 25 April 1965, p. 1.
76 ZIS *Press Release* no. 1109/64, 2 July 1964, p. 7, Pettman, *Zambia*, p. 194; *ARB: PSC*, 1965, p. 255; *Africa 1965*, no. 5, 5 March 1965, p. 6; Hall and Peyman, *Great Uhuru Railway*, pp. 66–8.
77 *Nat. Ass. Deb.* no. 3, cols. 134–7, 142–4, 23 April 1965. The minister of labour and social development (Mundia) insisted that Zambian policy was one of "positive neutrality not to interfere in the affairs of the Congo" (col. 137). Nevertheless, he was acutely embarrassed when, in February 1965, he accidentally encountered Tshombe in the lobby of a Nairobi hotel.
78 ZIS *Press Release* no. 467/65, 26 March 1965; *Africa 1965*, no. 13, 2 July 1965, p. 5; ZIS *Background* no. 36/65, pp. 3–4, 23 September 1965.
79 *Zambia News*, 2 May 1965, p. 7.
80 The Zambian ambassador in Zaire was recalled for "consultations" at this time, but this appears to have been more in connection with the forthcoming OAU summit (Decision No. 13) than with alternative routes (*Zambia Mail*, 15 October 1965, p. 8).
81 Tshombe reportedly spurned an invitation from Ian Smith to undertake joint contingency planning with Rhodesia (rather than Zambia) (*Africa 1965*, no. 20, 15 October 1965, p. 3).
82 The Lobito rail route comprised 620 miles in Zaire operated by the Belgian Compagnie du Chemin de Fer du Bas-Congo au Katanga (BCK) and 835 miles in Angola operated by the Anglo-Portuguese

Companhia do Caminho de Ferro de Benguela (CFB). The real bottleneck was on the BCK sector.
83 *Times of Zambia*, 12 October 1965, p. 7, and 16 October 1965, p. 1; *Zambia News*, 17 October 1965, p. 1.
84 *ARB: PSC*, 1965, p. 396.
85 *The Times*, 14 June 1965, p. 8; *Daily Times* (Lagos), 20 August 1965, p. 3; UN doc. A/PV. 1352, 11 October 1965, pp. 15–16.
86 *Zambia Mail*, 15 October 1965, p. 8. The heads of the other three African missions (in Accra, Lagos, and Addis Ababa) were appointed members of the delegation to the meetings (ZIS *Press Release* no. 1601/65, 6 October 1965). A Ghanaian delegation visited Lusaka, 1–2 October, to brief Kaunda (ZIS *Press Release* no. 1575/65, 1 October 1965).
87 For example, John Mwanakatwe, the minister of education: "There are very many Zambians and other nationals who believe, quite wrongly and without any justification, that this country is vulnerable economically in the event of a Unilateral Declaration of Independence by Rhodesia. On the contrary, I believe that a Rhodesian UDI would precipitate the worst constitutional and economic crisis, which would lead immediately to the emergence of a majority government in that country" (ZIS *Press Release* no. 1744/65, p. 33, 29 October 1965).
88 Thus, Kaunda reassured Zambians, on his departure for Accra, that they had nothing to worry about in the event of UDI as the government had taken "every possible precautionary measure" (*Times of Zambia*, 18 October 1965, p. 1).
89 Good, *UDI*, p. 95. A few weeks earlier Finance Minister Wina, a leading "nationalist," had announced at the Commonwealth Finance Ministers' Conference in Jamaica that the government was "now considering the possibility of pledging that we should match measure for measure or blow for blow even, any sanctions that the United Kingdom should invoke." He added: "Indeed such is the mood and sentiments of our people on this issue that we may have to go even further than that" (*Times of Zambia*, 24 September 1965, p. 1).
90 *Zambia Mail*, 15 October 1965, p. 2.
91 Kaunda succeeded in having the resolution drafted by the OAU foreign ministers debated in closed session, presumably to enable heads of state to speak more freely.
92 ZIS *Press Release* no. 1695, p. 10, 21 October 1965. Kaunda attended only the opening session, as he had to return home for the first anniversary celebrations of independence. It was normal practice in Zambia for the texts of important speeches, such as this one, to be cleared in cabinet in advance.

93 The British minister of defence reported to cabinet (on 7 October) that "the UK was simply not in a position to move in troops [to Rhodesia] unless we first got staging facilities from Zambia and to obtain these now would give Smith the excuse he is seeking" (Barbara Castle, *The Castle Diaries, 1964–70* [London: Weidenfeld and Nicolson, 1984], p. 61). Kaunda argued that British troops would deter UDI, not precipitate it.

94 ZIS *Press Release* no. 1710/65, pp. 22–3, 23 October 1965. Kaunda added that Zambia might support UN or OAU military action in Rhodesia "in certain circumstances."

95 OAU resolutions CM/Res. 62(V), 18 October 1965, and AHG/Res. 25/Rev. II, 22 October 1965; *Guardian*, 23 October 1965, p. 9 and 25 October 1965, p. 1; Nora McKeon, "The African States and the OAU," *International Affairs* 42:3 (July 1966), pp. 402–3; *New York Times*, 23 October 1965, p. 8. A second, secret resolution set up a watchdog Committee of Five (including Zambia). *Jeune Afrique* (28 November 1965, p. 12) alleged that the resolution also asked Zambia (and Malawi) to permit an African army to be stationed on its border with Rhodesia and that Kaunda offered his full cooperation.

96 *Guardian*, 23 October 1965, p. 9; Young, *Rhodesia and Independence*, pp. 254–5.

97 Prime Minister's Office, *Economic Aspects of a Declaration of Independence* (Salisbury: Government Printer, 1965), CSR 15–1965, pp. 3–4. Smith had revived this threat twice: on 8 and 18 October (*Southern Rhodesia: Documents relating to the negotiations between the United Kingdom and Southern Rhodesian Governments, November 1963 to November 1965* [London: HMSO, 1965], Cmnd. 2807, p. 85; *Rhodesia Herald*, 19 October 1965, p. 2). See also *U.S. News and World Report*, 8 November 1965, p. 70.

98 The letter was drafted in cabinet on 20 October, completed next day, and delivered to Lusaka by a Ministry of External Affairs official on the 22nd (*Times of Zambia*, 23 October 1965, p. 1). Actually, Rhodesian Intelligence had planned to leak the letter to Kaunda through John Brumer, their agent in State House, partly to test Kaunda's reactions in advance and perhaps influence his thinking, but also to establish Brumer's credentials. However, as a result of a mix-up, the External Affairs copy arrived first (Christie, *For the President's Eyes Only*, pp. 126–7).

99 ZIS *Press Release* no. 1785/65, pp. 7–9, 7 November 1965.

100 Ibid., no. 1738/65, 27 October 1965.

101 In part, this stemmed from an incident in February 1963, when Kaunda, on a visit to Malawi, was pointedly kept waiting for hours by Hastings Banda. See Fergus Macpherson, *Kenneth Kaunda of Zambia:*

The Times and the Man (Lusaka: Oxford University Press, 1974), p. 406; Kanyama Chiume, *Kwacha* (Nairobi: East African Publishing House, 1975), p. 156; Hall, *High Price of Principles*, p. 37.

102 Subsequent experience showed that shipping costs on the Great East Road–Malawi route were 20 per cent higher than via Lobito or Dar es Salaam, and the average transit time of forty-six days, much longer than by either of the other two routes (fourteen and eleven days respectively) (Richard L. Sklar, *Corporate Power in an African State: The Political Impact of Multinational Mining Companies in Zambia* [Berkeley: University of California Press, 1975], p. 161), despite the fact that the distance by road and rail between Ndola and Beira via Malawi (1,470 miles) was almost identical with that of the all-rail routes to Beira via Salisbury (1,460 miles) and to Lobito (1,470 miles), though 22 per cent longer than the Great North Road to Dar es Salaam (1,200 miles).

103 *Africa 1965*, no. 22, 12 November 1965, p. 4; *Times of Zambia*, 2 October 1965, p. 1, and 30 October 1965, p. 1. Banda was in Nairobi and had to be tracked down there. His second condition was that he be left to award the contracts which, in the case of the Salima transit depot, went to a Salisbury firm.

104 *Times of Zambia*, 4 November 1965, p. 1, 9 November 1965, p. 1, and 11 November 1965, p. 1.

CHAPTER 5

1 Ken Flower, *Serving Secretly: An Intelligence Chief on Record: Rhodesia into Zimbabwe, 1964 to 1981* (Harare: Quest Publishing, 1987), pp. 47–8, 51, 283–6; Denis Healey, *The Time of My Life* (London: Michael Joseph, 1989), p. 332. Although Bottomley had admitted in August that there would be no use of force (at least before UDI), his remarks were neither as categorical nor as authoritative as Wilson's BBC speech.

2 Rhodesia, Proclamation No. 51 of 1965: Emergency Powers Act (Cap.33), *Government Gazette* Extraordinary XLIII:63 (5 November 1965), Supplement, p. 1,289. In addition, some fifteen emergency regulations were promulgated. On the decision of the governor to sign the proclamations (undated) on 3 November, see Flower, *Serving Secretly*, pp. 52–5, Robert Good, *UDI: The International Politics of the Rhodesian Rebellion* (Princeton: Princeton University Press, 1973), pp. 16–17, and British *H.C. Deb.*, vol. 722, col. 744, 10 December 1965. Smith, as he later confessed, lied to the governor when he categorically denied that the declaration presaged a UDI.

3 Flower, *Serving Secretly*, pp. 52, 289; *Rhodesia Herald* (Salisbury), 5

November 1965, pp. 1, 2; *Guardian* (London), 6 November 1965, p. 1. See also Rhodesia *Leg. Ass. Deb.*, vol. 62, cols. 1943–55, 25 November 1965. On 5 November Rhodesia ceased rebroadcasting the BBC news, and two days earlier imposed import controls (*The Times* [London], 6 November 1965, p. 1).

4 Towards the end of October Ian Smyth, Canadian trade commissioner in Salisbury, warned Musakanya to expect UDI on 5 November, a prediction he later changed to 11 November. Smyth was exceedingly well informed as a result of the close personal relations he cultivated with Rhodesian cabinet ministers. He kept Musakanya fully informed of developments. So secret were his intelligence reports that, in some instances, they were not passed on even to Kaunda.

5 *Zambia News* (Ndola), 7 November 1965, p. 1.

6 Zambia Information Services (ZIS) *Press Release* no. 1785/65, pp. 5, 12, 17, 7 November 1965.

7 In declaring that "we are not in a position to say whether or not Mr. Smith will seize independence" (ibid., p. 6), Kaunda was undoubtedly anxious not to alarm the public unnecessarily. Kaunda's meeting with Wilson in Livingstone on 30 October, following the collapse of the Smith-Wilson negotiations, convinced Kaunda that UDI was inevitable. Any residual doubts concerning the imminence of UDI were removed when Roy Lewis, the *Times* correspondent in Salisbury, flew to Lusaka on 9 November to inform Kaunda of the precise date (letter to author, 9 July 1980).

8 Richard Hall in the *Guardian*, 13 November 1965, p. 9. An unsympathetic observer in State House was surprised at the absence of "a mood of gloom and foreboding. On the contrary, there was a heady excitement about ... plus a lot of ill-founded optimism about the imminent collapse of the 'rebel regime'" (Roy Christie, *For the President's Eyes Only: The Story of John Brumer Agent Extraordinary* [Johannesburg: Hugh Keartland, 1971], p. 138).

9 Richard Hall, *High Price of Principles: Kaunda and the White South* (Harmondsworth: Penguin, 1973), p. 126; Good, *UDI*, p. 20. Good records that: "At Chingola, white locomotive engineers ... celebrated the announcement of UDI by prolonged blasts on their whistles. A white labour union meeting at Mufulira mine turned into a 'bloody independence celebration.'" Racial tensions were a major concern immediately after UDI. The Rhodesians had singled out the Copperbelt as a promising target in their efforts to destabilize Zambia.

10 Flower, *Serving Secretly*, p. 57; Hall, *High Price of Principles*, p. 112; Good, *UDI*, p. 20; *Times of Zambia* (Ndola), 13 November 1965, p. 1; *Guardian*, 11 November 1965, p. 1; Colin Legum, ed., *Zambia: Independence and Beyond: The Speeches of Kenneth Kaunda* (London:

319 Notes to pages 106–8

Nelson, 1966), pp. 238–9. See also *Zambia Mail* (Lusaka), 15 October 1965, p. 1.
11 ZIS *Press Release* no. 1829/65, 12 November 1965; *Background* no. 47/65, p. 1, 14 November 1965.
12 ZIS *Press Release* no. 1825/65, 11 November 1965. John Brumer, the Rhodesian Intelligence agent in State House, claims to have toned down the draft text prepared by the attorney general, James Skinner. Brumer told Kaunda that "I don't like the many references in the speech to the possible use of force" (Christie, *For the President's Eyes Only*, pp. 139–40).
13 *Times of Zambia*, 12 November 1965, p. 1; Christie, *For the President's Eyes Only*, pp. 138–45. Among the officials consulted were: State House advisers (John Brumer, Dennis Grennan, Michael Talmage), civil servants (Mark Chona, Valentine Musakanya), and diplomats (Simon Katilungu, Sir Leslie Monson).
14 Good, *UDI*, p. 98; Hall, *High Price of Principles*, p. 129.
15 Good, *UDI*, p. 92. "The British were woefully negligent and incompetent" in having "no contingency economic plans ready for Zambia" when UDI was declared (*New York Times*, 18 August 1966, p. 12). "The storm clouds of UDI had been growing in the sky for nearly two years, yet even fewer preparations were made in London than in Salisbury, where the planning was lackadaisical on any reckoning" (Hall, *High Price of Principles*, p. 119).
16 Good, *UDI*, p. 98.
17 *Times of Zambia*, 12 November 1965, p. 1. Almost the full roster of sixteen ministers was present, including two ministers (A. Wina and Banda) who were en route to Dar es Salaam when UDI was declared and had to be recalled. The purpose of their trip was to finalize the contract for the British-Canadian survey of a rail link to Tanzania. It was initialed two days later (ZIS *Press Release* no. 1812/65, 11 November 1965 and no. 1890/65, 22 November 1965).
18 Rhodesian army chief Sam Putterill claimed that the despatch of white troops to the Zambian border was "a gesture of defiance against the prospects of a British invasion" (Flower, *Serving Secretly*, p. 57).
19 ZIS *Press Release* no. 1815/65, pp. 3, 4, 11 November 1965. Kaunda indicated that the force consisted of seven hundred (later revised to twelve hundred) officers and men of the Rhodesia Light Infantry, detachments of the Special Air Service and the Signals Corps, and "other personnel required to maintain a large body of troops in operational condition," along with "equipment for spanning rivers." Units had been posted to six strategic border points. Also, "in the past week, reconnaissance flights by Rhodesian Air Force aircraft

along the Zambian border have greatly increased. On the tenth of November, flights were carried out over the border by jet, piston-engined and helicopter aircraft." See also *Times of Zambia*, 13 November 1965, p. 1; UN doc. S/PV.1260, 13 November 1965, p. 17.

20 ZIS *Press Release* no. 1829/65, 12 November 1965; Christie, *For the President's Eyes Only*, p. 142. In the interests of speed, the statutory Defence Council, composed of cabinet ministers and military and police chiefs under the chairmanship of the president, was not convened.

21 ZIS *Background* no. 47/65, p. 1, 14 November 1965. Kaunda added that "nothing that is going to be done by my government is going to be a rash action."

22 *Times of Zambia*, 25 November 1965, p. 1; ZIS *Background* no. 49/65, p. 4, 25 November 1965. "On the Zambian side, troops are scrupulously obeying President Kaunda's instructions to avoid any accidental clashes. No defences are being constructed closer than two miles to Rhodesia" (*Daily Telegraph* [London], 16 November 1965, p. 26).

23 ZIS *Press Release* no. 1833/65, 13 November 1965; ZIS *Background* no. 47/65, p. 2, 14 November 1965. Within a few days the initial stringent foreign exchange regulations were partially relaxed (*Africa 1965* no. 23, 26 November 1965, p. 2).

24 Good, *UDI*, pp. 95, 96; *Sunday Times* (London), 5 December 1965, p. 11; ZIS *Background* no. 47/65, pp. 3–4, 14 November 1965.

25 *Zambia Mail*, 22 July 1966, p. 8; UN Security Council resolution S/RES.216, 12 November 1965. The Zambian spokesman called for rejection of the initial British draft as not "adequate to deal with the rebellion" and instead urged support for the stronger African draft (UN Security Council S/PV.1260, 13 November 1965, pp. 18–19).

26 Article 50 reads: "If preventive or enforcement measures against any state are taken by the Security Council, any other state ... which finds itself confronted with special economic problems arising from the carrying out of these measures shall have the right to consult the Security Council with regard to a solution of these problems."

27 John Hatch, *Two African Statesmen: Kaunda of Zambia and Nyerere of Tanzania* (London: Secker and Warburg, 1976), p. 227.

28 Richard L. Sklar, "Zambia's Response to the Rhodesian Unilateral Declaration of Independence," in William Tordoff, ed., *Politics in Zambia* (Manchester: Manchester University Press, 1974), pp. 323, 324; Good, *UDI*, p. 94; Hall, *High Price of Principles*, pp. 118–19; UN Security Council S/PV.1260, 13 November 1965, p. 15; Christie, *For the President's Eyes Only*, pp. 143, 145. Kapwepwe later argued that sanctions had never worked and could never work (OAU doc. ECM/PV.1(VI), 3 December 1965, p. 30).

29 ZIS *Background* no. 47/65, p. 3, 14 November 1965, and no. 48/65, pp. 1–2, 19 November 1965.
30 Good, *UDI*, pp. 96–7; Sklar, "Zambia's Response," p. 325.
31 Hatch, *Two African Statesmen*, p. 227. Good (*UDI*, p. 96) implies that Kaunda abandoned his ambivalence towards sanctions as early as 7 November.
32 ZIS *Press Release* no. 1833/65, 13 November 1965. It is not clear whether the appeal to importers was part of the original cabinet decision or a ministerial embellishment which could be justified as consistent with the general government goal of disengagement from Southern Africa.
33 UN Security Council S/PV.1260, 13 November 1965, pp. 15–19, and S/6929, 13 November 1965. Zambia did not participate in the debates culminating in the adoption of General Assembly resolution A/RES/2024 (XX), 11 November 1965.
34 Good, *UDI*, pp. 95–6, 97, 98; Christie, *For the President's Eyes Only*, p. 145. Barbara Castle cites a Foreign Office telegram which claimed that "Zambia had wanted to break off trade relations with Smith immediately after UDI" (*The Castle Diaries, 1964–70* [London: Weidenfeld and Nicolson, 1985], p. 131. This was confirmed by Kaunda (ZIS *Background* no. 12/66, p. 4, 14 May 1966). Wilson was furious to learn on 17 November that the Ministry of Defence had taken no action to provide Zambia with the military "oil bowsers" that he had promised Kaunda apparently at their meeting in Livingstone on 30 October (*Castle Diaries*, p. 69).
35 ZIS *Press Release* no. 1833/65, 13 November 1965; *Times of Zambia*, 17 November 1965, p. 11, 2 December 1965, p. 11, and 8 January 1966, p. 7.
36 On British policy on the use of force in Rhodesia, see Douglas G. Anglin and Timothy M. Shaw, *Zambia's Foreign Policy: Studies in Diplomacy and Dependence* (Boulder: Westview Press, 1979), pp. 113–21, 136–44, 146–54; James Callaghan, *Time and Chance* (London: Collins, 1987), p. 145; Healey, *The Time of My Life*, pp. 332–3; David Owen, *The Politics of Defence* (London: Cape, 1972), p. 116.
37 OAU doc. ECM/PV.1 (VI), 3 December 1965, p. 29. This was a view shared by Malcolm MacDonald, Britain's roving ambassador to Africa, provided the operation were handled imaginatively. Ken Flower was convinced that "senior Rhodesian military officers would not fight against British forces," but "it could not be guaranteed that there would be no bloodshed, for many of the middle and lower ranks of the Rhodesian Light Infantry (RLI), an all-white regular battalion, would willingly 'jump into the Makabusi' (a muddy river

on the outskirts of the city) for Smith, even if this meant going against their seniors." He also dismissed the widely propagated view that British commanders would refuse to fight Rhodesian forces with whom they had close personal service links (*Serving Secretly*, pp. 49–51, 55). ZIS *Press Release* no. 1710/65, 23 October 1965, pp. 22–3, and no. 1993/65, 8 December 1965, p. 1; *Daily Mail* (London), 8 December 1965, p. 6; *Sunday Times*, 5 December 1965, p. 11.

38 ZIS *Press Release* no. 1710/65, 23 October 1965, pp. 23, 24.

39 Christie, *For the President's Eyes Only*, p. 143; *Guardian*, 17 November 1965, p. 11; *Rhodesia Herald*, 19 November 1965, p. 9.

40 ZIS *Background* no. 50/65, p. 1, 3 December 1965; ZIS *Press Release* no. 1911/65, 26 November 1965. According to Good (*UDI*, p. 96), Kaunda warned Wilson that "the longer the rebellion continued, the greater was ... the danger of economic strangulation by a racist and rebellious regime deeply antithetical to everything Zambia stood for."

41 Harold Wilson, *Personal Record: The Labour Government 1964–1970* (Boston: Little Brown, 1971), p. 182.

42 Southern Rhodesia Act, 1965, 13 & 14 Eliz. II, c.76 and Southern Rhodesia (Constitution) Order, 1965, SI 1965 No. 1952, 16 November 1965.

43 ZIS *Background* no. 47/65, p. 3, 14 November 1965.

44 Christie, *For the President's Eyes Only*, p. 145; ZIS *Background* no. 47/65, p. 3, 14 November 1965. Following the Nairobi summit, Nyerere said the four presidents were "waiting to see what Britain is going to do." He added that if "we feel that Britain is not doing anything worth while ... it may be necessary to take the matter out of British hands" (*Rhodesia Herald*, 18 November 1965, p. 7).

45 This was the implication of Wilson's messages to Kaunda on 14 and 16 November 1965. Joe Garner, permanent under-secretary in the Commonwealth Relations Office at the time, defends the legal charade as necessary to "provide for all eventualities," even though it remained a complete "dead letter" (*The Commonwealth Office, 1925–68* [London: Heinemann, 1978], p. 392).

46 *Rhodesia Herald*, 7 December 1965, p. 3. "About 95 per cent of [white Zambian officers] are Rhodesian or South African. Many are on the Rhodesian Army Reserve" (*Daily Telegraph*, 16 November 1965, p. 26).

47 ZIS *Background* no. 47/65, p. 1, 14 November 1965, no. 48/65, p. 2, 17 November 1965, and no. 50/65, p. 1, 2 December 1965. Kaunda claims that "we thought this over very carefully," *Daily Mail*, 8 December 1965, pp. 1, 6.

48 Christie, *For the President's Eyes Only*, p. 145.

49 Wilson ruled out the use of force "unless, of course, our troops are asked for [by the governor] to preserve law and order and to avert a tragic action, subversion, murder, and so on" (*H.C. Deb.*, vol. 720, col. 360, 11 November 1965).
50 ZIS *Background* no. 47/65, pp. 4–5, 14 November 1965, and no. 48/65, pp. 2, 3, 17 November 1965; *Sunday Times*, 5 December 1965, p. 11.
51 On plans to set up a government-in-exile, see *Africa 1964* (London), no. 13, 26 June 1964, p. 4, no. 15, 24 July 1964, p. 2; *Africa 1965*, no. 18, 10 September 1965, p. 3; *The Times*, 6 November 1965, p. 1.
52 Christie, *For the President's Eyes Only*, p. 145; Good, *UDI*, p. 96. There is some uncertainty concerning the date of Kaunda's letter; Good says "almost immediately" after UDI, Patrick Keatley says "two days after UDI" (*Guardian*, 3 December 1965, p. 1), and Brumer implies three days after, in which case it crossed with Wilson's letter of 14 November.
53 Good, *UDI*, p. 97. On his departure from Salisbury on 12 November, British High Commissioner Jack Johnston assured Ken Flower that "we'll be back inside three months. Sanctions will have worked and legality be restored" (*Serving Secretly*, pp. 57–8).
54 It is not clear if the meeting took place Tuesday evening, 16 November or, more probably, on the Wednesday. The Zambian vice-president and foreign minister had been delayed in their return from Nairobi and so missed the regular Tuesday morning cabinet meeting.
55 Hall claims there was "a considerable conflict between Kaunda and Kapwepwe over the former's announcement, in anticipation of the OAU Defence Committee's meeting, that he was asking Britain to send in a military force" (*High Price of Principles*, pp. 127–8). Kapwepwe subsequently (20 November) stated that he supported the decision (*Zambia Mail*, 26 November 1965, "Mail Magazine," p. 12).
56 *Guardian*, 17 November 1965, p. 11, and 23 November 1965, p. 11. There was also talk of "a political boycott against London" (ibid., 16 November 1965, p. 11).
57 Ibid., 23 November 1965, p. 11. In reply to a press inquiry, Kaunda indicated that he would prefer British troops to take over Kariba in advance of any cut-off of power (ZIS *Background* no. 48/65, p. 2, 17 November 1965).
58 ZIS *Press Release* no. 1857/65, 17 November 1965, p. 1.
59 *Times of Zambia*, 23 November 1965, p. 1.
60 Anglin and Shaw, *Zambia's Foreign Policy*, pp. 127–8.
61 ZIS *Background* no. 47/65, p. 3, 14 November 1965.
62 Kwame Nkrumah, *Rhodesia File* (London: Panaf, 1976), p. 96–7. The

other countries contacted were the Congo, Guinea, Sudan, Tanzania, Uganda and Zaire.
63 OAU Resolutions AHG/Res. 25/Rev. II, 22 October 1965 and AHG/Res. 39, II, 25 October 1965. The latter ("secret") resolution was published in *Jeune Afrique* (Paris), no. 257, 28 November 1965, p. 12. *Jeune Afrique* claimed that, at Accra, Kaunda responded positively to a request to permit an OAU force to operate against Rhodesia from Zambian territory.
64 *Guardian*, 20 November 1965, pp. 1, 14, 23 November 1965, p. 11; *Times*, 20 November 1965, p. 7. "The Egyptians, Algerians and Ethiopians are the three governments most determined to see concrete action with military units" (*Guardian*, 24 November 1965, p. 11).
65 OAU doc. ECM/PV.1 (VI), 3 December 1965, pp. 14–18; *Guardian*, 23 November 1965, p. 11, 24 November 1965, p. 11 and 25 November 1965, p. 1; T.O. Elias, "The Legality of the OAU Council of Ministers' Resolution on Rhodesia in December 1965," *Nigerian Law Journal* 3 (1969), pp. 4–5. The subcommittee comprised the Kenyan foreign minister Joseph Murumbi, Egyptian under-secretary for foreign affairs, Dr L. Zayat (both hawks), and Zambian minister of home affairs, Mainza Chona. Mohamed Sahnoun, OAU assistant secretary general at the time, claims that proposals for an OAU army never envisaged an invasion of Rhodesia but only the provision of protection to Zambia against Rhodesian retaliation as a result of incursions by liberation movements based in Zambia (interview, 9 December 1980).
66 Personal interview with Ali M. Simbule, Zambian high commissioner to Tanzania, Dar es Salaam, 30 November 1965; Hall, *High Price of Principles*, pp. 128, 134. At the earlier eastern African summit on 15 November, Nyerere, curiously, had supported Obote (who advocated an OAU force) in principle and Kenyatta (who opposed it) in practice.
67 Hall, *High Price of Principles*, pp. 127–8; ZIS *Press Release* no. 1883/65, 22 November 1965; *Rhodesia Herald*, 23 November 1965, p. 4; *Times of Zambia*, 22 November 1965, p. 1, which refers to there being several ministers in attendance at State House.
68 Anglin and Shaw, *Zambia's Foreign Policy*, pp. 132–3.
69 Simbule interview. John Roberts, leader of the white opposition in Parliament, warned Kaunda that, if the Ethiopians landed at Ndola, the whites would flee through Chingola. Experiences in Zaire and in Tunisia (with Algerian guerillas) were very much in the minds of Zambian leaders.
70 Christie, *For the President's Eyes Only*, p. 145; ZIS *Press Release* no. 1857/65, 17 November 1965 p. 1; ZIS *Background* no. 48/65, p. 1,

17 November 1965 and no. 50/65, pp. 3–4, 2 December 1965. "Offers of troops are flowing in daily," Kaunda declared. "Only yesterday I received another one and ... for the first time this was from a non-Commonwealth country in Africa... Outside Africa a number of offers have already been made." (ZIS *Background* no. 49/65, p. 3, 17 November 1965). Zdenek Cervenka claims that Algeria, Egypt, Ethiopia, Ghana, Ivory Coast, Nigeria, Sudan and Zaire "pledged to send their armies to fight the Smith regime" (*The Unfinished Quest for Unity* [London: Julian Friedmann, 1977], p. 41). Actually, only Tanzania formally designated a unit – two companies – for service (only) in Zambia (Anglin and Shaw, *Zambia's Foreign Policy*, pp. 130–2).

71 OAU doc. ECM/PV.1 (VI), 3 December 1965, pp. 45, 46, also p. 29, and ECM/PV.2 (VI), 4 December 1965, pp. 50–1; ECM/res.14 (VI), 5 December 1965.

72 Interview with Maj.-Gen. Nathan A. Aferi, Ghana's chief of defence staff, who headed the mission (Lagos, 15 June 1971). The mission, which also included Nigerian, Egyptian, and Algerian members, visited Zambia from 6 to 12 February 1966 (*Times of Zambia*, 11 February 1966, p. 11).

73 Although Wilson dismissed OAU rhetoric as mere "masturbation," he was greatly agitated by the danger of "Egyptian MiGs and Ethiopian and Congolese troops" in Zambia. "The additional danger was the assassination of whites in Kenya and elsewhere by Chinese-trained terrorists" (Hugh Cudlipp's notes of a meeting with Wilson, 3 December 1965, *The Cecil King Diaries, 1965–1970* [London: Jonathan Cape, 1972], p. 43.)

74 See notes 36 and 37.

75 *Guardian*, 7 December 1965, p. 9, and 11 December 1965, p. 9; *The Times*, 26 November 1965, p. 13; *Cecil King Diaries*, p. 45; *Rhodesia Herald*, 2 December 1965, p. 1.

76 *Guardian*, 2 December 1965, p. 1.

77 *Cecil King Diaries*, pp. 44, 45; *H.C. Deb.*, vol. 720, col. 637, 12 November 1965; Wilson, *Personal Record*, pp. 181, 223; *Guardian*, 27 November 1965, p. 1, and 21 December 1965, p. 5; *Financial Times*, 18 November 1965, p. 9; *Daily Telegraph*, 4 December 1965, p. 18. Wilson had positioned the aircraft carrier HMS *Eagle* off the Tanzanian coast "so that Sea Vixens could blow up [Zambian] airfields" to prevent Egyptian MiGs landing (*Cecil King Diaries*, p. 45).

78 Hall, *High Price of Principles*, p. 134; *Financial Times*, 17 November 1965, p. 19. "Russia had no intention of making sacrifices to restore British colonialism in Rhodesia, assure an uninterrupted flow of copper to the West, protect foreign investments, or even support

Zambia, which, initially at least, she regarded as a neocolonial dependency of a capitalist mining empire" (Anglin and Shaw, *Zambia's Foreign Policy*, p. 136).

79 Castle, *Castle Diaries*, p. 72; *Keesing's Contemporary Archives, 1965*, p. 21136; Wilson, *Personal Record*, p. 182; *H.C. Deb.*, vol. 721, cols, 1433, 1435, 1 December 1965. According to an "authoritative source," the letter "did not contain an ultimatum to Britain that, if it did not send troops, Zambia would then call for other countries' assistance" (Reuters dispatch from Lusaka, 27 November 1965).

80 Castle, *Castle Diaries*, p. 73. *Guardian*, 27 November 1965, p. 1; Good, *UDI*, pp. 98, 99. The home affairs minister accused Britain of collusion with Rhodesia over UDI (*Zambia Mail*, 26 November 1965, p. 12). In denying this, Kaunda was constrained to admit that events leading to UDI were "so curious that ... one would wonder whether there was any connivance" (Zambia *Nat. Ass. Deb.* no. 5, col. 95, 9 December 1965). See also UN doc. S/PV.1260, p. 16, 13 November 1965.

81 *H.C. Deb.*, vol. 721, cols. 1430, 1433, 1 December 1965.

82 Good, *UDI*, p. 98; *Times of Zambia*, 24 November 1965, p. 1, and 25 November 1965, p. 1; *The Times*, 24 November 1965, p. 10, and 25 November 1965, p. 10. Good (p. 98) says MacDonald "came away impressed with the courage and responsibility of Zambia's leaders in the face of the most appalling uncertainties."

83 *H.C. Deb.*, vol. 721, col. 1435, 1 December 1965. Kaunda conceded that other OAU members were pressuring him (ZIS *Background* no. 49/65, p. 3, 25 November 1965 and no. 50/65, p. 4, 3 December 1965). He was considerably agitated by "the difficulties posed by the violent pressures" from the OAU (*Sunday Times*, 5 December 1965, p. 11).

84 The two messages were actually dispatched on 1 December, a day before the final Zambian decision (*Financial Times*, 2 December 1965, p. 16; *Zambia Mail*, 10 December 1965, p. 5), thus suggesting that they may have been Trollope ploys designed to pressure Kaunda. On 30 November the Tanzanian cabinet rejected a British request for overflight rights for troop transport aircraft en route to Zambia (*Financial Times*, 3 December 1965, p. 19). See also *Guardian*, 30 November 1965, p. 11. There were also rumours that the OAU Defence Committee had telegraphed Kaunda to urge rejection of any restrictions on his right to invite troops from other friendly sources.

85 *The Times*, 29 November 1965, p. 10; *Daily Telegraph* (London), 29 November 1965, p. 1.

86 *H.C. Deb.*, vol. 721, col. 1433, 1 December 1965; Good, *UDI*, p. 99, where the date is inaccurately given as 29 November; *Times of Zam-*

bia, 1 December 1965, p. 1; *Guardian*, 1 December 1965, p. 11 and 3 December 1965, p. 1; *Daily Telegraph*, 1 December 1965, p. 1. The duration of the two Kaunda-MacDonald meetings appears to have been 1 hour and 2½ hours.
87 Bottomley was accompanied by Sir Arthur Snelling, deputy undersecretary, Commonwealth Office, and Maj.-Gen. Fitzgeorge Balfour, director of military operations, Ministry of Defence.
88 *Times of Zambia*, 3 December 1965, p. 1. One session lasted from 9 p.m. until nearly midnight (ibid., 2 December 1965, p. 1).
89 *Guardian*, 2 December 1965, p. 1.
90 *H.C. Deb.*, vol. 721, col. 1433, 1 December 1965, and col. 1641, 2 December 1965; *Guardian*, 1 December 1965, p. 1. Primitive communications were a constant diplomatic constraint; on the evening of 11 November, Kaunda was forced to route his telephone calls to Obote, Nyerere, and Kenyatta through Salisbury (Christie, *For the President's Eyes Only*, p. 138).
91 "The only discussion [in cabinet] had been on ways of inducing Britain to change her mind" and authorize its troops to seize Kariba (*Daily Telegraph*, 4 December 1965, p. 1).
92 ZIS *Background* no. 49/65, pp. 2–3, 25 November 1965; *Times of Zambia*, 2 December 1965, p. 1.
93 "The hope that a limited operation south of the [Zambezi] might commit Britain unequivocally to a swift military solution of the UDI problem is less present in [Kaunda's] mind than in some of his more extreme cabinet ministers [though] he cannot have neglected it entirely" (*Sunday Times*, 5 December 1965, p. 11).
94 *H.C. Deb.*, vol. 721, cols. 1430, 1433–4, 1439–0, 1 December 1965; Castle, *Castle Diaries*, p. 73. Wilson added that, "while we are putting forces ... on a defensive basis, it must be clear that we have the power to provide a deterrent to a cutting-off of the electric supply and we must be prepared to use that power" since "Rhodesian [sic] copper is absolutely vital to our own industrial production" (*H.C. Deb.*, vol. 721, cols. 1433–4). Later, he explained that he would "take whatever action was necessary in order to fulfil the deterrent threat ... If that did mean a limited operation, we should be prepared to undertake that operation" (col. 1440).
95 *Nat. Ass. Deb.*, no. 5, col. 96, 9 December 1965; ZIS *Background* no. 50/65, p. 1, 3 December 1965.
96 *Sunday Times*, 5 December 1965, p. 11. Although Wilson continued to mislead Kaunda (and Nyerere) by assertions that he had never completely excluded the possibility of using force, it is clear that the most he ever contemplated was "simple sabotage of the Special Services type – 'two electricians with a pair of pliers'" (*Cecil King Diaries*, p. 44). See also Anglin and Shaw, *Zambia's Foreign Policy*, pp. 143–4.

97 *Rhodesia Herald*, 2 December 1965, p. 1. "It is feared in Whitehall that if Britain loses the race, mounting African extremist pressure may lead to the overthrow of President Kaunda." In a curiously convoluted statement, Kaunda defended the British against BBC claims that they were "trying to beat the OAU conference" (ZIS *Background* no. 50/65, p. 4, 3 December 1965). Cf. Good, *UDI*, pp. 100, 101; *Guardian*, 2 December 1965, p. 1.

98 Good, *UDI*, p. 99.

99 Based on Anglin and Shaw, *Zambia's Foreign Policy*, p. 40; *Guardian*, 2 December 1965, p. 1; ZIS *Background* no. 50/65, pp. 2–3, 3 December 1965.

100 *Rhodesia Herald*, 30 November 1965, p. 1; *Guardian*, 30 November 1965, p. 10; *Times of Zambia*, 1 December 1965, p. 1.

101 *H.C. Deb.*, vol 721, col. 1430, 1 December 1965; Wilson, *Personal Record*, p. 182; Castle, *Castle Diaries*, p. 73; *Times of Zambia*, 4 December 1965, p. 2. Subsequently, Kaunda asked for "a date in writing" when British troops would seize Kariba (ZIS *Background* no. 52/65, p. 3, 12 December 1965).

102 Although an official spokesman announced that the cabinet was unanimous in its rejection of the British troop offer (*Daily Telegraph*, 4 December 1965, p. 1), the debate that preceded the decision revealed deep divisions among ministers. These were perhaps less dramatic than some press accounts suggested, especially the alleged Kaunda-Kapwepwe split on this and other issues. Richard Hall claims that Arthur Wina, but not Kaunda, was among the minority prepared to trust the British, that Kamanga was "docile," but that Kapwepwe was "adamant" (*High Price of Principles*, pp. 128, 130). Another report states that Kapwepwe could "count on the support of at least four other cabinet members in his opposition to President Kaunda's policies" (*Daily Telegraph*, 6 December 1965, p. 24, 4 December 1965, p. 18). Among the militants were Sikota Wina, Nalumino Mundia, and Justin Chimba. See also Good, *UDI*, p. 104.

103 *Zambia Mail*, 3 December 1965, p. 1; Good, *UDI*, pp. 99, 101. A subsidiary British argument was the claim propagated by the rebel regime that the Kariba installations had already been mined. As so often in the case of Rhodesia, British intelligence here proved faulty (Hall, *High Price of Principles*, p. 139; *New York Times*, 9 December 1965, p. 6; *Times of Zambia*, 6 December 1965, p. 1, and 9 December 1965, p. 1; *Sunday Times*, 5 December 1965, p. 11).

104 Good, *UDI*, pp. 99–100; *Guardian*, 1 December 1965, p. 11; *Africa 1965*, no., 24, 10 December 1965, p. 2; Anglin and Shaw, *Zambia's Foreign Policy*, p. 139.

105 *Guardian*, 3 December 1965, p. 1. The full cabinet comprised four-

teen ministers in addition to the president and vice-president. Mainza Chona was among the absentees.
106 *Guardian*, 2 December 1965, p. 1 and 3 December 1965, p. 1; *Daily Telegraph*, 6 December 1965, p. 24.
107 At the opening session of the OAU Council of Ministers, Kapwepwe announced (on instructions) that "we have refused to have [British] troops stationed in Zambia unless they are in transit on their way to Kariba" (applause) (OAU doc. ECM/PV.1 [VI], 3 December 1965, p. 27).
108 *Guardian*, 4 December 1965, p. 9, and 6 December 1965, p. 10.
109 ZIS *Background* no. 50/65, pp. 1–4, 3 December 1965, and no. 52/65, pp. 1–5, 12 December 1965; *Daily Mail*, 8 December 1965, pp. 1, 6; ZIS *Press Release* no. 1977/65, 6 December 1965; *Guardian*, 9 December 1965, p. 1; *Nat. Ass. Deb.*, no. 5, cols. 95–8, 9 December 1965. Kaunda warned that any Rhodesian interference with jointly owned common services would be "a declaration of war on Zambia and I will not hesitate to order my country into action" (ibid., col. 93). Kaunda wrote to Wilson at least once and possibly twice between 5 and 8 December (*Times of Zambia*, 10 December 1965, p. 1; *Guardian*, 11 December 1965, p. 9). He reportedly gave Wilson ten days to comply with his request for troops for Kariba (*Financial Times*, 9 December 1965, p. 1). See also *Financial Times*, 21 December 1965, p. 6; *Times of Zambia*, 22 December 1965, p. 1; *Guardian*, 5 January 1966, p. 11.
110 *Times of Zambia*, 10 December 1965, p. 1; *Daily Telegraph*, 7 December 1965, p. 1. According to one report, Kaunda's letter of 8 December argued that only a British military presence would enable him to hold out against pressures within his cabinet for an appeal to the OAU. Kaunda was allegedly prepared to accept the British force subject to an undertaking that it would invest Kariba if and when there was a threat to the dam. (*Daily Telegraph*, 9 December 1965, p. 1).
111 Anglin and Shaw, *Zambia's Foreign Policy*, pp. 142, 145–6, and Decision No. 30. Denis Healey, British minister of defence, claims inaccurately that Britain "sent soldiers to guard the Kariba Dam" (*The Time of My Life*, p. 332).
112 *H.C. Deb.*, vol. 721, co. 14, 33, 1 December 1965. Wilson defined his purpose as "to fill up the Zambian airfields with [Javelins] so that Egyptian MiGs could not land" (*Cecil King Diary*, p. 45). Again, in reporting to cabinet on 29 November, he said that he "personally didn't think Smith was going to attack Zambia, but [sending the RAF to Zambia] was a good excuse for giving us squatters' rights and keeping other people out" (Castle, *Castle Diaries*, p. 71). Chapman

Pincher reported that "officially the jets were being sent out to defend Zambia's airspace, but in fact their purpose was simply to occupy the airfields and so prevent the Russians from doing so" (*Inside Story: A Documentary of the Pursuit of Power* [London: Sidgwick and Jackson, 1978], p. 29). See also *Guardian*, 4 December 1965, p. 9, and 6 December 1965, p. 10.

113 *Sunday Times*, 5 December 1965, p. 11; Wilson, *Personal Record*, p. 182; OAU doc. ECM/PV.1 (VI), 3 December 1965, p. 27. There was some speculation that Rhodesia might attempt to seize a border town, such as Livingstone. However, in response to a press inquiry, "Do you fear an attack on Zambia?" Kaunda replied: "From the air, yes. Not on the ground. There they know they cannot succeed by reason of our ground forces here" (*Daily Mail*, 8 December 1965, p. 6). Two days later he warned of "probable and serious damage from the air" (*Nat. Ass. Deb.*, no. 5, col. 95, 9 December 1965). He also worried about a Stanleyville-type parachute descent on the Copperbelt by Rhodesia's crack Special Air Service Regiment, on the pretext of protecting whites. C Squadron of the SAS had been stationed in Ndola up to the end of the Federation (*Africa 1965* no. 15, 30 July 1965, p. 4).

114 ZIS *Background* no. 50/65, p. 1, 3 December 1965; *H.C. Deb.*, vol. 721, cols. 1429, 1433, 1 December 1965.

115 *Zambia-Rhodesia: The Economic Ties and Their Financial Effects: The History to the End of Federation* (Lusaka: Ministry of Finance, June 1968), pp. 14–18, mimeo. The estimated compensation owing to Zambia for movable air force assets alone was $6 million.

116 The Zambian request had initially specified that the number of planes "should not exceed thirty" (OAU doc. ECM/PV.1 [VI], 3 December 1965, p. 27).

117 *Times of Zambia*, 8 December 1965, p. 1; *The Times*, 30 December 1965, p. 6. The existing radar could not detect incoming aircraft until they were virtually over the airport. Moreover, planes in Zambian air space were subject to rebel operational control from Salisbury. This included the Javelins (*Daily Telegraph*, 4 December 1965, p. 13; *Sunday Times*, 5 December 1965, p. 11).

118 *Guardian*, 30 December 1965, p. 7.

119 *Daily Telegraph*, 4 December 1965, p. 18, and 6 December 1965, p. 19; *Times of Zambia*, 6 December 1965, p. 1, and 8 December, 1965, p. 1; Good, *UDI*, p. 104. Hall argues that this was the only way Kapwepwe could "find to voice his displeasure" with the decision which had been taken in his absence (*High Price of Principles*, p. 131). The British defence minister admitted that the Javelins were not first-strike weapons, but he insisted that they could take out the

Hunters and would later be replaced by Lightnings (Castle, *Castle Diaries*, pp. 71–2).

120 Tanzania Information Services *Press Release* C/3583/65, 1 December 1965; *Daily Telegraph*, 3 December 1965, p. 32; *Cecil King Diary*, pp. 44–5; *H.C. Deb.*, vol. 721, col. 1641, 2 December 1965. Nyerere later conceded that RAF protection was essential (*Freedom and Socialism*, p. 126).

121 Kapwepwe revealed that the British initially insisted that RAF protection was conditional on Zambia undertaking not to invite in troops or air forces "from the OAU or from any other part of the world." He added: "We turned them down; we cannot accept those conditions ... We would like to die as people with principles" (OAU doc. ECM/PV.1 [VI], 3 December 1965, pp. 27–8).

122 Kapwepwe announced on arrival in Addis Ababa (by which time agreement had been reached with the British) that: "Zambia is not accepting British conditions that, once RAF planes go in, no other troops should be asked to come to Zambia from anywhere else. Permission ... will be given to fly to Zambia when this point is cleared up. Britain is still hedging around. As long as this continues, we are not accepting the planes" (Reuters dispatch from Addis Ababa, 3 December 1965). On his return to Lusaka he congratulated Kaunda for standing firm "without selling his sovereignty to Britain" (*Rhodesia Herald*, 6 December 1965, p. 1).

123 *Nat. Ass. Deb.*, no. 5, col. 96, 9 December 1965.

124 *Guardian*, 6 December 1965, p. 10; *The Times*, 3 December 1965, p. 1.

125 ZIS *Background* no. 50/65, p. 1, 3 December 1965; *Nat. Ass. Deb.*, no. 5, cols. 96, 97, 9 December 1965; *Guardian*, 11 December 1965, p. 9; *H.C. Deb.*, vol. 722, col. 334, 16 December 1965. The final cost to the British was $7,420,000, including $3,780,000 to airlift fuel into Zambia for the Javelins (*H.C. Deb.*, vol. 734, col. 45, 20 October 1966).

126 Wilson, *Personal Record*, p. 182; *Guardian*, 23 November 1965, pp. 11. The RAF radar coverage extended only to the Rhodesian border. The former head of the RRAF claimed that RAF bombers could have maintained a permanent watch over the RRAF's two airbases, thus neutralizing the RRAF "without a shot being fired in anger" (Flower, *Serving Secretly*, p. 52).

127 Castle, *Castle Diaries*, p. 71.

128 *H.C. Deb.*, vol. 721, col. 1440, 1 December 1965; *Times of Zambia*, 3 December 1965, p. 1; *Guardian*, 3 December 1965, p. 1; ZIS *Background* no. 50/65, p. 3, 2 December 1965, and no. 52/65, p. 1, 12 December 1965.

129 A resolution calling for the cancellation of the agreement and the immediate withdrawal of the RAF was introduced in caucus but not adopted (*Guardian*, 7 December 1965, p. 9).
130 *Times of Zambia*, 25 January 1966, p. 7 and 16 August 1966, p. 7; *Zambia News*, 8 May 1966, p. 1.
131 ZIS *Press Release* no. 1557/66, 24 August 1966; *Guardian*, 24 August 1966, p. 17; *Daily Telegraph*, 26 August 1966, p. 1.

CHAPTER 6

1 The government specifically repudiated press reports that it had abandoned its request for British troops to guard Kariba (Zambia Information Services [ZIS] *Press Release* no. 1977/65, 6 December 1965; *Background* no. 52/65, p. 3, 12 December 1965). On the contrary, Kaunda renewed his appeal in a letter to Wilson on 8 December (*The Times* [London], 9 December 1965, p. 10; *Guardian* [London], 9 December 1965, p. 1).
2 For informed speculation on the last scenario, see Richard L. Sklar, *Corporate Power in an African State: The Political Impact of Multinational Mining Companies in Zambia* (Berkeley: University of California Press, 1975), pp. 153–4.
3 The original members, in addition to Kapwepwe, were Grey Zulu and Solomon Kalulu along with Goundrey. In May Reuben Kamanga and Dingiswayo Banda were added.
4 *Africa 1965* (London) no. 20, 15 October 1965, p. 2; ZIS *Press Release* no. 255/66, p. 2, 10 February 1966. Ian Aldridge, an under-secretary in the Cabinet Office, headed the CPO until his retirement in October. Sir Norman Kipping, retiring director general of the Federation of British Industries, appears to have recommended an organization along the lines of the CPO, as restructured in mid-December, during the course of his visit to Lusaka, 21–27 November 1965.
5 *Observer* (London), 5 December 1965, p. 2; *Guardian*, 26 November 1965, p. 19, and 7 December 1965, p. 9; *Zambia News* (Ndola), 28 November 1965, p. 7; *Zambia Mail* (Lusaka), 7 January 1966, p. 4.
6 ZIS *Background* no. 47/65, pp. 2–3, 14 November 1965; Zambia *Nat. Ass. Deb.* no. 5. cols. 99–100, 9 December 1965, and cols. 241–2, 16 December 1965; *Guardian*, 11 December 1965, p. 9. Kaunda convened a special UNIP parliamentary caucus on 6 December, "to give full details of what steps government has taken ever since UDI to safeguard the sovereign integrity of the Republic and also to brief MPs on the latest talks and exchange of letters between the President and the British government" (ZIS *Press Release* no. 1951/65, 3 December 1965). He evidently succeeded in persuading members to

reject a motion calling for an immediate RAF withdrawal (*Guardian*, 7 December 1965, p. 1).
7 *Guardian*, 24 December 1965, p. 9. The rate of exodus of whites was watched closely and anxiously as the nearest equivalent to a Gallup poll of expatriate opinion.
8 OAU doc. ECM/Res. 13 (VI), para. 2.
9 "I have always maintained," Kaunda declared, "that Rhodesia is a British responsibility and as such it is Britain's duty to get us out of the situation caused by the illegal declaration of independence" (ZIS *Press Release* no. 1995/65, 8 December 1965).
10 *Daily Mail* (London), 8 December 1965, p. 6. Later he asked: "If we don't have the cooperation of Britain, how are we going to fight Africa's battle?" (ZIS *Background* no. 56/65, p. 4, 30 December 1965).
11 J.D.B. Miller, *Survey of Commonwealth Affairs: Problems of Expansion and Attrition, 1953–1969* (London: Oxford University Press, 1974), pp. 214–15; Arnold Smith with Clyde Sanger, *Stitches in Time: The Commonwealth in World Politics* (London: André Deutsch, 1981), pp. 31–2; *Africa 1965* no. 24, 10 December 1965, p. 1. Kapwepwe did, however, insist that the resolution should not be implemented immediately, but be delayed for "two weeks or one month" to enable Britain to respond (OAU doc. ECM/PV.1 [VI], 3 December 1965, p. 58).
12 *The Times*, 6 December 1965, p. 8. Kapwepwe is reported to have persuaded a reluctant Ghana also to withdraw from the Commonwealth, which it attempted to do, until talked out of it by the Commonwealth secretary general. The *Verbatim Records* of the meeting contain no mention of the issue of Commonwealth withdrawal being raised.
13 *The Times*, 9 December 1965, p. 9; Robert C. Good, *UDI: The International Politics of the Rhodesian Rebellion* (Princeton: Princeton University Press, 1973), p. 104.
14 There is some evidence to suggest that initially Kaunda, like Kapwepwe, was persuaded by Nyerere's eloquence – until the British intervened to warn of the consequences. Kaunda later described the OAU decision, somewhat contemptuously, as the "lightest of measures" it might have adopted (ZIS *Background* no. 56/65, p. 4, 30 December 1965).
15 ZIS *Press Release* no. 2031/65, 15 December 1965.
16 *Rhodesia Herald* (Salisbury) 6 December 1965, p. 1; *The Times*, 9 December 1965, p. 9; ZIS *Background* no. 56/65, p. 4, 30 December 1965; T.O. Elias, "The Legality of the OAU Council of Ministers' Resolution on Rhodesia in December 1965," *Nigerian Law Journal* 3 (1969), pp. 6–12.

17 Julius Nyerere, *Freedom and Socialism: Selections from Writings and Speeches, 1965–1967* (Dar es Salaam: Oxford University Press, 1968), pp. 129–32.
18 *Rhodesia Herald*, 6 December 1965, p. 1.
19 *New York Times*, 9 December 1965, p. 5, and 12 December 1965, p. 11; *The Times*, 13 December 1965, p. 7; ZIS *Background* no. 52/65, p. 3, 12 December 1965. George Ivan Smith, a former special representative of the UN secretary general, conveyed the concerns of Kaunda (whom he met on 7 December) to Nyerere on 9 December (personal interview, London, 22 January 1980). The Tanzanian decision to break relations with Britain was taken by Nyerere personally, without consulting his cabinet and despite the opposition of some ministers (see William Tordoff, ed., *Politics in Zambia* [Manchester: Manchester University Press, 1974], pp. 77, 177).
20 Arthur Bottomley, British *H.C. Deb.*, vol. 722, col. 388, 7 December 1965; *The Times*, 6 December 1965, p. 8; Harold Wilson, *Personal Record: The Labour Government 1964–1970* (Boston: Little Brown, 1971), pp. 185–6. Bottomley's insinuations infuriated Kaunda (ZIS *Background* no. 52/65, p. 4, 12 December 1965). Wilson addressed the General Assembly on 16 December.
21 *Times of Zambia* (Ndola), 7 December 1965, p. 1; *Zambia News*, 12 December 1965, p. 1. The caucus, somewhat ambiguously, "noted with satisfaction" the OAU resolution.
22 *Rhodesia Herald*, 11 December 1965, p. 1; *Zambia Mail*, 17 December 1965, p. 5; *Guardian*, 11 December 1965, p. 1. Six heads of mission were recalled: three from Africa (Accra, Lagos, and Kinshasa, but not Addis Ababa, Cairo, or Dar es Salaam) and three from overseas (London, Washington, and New York, but not Moscow). The only African states with missions in Lusaka at the time were Egypt, Ghana, and Zaire.
23 ZIS *Press Release* no. 1995/65, 8 December 1965, and no. 2031/65, 15 December 1965.
24 Nyerere, *Freedom and Socialism*, p. 129. Nyerere denied that Kaunda had tried to dissuade him. Yet on two occasions he inquired rhetorically of the Zambian high commissioner: "Why doesn't Kaunda defy Britain?" He appears never to have understood what it meant to be a landlocked state.
25 ZIS *Background* no. 56/65, p. 4, 30 December 1965. Sékou Touré of Guinea was one president who wrote to urge Kaunda (and others) to implement the OAU decision. In February 1966 a diplomatic mission from Zambia visited Guinea (and Mali) to explain Lusaka's stand.
26 Nathan Shamuyarira, *National Liberation through Self-Reliance in Rhodesia, 1956–1972* (Ph.D. thesis, Princeton University, 1976),

I:445. Originally mooted by Sierra Leone, the summit proposal was taken up actively by Haile Selassie, Kenyatta, and Obote at their 19 December meeting in Nairobi and subsequently endorsed by seventeen of the thirty-six OAU members (*The Times*, 20 December 1965, p. 8).

27 *The Times*, 8 December 1965, p. 10; *The Economist*, 11 December 1965, p. 1185; Paul Martin (acting Canadian prime minister), personal message to heads of Commonwealth African governments, 6 December 1965. The Commonwealth secretary general also dispatched a circular letter to forestall an incipient movement to withdraw from the Commonwealth (Smith, *Stitches in Time*, pp. 31–2).

28 Good, *UDI*, p. 104.

29 ZIS *Press Release* no. 1995/65, 8 December 1965. The final announcement maintained that Zambia did "not wish her peculiar problem ... to influence the decision of others who may be in a position" to sever diplomatic relations with Britain (ibid., no. 2031/65, 15 December 1965).

30 In a presidential statement to the National Assembly, Kenyatta declared: "We believe that Zambia's interests must be taken into consideration at all times ... We are particularly concerned that the Zambian Government has expressed serious doubt about the wisdom of breaking diplomatic relations with Britain" (House of Representatives, *Official Report*, 10 December 1965, cols. 1050–1).

31 The nine comprised two Commonwealth members (Ghana and Tanzania), four francophone states (Congo, Guinea, Mali, and Mauretania) and three Arab North African states (Algeria, Egypt, and the Sudan). Somalia had broken relations with Britain earlier.

32 The *Times of Zambia*, 15 December 1965, p. 1, referred to the decision as "a grave departure from Zambia's policy towards Britain as 'most favoured nation'."

33 In justifying his demand that British troops should take over Kariba, Kaunda explained that "the alternative might be to send American troops there. But ... America might say 'No'... What is left to us except to go to ... [the] Soviet Union? ... this would mean ... a shooting war based on ideologies ... This we are trying to avoid if we can, but much will depend on what Britain does" (ZIS *Background* no. 50/65, p. 2, 3 December 1965). Patrick Keatley claimed, on the basis of "a private discussion with leading Zambian sources," that "If Mr. Wilson continues to balk at action on the Kariba issue, there is a clear intention on the part of the Kaunda administration to bring in either the Americans or the Russians, or an OAU scratch force, or all three" (*Guardian*, 15 December 1965, p. 1).

34 *Daily Telegraph* (London), 29 November 1965, p. 1.

35 Vernon J. Mwaanga, *An Extraordinary Life* (Lusaka: Multimedia Publications, 1982), p. 112. Mark Chona visited Moscow on 7–9 December 1965 on a mission inspection tour.
36 Smith, *Stitches in Time*, pp. 29–30; *The Times*, 30 November 1965, p. 16; *West Africa* (London) no. 2532, 11 December, p. 1414.
37 ZIS *Press Release* no. 2031/65, 15 December 1965.
38 Wilson, *Personal Record*, pp. 182–3; Ken Flower, *Serving Secretly: An Intelligence Chief on Record: Rhodesia into Zimbabwe 1964–1981* (Harare: Quest Publishing, 1987), pp. 102–3. That Wilson considered that there was some substance to the threat of Soviet intervention seems to be confirmed by his alarmist report to Parliament on 20 December alleging, without any substantiation, that "in the last week, we have been within inches of very serious intervention by other countries" (*H.C. Deb.* vol. 722, col. 1700).
39 The two decisions were announced in the same press statement, which emphasized that the Zambian initiative was not intended in any way to undermine "the important decision of the OAU" (on relations with Britain) to which Zambia was a party (ZIS *Press Release* no. 2031/65, 15 December 1965).
40 Kapwepwe handed Wilson a personal message from Kaunda, requesting a "definite answer" to his demand for British troops to protect Kariba (*Times of Zambia*, 22 December 1965, p. 1). As arrangements had already been made to visit Moscow and Washington, it is likely that these visits would have taken place even if Wilson had unexpectedly given in to Kaunda's demand.
41 *H.C. Deb.*, vol. 722, col. 1917, 21 December 1965. Kapwepwe recorded in his diary, after his meeting with Wilson on 21 December, that he was "a politician without principles" who "went on talking a lot of nothingness ... We got nothing from him. But we discovered that he was helping Zambia ... simply because ... if Zambia went broke Britain would also crack ... it was purely the old exploitation" (Goodwin Mwangilwa, *The Kapwepwe Diaries* [Lusaka: Multimedia Publications, 1986], p. 61).
42 Ibid., p. 60. Despite various deliberately ambiguous statements, it appears that there was never any intention of asking for Soviet or American troops or arms (*Guardian*, 21 December 1965, p. 5; *The Economist*, 18 December 1965, p. 1310).
43 *New York Times*, 15 December 1965, p. 1, and 20 December 1965, p. 20; *Guardian*, 21 December 1965, p. 5; *Times of Zambia*, 20 December 1965, p. 7, and 22 December 1965, p. 1.
44 As the mission to Moscow considered it was also acting on behalf of the OAU, it returned via Addis Ababa to report to the OAU secretary general.

45 *Africa 1965* no. 25, 24 December 1965, p. 3. For Kapwepwe's uninhibited comments on the US mission, see Mwangilwa, *Kapwepwe Diaries*, p. 61. Kapwepwe was accompanied to Washington (22–7 December) and New York (22, 27–8 December) by Grey Zulu and Wina by Elijah Mudenda to Moscow (22–25 December).

46 US Department of State *Press Release* no. 296, 17 December 1965 and US–Zambia joint communiqué, 27 December 1965 (*Department of State Bulletin* 54(1384), 3 January 1966, p. 27, and 54(1386), 17 January 1966, pp. 85–6). Good describes the Great North Road as "a euphemism for the most important section of an endless gravel track winding more than 1,100 miles from central Zambia to Dar es Salaam ... It was soon to become the famous 'hell run,' a vital and dangerous truck route for the import of fuel oil" (*UDI*, p. 90).

47 Anthony Lake, *The "Tar Baby" Option: American Policy toward Southern Rhodesia* (New York: Columbia University Press, 1976), pp. 82–93; *Guardian*, 29 December 1965, p. 7. One Zambian official stated that the mission to Washington would be "an acid test of America's true intentions in Africa" (*New York Times*, 15 December 1965, p. 1). A State Department briefing paper for President Johnson explained that "We look to the UK to carry the initiative" and "We cannot undertake an open-end commitment to bear the costs of a Zambian shutdown," especially as sanctions might be "neither quick nor lethal" ("Visit of Prime Minister Wilson, December 15–19, 1965: Southern Rhodesia," WMP/BP-16, 15 December 1965).

48 ZIS *Background* no. 55/65, 28 December 1965; Mwaanga, *An Extraordinary Life*, p. 110; Richard Hall, *The High Price of Principles: Kaunda and the White South* (Harmondsworth: Penguin, 1973), p. 134; Jan Pettman, *Zambia: Security and Conflict* (London: Julian Friedman, 1974), pp. 202–3. Publicly Kaunda pronounced the Moscow trip "very, very successful" (ZIS *Background* no. 56/65, p. 1, 30 December 1965). On his return, Wina stated that "all aspects" of UDI had been discussed, "including its effects on Zambia, economically, politically, and militarily" (*Times of Zambia*, 25 December 1965, p. 1). The Soviet ambassador to Zambia at the time subsequently claimed that both Zambia and the USSR were to blame for the failure of the mission (interview with Ambassador Sergei Slipchenko, Ife, 1 June 1983).

49 *The Economist*, 18 December 1965, p. 1299; *Daily Telegraph*, 24 December 1965, p. 20; *Mizan* (London) 8:3 (May/June 1966), p. 140. Lusaka and Moscow continued to differ on two important points: whether Rhodesia was primarily a British or an OAU responsibility, and whether Wilson was conniving with Smith.

50 UN doc. S/RES.217, 20 November 1965; *H.C. Deb.*, vol. 721, cols.

247–50, 23 November 1965, and cols. 1430–1, 1 December 1965; Lake, *"Tar Baby" Option*, pp. 85–7. The OAU Defence Committee (OAU doc. SC/Rhodesia/Res.1, 20 November 1965) and the Council of Minister (ECM/Res.13 [VI], 3 December 1965) also resolved to institute comprehensive sanctions. In 1965 Zambia accounted for 25.5 per cent of Rhodesia's domestic exports, Britain took 22.4 per cent and South Africa a mere 9.7 per cent (*Economic Survey of Rhodesia for 1965* [Salisbury: Government Printer, 1966], CSR35-1966, pp. 19, 51).

51 Kaunda also felt that for Zambia not to support British sanctions would obviously be a "sell-out action" (ZIS *Background* no. 48/65, p. 2, 17 November 1965). "My Foreign Minister, Simon Kapwepwe," Kaunda revealed to a British journalist, "toured the foreign embassies and legations in Lusaka to impress on them that we were firm on [sanctions], and would they please be so too" (*Sunday Times* [London], 5 December 1965, p. 11). Kaunda was particularly suspicious of Japanese sanction-busting.

52 Good, *UDI*, pp. 96–8; Roy Christie, *For the President's Eyes Only: The Story of John Brumer Agent Extraordinary* (Johannesburg: Hugh Keartland, 1971), p. 145. On 17 November Wilson rejected out of hand a joint Foreign Office/Ministry of Fuel and Power study which dismissed oil sanctions completely as "ineffective" and likely to "do more harm than good" (Barbara Castle, *The Castle Diaries, 1964–70* [London: Weidenfeld and Nicolson, 1985], pp. 68–9).

53 *Nat. Ass. Deb.* no. 5, col. 94, 9 December 1965; *Sunday Times*, 5 December 1965, p. 11; *Guardian*, 6 December 1965, p. 10; *The Times*, 13 December 1965, p. 7. In a memorandum to the Commonwealth senior trade officials meeting in London on 29 November 1965, Zambia asserted: "No government should regard Zambia's difficult position *vis-à-vis* Rhodesia as a reason for not taking strong measures against the Smith regime." On the other hand, the Zambian minister of agriculture accused the British of imposing an oil embargo knowing that it "would hurt Zambia more" than Rhodesia (*Times of Zambia*, 3 January 1966, p. 7).

54 ZIS *Press Release* no. 1971/65 and no. 1976/65, 6 December 1965; *Times of Zambia*, 17 December 1965, p. 1. The minister of commerce and industry emphasized that import licences for "essential commodities would be issued freely" and removed altogether "at the earliest opportunity." Kaunda commented that "we cannot free ourselves overnight from ties with Rhodesia, though the time will come when this may be possible" (*Daily Mail*, 8 December 1965, p. 6).

55 Good, *UDI*, p. 96; UN doc. S/PV.1260, 13 November 1965, p. 17. Kaunda was particularly critical of Britain's failure to prevent the BP

tanker *British Security* discharging 12,000 tons of oil at Beira on 13 December (*Nat. Ass. Deb.* no. 5, col. 94, 9 December 1965; *The Times*, 6 December 1965, p. 8, and 14 December 1965, p. 10). UNIP's National Council described British inaction as "the height of international trickery" (*Times of Zambia*, 14 December 1965, p. 1).

56 Arnold Smith, Commonwealth secretary general, who conferred with Kaunda on 15 November, noted that "the dwindling of oil supplies was his most immediate anxiety" (*Stitches in Time*, p. 29). The *Daily Telegraph* reported from Lusaka that "the main Zambian concern now is continuation of petrol supplies" (24 November 1965, p. 1). See also Lake, *"Tar Baby" Option*, p. 88, and Good, *UDI*, p. 96.

57 Zambian oil stocks declined from "25 days' petrol consumption and 10 days for other fuels" at the end of October 1965 to "13 days' consumption of petrol and 7 days for other products" on 11 December; by contrast, Rhodesian supplies increased from 27 days' petrol consumption and 14 days of other fuels on 14 October to "about three months'" supply on 20 November. Moreover, the international oil-marketing companies in Zambia were "stockpiling all the incoming fuel and starving Zambia," and indulging in other obstructionist activities in addition to reporting their stock figures regularly to Salisbury (Jorge Jardim, *Sanctions Double-Cross: Oil to Rhodesia* [Lisbon: Intervençao, 1978], pp. 19, 21, 24–5, 61–2).

58 When "difficulties" were advanced in the British cabinet as explanations for the delay in mounting the Zambian oil airlift, Barbara Castle's reactions were: "Why aren't we ready now after all this time?" (7 December) and "Why we hadn't made our detailed preparations earlier I shall never know" (14 December) (*The Castle Diaries*, pp. 76, 77). Arnold Smith charges that sanctions were "applied like a course of inoculations" (*Stitches in Time*, p. 59). American officials urged that an oil embargo be announced prior to the OAU meeting of 3–5 December (Lake, *"Tar Baby" Option*, p. 88). Actually, Wilson advanced the date by two or three weeks in response to the OAU threat to break diplomatic relations on 15 December. This largely explains the acute oil shortage Zambia experienced in early January 1966.

59 Lake, *"Tar Baby" Option*, pp. 89–90; Wilson, *Personal Record*, p. 187. The American embassy in Lusaka worked hard to secure US support for the airlift. Subsequently, Kaunda wrote Johnson personally to stress the urgency of American involvement (Good, *UDI*, p. 108).

60 According to Martin Bailey, Cledwyn Hughes, British minister of state for Commonwealth relations, who was then in Lusaka, "picked up the phone at the British High Commission to be greeted with a howl of static. To begin with he didn't understand a word. It turned

out to be George Brown [deputy prime minister] who was having to shout down the phone from London to tell him that Britain had agreed to oil sanctions" (*New Statesman* [London] 8 December 1978, p. 782). See also Good, *UDI*, p. 107.
61 Good, *UDI*, p. 108.
62 Ibid., pp. 107–8.
63 Kaunda's telegram requesting Canadian participation in the airlift reached Prime Minister Pearson on 19 December. It was warmly seconded by Wilson who arrived in Ottawa that same day. The cabinet formally authorized a Canadian contribution the next day, though initially for only a month. Zambian hopes that the Soviet Union might join in providing planes for the airlift were doomed to disappointment.
64 *The Times*, 23 November 1965, p. 10, and 16 December 1965. p. 10; *The Economist*, 25 December 1965, p. 1411. Following the Mbeya meeting of 11 December, Nyerere reiterated his pledge to Kaunda in writing. He also offered to fly to Washington and Ottawa if necessary to appeal for help for Zambia.
65 ZIS *Background* no. 49/65, 26 November 1965, p. 4. The prickly Zairien military leader reacted to Kaunda's criticism by promptly expelling the Zambian ambassador, though the order was soon rescinded. A personal letter from Kaunda appealing for help in transporting oil through Zaire was delivered to Mobutu on 21 December (*Rhodesia Herald*, 22 December 1965, p. 1, and 23 December 1965, p. 1).
66 Good, *UDI*, p. 107.
67 Flower, *Serving Secretly*, pp. 31–4, 63–4. Barbara Castle's diary entry on the cabinet meeting of 17 November noted that Wilson "doubted if either South Africa or Portugal would want to run foul of the UN for their own reasons – nor would private oil companies"; on 21 December he reported that "Portugal and South Africa had toed the line" (*Castle Diaries*, pp. 69, 90). On the day the oil ban was imposed, "sources close to the British government" – presumably members of the British ministerial delegation then in Lusaka – dismissed the threat that South Africa might supply Rhodesia from its strategic oil reserve, claimed that Portugal would be a "reluctant contributor," and predicted that sanctions would take effect "within the next crucial three weeks" (*Times of Zambia*, 18 December 1965, p. 1). For an optimistic Zambian view, see the *Observer*, 19 December 1965, p. 2.
68 Hugh Thomas, ed., *The Crisis in the Civil Service* (London: Anthony Blond, 1968), pp. 67, 97–8; Wilfred Beckerman, ed., *The Labour Government's Economic Record: 1964–1970* (London: Duckworth,

1972), p. 144. An American official complained that the British "never seemed to have done their homework" (Lake, *"Tar Baby" Option*, p. 92). Arnold Smith accused Wilson of being "susceptible to illusory predictions of imminent success" (*Stitches in Time*, p. 53).

69 John Day, manager of Shell Zambia Ltd., a subsidiary of Shell Rhodesia (Pvt.) Limited, was seconded to the Contingency Planning Organization as oil liaison officer.

70 James W. Vernon, an assistant under-secretary in the Department of Economic Affairs, was sent out to Lusaka as economic adviser to the British High Commission to negotiate details of the airlift with the CPO. Kaunda refused to receive Cledwyn Hughes (minister of state for Commonwealth relations), who headed a contingency planning mission to Lusaka (15–19 December) until the final day of the visit, though there was close and continuous consultation at the official level, and some contact at ministerial level.

71 Although the UNIP National Council, meeting on 11–13 December, adopted a resolution condemning Britain for failing to implement oil sanctions, there is no evidence that Kaunda consulted it on the implications of such action for Zambia.

72 Good, *UDI*, p. 108. The Hughes team negotiated with Finance Minister Arthur Wina who acted on behalf of the Zambian cabinet. At one stage the British took Wina aside and asked him bluntly how he thought Zambia could preserve any credibility with the OAU and the UN if it refused to go along with oil sanctions. This appears to have been the crucial argument in the subsequent cabinet debate.

73 *New York Times*, 15 December 1965, p. 9.

74 The British also refused to suggest a date by which sanctions were expected to be effective (*Financial Times* [London] December 1965, p. 14). Both Kaunda and Nyerere were reportedly prepared to give sanctions a five-month trial – until 15 May 1966 (*Observer*, 12 December 1965, p. 12; *Guardian*, 23 December 1965, p. 1). George Ivan Smith, U Thant's former special representative to Central and Southern Africa, also cited 15 May as the deadline, following meetings with Kaunda (7 December) and Nyerere (9 December).

75 Good, *UDI*, 108. Kapwepwe also mentioned a figure of 7,000 tons per month by road (*The Times*, 30 December 1965, p. 6). Publicly the British agreed to meet "Zambia's minimum requirements in the shortest possible time" ("Joint Communiqué on Zambian-British Talks," 19 December 1965). Negotiations between Zambian and British officials on the airlift tonnage had reached a deadlock (with the British offering 12,500 tons and the Zambians holding out for 16,000 tons, or at least a minimum of 14,000 tons) when a telephone call came through from London announcing Wilson's deci-

sion on oil sanctions. The British official (Vernon) immediately agreed to the 14,000 ton figure.
76 The ration for the first forty days was four gallons per motorist (ZIS *Press Release* no. 2085/65, 22 December 1965). Even so, supplies ran out temporarily in many centres by 7 January (*Daily Telegraph*, 8 January 1966, p. 22). On 21 December Wilson optimistically predicted that rationing would be off by Christmas (Castle, *Castle Diaries*, p. 90).
77 The British airlift (Nairobi/Dar es Salaam to Lusaka/Ndola) delivered 5.4 million gallons between 19 December 1965 and 31 October 1966; the American airlift (Kinshasa to Lubumbashi) carried 3.2 million gallons (4 January–30 April 1966); and the Canadian airlift (Kinshasa to Lusaka/Ndola) accounted for 1.1 million gallons (27 December 1965–30 April 1966).
78 Hall, *High Price of Principles*, p. 119; Good, *UDI*, p. 92; Smith, *Stitches in Time*, p. 58; Lake, *"Tar Baby" Option*, p. 80.
79 Good, *UDI*, pp. 96–9; *Daily Telegraph*, 24 November 1965, p. 1; *The Times*, 29 November 1965, p. 10. MacDonald's first mission to Lusaka was 22–28 November.
80 Snelling accompanied Arthur Bottomley, secretary of state for Commonwealth relations, 1–3 December.
81 "Joint Communiqué on Zambian-British Talks," 19 December 1965.
82 ZIS *Press Release* no. 3/66, 3 January 1966. Earlier Kapwepwe had predicted "about twelve years" (OAU doc. ECM/PV.1 [VI], 3 December 1965, p. 45).
83 *Zambia News*, 28 November 1965, p. 7; also, *Nat. Ass. Deb.* no. 5, cols. 93, 98, 9 December 1965. On the other hand Wilson was anxious that any diversion of trade that did occur should benefit Britain; this was the purpose of the mission of Sir Norman Kipping to Lusaka, 21–27 November (Wilson, *Personal Record*, p. 182).
84 ZIS *Press Release* no. 1857/65, p. 1, and *Background* no. 48/65, p. 3, 17 November 1965, and no. 50/65, p. 4, 3 December 1965.
85 Good, *UDI*, p. 97.
86 Ibid., pp. 93, 97, 98.
87 Zambia eventually contributed $6.2 million in grants and loans to develop Tanzanian port facilities (ZIS *Press Release* no. 88/68, 12 January 1968).
88 Smith, *Stitches in Time*, pp. 29–30; *West Africa* no. 2532, 11 December 1965, p. 1414. At the OAU Council of Ministers, Kapwepwe thanked Zambia's neighbours for their support but asked of the other members that "when we knock at your doors, please be ready to open your doors." He received loud applause but little else (ECM/PV.2 [VI], 4 December 1965, p. 51).

89 Good, *UDI*, p. 111; *Times of Zambia*, 16 December 1965, p. 1; *Daily Telegraph*, 17 December 1965, p. 21; *Africa 1965* no. 24, 10 December 1965, p. 6.
90 The Hughes-Foley mission included some twenty Treasury and Economic Affairs experts (*Times of Zambia*, 17 December 1965, p. 1), among them Sir Arthur Snelling and Dudley Seers, director general of the Economic Planning Staff, Ministry of Overseas Development.
91 See note 70. The Zambians also cancelled without explanation both a public address and a radio broadcast which Hughes had been scheduled to deliver (*Daily Telegraph*, 18 December 1965, p. 11, and 20 December 1965, p. 20); *Times of Zambia*, 20 December 1965, p. 1). Kaunda was greatly embarrassed when, on the occasion of the arrival of the first RAF oil plane on 19 December, he accidentally encountered Hughes at the airport (*Daily Telegraph*, 20 December 1965, p. 20).
92 *Daily Telegraph*, 17 December 1965, p. 21; Good, *UDI*, p. 116. In the course of the negotiations, Knaggs (who was British) acquired the sobriquet "Mr Snaggs" from the British team.
93 ZIS *Press Release* no. 1857/65, p. 1, and *Background* no. 48/65, p. 3, 17 November 1965, and no. 50/65, p. 4, 3 December 1965; Good, *UDI*, pp. 97, 121; *Africa 1965* no. 24, 10 December 1965, p. 6. In an interview in the London *Daily Mail*, Kaunda declared: "We have asked Britain to pay for all external contingency planning because Rhodesia is her baby" (8 December 1965, p. 6).
94 *Financial Times*, 21 December 1965, p. 14; *Guardian*, 21 December 1965, p. 5; Good, *UDI*, p. 121; "Joint Communiqué on Zambian-British Talks," 19 December 1965.
95 $9.8 million out of an estimated $28 million (*Daily Telegraph*, 17 December 1965, p. 21).
96 Good, *UDI*, p. 116; Hall, *High Price of Principles*, p. 148.
97 Bottomley encouraged the Zambian ministerial missions to seek further economic assistance in Washington and Moscow (*The Times*, 21 December 1965, p. 7).
98 *Rhodesia Herald*, 20 December 1965, p. 1. The royalty on coal increased from 14¢ a short ton to $14. At the same time, an export tax of $22.40 per ton was introduced for coke.
99 Rhodesia *Leg. Ass. Deb.* vol. 61, cols. 1060–62, 8 July 1965; Rhodesian government statement, 13 November 1965 (*Zambia News*, 14 November 1965, p. 7).
100 *Rhodesia Herald*, 9 December 1965, p. 5.
101 ZIS *Press Release* no. 1996/65, 8 December 1965 and no. 2095/65, 24 December 1965. In 1965 Zambia's imports from Rhodesia were eight times the value of its exports to that country. On 16 Decem-

ber Zambia blocked payments to Rhodesia of rents, interest, dividends, profits, and capital (amounting to nearly $8 million in 1964); Rhodesia replied in kind the next day, though only $2.5 million was involved (*Times of Zambia*, 17 December 1965, p. 1; *Rhodesia Herald*, 18 December 1965, p. 7).

102 *Rhodesia Herald*, 20 December 1965, pp. 1, 2. See also *The Times*, 21 December 1965, p. 1, and 30 December 1965, p. 8. The surcharges were backdated to 17 December, the day oil sanctions were imposed.

103 Immediately following the Smith broadcast, a government spokesman in Lusaka characterized this first "direct economic attack on Zambia" as an act of desperation (*Times of Zambia*, 20 December 1965, p. 1). In London, Finance Minister Wina denounced the surcharge as "clear and calculated robbery" with a view to "holding Zambia to ransom for whatever sanctions the world applies" (*Rhodesia Herald*, 21 December 1965, p. 2).

104 ZIS *Background* no. 53/65, 22 December 1965; Good, *UDI*, p. 112. Good quotes a slightly more qualified text which reads: "We shall, *as and when appropriate*, take *further* measures *in order to show* ..." (pp. 111–12).

105 *New York Times*, 2 January 1966, p. 11.

106 ZIS *Press Release* no. 1996/65, 8 December 1965; *Africa 1966* no. 1, 7 January 1966, p. 3. The source may have been John Brumer, the Rhodesian agent serving as Kaunda's personal adviser, though Christie makes no mention of this in *For the President's Eyes Only*.

107 Kaunda's "first action" following the Smith broadcast was to communicate with the British government "personally" (ZIS *Background* no. 53/65, 23 December 1965). Four senior Zambian ministers were in London at the time conferring with Bottomley (on 20 December) and Wilson (on 21 December).

108 "Advice from London was filled with caution. The Americans ... were equally apprehensive" (Good, *UDI*, p. 111). At Washington's behest, Good sought out a meeting with Kaunda urgently only hours before the broadcast. See also *Financial Times*, 3 January 1966, p. 11.

109 *Times of Zambia*, 21 December 1965, p. 1; *Guardian*, 4 January 1966, p. 1. Kaunda later reported that the mining companies had been "very cooperative indeed" (ZIS *Background* no. 56/65, p. 3, 30 December 1965). Although the mines had an obvious vested interest in preserving Zambia's close economic integration with Rhodesia, they proved remarkably supportive of Lusaka's efforts at disengagement. The Wankie Colliery Company was an AAC subsidiary (as well as a minority shareholder in two Copperbelt mines). In 1965 Zambia provided 38 per cent of the market for Wankie coal.

110 *New York Times*, 15 December 1965, p. 9; *Financial Times*, 3 January 1966, p. 11, 5 January 1966, p. 6, and 20 January 1966, p. 7; ZIS *Background* no. 1/66, p. 2, 2 January 1966. Rhodesia Railways was also keenly concerned as its Zambian section consumed one-third of the coal imports (*Rhodesia Herald*, 22 December 1965, p. 13; *Financial Times*, 22 December 1965, p. 6).

111 *Daily Telegraph*, 29 December 1965, p. 11. As Lusaka appears to have had prior intimation of Salisbury's intentions (*Africa 1966*, no. 1, 7 January 1966, p. 3), it is probable that Kaunda consulted his senior ministers before their departure for London on 19 December.

112 Nearly $300,000 in royalties was paid out during this period (*Daily Telegraph*, 7 January 1966, p. 23).

113 ZIS *Background* no. 53/65, 22 December 1965; Good, *UDI*, p. 111. In London, Wina declared that "Zambia cannot sit by and see our life squeezed out" (*Rhodesia Herald*, 21 December 1965, p. 2). Zambian ministers told Wilson that they feared increased coal charges would be followed by punitive increases in freight and electricity tariffs (*The Times*, 22 December 1965, p. 7, and 30 December 1965, p. 6).

114 ZIS *Background* no. 53/65, 22 December 1965, and no. 56/65, p. 2, 30 December 1965; *Times of Zambia*, 30 December 1965, pp. 1, 6; *Daily Telegraph*, 31 December 1965, p. 16, 1 January 1966, p. 19, and 4 January 1966, p. 1; *Financial Times*, 1 January 1966, p. 5.

115 ZIS *Background* no. 53/65, 22 December 1965; *Guardian*, 24 December 1965, p. 9; *Financial Times*, 3 January 1966, p. 11. Smith expected his surcharge to earn $27.7 million a year; if Zambia were to deny Rhodesia an additional 10 per cent or a total of $30.5 million, it would have had to reduce imports from Rhodesia by 31 per cent.

116 Richard Sklar claims that "the possibility of a total break with Rhodesia was seriously considered by the Zambian cabinet in December 1965" (*Corporate Power in an African State*, p. 153); Good indicates that Kaunda's "first reaction was to give no ground ... Zambia would respond by imposing a total embargo against Rhodesia" (*UDI*, p. 111). See also Castle, *Castle Diaries*, p. 131; *Financial Times*, 3 January 1966, p. 11, 7 January 1966, p. 21, and 16 March 1966, p. 19; *Times of Zambia*, 9 December 1967, p. 6; *New York Times*, 18 August 1966, p. 12.

117 Good, *UDI*, p. 111; *Guardian*, 24 December 1965, p. 9. Good also mentions a suggestion that only 20 per cent of copper should be diverted; this would have cost Salisbury only $3 million.

118 Arthur Wina stated that: "Our target is to stop buying Wankie coal as soon as alternative sources are available" (*Financial Times*, 21 December 1965, p. 14).

119 *The Economist*, 25 December 1965, p. 1432; *Rhodesia Herald*, 10 December 1965, p. 1; *Financial Times*, 1 January 1966, p. 5 and 1 February 1966, p. 16. On 30 December, Kaunda declared that "we can survive without Rhodesian coal if we can use the stocks that we have at the moment to keep us going for a couple of weeks"; three days later, he admitted that, "for a short time," the mines would be unable to operate at full capacity. He also warmly welcomed Prime Minister Verwoerd's offer of South African coal (ZIS *Background* no. 56/65, p. 3, 30 December 1965, and no. 1/66, p. 2, 2 January 1966; *Guardian*, 1 January 1966, p. 1).

120 Following the surcharge announcement, "President Kaunda wanted an immediate ban on importing coal from Rhodesia but was dissuaded from acting at once "(*Daily Telegraph*, 31 December 1965, p. 16; also, 29 December 1965, p. 11). The previous day, a *Times* correspondent warned that: "The only way to prevent this hari-kiri by Zambia seems to be for the British government to offer to pay the surcharge" (30 December 1965, p. 6). The *Times of Zambia* urged editorially (21 December 1965, p. 10) that "all coal imports from Rhodesia must be stopped. The country cannot be blackmailed into rescuing an illegal regime it utterly condemns." This was echoed by the *Zambia Mail* (24 December 1965, p. 2).

121 Good comments: "As the time for Kaunda's broadcast approached it was not clear – perhaps not even to the President himself – what he would say" (*UDI*, p. 111).

122 ZIS *Background* no. 53/65, 22 December 1965.

123 Smith confirmed on 24 December that Zambia would receive no further coal unless it paid the new royalty (*Rhodesia Herald*, 25 December, 1965, p. 1). This led to renewed cabinet consideration of the coal issue on 28 December with "almost irresistible" pressure on Kaunda to refuse to pay the surcharge (*Daily Telegraph*, 29 December 1965, p. 11; *The Times* 30 December 1965, p. 6).

124 *New York Times*, 2 January 1966, p. 11.

125 ZIS *Background* no. 1/66, pp. 1, 22 January 1966; *Daily Telegraph*, 4 January 1966, p. 1, and 7 January 1966, p. 23.

126 ZIS *Press Release* no. 1/66, 2 January 1966. Kaunda concluded that "the rebels are beginning very seriously to feel the pinch of economic sanctions" (ZIS *Background* no. 1/66, p. 1, 2 January 1966).

127 Six months earlier, the joint Anglo-American feasibility plan drafted in Washington, 20 May 1965, had identified Beira as well as Lourenço Marques and Luanda as potential airlift bases, but no steps had been taken to investigate their facilities. According to Barbara Castle, Wilson reported to the cabinet on 21 December that the airlift "bottleneck was at Dar, which could only take four planes, and

Portugal ought to be approached for facilities at Beira" (*Castle Diaries*, p. 78).

128 Alberto Franco Nogueira, *Diálogos Interditos: A Político Externa Portuguesa e a Guerra de África* (Lisbon: Editorial Intervenção, 1979), II:109–15. The request was approved on 28 December, subject to several acceptable conditions, and conveyed to the Zambian ambassador in Washington (ibid., pp. 115–18). Bottomley informed Kapwepwe of Portugal's agreement when the latter passed through London on 29 December on his return from Washington (Mwangilwa, *Kapwepwe Diaries*, p. 62).

129 *Rhodesia Herald*, 20 December 1965, pp. 1–2; *Times of Zambia*, 24 December 1965, p. 1.

130 See note 57. On 23 December, the day gasoline rationing was introduced, eighteen Zambia Airways flights were cancelled (ZIS *Press Release* no. 2085/65, 22 December 1965; *Times of Zambia*, 24 December 1965, p. 1). Incoming intercontinental flights were monitored in case there were insufficient supplies of fuel for the return trip.

131 *Rhodesia Herald*, 22 December 1965, p. 1.

132 Although Zambia sponsored and voted for the annual UN General Assembly resolution condemning Portuguese colonial policy, its delegate explained afterwards that there were "certain aspects of it which are not relevant to us as a landlocked country" – presumably the call to boycott all trade with Portugal. He then added: "Zambia bears no malice towards any nation. We have assured our neighbours of our goodwill towards them, and this assurance still stands and will continue. We shall always reciprocate good gestures from all nations" (UN doc. A/RES. 2107 [XX] and A/PV.1407, pp. 5–6, 21 December 1965). On 15 December the 3,400 Mozambican refugees who had recently crossed into Zambia were warned that they would not be allowed "to turn their camp into a subversion training centre" (ZIS *Press Release* no. 2056/65, 17 December 1965).

133 For the text of this letter, see Jardim, *Sanctions Double-Cross*, pp. 53–4.

134 Nogueira, *Diálogos Interditos*, II:115. The actual meeting may have taken place on 24 December. Franco Nogueira noted that Kapwepwe's request differed in some details from the one Ross had submitted.

135 Jardim, *Sanctions Double-Cross*, p. 53. Beira was 526 air miles from Lusaka and 625 miles from Ndola, Dar es Salaam 935 and 810 miles respectively, Nairobi 1,128 and 965 miles, Lobito 1,025 and 1,030 miles, and Kinshasa 1,163 and 1,080 miles. Actual flight paths were in some cases considerably longer as a result of Portuguese restrictions on overflights of operational areas.

136 *Financial Times*, 14 January 1966, p. 8.

137 Francistown in Bechuanaland (Botswana), although only 260 miles from Livingstone or 330 miles if overflights of Rhodesia were avoided, appears not to have been seriously considered at this time, though it was later (*Financial Times*, 1 February 1966, p. 16). It lacked adequate facilities and relied on South Africa for its oil. Contingency planners from the first had ruled out the use of South African bases. At one stage, consideration was even given to Blantyre in Malawi (437 miles from Lusaka).

138 Jardim, *Sanctions Double-Cross*, p. 53.

139 *Diálogos Interditos*, II:118. It is unclear whether Salazar raised this point specifically when he received Ross on 17 December. However, three days later, in a memorandum drafted by Jardim, Salazar directed: "As to helping Zambia, Portugal did not recognize the United Kingdom as qualified to speak for a country which, being independent, had a personality and voice of its own" (Jardim, *Sanctions Double-Cross*, p. 32). At the same time, Salazar resisted strong pressures from within his administration to "use the opportunity to force Zambia to accept, at least, the re-establishment of consular relations" (Jorge Jardim, *Moçambique: Terra Queimada* [Lisbon: Intervenção, 1978], p. 75).

140 Jardim, *Sanctions Double-Cross*, pp. 53–4. For some unexplained reason, Kaunda's letter of 23 December did not reach Lisbon until 14 January 1966. The reply was sent on 18 January.

141 Nogueira, *Dialogos Interditos*, II:115–16; Jardim, *Sanctions Double-Cross*, pp. 55, 58–61; Jardim, *Moçambique*, pp. 75–6.

142 Flower, *Serving Secretly*, pp. 65–8; Good, *UDI*, p. 134n. The alleged British military threat was an invention of Jorge Jardim for his own commercial reasons.

143 Jardim, *Sanctions Double-Cross*, pp. 60, 61. There is evidence to suggest that the Portuguese position might have been more flexible if Zambia had been willing to accord a greater measure of political recognition – preferably the reception of a Portuguese consul but at least direct ministerial contact.

144 ZIS *Press Release* no. 331/66, 18 February 1966; *Portuguese Foreign Policy, 1965–1967* (Lisbon: Ministry of Foreign Affairs, [1968]), pp. 43, 58; Jardim, *Sanctions Double-Cross*, pp. 59, 60. The shipment of oil to Zambia via Malawi began on 26 January (*Daily Telegraph*, 5 March 1966, p. 15).

145 *Financial Times*, 21 January 1966, p. 9, and 26 January 1966, p. 16.

146 Tanzania Information Services *Press Release* no. C/3583/65, 1 December 1965.

147 "Whatever happens as regards our relations with Britain," Nyerere declared in Parliament on 14 December, "our commitment to

Zambia remains. We continue to be ready to allow the transit of any goods or personnel, from any place, needed by Zambia to protect her interests and pursue the fight against Smith at the same time. No one can drive a wedge between Zambia and Tanzania" (*Freedom and Socialism*, p. 126).

148 *The Economist*, 25 December 1965, p. 1,411. This enabled the airlift to begin on 19 December rather than two weeks later.

149 Good, *UDI*, p. 109; *Times of Zambia*, 24 December 1965, p. 1; *Daily Telegraph*, 24 December 1965, p. 1. HMS *Dido* discharged her cargo and hastily put to sea that same day. Her captain had somewhat naïvely invited Nyerere to lunch. A second frigate, HMS *Berwick*, was diverted to Mombasa. *The Standard* (Dar es Salaam) initially welcomed the warship editorially and praised the RAF (23 December 1965, p. 4).

150 *Daily Telegraph*, 24 December 1965, p. 1. Although the Zambian high commissioner in Dar es Salaam personally secured clearance from Nyerere for RAF oil planes to be based there, the Tanzanian government subsequently gave failure to secure clearance as its reason for refusing permission. Some ninety-six RAF airmen were based in Dar es Salaam, servicing the airlift. Tanzania also banned the direct delivery of oil drums bought in South Africa; instead, they reached Dar es Salaam via Beira, Blantyre, and Lusaka (Good, *UDI*, p. 109).

151 ZIS *Press Release* no. 2121/65, 29 December 1965; *The Times*, 29 December 1965, p. 5. The changeover was completed on 3 January 1966, nearly a week ahead of schedule; in the meantime, RAF personnel wore civilian clothes.

152 *Rhodesia Herald*, 25 December 1965, p. 1.

153 ZIS *Press Release* no. 2121/65, 29 December 1965; ZIS *Background* no. 56/65, pp. 1, 2, 30 December 1965; *Zambia News*, 2 January 1966, p. 2. The mission was headed by Reuben Kamanga and included Nalumino Mundia, in the absence overseas of Kapwepwe.

154 Shamuyarira, *National Liberation through Self-Reliance*, I:445; *Times of Zambia*, 23 December 1965, p. 1; ZIS *Background* no. 56/65, pp. 4–5, 30 December 1965, also no. 52/65, p. 2, 12 December 1965.

155 ZIS *Press Release* no. 42/66, 7 January 1966.

156 *Guardian*, 10 January 1966, p. 1. Pearson also wrote to Balewa on 3 January indicating that he thought it "especially important" that Kaunda, Nyerere, and Kenyatta attend (L.B. Pearson Papers). Senator Dan Ibekwe, Nigerian minister of state for Commonwealth relations, arrived in Lusaka on 7 January, a few hours after the announcement of the Zambian decision (*Times of Zambia*, 8 January 1966, p. 1). He also raised the question of basing Nigerian troops in

350 Notes to pages 175–6

Zambia. At one stage Nigeria proposed that the conference meet in Lusaka, but the Zambian government indicated that it was too preoccupied with immediate issues to organize it.

157 *Daily Telegraph*, 7 January 1966, p. 23 and 10 January 1966, p. 24.
158 ZIS *Background* no. 56/65, p. 4, 30 December 1965; *Daily Telegraph* 8 January 1966, p. 22; ZIS *Press Release* no. 42/66, 7 January 1966. The Lagos conference was no doubt one of the items Kaunda and Kapwepwe discussed during their lengthy session in Kitwe on 1 January 1966 (*Guardian*, 1 January 1966, p. 1). In addition to Kamanga, the delegation included the minister of home affairs, the minister of state for Commonwealth affairs, the Zambian high commissioner to Nigeria, and other officials.
159 ZIS *Background* no. 56/65, p. 5, 30 December 1965. Nigeria generously agreed to divert four diesel electric locomotives and fifty-seven road tankers it had on order to Zambia (ZIS *Press Release* no. 316/66, 17 February 1966; *Times of Zambia*, 23 February 1966, p. 9; *Daily Telegraph*, 15 February 1966, p. 19).
160 ZIS *Background* no. 56/65, p. 4, 30 December 1965. Kaunda had earlier stated categorically: "I certainly cannot leave the country" (ibid., no. 52/65, p. 2, 12 December 1965).
161 Pearson is reported to have offered to send an RCAF plane to pick Kaunda up (*Guardian*, 10 January 1966, p. 1). Wilson did manage to send a plane to Malawi for Dr Banda.
162 *Daily Graphic* (Accra), 14 January 1966, p. 12; *Zambia Mail*, 14 January 1966, p. 1.
163 Wilson claimed the conference "ended in an atmosphere of unity, even euphoria" (*Personal Record*, p. 196). Pearson, in a diary entry, noted that it was "the best diplomatic performance by [Wilson] that I have ever seen ... He made the most of the 'Now, this is most secret, even my cabinet colleagues don't know a word of it' routine" (*Mike: The Memoirs of the Right Honourable Lester B. Pearson* [Toronto: University of Toronto Press, 1975], III:285).
164 Commonwealth Prime Ministers' Meeting in Lagos, 1966, *Final Communique, January 1966* (London: HMSO, 1966), Cmnd. 2890, p. 5. On the controversy concerning the origin of this phrase, see Wilson, *Personal Record*, p. 196; Smith, *Stitches in Time*, p. 56; Thomas, *Crisis in the Civil Service*, pp. 97–8; Good, *UDI*, pp. 120–1; Joe Garner, *The Commonwealth Office, 1925–68* (London: Heinemann, 1978), p. 394; Chapman Pincher, *Inside Story: A Documentary of the Pursuit of Power* (London: Sidgwick and Jackson, 1978), p. 16.
165 This was eventually instituted following the adoption of UN Security Council resolution S/RES/221 on 9 April 1966. See Good, *UDI*, pp. 132–45.

166. *Keesing's Contemporary Archives* (London) XV (1965–66), pp. 21130–1; Garner, *Commonwealth Office*, p. 56; Good, *UDI*, pp. 128–32; Flower, *Serving Secretly*, pp. 63–4.
167. The index of imports from Rhodesia was 64 for December 1965 and 61 for January 1966 (using September 1965 as the base month), and 73 and 69 respectively (using November 1965=100). See Figure 2.
168. Cmnd. 2890, p. 5; *Zambia Mail*, 18 February 1966, p. 1; *Guardian*, 5 January 1966, p. 11; ZIS *Press Release* no. 2/66, 2 January 1966, and no. 28/66, 6 January 1966, pp. 4–9. Kapwepwe argued with considerable prescience that it would be "cheaper to use force than to impose economic sanctions" as, if not stopped soon, the Smith regime would "last for at least 15 years" (ibid., no. 3/66, 3 January 1966).
169. ZIS *Background* no. 56/65, 30 December 1965, p. 5.
170. *H.C. Deb.*, vol. 722, col. 771, 10 December 1965, and vol. 720, col. 633, 12 November 1965; *Nat. Ass. Deb.* no. 5, cols. 94–5, 9 December 1965. The Zambian government had not yet recovered from the shock of the Lord Chancellor's offer to negotiate with Smith (*H.L. Deb.*, vol. 271, col. 131, 7 December 1965; Barbara Castle, *Castle Diaries*, p. 76). One Zambian minister commented that "Kenneth has been dealing with London in good faith and his reward is to be made to look like a Tshombe" (*Guardian*, 11 December 1965, p. 1).
171. *Guardian*, 3 January 1966, p. 1; *Times of Zambia*, 3 January 1966, p. 7, and 5 January 1966, p. 1.
172. *Sun* (London), 5 January 1966, p. 1; Good, *UDI*, pp. 113–18, 293; *Times of Zambia*, 18 December 1965, p. 1. According to Dudley Seers, British planning "fantasies" included "estimates of how fast the [Rhodesian] national income would fall, prices rise, unemployment grow, etc., each month until the Ides of March" (Thomas, *Crisis in the Civil Service*, pp. 97, 98).
173. Variously characterized as the "quick kill" (a term in circulation as early as a week after UDI), the *coup de grâce*, the crunch, the knockout blow, or simply the cut-off.
174. The only Zambian official present was Mark Chona, the permanent secretary in the Ministry of Foreign Affairs, who had just returned from the Lagos conference. Wilson was accompanied by Arthur Bottomley, Malcolm MacDonald, Sir Leslie Monson, and other officials.
175. On the Wilson visit, see Wilson, *Personal Record*, p. 196; Good, *UDI*, pp. 121–2; Hall, *High Price of Principles*, pp. 135–6; *Zambia Mail*, 14 January 1966, pp. 1, 8. Wilson's entourage numbered thirty-seven.
176. Thomas, *Crisis in the Civil Service*, p. 98; Good, *UDI*, p. 115. See also note 68.

177 This was made clear to the author in a conversation with Wilson in Lusaka, 13 January 1966.
178 Good, *UDI*, p. 122; Wilson, *Personal Record*, p. 198; *Times of Zambia*, 14 January 1966, p. 1; *Daily Telegraph*, 15 January 1966, p. 1. On his return home, Wilson reiterated that "Rhodesia's future course cannot be negotiated with the regime which illegally claims to govern the country" (*H.C. Deb.*, vol 723, col. 40, 25 January 1966).
179 *Financial Times*, 3 January 1966, p. 11, and 11 January 1966, pp. 1, 8; *Times of Zambia*, 13 January 1966, p. 1; Good, *UDI*, p. 115. British officials repeatedly expressed the need to "calm" Kaunda down. Kaunda claimed publicly (and privately in correspondence with Wilson) that "Zambia is fully prepared, or is just about to be" for a complete rupture with Rhodesia. He conceded that, "for a short time," Zambia might not be able "to operate the mines 100 per cent" (ZIS *Background* no. 1/66, p. 2, 2 January 1966).
180 Good, *UDI*, pp. 121, 122; Hall, *High Price of Principles*, pp. 135–6. Good notes that "high ranking American officials scoffed when presented with this fanciful picture. It was a classic instance of the policy wish fathering the intelligence estimate" (*UDI*, p. 115). Good himself (p. 293) considered Wilson's strategy "a fanciful and irresponsible *scenario* for it assumed that Zambia should accept a level of risk which Britain itself had refused." See also Lake, *"Tar Baby" Option*, p. 93. British planners immediately prior to Lagos and Lusaka envisaged a cut-off date "some time in February."
181 *Financial Times*, 7 January 1966, p. 21, 27 January 1966, p. 16, and 16 March 1966, p. 9.
182 Ibid., 7 January 1966, p. 21; Good, *UDI*, pp. 116, 121.
183 Tom Stacy, "Who will fall first – Smith or Kaunda?," *Evening Standard* (London), 27 January 1966, p. 7; *Daily Telegraph*, 1 January 1966, p. 14; Good, *UDI*, p. 118 (the quotation represents Good's paraphrase of Kaunda's words). Good notes that a recent US transport survey estimated that the minimum necessary improvements in the Great East Road would take four to six months to complete.
184 *Guardian*, 23 December 1965, p. 1; Good, *UDI*, pp. 124, 293. "The only way quickly to bring the full force of sanctions into play against Rhodesia was to give Zambia a guarantee that *in extremis* ... there would be a recourse to force – which the sanctions policy was devised in the first place to avoid" (Good, p. 125).
185 This appears to be what Kapwepwe was alluding to in his puzzling diary entry for 13 January: "Mr. Wilson had nothing real to tell President Kaunda. He was still confused. But he agreed in privacy that force had to be used sometime at a later stage, 15th March was

fixed for the last Rhodesian section – and thereafter to use force or other method" (Mwangilwa, *Kapwepwe Diaries*, p. 62).
186 Hall, *High Price of Principles*, pp. 136, 139, 153; ZIS, *Press Release* no. 681/66, 21 April 1966, p. 2; *New York Times*, 18 August 1966, p. 12. Malcolm MacDonald visited Lusaka on 23 February to inform Kaunda of the actual date of the election, five days before the public announcement (Good, *UDI*, p. 155).
187 *The Times*, 14 January 1966, p. 9; Good, *UDI*, pp. 113, 122. Wilson stated at his Lusaka press conference that "We have never ruled out the use of force in appropriate circumstances, provided it is understood that this would be for the purpose of restoring law and order and not for securing a solution to the constitutional problems" (*Financial Times*, 14 January 1966, p. 8). The British professed to believe that, once the Rhodesian oil supplies ran out, the security forces would be immobilized, thus creating a serious internal security problem.
188 ZIS *Press Release* no. 104/66, 18 January 1966, and no. 154/66, 25 January 1966; *Times of Zambia*, 19 January 1966, p. 1; *The Times*, 19 January 1966, p. 10; Hall, *High Price of Principles*, pp. 139–40. The mission visited Zambia, 19–24 January – two weeks ahead of a similar OAU mission, 6–12 February. It was headed by Maj.-Gen. J.E.F. Willoughby, officer commanding Britain's Middle East Ground Forces, and a classic "Colonel Blimp." Following his visit to Kariba, he sent a message to his military friends in Rhodesia: "Tell [Maj.-Gen.] Sam Putterill [Rhodesian Army Commander] I would much rather be drinking a beer with him in some pub than observing him from this distance through a pair of binoculars" (Flower, *Serving Secretly*, p. 57). One report suggests that some "Zambian officials" misinterpreted the despatch of the mission as evidence that "Britain had now accepted the need to move into Rhodesia" (*Daily Telegraph*, 19 January 1966, p. 1).
189 From 23 January to 10 February, the 2nd battalion of the Scots Guards was on seventy-two hours' notice to take off for Zambia (*Daily Telegraph*, 10 February 1966, p. 25, and 11 February 1966, p. 23).
190 *The Times*, 14 January 1966, p. 10; Good, *UDI*, p. 122.
191 *Times of Zambia*, 14 January 1966, p. 1; *Observer*, 16 January 1966, p. 2; *Zambia Mail*, 14 January 1966, "Mail Magazine," pp. 6–7.
192 Hall, *High Price of Principles*, p. 136. This was a familiar Kaunda theme prior to UDI (ZIS *Background* no. 37/65, p. 2, 30 September 1965).

CHAPTER 7

1 *Times of Zambia* (Ndola), 28 January 1966, p. 1 and 31 January 1966, p. 1; *Guardian* (London), 12 February 1966, p. 1.
2 Richard Hall, *The High Price of Principles: Kaunda and the White South* (Harmondsworth: Penguin, 1973), pp. 125–7; Robert C. Good, *UDI: The International Politics of the Rhodesian Rebellion* (Princeton: Princeton University Press, 1973), pp. 97–8, 108, 112, 115; *Observer* (London), 4 December 1965, p. 12.
3 Hall, *High Price of Principles*, pp. 136, 139.
4 Zambia Information Services (ZIS) *Press Release* no. 254/66, 10 February 1966, p. 1.
5 At least four of the fifteen ministers were absent abroad: Banda (Transport and Works), Kalulu (Lands and Natural Resources), S. Wina (Local Government and Housing), and Changufu (Information and Postal Services).
6 *Financial Times* (London), 21 January 1966, p. 10; *Times of Zambia*, 26 January 1966, p. 1. Kapwepwe notes that the next day, "Kaunda and Nyerere had full discussion over international problems including Rhodesia" (Goodwin Mwangilwa, *The Kapwepwe Diaries* [Lusaka: Multimedia Publications, 1986], p. 63). It is unclear if Vernon Mwaanga, Zambian ambassador to Moscow who had returned to Lusaka on 19 January on other business, was consulted on possible Soviet assistance.
7 ZIS *Press Release* no. 190/66, 28 January 1966; *The Economist* (London), 5 February 1966, pp. 561–2. The next day Vice-President Kamanga, whose personal behaviour had become a political embarrassment, was posted to the United Nations for six months (ZIS *Press Release* no. 191/66, 29 January 1966), though he flatly refused to go.
8 Commonwealth Continuing Committee on Sanctions, "Essential Requirements of Zambia" (Memorandum by the Government of Zambia), January 1966.
9 Good, *UDI*, pp. 110, 124, 134n; *Financial Times*, 14 January 1966, p. 8, and 26 January 1966, p. 16. Zambian interest in Beira (and briefly, Francistown) may have been reinforced by the decision of the three East African governments on 14 January to ban aircraft of Central African Airways (and Zambia Airways) from their skies and airfields (ZIS *Press Release* no. 157/66, 25 January 1966).
10 A strike by white miners on 7 February culminated in the "restriction" of one of their leaders (*Africa Research Bulletin: Political, Social and Cultural Series* [ARB: PSC], 1966, pp. 479, 502; *Daily Telegraph* (London), 18 February 1966, p. 14). Kaunda perceived the threatened industrial chaos as the work of "a handful of self-seeking

individuals ... working hand in hand with our enemies [to] disrupt the economy of the country" and "destroy the people's government" (ZIS *Background* no. 7/66, pp. 1, 2, 10 February 1966; ZIS *Press Release* no. 365/66, 22 February 1966, p. 1, and no. 402/66, 26 February 1966, p. 1).

11 "I do not pretend that we shall be able to maintain mineral production at its present level in every contingency," Kamanga declared in one of his weekly broadcasts to the nation. "But specific plans have been made and are being put into effect to maintain a reasonable level of production" (ZIS *Press Release* no. 254/66, 10 February 1966, p. 4). See also *Financial Times*, 1 February 1966, p. 16, and 18 February 1966, p. 15; Good, *UDI*, p. 124.

12 Good, *UDI*, p. 124.

13 ZIS *Press Release* nos. 1971/65 and 1976/65, 6 December 1965, no. 2095/65, 24 December 1965; *Times of Zambia*, 17 December 1965, p. 1. Rhodesian citizens entering Zambia were required to sign "a declaration of disavowal of the illegal regime of the rebels in Southern Rhodesia" (Republic of Zambia, *Government Gazette* I:86, 1 December 1965, p. 1,113).

14 *Zambia News*, 28 November 1965, p. 7; *Times of Zambia*, 1 December 1965, p. 6; ZIS *Press Release* no. 187/66, 29 January 1966, pp. 10–12; Zambia *Nat. Ass. Deb.* no. 5, col. 93, 9 December 1965.

15 ZIS *Press Release* no. 1954/65, 3 December 1965, and no. 122/66, 20 January 1966.

16 *Times of Zambia*, 11 August 1966, p. 1.

17 Ibid., 27 January 1966, p. 1, 31 January 1966, p. 6, 5 February 1966, p. 7, and 7 February 1966, p. 7; *Financial Times*, 27 January 1966, p. 16, and 8 February 1966, p. 16; *Zambia News*, 30 January 1966 p. 7, and 20 February 1966, p. 7. There is some evidence to suggest that the import restriction policy was formally sanctioned by the cabinet on 18 January. The aim was to reduce imports to 65 per cent of the 1964 level, or $56 million. The actual figure for 1966 was $65 million, which in real terms represented an even greater reduction than hoped for. Arthur Wina, who was appointed acting minister of commerce and industry on 28 January while retaining his finance portfolio, is credited with revising the policy.

18 ZIS *Press Release* no. 208/66, 3 February 1966, p. 4.

19 Good, *UDI*, p. 124; ZIS *Press Release* no. 254/66, 10 February 1966, p. 2; *Financial Times*, 11 February 1966, p. 9.

20 *Times of Zambia*, 27 January 1966, p. 9; ZIS *Press Release* no. 187/66, 29 January 1966, pp. 8–11.

21 Good, *UDI*, p. 124. The British mission visited Zambia from 23 to 28 January (*Financial Times*, 16 February 1966, p. 16, and 18 February

1966, p. 6). Malcolm MacDonald returned to Lusaka on 5 February, but does not appear to have been involved with this issue. On the other hand, the visit of John Msonthi, Malawi's minister of transport and communications, to Lusaka, 26–7 January, was relevant.
22 *Financial Times*, 4 February 1966, p. 10, and 8 February 1966, p. 16.
23 ZIS *Press Release* no. 544/66, 24 March 1966, p. 1; *Zambia News*, 13 February 1966, p. 2, and 20 February 1966, p. 7. In the absence of a definitive list of importers, letters were sent to companies whose names appeared in bold type in the national telephone directory.
24 ZIS *Press Release* no. 254/66, 10 February 1966, pp. 2–3, and no. 544/66, 24 March 1966, p. 1. One measure of white morale was the mining companies' report that, during December 1965 and January 1966, expatriate resignations in the industry had increased by about 60 per cent and engagements had fallen by about 10 per cent over the average rates since January 1965 (*Times of Zambia*, 24 February 1966, p. 9).
25 ZIS *Press Release* no. 254/66, 10 February 1966, p. 2, and no. 544/66, 24 March 1966, p. 1. The actual countries named were Angola, Zaire, Malawi, and the three East African countries.
26 ZIS *Press Release* no. 229/66, 8 February 1966. The missions visited Egypt, Italy, West Germany, the Netherlands, Denmark, Sweden, Czechoslovakia, Hong Kong, and Japan between 13 and 27 February. Zambia received trade delegations from Britain (23–28 January), Tanzania (6–13 February) and, in March 1966, Canada, Japan, and Singapore.
27 *Zambia News*, 20 February 1966, p. 7, and 17 April 1966, p. 3; *Financial Times*, 24 February 1966, p. 12; *Nat. Ass. Deb.* no. 10, cols. 348–9, 21 June 1967. In April an attempt was made to tighten import route control (ZIS *Press Release* no. 681/66, 21 April 1966, p. 10).
28 For an early indication of some reconsideration of this commitment, see *Financial Times*, 4 February 1966, p. 10. The 15 February deadline had never been publicly confirmed. In fact, Lusaka angrily dismissed reference to this date in the Salisbury press as "pure speculation" (ZIS *Press Release* no. 255/66, 10 February 1966, p. 2). The British also played down the date.
29 *Financial Times*, 31 January 1966, p. 1, 4 February 1966, p. 10, 10 February 1966, p. 9 and 12 February 1966, p. 9; *Guardian*, 10 February 1966, p. 11; *Times of Zambia*, 7 February 1966, p. 1. MacDonald visited Lusaka from 5 to 8 February. Press reports that he returned to London (on 8 February) with an ultimatum from Kaunda giving Wilson one week to topple Smith proved groundless. Good claims that the British had had "second thoughts" about the 15 February date but "were reluctant to reopen the question with Lusaka" (*UDI*, p. 124).

30 Five ministers were overseas and the remainder were scattered throughout the country on a major "meet the people" operation, from 10 to 20 February, to explain "what the government has been doing about development and the Rhodesian situation" (ZIS *Press Release* no. 224/66, 6 February 1966; *Times of Zambia*, 10 February 1966, p. 7). Only the president and the vice-president remained in Lusaka, though it was announced that ministers would be "accessible" for "vital duties."

31 *Rhodesia Herald*, 8 February 1966, p. 1; *Guardian*, 11 February 1966, p. 14; ZIS *Press Release* no. 255/66, 10 February 1966. The government suspected that the strike of white miners on 7 February was part of a carefully orchestrated Rhodesian plot to destabilize it on the eve of the planned break in relations (see note 10).

32 On 20 January Kamanga announced that "the illegal regime in Rhodesia is starting to crack" and on 17 February that its economy was "crumbling" and the outlook "bleak" (ZIS *Press Release* no. 125/66, 20 January 1966, p. 6, and no. 313/66, 17 February 1966, p. 5).

33 Good, *UDI*, pp. 126–49; ZIS *Background* no. 7/66, p. 4, 10 February 1966; *Times of Zambia*, 15 February 1966, p. 1. The first large shipment of South African oil reached Rhodesia, ironically, on 15 February.

34 Some difference in emphasis was evident in the views of Kaunda and Kapwepwe. The former declared in a BBC broadcast that he had no doubt about the power of economic sanctions to bring down the Smith regime "if it were not for the fact that Rhodesia is receiving formidable aid from South Africa" (*Times of Zambia*, 15 February 1966, p. 1), whereas the latter asserted that "Zambia has never at any time believed that sanctions alone would topple the rebel regime" (*Zambia Mail*, 18 February 1966, p. 1).

35 *Times of Zambia*, 28 February 1966, p. 1; *New York Times*, 20 March 1966, p. 27; *Financial Times*, 23 March 1966, p. 17; Good, *UDI*, pp. 153–4. Following his mission to Rhodesia, Selwyn Lloyd (Conservative shadow Commonwealth secretary) met with Kaunda, Kamanga, and Kapwepwe in Lusaka on 16 February, and impressed on them both the futility of sanctions and the necessity of initiating negotiations with Smith without pre-conditions (*Daily Telegraph*, 18 February 1966, p. 22).

36 *Times of Zambia*, 16 February 1966, p. 2; ZIS *Press Release* no. 229/66, 8 February 1966. The delegation to the OAU meeting included the heads of mission in Addis Ababa, Cairo, and Dar es Salaam along with a senior official from New York (ZIS *Press Release* no. 372/66, 24 February 1966).

37 ZIS *Press Release* No. 372/66, 24 February 1966; *ARB: PSC*, 1966, p.

462. The military mission, headed by Ghanaian Maj.-Gen. Nathan Aferi, visited Zambia, from 6 to 12 February. Its report questioned the feasibility of an OAU army liberating Rhodesia (Douglas G. Anglin and Timothy M. Shaw, *Zambia's Foreign Policy: Studies in Diplomacy and Dependence* [Boulder: Westview Press, 1979], pp. 128–9). See Decision no. 19.

38 *Times of Zambia*, 18 February 1966, p. 1; *The Times* (London), 23 February 1966, p. 9; Good, *UDI*, p. 155. MacDonald's hasty return may have been prompted in part by the statement of Home Affairs Minister Mainza Chona in Addis Ababa on 21 February that "Zambia will tell the Committee [of Five] that the economic sanctions are not working and that pressure must be put on Britain to use force right now" (*Times of Zambia*, 22 February 1966, p. 1).

39 Based on Good's paraphrase (*UDI*, p. 155).

40 *Times of Zambia*, 28 February 1966, p. 1. The meeting convened following the president's broadcast to the nation on the emergency measures he had taken to end the strike of expatriate miners. It is not clear how many ministers attended, though the full cabinet was not present.

41 The appeals for the use of force were softened, not silenced (*Times of Zambia*, 28 February 1966, p. 1, and 7 March 1966, p. 1).

42 *Times of Zambia*, 28 February 1966, p. 1; *Observer*, 22 May 1966, p. 2.

43 OAU Res. CM/Res. 75 (VI), 5 March 1966.

44 Mwangilwa, *Kapwepwe Diaries*, p. 67. Despite the deletion of the controversial clause that would have sanctioned the restoration of relations with Britain, the resolution received the support of only twenty-three of the thirty-six member states. Four (Guinea, Kenya, Mali, and Tanzania) had previously walked out in protest at the seating of the new Ghana regime that overthrew Nkrumah, four (Algeria, Congo Brazzaville, Egypt, and Somalia) withdrew in opposition to the resolution, which was variously characterized as "flabby," "irresponsible," and "submissive," Mauretania formally declared itself a "non-participant," Sudan abstained, and three others were absent (*New York Times*, 5 March 1966, p. 2, and 6 March 1966, p. 9; *ARB: PSC*, 1966, p. 483).

45 OAU Res. CM/Res. 75 (VI); *Times of Zambia*, 3 March 1966, p. 1, and 7 March 1966, p. 1. It is significant that no West African state, either anglophone or francophone, accepted membership on the committee.

46 Good, *UDI*, pp. 115, 117; *Financial Times*, 24 February 1966, p. 2 and 16 March 1966, p. 19. Smith did his best to fan Zambian frustrations with the British. "The tragedy," he declared in a broadcast, "is that this newly independent country ... is being dragged down

into economic ruin and political chaos in order to satisfy the whims of certain British politicians ... Zambia and its economy are mere pawns in the game as far as the British politicians are concerned" (*Guardian*, 11 February 1966, p. 14). Two days earlier the *Rhodesia Herald* (8 February 1966, p. 1) headlined its lead story: "Zambia's economy is threatened by planned break with Rhodesia" (ZIS *Press Release* no. 255/66, 10 February 1966, p. 1). See also note 10.

47 Good, *UDI*, pp. 124, 161; Hall, *High Price of Principles*, p. 148; *Financial Times*, 4 February 1966, p. 10, and 16 March 1966, p. 19; *Times of Zambia*, 15 February 1966, p. 1; *Zambia Mail*, 18 February 1966, p. 1; *Observer*, 20 February 1966, p. 4.

48 *Nat. Ass. Deb.* no. 6, cols. 4–5, 7, 8 March 1966; ZIS *Press Release* no. 330/66, 18 February 1966; Hall, *High Price of Principles*, pp. 147–8.

49 *Zambia Mail*, 18 February 1966, p. 1; ZIS *Press Release* no. 426/66, 3 March 1966, p. 2, and no. 476/66, 10 March 1966, p. 9; *Nat. Ass. Deb.* no. 6, cols. 5–6, 8 March 1966; K.D. Kaunda, "A racial holocaust in Central Africa?" *Punch* (London), 9 March 1966, p. 334; *Financial Times*, 19 March 1966, p. 9.

50 See Derek Taylor's sobering analyses (*Times of Zambia*, 25 February 1966, p. 9, and 26 February 1966, p. 7); also *Daily Telegraph*, 2 March 1966, p. 22. Kaunda conferred with Selwyn Lloyd on 16 February on his return from Rhodesia, and with Sir Ronald Prain, RST chairman, early in March following his midnight visit to Moamba rail junction in Mozambique to check at first hand on the routing of oil trains (*Observer*, 19 November 1978, p. 13).

51 *Financial Times*, 17 February 1966, p. 10; Good, *UDI*, pp. 127–8, 131.

52 The Commonwealth Sanctions Committee met on 23 February (and its Sub-Committee on Cooperation with Zambia two days later). The OAU Council of Ministers met from 28 February to 6 March. Consultations were also held with Sir William McFadzean, chairman of British Insulated Callender's Cables, a major consumer of Zambian copper, during his visit to Zambia in early March. Party officials and the public were not entirely neglected; cabinet members toured the country on a "meet the people" campaign from 10 to 20 February, and Kaunda visited the Copperbelt on a similar "Operation Capitao" on 6 and 7 March.

53 ZIS *Background* no. 7/66, p.3, 10 February 1966; *Times of Zambia*, 15 February 1966; p. 1; Kaunda, "Racial holocaust," p. 335.

54 *Financial Times*, 16 March 1966, p. 19 (based on an interview with Arthur Wina).

55 *Nat. Ass. Deb.* no. 6, col. 3, 8 March 1966.

56 *Financial Times*, 16 March 1966, p. 19, and 23 March 1966, p. 17.

Article 50 of the UN Charter entitled countries "confronted with special economic problems ... to consult the Security Council."

57 ZIS *Press Release* no. 584/66, 2 April 1966, and *Background* no. 9/66, p. 1, 1 April 1966; Hall, *High Price of Principles*, p. 150; Good, *UDI*, p. 155. In a letter to Wilson on 7 April, Kaunda undertook to put his own detailed ideas on paper, though it appears that he did not do so before the offer was overtaken by events. On pre-election expectations, see also *Times of Zambia*, 28 February 1966; p. 1; *New York Times*, 20 March 1966, p. 27; *Financial Times*, 23 March 1966, p. 17.

58 Hall, *High Price of Principles*, pp. 139, 153; Good, *UDI*, p. 155; ZIS *Press Release* no. 681/66, 21 April 1966, p. 2.

59 *Times of Zambia*, 29 April 1966, p. 1; *Zambia Mail*, 29 April 1966, p. 12. A week earlier Kamanga had declared on television that "our patience is not inexhaustible and, now that three weeks have passed since the British general elections, we are waiting anxiously for evidence of a new British initiative to bring about the removal of the rebel regime and the introduction of democratic constitutional government in Rhodesia" (ZIS *Press Release* No. 681/66, 21 April 1966, p. 2).

60 *Times of Zambia*, 30 April 1966, p. 1. MacDonald subsequently confessed that he found the task of constantly justifying Wilson's Rhodesian policy to Kaunda both difficult and disagreeable as he neither fully agreed with it nor wholly trusted Wilson's promises. In the case of the infamous "talks about talks," MacDonald dutifully assured Kaunda categorically that these were not a prelude to a "sell-out," even though this is what MacDonald feared they were. He did so partly because he had been so instructed and partly in the (vain) hope that the firmer the commitment, the more likely Wilson would respect it.

61 British *H. C. Deb.* vol. 727, cols. 743–4, 27 April 1966; Hall, *High Price of Principles*, pp. 148–53; Good, *UDI*, pp. 154, 293. Kaunda had earlier denounced the Conservative call for negotiations as morally and politically indefensible (*Times of Zambia*, 2 April 1966, p. 1; *Financial Times*, 19 March 1966, p. 9). Many Labour MPs were also reluctant to get drawn further into the Rhodesian imbroglio.

62 Kaunda's suspicions may have been aroused earlier by a mysterious visit to Salisbury, 14–23 March, by Duncan Watson, under-secretary of state in the Commonwealth Relations Office, ostensibly to "check on the accommodation and administrative arrangements" of the British High Commission but actually to sound out Smith on a sell-out (*Daily Telegraph*, 16 March 1966, p. 1, and 24 March 1966, p. 23).

63 Good, *UDI*, p. 235; David Martin and Phyllis Johnston, *The Struggle for Zimbabwe: The Chimurenga War* (London: Faber and Faber, 1981),

pp. 9–12; Flower, *Serving Secretly*, pp. 105–7. "Are they going to wait until thousands of people are killed?" Kaunda asked angrily (ZIS *Press Release* no. 773/66, 30 April 1966, p. 1).

64 Hall, *High Price of Principles*, pp. 151–3; Good, *UDI*, pp. 154–6, 161; *Times of Zambia*, 30 April 1966, p. 1; ZIS *Press Release* no. 773/66, 30 April 1966, and *Background* no. 34/67, p. 2, 4 November 1967; *Observer*, 1 May 1966, p. 1, and 22 May 1966, p. 2.

65 In May a deliberately provoked railway payments crisis with Rhodesia halted all traffic between the two countries; in July Kaunda threatened to quit the Commonwealth and personally boycotted the Commonwealth conference in September. On the concept of a "protracted conflict," see Michael Brecher, "International Crises and Protracted Conflicts," *International Interactions* 11:3–4 (1984), pp. 237–97.

CHAPTER 8

1 Prime Minister's Office, *Economic Aspects of a Declaration of Independence* (Salisbury: Government Printer, 1965), CSR 15–1965, pp. 3–4. Smith asked the white electorate for "a blank cheque to run this country in what we consider to be the best interests." His claim that "the reason for the election had nothing to do with a UDI" was rightly treated with scepticism (*Rhodesia Herald* [Salisbury], 22 April 1965, p. 1).

2 Michael Brecher, "A Theoretical Approach to International Crisis Behaviour," *Jerusalem Journal of International Relations* 3:2–3 (Winter–Spring 1978), pp. 7–8.

3 *Times of Zambia* (Ndola), 24 November 1965, p. 1, 26 November 1965, p. 1, and 29 November 1965, p. 1.

4 Ole R. Holsti and Alexander L. George, "The Effects of Stress on the Performance of Foreign Policy Makers," *Political Science Annual* 6 (1975), p. 262.

5 Brumer noted, the day after UDI, that Kaunda "looked very weary and drawn from the tension of the past 24 hours" (Roy Christie, *For the President's Eyes Only: The Story of John Brumer Agent Extraordinary* [Johannesburg: Hugh Keartland, 1971], p. 142. Hall observed that the prospects UDI posed were "little short of terrifying for Kenneth Kaunda" (Richard Hall and Hugh Peyman, *The Great Uhuru Railway: China's Showpiece in Africa* [London: Victor Gollancz, 1976], p. 76).

6 *Sunday Times* (London), 5 December 1965, p. 11; British *H. C. Deb.*, 1965–66, vol. 721, col. 1435, 1 December 1965. See also Robert C. Good, *UDI: The International Politics of the Rhodesian Rebellion* (Princeton: Princeton University Press, 1973), pp. 98, 99; Arnold Smith

with Clyde Sanger, *Stitches in Time: The Commonwealth in World Affairs* (London: André Deutsch, 1981), p. 29.
7 Michael Brecher, *Decisions in Crisis: Israel, 1967 and 1973* (Berkeley: University of California Press, 1980), pp. 20 n23, 78.
8 A further, and somewhat more questionable, breakdown of threatened values into sixteen elements is found in Table A39.
9 As was noted in chapter 4 (but not fully reflected in the data derived from public statements), time pressures were also experienced in connection with the contingency planning during the run-up to UDI; see especially Decisions No. 7, 8, 9, 11, and 14.
10 Christie, *For the President's Eyes Only*, pp. 143, 145. A Canadian diplomat in Lusaka reported on 23 November 1965 that the government feared that "if economic sanctions do not defeat the Smith government in 3 or 4 months, then UDI will succeed."
11 Good, *UDI*, p. 96, "Britain's policy ... needed above all time for sanctions to take their toll ... It was precisely Kaunda's objective to deny this time and to force the pace of Britain's response" (p. 99).
12 Richard Hall, *The High Price of Principles: Kaunda and the White South* (Harmondsworth: Penguin, 1973), p. 127. Kaunda saw the Rhodesian crisis as global in scope. "How many of you gentlemen," he inquired at a press conference, "realize how close we are to a third world war? I personally realize it" (Zambia Information Services [ZIS], *Background* no. 49/65, p. 2, 25 November 1965).
13 Ibid., no. 50/65, p. 4, 2 December 1965; *Sunday Times*, 5 December 1965, p. 11.
14 OAU doc. ECM/PV.1 (VI), 3 December 1965, p. 28.
15 Brecher, *Decisions in Crisis*, p. 5.
16 *Central African Mail* (Ndola), 9 April 1965, p. 8.
17 ZIS *Background* no. 19/65, p. 1, 3 June 1965.
18 Hall, *High Price of Principles*, pp. 112, 125-7; *Daily Telegraph* (London), 16 November 1965, p.26.
19 *Sunday Express* (Johannesburg), 10 October 1965, p. 2.
20 Although Kaunda stated that UDI would "virtually mean war," he later explained that he meant economic rather than military aggression (ZIS *Press Release* no. 722/65, 6 May 1965, p. 2).
21 ZIS *Press Release* no. 1785/65, 7 November 1965, pp. 6-8; ZIS *Background* no. 48/65, p. 1, 17 November 1965, and no. 56/65, pp. 3, 4, 30 December 1965; *Sunday Times*, 5 December 1965, p. 11; Zambia *Nat. Ass. Deb.* no. 5, col. 93, 9 December 1965.
22 ZIS *Press Release* no. 1815/65, 11 November 1965, p. 4. "We should not take chances," Kaunda explained, on "any misbehaviour of the rebel troops" (ZIS *Background* no. 47/65, p. 1, 14 November 1965).

23 ZIS *Press Release* no. 1785/65, 7 November 1965, p. 8.
24 *Nat. Ass. Deb.* no. 5, col. 96, 9 December 1965; also ZIS *Background* no. 50/65, p. 1, 2 December 1965. Malcolm MacDonald claimed that Kaunda resisted the stationing of British troops in Zambia for defensive purposes in part because they might precipitate rather than deter a Rhodesian attack, which Kaunda genuinely feared (interview with MacDonald, 10 May 1978; see also *Guardian* [London], 30 November 1965, p. 10).
25 *Daily Mail* (London), 8 December 1965, p. 6. "As our great weakness was in the air," Kaunda explained, "I wanted this protection first of all" (*Sunday Times*, 5 December 1965, p. 11). Even Wilson recognized that the threat of a "possible Rhodesian pre-emptive strike against Lusaka and the mines" had to be taken seriously (Harold Wilson, *Personal Record: The Labour Government, 1964–1970* [Boston: Little Brown, 1971], p. 182).
26 ZIS *Background* no. 50/65, p. 1, 2 December 1965.
27 Jan Pettman, *Zambia: Security and Conflict* (London: Julian Friedmann, 1974), pp. 25, 195; Hall, *High Price of Principles*, p. 107.
28 *Nat. Ass. Deb.* no. 5, cols. 95, 96, 9 December 1965. There was also some concern about a possible South African air strike. Significantly, the first SAAF fighters arrived at the new Caprivi air base two days after UDI (OAU doc. ECM/PV.1 [VI], 3 December 1965, p. 26). Kaunda attempted to reassure the public: "We do not worry about such things. We do not intend to be intimidated" (ZIS *Background* no. 47/65, p. 1, 14 November 1965). Kapwepwe, however, later charged that Pretoria "almost made an agreement with Rhodesia to bomb our airports" (*Financial Times* [London], 3 December 1965, p. 26).
29 *Observer* (London), 5 December 1965, p. 2; *Daily Telegraph*, 17 January 1966, p. 14. In a telephone conversation with Sir Ronald Prain, the chairman of RST, a few days after UDI, Kaunda said that Kariba was a "nightmare"; Prain told him there was nothing to worry about (interview with Prain, 25 July 1978).
30 ZIS *Press Release* no. 1911/65, 26 November 1965, p. 1; *Times of Zambia*, 27 November 1965, p. 1.
31 *Nat. Ass. Deb.* no. 5, col. 93, 9 December 1965. "What is to prevent one saboteur ... from committing the mildest but most obvious bit of sabotage within the Kariba generating station? Such an act would instantly create a *causus belli*" (*Sunday Times*, 5 December 1965, p. 11, based on an interview with Kaunda).
32 *Observer*, 5 December 1965, p. 2.

CHAPTER 9

1 Michael Brecher, *Decisions in Crisis: Israel, 1967 and 1973* (Berkeley: University of California Press, 1980), pp. 343, 375–8, 397, 399, 402–3.
2 Ibid., p. 27. There is little direct evidence available on the relationship between stress and the size of the information-consuming body, though it can be assumed to correspond closely to the "effective decisional forum" analysed below.
3 Among the hypotheses generated elsewhere are: "The greater the crisis, the greater the felt need for information" (Glenn D. Paige, *The Korean Decision* [New York: Free Press, 1968], p. 292); under conditions of high stress, the "search for information about the crisis situation and alternative courses of action is likely to become more active" (Ole R. Holsti and Alexander L. George, "The Effects of Stress on the Performance of Foreign Policy-Makers," *Political Science Annual* 6 [1975], p. 280); "As crisis-induced stress rises, the quest for information about the threatening events tends to become more thorough" (Brecher, *Decisions in Crisis*, p. 397).
4 Zambia Information Services (ZIS), *Background* no. 47/65, p. 4, 14 November 1965; no. 48/65, p. 1, 17 November 1965; no. 49/65, p. 3, 25 November 1965; no. 50/65, pp. 2–3, 3 December 1965; no. 52/65, pp. 1–3, 12 December 1965; no. 56/65, p. 2, 30 December 1965. "Up to now, we do not know what is going to happen" (ZIS *Press Release* no. 1857/65, 17 November 1965, p. 1).
5 Robert C. Good, *UDI: The International Politics of the Rhodesian Rebellion* (Princeton: Princeton University Press, 1973), p. 98.
6 *Sunday Times* (London), 5 December 1965, p. 11. Richard Hall interpreted this response as an admission that serious divisions existed within the cabinet (*The High Price of Principles: Kaunda and the White South* [Harmondsworth: Penguin, 1973], p. 130).
7 The modes show the shift in the extent of the information probes more clearly than the medians. The modal category for the pre-crisis period is "minimal" and for the crisis period "thorough."
8 *Zambia Mail* (Ndola), 17 December 1965, p. 5; *Guardian* (London), 11 December 1965, p. 1. Similar action had been taken prior to the OAU summit in Accra in October (Decision No. 12), another occasion when Zambia was resisting OAU pressure (*Zambia Mail*, 15 October 1965, p. 8).
9 Nairobi (November 15), Washington (December 22–8), Moscow (December 22–5), and Dar es Salaam (December 28).
10 Kaunda wrote Wilson on 14, 17, 22, and 26 November and 2 and 8

December 1965. He also wrote to Lyndon B. Johnson, Joseph Mobutu, Lester B. Pearson, and Antonio Salazar as well as all African heads of state at least once.

11 Charles F. Hermann, ed., *International Crisis: Insights from Behavioral Research* (New York: Free Press, 1972), p. 202.
12 Brecher, *Decisions in Crisis*, pp. 397, 399.
13 "Receptivity" is defined operationally in terms, not of whether factual inputs are digested or disregarded, but of the extent to which they are accepted or rejected on their objective merits rather than being "filtered through a prism heavily influenced by past experience, ideology, etc." (ibid., p. 362).
14 Zambia *Nat. Ass. Deb.* no. 5, col. 92, 9 December 1965.
15 Distrust can be distinguished from non-receptivity in that it represents a judgment on sources of information rather than on the information itself.
16 Brecher, *Decisions in Crisis*, p. 399. Institutional meetings are characterized as having "permanence in organizational form; legal authorization to make decisions; and relative stability in composition" (p. 83).
17 For example, the *Times of Zambia* (Ndola) (2 December 1965, p. 1) reported that one cabinet consultation with a British ministerial delegation ended "shortly before midnight tonight, after nearly three hours of talks." Similarly, the *Daily Telegraph* (London) (8 January 1966, p. 22) noted "a 3 a.m. meeting today between President Kaunda and some of his ministers." There were also late-night sessions at State House during both the pre-crisis and the post-crisis periods (Decisions No. 4 and 33) (*Times of Zambia*, 28 February 1966, p. 1).
18 Brecher, *Decisions in Crisis*, p. 399.
19 Avi Shlaim notes that "declining stress was accompanied only by a slow and partial contraction of the consultative circle" (*The United States and the Berlin Blockade, 1948–1949: A Study in Crisis Decision Making* [Berkeley: University of California Press, 1983], p. 412). The limited number of cases in the post-crisis period of the Zambian study makes it difficult to draw firm conclusions based on them.
20 For the crisis period, the scope of consultations was "moderate" or "extensive" in nine of the thirteen cases in which the decision time was deemed "brief," compared with only one of four pre-crisis (and one out of one post-crisis) cases.
21 "These contingency plans, of course, were made, and continue to be made, in conjunction with the British and American governments" (K.D. Kaunda, *Nat. Ass. Deb.* no. 5, col. 92, 9 December 1965).

"There is a continuous flow and exchange of letters and communications and what not" with the British (Kaunda, ZIS *Background* no. 48/65, p. 3, 19 November 1965).

22 Glenn D. Paige, "Comparative Case Analysis of Crisis Decisions: Korea and Cuba," in Hermann, *International Crises*, p. 52.

23 Alan Dowty reports that in the 1958 US crisis over Lebanon, "there was as much or more consultation when decision time was most limited" (*Middle East Crisis: US Decision-Making in 1958, 1970, and 1973* [Berkeley: University of California Press, 1984], p. 347).

24 Holsti and George suggest that "as stress increases, both the frequency and intensity of interaction tend to rise" ("The Effects of Stress," p. 289). Avi Shlaim notes "a deeper involvement of the top decision makers in the consultative process" and "an intensification of inter-Allied consultations at all levels" during the crisis period, though only "a slow and barely perceptive move from the frequent, highly intensive ... patterns of consultation" in the post-crisis period (*The United States and the Berlin Blockade*, p. 412).

25 These motives differ somewhat in their definitions from those Alexander L. George has advanced, namely, understanding and support, political legitimacy and emotional support in addition to cognitive needs (*Presidential Decision Making in Foreign Policy: The Effective Use of Information and Advice* [Boulder: Westview Press, 1980], p. 81). See also Shlaim, *United States and the Berlin Blockade*, pp. 273–6.

26 Paige, *The Korean Decision*, p. 281; Brecher, *Decisions in Crisis*, pp. 377, 399.

27 Holsti and George, "The Effects of Stress," p. 288; Brecher, *Decisions in Crisis*, pp. 356, 377, 399. In an earlier study Brecher reported that the size of the decisional unit, under conditions of enhanced threat, was "slightly larger in two of the three reported cases of economically developing and underdeveloped crisis actors" (*Jerusalem Journal of International Relations* 3:1–2 [Winter–Spring 1978], p. 274).

28 A pre-crisis example of this was Decision No. 4 on coal-mining. Kaunda may also have felt that his cabinet would prove more supportive and manageable than his senior ministers.

29 For the distinction between decision taking and decision making, see Bahgat Korany, *How Foreign Policy Decisions Are Made in the Third World* (Boulder: Westview Press, 1986), pp. 171–2.

30 Holsti and George note that the acceptance of a decision by those whose political support is necessary or desirable may have several dimensions: "agreement with the decision because it is persuasively explained; acceptance because it is authoritatively made and announced; acceptance because of the quality of the procedures

followed in arriving at the decision" ("The Effects of Stress," pp. 270, 273 n12).
31 Cited in Brecher, *Decisions in Crisis*, p. 376.
32 Holsti and George, "The Effects of Stress," pp. 267, 289–90. The minor cabinet crisis in January 1966 that resulted in the dismissal of two ministers had nothing to do with the UDI crisis, though it is perhaps significant that it came to a head only during the post-crisis period.
33 Shlaim, *The United States and the Berlin Blockade*, p. 415; Holsti and George, "The Effects of Stress," pp. 280–1, 290–1.
34 Brecher, *Decisions in Crisis*, p. 358.
35 Ibid., p. 399; Holsti and George, "The Effects of Stress," pp. 288–9. Brecher adds (p. 402) that, as stress declines, "the search for options tends to become less extensive."
36 Brecher, *Decisions in Crisis*, p. 360
37 Ibid., p. 377; Holsti and George, "The Effects of Stress," p. 280.
38 Ole R. Holsti, *Crisis, Escalation, War* (Montreal: McGill-Queen's University Press, 1972), p. 121.
39 Holsti and George, "The Effects of Stress," pp. 280, 282, 291.
40 Ole R. Holsti, "Theories of Crisis Decision Making," in Paul Gordon Lauren, ed. *Diplomacy: New Approaches in History, Theory, and Policy* (New York: Free Press, 1979), pp. 405, 410. See also Holsti and George, "The Effects of Stress," pp. 277–8, 288.
41 Holsti and George note (p. 256 n1) that their analysis is largely drawn from American experience and may have "more limited applicability for other nations (e.g. in small countries that have small or virtually non-existent foreign policy bureaucracies)."
42 Holsti, "Theories of Crisis Decision Making," pp. 107–9; Alexander L George, *Presidential Decision Making in Foreign Policy*, pp. 48–9; Holsti and George, "The Effects of Stress," pp. 279–80.
43 Holsti and George, "The Effects of Stress," p. 278; Shlaim, *The United States and the Berlin Blockade*, pp. 403–4.
44 David A. Hamburg and Alexander L. George, "Nuclear Crisis Management," *Bulletin of the Atomic Scientists* 40:6 (June/July 1984), p. 25.
45 Maurice A. East, "Size and Foreign Policy Behaviour: A Test of Two Models," *World Politics* 25:4 (July 1973), pp. 559, 568, 576.
46 *Nat. Ass. Deb.* no. 5, col. 92, 9 December 1965. Kaunda questioned the theoretical basis of British sanctions on the grounds that it "seems to me to misunderstand the nature of the European community in Rhodesia" (*Punch* [London], 9 March 1966, p. 335).
47 Hall, *The High Price of Principles*, pp. 44–5, 136, 139, 150.
48 Hamburg and George, "Nuclear Crisis Management," p. 25.
49 Douglas G. Anglin and Timothy M. Shaw, *Zambia's Foreign Policy:*

Studies in Diplomacy and Dependence (Boulder: Westview, 1979), pp. 146–50. The minister of home affairs confidently asserted that the conquest of Rhodesia would be as easy as "crushing a louse" (ZIS *Press Release* no. 1993/65, 8 December 1965, p. 1).

50 Hamburg and George, "Nuclear Crisis Management," p. 25.
51 Ibid.
52 Good, *UDI*, p. 108.
53 Shlaim and, somewhat more cautiously, Brecher also challenge Holsti's sweeping generalizations (*United States and the Berlin Blockade*, pp. 422–3; *Decisions in Crisis*, pp. 346–7).
54 Hugh Thomas, ed., *The Crisis in the Civil Service* (London: Anthony Blond, 1968), p. 98.
55 With increasing stress, fourteen hypotheses are confirmed strongly and three disconfirmed strongly. The comparable figures under conditions of diminishing stress are nine and eight.
56 Brecher, *Decisions in Crisis*, pp. 399, 402; Holsti and George, "The Effects of Stress," pp. 280, 290.
57 Brecher, *Decisions in Crisis*, pp. 399, 402.

CHAPTER 10

1 Ole R. Holsti and Alexander L. George, "The Effects of Stress on the Performance of Foreign Policy Makers," *Political Science Annual* 6(1975), p. 269.
2 "As crisis-induced stress begins to rise, the number and variety of core inputs to decision increase sharply" and, as it declines, they are reduced (Michael Brecher, *Decisions in Crisis: Israel, 1967 and 1973* [Berkeley: University of California Press, 1980], p. 402).
3 Brecher, *Decisions in Crisis*, pp. 383–96, 402; Alan Dowty, *Middle East Crisis: US Decision-Making in 1958, 1970 and 1973* (Berkeley: University of California Press, 1984), p. 355. A comparison of perceived "importance" using average values on Brecher's 5-point scale points to the relative insensitivity of Zambian behavioural patterns to changing conditions of stress:

Decision Makers	Period			Average
	Pre-Crisis	Crisis	Post-Crisis	
Israelis	1.6	3.2	2.5	2.8
Americans	2.2	3.8	2.6	3.0
Zambians	2.5	3.4	3.2	3.0

On the whole, Zambian decision makers appear to have judged the importance of choices to be greater (and their costs lower) than American and Israeli decision makers. This may in part reflect the greater experience of the Israelis in coping with international crises.

4 Brecher, *Decisions in Crisis*, p. 402. Dowty's crises revealed no clear patterns (*Middle East Crisis*, p. 355).

5 The contrast between the substance of the Zambian decisions and that of the two Middle East studies is evident from the following data on the relative emphasis on the various issue areas in decisions:

	Issue Areas			
Decision Actors	Military-security %	Political-diplomatic %	Cultural-status %	Economic-developmental %
Israelis	54	39	5	2
Americans	48	50	0	2
Zambians	11	40	17	32

(Brecher, *Decisions in Crisis*, pp. 382–95 and Dowty, *Middle East Crisis*, pp. 356–61).

6 Zambia *Nat. Ass. Deb.* no. 5, col. 93, 9 December 1965.

7 Zambia Information Services (ZIS), *Background* no. 49/65, pp. 2–3, 25 November 1965.

8 As earlier noted, a similar conclusion was reached concerning core inputs. The perceived scope of inputs and outputs (domains) can be seen by comparing tables A30 and A33, section b.

9 This confirms Dowty's findings but not Brecher's, except partially for the period of rising tension (*Middle East Crisis*, p. 355; *Decisions in Crisis*, pp. 382–96, 403). The following is a comparison of the average number of domains per decision for the three studies:

	Period			Overall
Actors	Pre-Crisis	Crisis	Post-Crisis	Average
Israel	1.0	2.0	2.3	2.0
United States	2.1	3.5	2.1	2.7
Zambia	2.4	3.0	2.8	2.7

10 ZIS *Press Release* no. 700/65, p. 15, 5 May 1965, and no. 1785/65, p. 16, 7 November 1965.

11 Bahgat Korany, "Foreign Policy in the Third World: An Introduction," *International Political Science Review* 5:1 (1984), p. 12.
12 Brecher (*Decisions in Crisis*, pp. 382–98, 403), and Dowty (*Middle East Crisis*, pp. 355–61) report a steady increase in preferences for rational decisional processes over the course of their crises:

Actors	Rational Processes by Crisis Period			
	Pre-Crisis %	Crisis %	Post-Crisis %	Average %
Israelis	0	53	60	51
Americans	64	90	93	84
Zambians	71	56	75	65

Both Middle East studies record a greater salience of routine procedures (19 and 10 per cent respectively overall compared with 3 per cent for Zambia). The prominence Brecher accords affective processes (30 per cent) is comparable to the 32 per cent evinced here; both are substantially higher than the mere 6 per cent attributed to the "rational" American decision makers.

13 Only 21 per cent of the decisions were physical or verbal/physical compared to with 49 per cent in the case of the United States in the Dowty study and 65 per cent in the case of Israel in the Brecher study. Maurice A. East claims that, contrary to conventional thinking, "small states do not initiate as much verbal behaviour as large states" (and small developing states generate even less). This is confirmed in the case of Israel but not in the case of Zambia ("Size and Foreign Policy Behavior: A Test of Two Models," *World Politics* 25:4 [July 1973], pp. 566, 576).
14 Brecher, *Decisions in Crisis*, p. 403; Dowty, *Middle East Crisis*, p. 362.
15 *Nat. Ass. Deb.* no. 5, col. 97, 9 December 1965. A few months later Kaunda reiterated that "we in Zambia have a record of having been right so frequently in the past that we fear we are about to be proved right again" (ibid., no. 6, cols. 3–4, 8 March 1966). See also *Punch* (London), 9 March 1966, p. 335. On the other hand, Kaunda misled the OAU summit in October 1965 by claiming that the advocates of UDI were merely "a lunatic fringe who do not represent ... even the majority of white people who have been cowed into silence" (Colin Legum, ed., *Zambia: Independence and Beyond: The Speeches of Kenneth Kaunda* [London: Nelson, 1966], p. 228).
16 Robert C. Good, *UDI: The International Politics of the Rhodesian Rebel-*

lion (Princeton: Princeton University Press, 1973), p. 96. The cabinet secretary had earlier warned the British that they were "underestimating the force of white nationalism" in Rhodesia, and that UDI would be "a long drawn-out affair" (ibid., p. 94). Kapwepwe predicted twelve to fifteen years (OAU doc. ECM/PV.1 [VI], 3 December 1965, p. 46; ZIS *Press Release* no. 3/66, 3 January 1966).

17 Good, *UDI*, p. 96. Kapwepwe later claimed that, as a result of "applying pressure on Britain to take effective measures ... 90% of the sanctions called for had been applied" (*Africa Research Bulletin: Economic, Financial and Technical*, 1966, p. 460).

18 Arnold Smith with Clyde Sanger, *Stitches in Time: The Commonwealth in World Politics* (London: André Deutsch, 1981), p. 58. Malcolm MacDonald was highly critical of the failure of the British government to take military action immediately after UDI. Douglas G. Anglin and Timothy M. Shaw, *Zambia's Foreign Policy: Studies in Diplomacy and Dependence* (Boulder: Westview Press, 1979), pp. 152–4; Good, *UDI*, pp. 55–65.

19 James Callaghan, *Time and Chance* (London: Collins, 1987), p. 145. Two other Labour ministers have since admitted that Britain missed her opportunity: David Owen (*The Politics of Defence* [London: Cape, 1972], p. 116) and Cledwyn Hughes (personal interview, 31 July 1978).

20 Bahgat Korany and Ali E. Hillal Dessouki, *The Foreign Policies of Arab States: The Challenge of Change*, 2nd ed. (Boulder: Westview Press, 1991), p. 11; Harold and Margaret Sprout, "Environmental factors in the study of international politics," *Journal of Conflict Resolution* 1:4 (December 1957), pp. 318–19; Michael Brecher et al., "A framework for research on foreign policy behavior," *Journal of Conflict Resolution* 13:1 (March 1969), pp. 81, 86.

21 Anglin and Shaw, *Zambia's Foreign Policy*, p. 142.

22 Harold Wilson, *Personal Record: The Labour Government, 1964–1970* (Boston: Little Brown, 1971), pp. 182–3; British *H.C. Deb.*, vol. 721, col. 1433, 1 December 1965; ZIS *Background* no. 1/66, 2 January 1966, p. 2; Barbara Castle, *The Castle Diaries, 1964–70* (London: Weidenfeld and Nicolson, 1985), p. 73.

23 Richard L. Sklar, *Corporate Power in an African State: The Political Impact of Multinational Mining Companies in Zambia* (Berkeley: University of California Press, 1975), p. 153. See also Castle, *The Castle Diaries*, p. 131; ZIS *Background* no. 12/66, p. 4, 14 May 1966.

24 East concludes that, when controlling for size and level of development, small developing states exhibit the lowest percentage of any category in terms of conflictual non-verbal (high-risk) behaviour ("Size and Foreign Policy Behaviour," pp. 571, 576). Zambia

certainly did not eschew risks, even though there were limits to the risks it was prepared to run.

25 Sklar, *Corporate Power in an African State*, pp. 148–55.
26 "The Effects of Stress," p. 269.

CHAPTER 11

1 The six books previously published are: Michael Brecher, *Decisions in Crisis: Israel, 1967 and 1973* (1980); Avi Shlaim, *The United States and the Berlin Blockade, 1948–1949: A Study in Crisis Decision Making* (1983); Alan Dowty, *Middle East Crisis: US Decision-Making in 1958, 1970, and 1973* (1984); Karen Dawisha, *The Kremlin and the Prague Spring* (1984); Geoffrey Jukes, *Hitler's Stalingrad Decisions* (1985); and Steven A. Hoffmann, *India and the China Crisis* (1990). Several other crises are dealt with more briefly in the *Jerusalem Journal of International Relations* 3:2–3 (Winter–Spring 1978): Frederic S. Pearson and R.E. Doerga, "The Netherlands and the 1940 Nazi Invasion" (pp. 25–50); Yoram Shapira, "The 1954 Guatemala Crisis" (pp. 81–116); Ya'acov Vertzberger, "India's Border Crisis with China, 1962" (pp. 117–42); Joseph Frankel, "Britain's Behaviour in the Cyprus Crisis, 1974" (pp. 229–44); and A.I. Dawisha, "Syria's Intervention in Lebanon, 1975–1976" (pp. 245–63).

2 No Independence Before Majority (African) Rule.

3 This point was also noted by Joseph Frankel in his study of "Britain's Behaviour in the Cyprus Crisis, 1974" (p. 244).

4 Dowty, *Middle East Crisis*, pp. 374–5.

5 Maurice East, "Size and Foreign Policy Behavior: A Test of Two Models," *World Politics* 25:4 (July 1973), pp. 557–8, 560. Bahgat Korany and Ali E. Hillal Dessouki also argue that the foreign policies of developed and developing states are qualitatively and not simply quantitatively different as a result, in the case of the latter, of such special features as "modernization, the low level of political institutionalization at home, and dependency status in the global stratification system abroad" (*The Foreign Policies of Arab States*, 2nd ed. [Boulder: Westview, 1991], p. 9).

6 Kenneth Kaunda, *A Humanist in Africa: Letters to Colin Morris* (London: Longmans, 1966), p. 29.

7 East, "Size and Foreign Policy Behavior," pp. 559, 568, 576; Robert L. Rothstein, *The Weak in the World of the Strong: The Developing Countries in the International System* (New York: Columbia University Press, 1977), pp. 90, 106; Donald Rothchild and Robert L. Curry, *Scarcity, Choice, and Public Policy in Middle Africa* (Berkeley: University of California Press, 1978), p. 23.

8 See the discussion of "cognitive performance" (chapter 9) and of "quality of decisions" (chapter 10).
9 Rothstein, *Weak in the World of the Strong*, p. 106.
10 *Zambia Mail* (Lusaka), 31 December 1965, p. 1; 14 January 1966, p. 2; 11 March 1966, p. 1; Zambia Information Service (ZIS), *Press Release* no. 224/66, 6 February 1966.
11 Initially, one kwacha was worth $1.40. By 1994 it was worth less than one-fifth of a cent.
12 For an instructive characterization of the substance and style of Zambian foreign policy into the 1990s, see Stephen Chan, *Kaunda and Southern Africa: Image and Reality in Foreign Policy* (London: British Academic Press, 1992).
13 Bahgat Korany, "Foreign Policy in the Third World: An Introduction," *International Political Science Review* 5:1 (1984), p. 15. See Appendix 1.
14 Michael D. Wallace and Peter Suedfeld hypothesize that "lengthy tenure in high office" is a contributing factor to "the ability to maintain conceptual complexity under the stress of crisis" ("Leadership Performance in Crisis: The Longevity-Complexity Link," *International Studies Quarterly* 32:4 [December 1988], pp. 439, 447).

APPENDIX 1

1 This section draws upon Douglas G. Anglin, "Zambian Crisis Behavior: Rhodesia's Unilateral Declaration of Independence," *International Studies Quarterly* 24:4 (December 1980), pp. 588–91.
2 The coding was undertaken by the author. Although this eliminated the problem of intercoder reliability, it introduced an additional element of uncertainty. The author wishes to acknowledge the valuable assistance of Kathleen Morris Kallio at an earlier stage.
3 Jan Kees von Donge, writing in the early 1980s, characterized Kaunda as "a long-winded, repetitive, sometimes stammering speaker," some of whose speeches were "to a large extent, purely rhetorical," though they contained "flashes of meaningful insights as well" ("Nadine Gordimer's 'A Guest of Honour': A Failure to Understand Zambian Society," *Journal of Southern African Affairs* 9:1 [October 1982], p. 89).
4 For purposes of the model, the three crisis perceptions are viewed as "logically independent." Since they are in reality interrelated, a problem of multi-collinearity exists when seeking to "differentiate and rank order their importance in the explanation of behaviour and choice" (Michael Brecher, "A Theoretical Approach to Interna-

tional Crisis Behaviour," *Jerusalem Journal of International Relations* 3:2–3 (Winter–Spring 1978), p. 20 n7).
5 Michael Brecher, "Toward a Theory of International Crisis Behavior," *International Studies Quarterly* 21:1 (March 1977), pp. 66–7. The original Brecher dimensions of gravity of a crisis were (in rank-order): survival of population, independence as international actor, territorial integrity, autonomy of political system, economic interest, influence in international system(s), and societal stability. A subsequent revision lists: threat to existence, threat of grave damage, threat to influence in the international system, threat to territorial integrity, threat to political or social system, threat to economic interests, and threat (limited) to population and property.
6 UN doc. A/PV.1357, p. 5, 12 October 1965.
7 Zambia Information Service (ZIS), *Press Release* no. 1785/65, 7 November 1965, p. 2, and *Background* no. 47/65, 14 November 1965, p. 6. Kaunda also attempted, on one occasion, to minimize the threat posed by the Rhodesian coal surcharge (ibid., no. 56/65, 30 December 1965, p. 3).
8 *Times of Zambia*, 1 July 1985, p. 4.
9 Baghat Korany, "Foreign Policy in the Third World: An Introduction," *International Political Science Review* 5:1 (1984), p. 15.
10 Ole R. Holsti, *Content Analysis for the Social Sciences and Humanities* (Reading, MA: Addison-Wesley Publications, 1969); Robert. C. North et al., *Content Analysis: A Handbook with Applications for the Study of International Crisis* (Evanston: Northwestern University Press, 1963).

Index

AAC (Anglo-American Corporation), 25–6, 56, 57, 164; and coal, 61, 64–5, 306n35, 307nn41, 45
Aferi, Maj.-Gen. Nathan A., 325n72, 358n37
African National Congress, Northern Rhodesia, 21, 28, 93
African states, 110, 128; advice to, 96, 97, 98, 112, 125, 145; militancy, 96, 97, 98, 112, 122, 128, 145. *See also* individual states
Airfield survey, 58, 87–9, 168, 313n65
Airlift, Anglo-American-Canadian, 18, 58, 83, 87, 313n64, 339n58
– air transport, 57, 157, 342n77; American, 58, 149, 150, 153, 154, 198, 305n22; British, 58, 154, 160, 173; Canadian, 58, 87–8, 154, 156, 187, 198, 340n63; Soviet, 58, 149, 151, 305n22, 340n63
– base facilities: Beira, 154, 168–71, 187, 198, 346n127; Dar es Salaam, 154, 168, 169, 170, 172–3, 340n64; Kinshasa, 154, 159, 170, 340n65
– contingency planning, 54–8, 305n19; airlift capacity, 55, 89, 154–5, 156–7, 341n75, 342n77
– operations, 58, 89, 153, 157, 168, 186, 187, 188, 339nn58, 60; financing, 86–7, 156, 161, 331n125
Airlift cargo: coal, 156, 166; copper, 55, 188; oil, 55, 156–7, 341n75
Aldridge, Ian, 332n4
Algeria, 121, 197, 324nn64, 69, 325nn70, 72, 335n31, 358n44
Alport, Lord, 300n56
Alternative policy options, 8, 225–8, 230, 276–7; evaluation, 8, 10, 227–8, 234, 276–7; extent of search, 8, 10, 226–7, 233–4, 276–7; range of options, 8, 10, 227, 276
Alternative sources of supply. *See* Economic disengagement
Anglo-American consultations, 81; Canadian observers, 55, 84; London, 84, 86, 88–9, 101, 102, 217; Washington, 55, 57, 58, 82, 87
Angola, 69, 81, 82, 101, 171, 356n25; route to sea, 55, 63, 76, 93, 314n82. *See also* Benguela Railway; Lobito
Arms in transit seized by: Portugal, 77, 78–9, 90, 92, 312nn48, 51; Rhodesia, 90–2, 99–100, 312n48; Zambia, 80, 312n51

Bailey, Martin, 339n60
Balewa, Alhaji Sir Abubakar Tafawa, 174, 349n156
Balfour, Maj.-Gen. Fitzgeorge, 327n87
Banda, Dingiswayo, 30, 32, 105, 299n47, 307n48, 310n22, 332n3
Banda, Dr Hastings Kamuzu, 69, 76, 83, 92, 98, 102, 171, 317n103, 350n161. *See also* Kaunda, relations with Dr Banda
Bank of Zambia, 110
Barotseland, 37, 43
Basic values, Zambian, 4, 5, 50, 90, 211, 246, 258–9, 262–3, 290, 375n5
BBC, 60, 202, 318n3
Bechuanaland (Botswana), 49
Beira: airport, 168, 169, 187; pipeline, 176; port, 78, 101, 102, 171, 176, 317n102, 339n55, 347n135, 349n150. *See also* Airlift, base facilities
Beira Convention (1950), 77, 90
Belief systems, 37–44
Benguela Railway, 55, 63, 64, 65, 101, 166, 314n82; appeals to Portuguese, 77–80, 81–2, 95, 168. *See also* Lobito
Bercovitch, Jacob, xiv
Blantyre, 170, 348n135, 349n150
Bottomley, Arthur, 83, 179, 301n69, 334n20, 343n97, 344n107, 347n128; non-use of force, 308n2, 317n1; visit to Zambia, 127, 129, 131, 342n80, 351n174

Brecher, Michael, xiii, 4, 207, 293nn13, 16, 366n27, 368n53, 370n12, 374n5; hypotheses, 216, 218, 219, 220, 223, 224, 226, 227, 233–4, 236, 237, 244, 367n35, 368n2
Britain: general elections, 17, 19, 181, 185, 195, 202, 353n186; incompetence, 107, 155, 179, 233, 249, 319n15, 338n52, 339n58, 341n68, 352n180; lack of political will, 107, 109–10, 117, 140, 152, 217, 326n80
Britain and Rhodesia, 48, 90, 92, 117, 149, 165
– negotiations: post-UDI, 19, 156, 179, 202, 318n7, 352nn177, 178, 360nn60, 62; pre-UDI, 67, 86, 92, 313n64
– sanctions, 109–10, 151, 180; belief in sanctions, 120, 126, 132, 152, 155, 158, 323n53, 338n52; discounts sanction-busting, 176, 181, 195, 200, 241
Britain and Zambia, 190, 338n50, 342n83
– dependence on Zambian copper supply, 87, 141, 149, 152, 166, 188, 243, 252, 327n94, 336n41, 359n52; jobs at stake, 55, 304n18
– efforts to restrain Zambia, 114, 126–7, 164, 167, 180, 195, 231, 344n108
– fears Zambia precipi-

tating UDI, 49–50, 57, 62, 63, 82, 86, 87, 105, 316n93
– perceptions of Kaunda as irresponsible, 49, 58, 86, 111, 126, 128, 152, 164, 181, 352n179; fears overthrow of Kaunda, 300n56, 328n97
– response to illegal Rhodesian actions against Zambia: arms seizure, 90, 92; coal royalty, 165
Britain and troop deployment in Zambia
– British troop offers, 127, 128, 134, 135, 178, 181–2, 353n189; defensive role, 127, 133; motives, 126, 132, 134, 178, 181–2
– other foreign forces, seek exclusion, 121, 125, 126, 127, 132, 134, 146, 147, 149, 325nn72, 73, 336n38; especially air forces, 126, 134, 135, 329n112
Britain and use of force in Rhodesia
– military reconnaissance mission, 134, 182, 353n188
– opposition: post-UDI, 116, 117, 120, 126, 147, 371n18; pre-UDI, 59, 60, 67, 103, 206, 308n2, 316n93, 317n1
– reassuring Rhodesia, 68, 103, 136, 138, 213, 308n2, 317n1
British Ministry of Defence, 321n34
British National Export Council, 190
British Security, 339n55
British South Africa Company, 20, 36, 43

Brown, George, 340n60
Brumer, John, 107, 108, 316n98, 318n8, 319nn12, 13, 323n52, 344n106, 361n5
Buch, Frank, 305n21
Business community: expatriate, 25–6, 190, 220–1, 251; Zambian, 26–7, 297n30. *See also* Mining companies
"Buy Zambian" campaign, 189

Callaghan, James, 241
Canada, 49, 55, 58, 75, 81, 84, 87–8, 146, 350n161. *See also* Airlift, air transport
Capital Fund Estimates: coal prospecting, 61; Mpulungu, 75
Caprivi Strip, 213, 363n28
Carver, Lord, xii
Castle, Barbara, 127, 321n34, 339n58
Central African Airways, 354n9
Cervenka, Zdenek, 325n70
"cha-cha-cha" campaign, 36, 299n52
Changufu, Lewis M., 31, 299nn46, 47
Chimba, M. Justin, 30, 31, 299n47, 328n102
China, 147, 325n73
Chirundu, 106
Choice, dimensions, 9, 10, 205, 235–40, 280–4, 288; activity and novelty, 9, 239–40, 287; complexity, 9, 237, 286; core inputs, 9, 236, 285; costs and importance, 9, 236–7, 285, 368n3; mental process, 9, 239, 287; systemic domain, 9, 237–9, 286, 369nn8, 9

Chona, Mainza M., 30, 32, 44, 105, 299nn47, 49, 326n80, 329n105, 358n38, 368n49; OAU Defence Committee, 123, 130–1, 324n65, 358n38
Chona, Mark, 296n23, 303n13, 319n13, 336n35, 351n174
Christianity, 19; Kaunda and, 38, 39, 83, 300n63
Clapham, Christopher, xii, xiii
Coal royalty: increase, 18, 131, 157, 161, 162–7, 168, 308n53, 343n98, 344n102, 345n112, 346n123; Rhodesian climbdown, 163, 167, 177–8, 198, 242, 346n126; Wankie coal ban considered, 163, 166, 346nn119, 120; Zambian response, 162, 163, 164–7, 212, 230–1, 344nn103, 104, 345nn112, 113, 117, 346n121
Coal supplies
– alternate foreign sources, 166; South Africa, 63, 65, 164, 166, 307n45, 346n119; Tanzania, 64, 166, 307nn48, 49
– dependence on, 22, 56, 60, 66; thermal generators, 56, 61, 306n32
– domestic sources, 54, 61, 64; Nkandabwe, 61, 64, 66, 84, 166, 308n54; Maamba, 66
– stockpiling, 63–4, 65, 308n52
– substitutes: aircraft engines, 63; charcoal, 63, 64; heavy fuel oil, 63, 166, 188, 307n43; wood, 63, 64, 307n41
– threat to, 18, 83, 162
– Wankie, 60, 61, 66, 162, 164
Cognitive performance, 10, 217, 228–33, 272, 274, 276, 293n13; "lessons of history," 230–1. *See also* Zambia and UDI, insights into settler mentality; Quality of Zambian decisions
Cold War: fear of ideological conflict, 39, 58, 98, 115, 119, 123, 125, 126, 129, 147, 149, 246, 330n112, 335n33, 336n38; third world war, 238, 362n12
Common services, 49, 69, 90, 99–100, 237, 329n109. *See also* Rhodesia Railways
Commonwealth, 41, 42, 93, 110, 146; conferences, 59, 148, 174–6, 183, 302n75, 315n89, 338n53, 349n156, 350n158; economic assistance to Zambia, 148, 159, 175, 187, 188, 200; force for Rhodesia, 59, 134; Zambian threats to withdraw, 144, 146, 175, 302n75, 333n12, 335n27, 361n65. *See also* Arnold Smith
Commonwealth Relations Office, 146, 200, 322n45
Commonwealth Sanctions Committee, 176, 182, 187, 188, 190, 195, 359n52; Subcommittee on Cooperation with Zambia, 188, 190, 359n52

Comparative findings on crisis decision making, 368n3, 369nn5, 9, 370n12
Conservative Party, British, 35, 127, 132, 152, 194, 202, 357n35, 360n61
Consultative pattern, 8, 10, 219–23, 272–4, 365nn16, 17; breadth, 8, 10, 24–9, 220, 273, 365nn19, 20; intensity of consultation, 221, 274; motivation, 221–3, 274; participation, 8, 10, 220–1, 273
Content analysis, 11, 208, 253, 257–60, 289–90; speech file, 11, 257, 289; speeches as faithful reflections of reality, 253, 259. *See also* Stress
Contingency planning, 304n17
– post-UDI, 124–5; conflicting objectives, 114, 158, 184
– pre-UDI, 18, 47–8, 50–1, 57, 60, 61–2, 64, 104, 107, 319n15; surveys, 55, 56, 58, 75, 77–8, 84, 311n37, 312n45. *See also* Anglo-American consultations; Secrecy
Contingency Planning Organization (CPO), 154, 155, 159, 160, 164, 169, 179, 186, 190, 200; establishment, 85, 141–2, 154, 332n4
Coping mechanisms, 6, 8, 206, 216–28, 264–71
Copper: exports, maintaining minimum, 166, 188; highgrading, 56; mixed blessing, 252; price, 22, 25, 246, 294n10; US strategic reserve, 56, 305n20. *See also* Britain and Zambia: dependence on Zambian copper supply
Copper mines: "care and maintenance plans," 19, 60, 178; closures, 56; cuts, 54, 56, 62, 185, 188, 346n119, 355n11; miners, 22; unemployment threat, 185, 186
Cornwall, F.W., 306n35
Crises, international, 3, 4–5, 6, 10, 205, 293n16; economic threat, 5, 146. *See also* Basic values; Military hostilities; Time constraints
Crisis decisions, 11, 14–16; issue areas, 12–13, 16, 237; policy objectives, 12, 14–16
Currency, xvi
Curry, Robert L., 249
Cyprus base, 60

Dar es Salaam, 104, 122, 309n9, 349n150; airport, 154, 168, 169, 170, 347n135; port, 77, 83, 84, 93, 157, 198, 311n38 317n102
Day, John, 341n69
Decisional forum, 8, 10, 223–5
– authority pattern, 10, 224–5, 275, 366n30
– formal and effective, 8, 13, 224
– size and structure, 10, 223, 274; cabinet, 57, 65, 79, 95, 99, 102, 110, 120, 124, 133, 146, 149, 155, 186, 190; ministerial, 50, 51, 59, 72, 75, 85, 88, 105, 160, 179, 196, 201; presidential, 59, 91, 108, 164, 170, 173, 175
Dessouki, Ali E. Hillal, 291n5, 372n1
Dominion, Leon, 309n14
Dowty, Alan, 244, 366n23, 369n4, 370nn12, 13
Dumont, René, 38

East, Maurice, A., 229–30, 248, 370n13, 371n24
East Africa, 74, 87, 107, 313n59, 354n9; Nairobi summit, 116, 120, 130, 322n44, 323nn54, 56 324n66
East African Railways, 311n32
Economic assistance to Zambia
– appeals elsewhere: Africa, 85, 102, 159, 196, 342nn87, 88; Commonwealth, 148, 159, 175, 187, 200; superpowers, 149–51, 159, 343n97; United Nations, 159
– British response, 86–7, 114, 157–8, 159, 160–1, 165, 181
– financing: defence costs, 136, 137–8, 330n115, 331n125; oil airlift, 86–7, 156, 161; third country projects, 83–4, 161, 343nn93, 95
– Zambian appeals: post-UDI, 114, 127, 157, 159, 160–1, 163; pre-UDI, 83–6; preparing for the "quick kill," 180–1, 186, 225
Economic disengagement, 151–2, 189, 190, 192, 201, 307n39, 338n54
– alternative routes, 54,

Index

56, 68–9, 113, 152, 158, 184, 186, 198, 226; mileages, 311n32, 314n82, 317n102. *See also* Contingency planning, pre-UDI surveys; Great East Road; Great North Road
- alternative sources of supply, 113, 152, 158, 189, 192–3, 338n54, 345n118, 356n27. *See also* Coal supplies

Egypt: British fears, 121, 126, 132, 324n64, 325nn72, 77; OAU, 122, 197, 335n31; and Zambia, 195, 197, 334n22

Electricity supply: aircraft engines, 63; thermal generation, 56, 61; Zaire, 93. *See also* Kariba

"Essential Requirements of Zambia," 182, 185, 186–9

Ethiopia, 197, 324n69; British fears, 121, 324n64, 325n73; OAU, 325n70, 335n26

Expatriates in Zambia, 19, 232, 301n73
- attitudes: loyalty, 17, 27, 51, 106, 118, 213, 301n73, 303n12, 318n9, 322n46; morale, 28, 187–8, 190, 232, 333n7, 356n24; political strikes, 207, 232, 354n10, 357n31, 358n40; racism, 318n9; threat of exodus, 83, 115, 124, 185, 236
- occupations: business, 25–6, 220–1, 251; civil servants, 17, 19, 24, 51, 106, 303n12; commercial farmers,

101; military, 17, 27, 106, 118, 213, 301n73, 322n46; miners, 19, 22, 28, 106, 187–8, 232, 301n73, 318n9, 356n24; presidential advisers, 24, 319n13; railwaymen, 19, 70–1, 83, 106, 207, 232, 318n9

Federation of Rhodesia and Nyasaland, 21, 35, 158; defederation, 69, 135–6, 137, 213, 301n74, 330n115
Feruka, 111, 176
First National Development Plan, 85, 111, 190. *See also* Transitional Development Plan
Flower, Ken, 321n37
Foley, Maurice, 158, 160, 343n90
Franco Nogueira, Alberto, 81, 95, 168, 170, 312n53
Francistown, 348n137, 354n9
Fredericks, Wayne, 64
FRELIMO (*Frente de Libertação de Moçambique*), 77, 79, 80, 312n51

Gandhi, Mahatma, 39, 115, 300n63
Garner, Joe, 322n45
Gauron, S.F., 312n45
George, Alexander L., 207, 224, 235, 244, 366nn24, 25, 30
Gibbs, Sir Humphrey: post-UDI, 117, 118, 127, 149, 179; pre-UDI, 103, 317n2
Good, Robert, 65, 82, 114, 153, 163, 188, 198, 217, 240, 323n52, 326n82, 345nn116, 117,

352nn180, 183, 356n29
Goundrey, Gordon, 142, 332n2
Great East Road, 92, 101, 187, 317n102, 352n183
Great North Road, 68, 83, 84, 92, 150, 187, 198, 199, 313n59, 317n102, 337n46; "hell-run," 180, 198, 337n46
Grennan, Dennis, 319n13
Guinea, 81, 195, 324n62, 334n25, 335n31, 358n44

Haile Selassie, Emperor, 335n26
Hall, Richard: on Kaunda, 26, 38, 259; on cabinet differences, 323n55, 328n102, 330n119, 364n6
Heath, Kenneth, 306n35
Hermann, Charles, 4, 218
Hoganson-Bright report, 75, 78, 87, 311n37
Holsti, Ole R., 207, 223, 228–9, 233, 235, 244, 366nn24, 30, 367n41
Huggins, Godfrey, 21
Hughes, Cledwyn, 158, 160, 339n60, 341nn70, 72, 343nn90, 91, 371n19
Hypotheses, 7–8, 216, 218–28, 230, 233–4, 236–40, 244, 278–9, 288, 364n3, 368n55

Ibekwe, Senator Dan, 349n156
India, 34, 39, 246
Industrial Development Corporation, 186, 297n32
Information processing, 8, 10, 216–18; extent

of quest, 8, 10,
217–18, 272, 364n7;
receptivity, 8, 10,
218–19, 272,
365nn13, 15
Interest groups, 27–9.
See also Business community; Public opinion
International Crisis Behaviour Project (ICB),
3–4; crisis model,
6–11, 247; research
questions, 10, 216–33,
247
International Monetary
Fund, 253
Israel, 237, 246–7,
368n3, 369nn5, 9,
370nn12,13

Japanese sanction busting, 338n51
Jardim, Jorge,
348nn139, 142
Johnson, Jack, 323n53
Johnson, Lyndon B.,
150, 153, 339n59,
365n10

Kabwe mine, 56
Kafue hydro-electric
scheme, 54
Kalemie (Albertville), 93
Kalulu, Solomon, 30,
299n47, 332n3
Kamanga, Reuben, 30,
44, 299nn46, 47; East
Africa missions, 116,
130, 173, 323n54,
349n153; ministerial
consultations, 32, 105,
128, 328n102, 332n3;
policy on Rhodesia,
176, 177, 189, 192,
357nn32, 25, 360n59;
UN posting, 187,
354n7
Kambona, Oscar, 122
Kapiri Mposhi, 80
Kapwepwe, Simon, 30,
32, 225, 299nn46, 47

– and belief system,
41–2, 305n24; alleged
extremism, 41, 42,
114, 126, 129, 150,
248, 301nn68, 69;
compared with Kaunda, 40–1, 251,
301n74, 302n75,
357n34; nationalism,
41, 110–11, 137, 155,
166, 179; pan-Africanism, 41–2, 120, 124,
197, 342n88
– and Britain, 42, 120,
160, 178, 179, 202,
301n74, 336n41; British troops, 128,
129–31, 328n102;
diplomatic break,
143–4, 333nn11, 14;
RAF, 136, 137, 138,
330n119, 331n121
– and Commonwealth,
41, 42, 143, 175,
302n75, 333n12
– and Rhodesia, 158,
212, 259, 354n6; contingency planning,
142, 307n48, 332n3;
"quick kill," 183, 199;
sanctions, 110–11,
320n28, 338n51,
357nn34, 35; use of
force, 125, 177,
306n27, 351n168
– and Portugal, 81, 95,
169, 171, 312n53,
347nn128, 134
– and South Africa,
363n28
– external travels, 83,
96, 105, 116, 120,
129, 134, 150, 196,
337n45
Kariba dam and power
station, 18, 294n3
– Zambian fears, 51, 83,
148, 162, 184, 188,
214–5, 259, 363n29;
British response to,
116, 117, 134,
353n188; mines,

328n102; pylons sabotaged, 117, 127, 131,
215; security threat,
106, 117, 120
Kasavubu, Joseph, 94
Katanga, 93, 94; Pedicle,
93, 314n74
Katilungu, Simon, 107,
319n13
Kaunda, Kenneth D., xiv,
xv, 30, 34, 36, 37,
299nn46, 47, 300n56,
373n14
– belief system, 37–40,
41, 83, 301nn70, 71;
contradictions, 39–40,
301n67; non-racialism, 38, 39, 42, 250,
300n60; non-violence,
39, 115
– crisis-induced stress,
107, 208, 211–15,
217, 224–5, 228, 250
– fear of racial/ideological war, 39, 98, 115,
118, 123, 129, 212,
238, 362n12
– presidential role in
foreign policy, 24,
224, 250–1, 295n13;
consensus style, 23–4,
224, 225, 250,
295n15, 366n28; expatriate advisers, 24,
107, 319n13,
344n106
– public statements,
373n3; broadcasts,
49–50, 51, 57, 104–5,
106, 163, 357n34;
party rallies, 112,
143, 303n11; press
conferences, 121,
130, 131, 143,
298n35
– soundness of judgments, 240–1,
370n15; concern with
image, 112, 145, 156
Kaunda, relations with Dr
Banda, 92, 101,
316n101. *See also* Ban-

da, Dr Hastings Kamuzu; Malawi
Kaunda, relations with Julius Nyerere, 171–2, 174, 222, 252
– consultations, 59, 104–5, 148, 155, 186, 221; military confrontation with Rhodesia, 128, 136–7
– contingency support, 54, 84–5, 172; cooperation with Britain, 144, 145, 159, 172–3; oil airlift, 88, 160, 169
– meetings: Dar es Salaam, 84–5, 104, 309n9; London, 54; Lusaka, 186; Mbeya, 144, 148, 159, 169, 172, 340n64
Kaunda, relations with Ian Smith: correspondence, 52, 90–2, 99–100, 304n16, 313n56, 316n98; perceptions of, 35–6, 38, 100, 107, 135, 165, 167
Kaunda, relations with Harold Wilson: correspondence, 64, 114, 120–1, 126, 127, 128, 130–1, 134, 138, 195–6, 323n52, 326n79, 329nn109, 110, 360n57, 364n10; meetings: 49, 55, 59, 60, 61, 64, 178–83, 318n7, 321n34; restraint on public statements on Rhodesia, 24, 49–50, 51, 105, 110, 117, 231, 303n9
Kaunda and British Labour government
– confidence misplaced, 25, 37, 39, 179, 184, 185, 202, 252, 306n31, 351n170
– faith in Labour Party leaders, 25, 27, 35, 36, 38–9, 158, 182–3, 184, 185, 193, 200, 202, 219, 231
– supports Labour election campaign: post-election expectations, 196, 197, 200, 202, 360nn57, 59; restraint in public criticism, 181, 182, 196, 202, 231; urges OAU restraint, 194, 196
Keatley, Patrick, 323n52
Kemp, Arthur R., 310n21
Kenya, 59, 116, 325n73, 356n25; and OAU, 96, 122, 146, 197, 358n44
Kenyatta, Jomo, 324n66, 335nn26, 30, 349n156
Khama, Seretse, 49
Kigoma, 74, 311nn32, 38
Kinshasa, 94, 154, 159, 170, 342n77
Kipping, Sir Norman, 332n4, 342n83
Knaggs, Kenneth J., 142, 154, 160, 310n20, 343n92
Konoso, D.K., 31, 34
Korany, Bahgat, xi, xii, xiii, 32, 239, 253, 291n5, 372n5

Labour Party, British, 17, 25, 34, 35, 39, 185, 202, 219, 231, 360n61
Lenshina, Alice, 36
Leopold Walford Limited, 79
Lewis, Roy, 318n7
Liberation movements, criticism of, 41, 80, 111, 118; restrictions on, 118, 227, 232, 312n51
Liberation of Zimbabwe, 59, 114, 115–16, 119, 120, 158, 246

Livingstone, 63, 65, 106, 321n34, 330n113; airport, 136, 348n137
Lloyd, Selwyn, 357n35, 359n50
Lobito, 347n135; port, 63, 64, 77, 78, 170; rail route, 65, 79, 93, 95, 168, 312n45, 314n82
"long haul," 19, 185, 197–202
LONRHO, 26
Lourenço Marques (Maputo), 171, 346n127
Luanda, 346n127
Luangwa River bridge, 101
Lubumbashi, 94, 305n22, 342n77
Lumpa Church, 36
Lusaka airport, 62, 168, 347n135

MacDonald, Malcolm, 321n37, 360n60, 371n18; economic issues, 152, 157, 160, 186, 193, 195, 327n86, 351n174, 356n21, 358n38, 363n24; military issues, 121, 126–31, 134, 326n82, 356n29; political issues, 175, 202, 353n186
McFadzean, Sir William, 359n52
McLean, A.D., 310n20
Malawi, 48, 77, 83, 92, 98, 171, 311n40, 316nn95, 101, 350n161, 356nn21, 25; facilities, 101, 102, 317n103; Malawi Railway, 101; routes to sea, 69, 76, 92, 101–2, 168, 171, 187, 317n102, 348nn137, 144
Mali, 334n25, 335n31, 358n44

Margolian, Michael, xiv
Martin, Paul, 335n27
Matadi, 93
Matoka, Peter W., 30, 81, 299n49
Mauretania, 335n31, 358n44
Mbeya meeting, 144, 148, 159, 169, 172
"Meet the people" campaigns, 29, 95, 143, 200, 251, 303n11, 357n30, 359n52; "Operation Capitao," 359n52
Military hostilities, likelihood of, 4–5, 213–15, 262; military imbalance, 135–6, 213, 263
Military missions to Zambia: British, 134, 182, 353n188; OAU, 125, 195, 325n72, 358n37
Mining companies, 25–6, 84, 145, 155, 251; contingency planning, 57, 63, 64, 75, 159, 200; cooperative, 296n25, 297nn26, 27; lobbying, 79, 94, 164, 344n109
Mineral royalty, 24, 295n16
Ministerial missions, 147–50: Cairo, 195; London, 149, 336nn40, 41, 345n113; Moscow, 149–51, 336n42; Washington, 149–50, 336n42
Moambo, 359n50
Mobutu, Joseph, 94, 154, 169, 340n65, 365n10
Molteno, Robert, 26–7, 29
Monson, Sir Leslie, 107, 128, 202, 217, 319n13, 351n174
Mozambique, 69, 77, 81, 171, 347n132; fear of British invasion, 171; rail routes, 76, 77, 78, 101
Mpulungu, 74–6, 311nn32, 38
Msonthi, John, 356n21
Mudenda, Elijah, 30, 337n45
Mulaisho, Dominic, 296n23, 303n13
Munali School, 34, 300n60
Mundia, Nalumino, 30, 32, 299n47, 306n27, 310n22, 314n77, 328n102, 349n153
Murumbi, Joseph, 59, 96, 324n65
Musakanya, Valentine, 79, 82–3, 84, 85, 142, 296n23, 303n13, 318n4, 319n13
Mwanakative, John, 30, 299n49, 315n87
Mwaanga, Vernon, 354n6
Mwiinga, Ditton, 306n27, 350n158

Nairobi, 116, 335n26, 347n135. See also East Africa
Nalilungwe, Mubiana, 31, 299n46
Nasser, Abdul, 122, 137, 251
National Coal Supply Commission, 63, 65
National Progress Party, 28, 298n40, 307n39, 324n69
Ndola, 128, 133, 136, 168, 311n32, 317n102, 347n135
Nigeria, 122, 174, 325nn70, 72, 349n156, 350n159
Nkrumah, Kwame, 251, 358n44; and Britain, 335n31; and Commonwealth, 59, 175, 333n12; and Zambia, 122, 128, 175, 305n24, 315n86, 325n70
Nogueira, Franco. See Franco Nogueira
Northern Rhodesia, 20, 69, 93; colonial rule, 33–4; racialism, 33–4
Northern Rhodesia Regiment, 301n74
Nyerere, Julius, 103, 174, 222, 251, 252, 349n156, 358n44
– helpful to Zambia, 88, 145, 154, 172, 173, 197, 331n120, 340n64, 348n147, 349n148; unhelpful, 84–5, 136–7, 144, 159, 168, 169, 172, 222, 326n84, 334n24, 349nn149, 150, 151, 354n9
– relations with Britain, 59, 136, 172–3, 322n44, 341n74; diplomatic break, 144–5, 146, 159, 172, 333n14, 334n19
– relations with Rhodesia, 105, 128, 324n66

Oakshott, Robert, 312n45
OAU (Organization of African Unity), 335n26; Accra summit, 96–8, 122, 315n91; Council of Ministers, 96, 98; (Dec. 1965), 122, 125, 127, 132, 143, 175, 324n63, 338n50; (Feb. 1966), 194, 196–7, 201, 359n52; Defence Committee (of Five), 316n95, 324n63; (Nov. 1965), 121, 122, 123, 125, 326n84, 338n50; (Feb. 1966), 195;

secretary general, 96, 122, 336n44
OAU and Rhodesia, 150, 252; diplomatic sanctions against Britain, 98, 134, 143–4, 145, 194, 335nn26, 31; economic sanctions, 96, 98, 197, 252, 338n50; military base in Zambia, 42, 96, 98, 124, 316n95, 324n65; military intervention, 96, 122–3, 124, 125, 316n95, 324n63; military mission, 125, 195, 325n72, 358n37
Obote, Milton, 59, 324n66, 335n26
Oil companies, 153, 339n57; Shell Oil Company, 84, 87, 101–2, 341n69
Oil pipelines: Dar es Salaam–Ndola, 157, 199; Beira–Feruka, 176
Oil sanctions against Rhodesia, 151, 153, 339n58
– Britain, 153, 156–7, 339n60, 341n75; confidence in effectiveness, 155, 181
– sanction-busting, 33, 198, 199–200, 201, 338nn51, 55, 359n50; Portugal, 176, 181; South Africa, 176–7, 181, 201, 241, 357n33
Oppenheimer, Harry, 64, 306n35, 307n45
Owen, David, 371n19

Paige, Glenn D., 221, 223
Pearson, Lester B., 49, 365n10; airlift, 187, 340n63; Lagos conference, 174, 175, 349n156, 350nn161, 163

Pettman, Jan, 27, 298n37
Pioneer Industries Act, 189
Portugal: and Rhodesia, 48, 67, 78–81, 118, 303n5, 308n1, 311n39; Rhodesian sanctions, 170, 176, 181, 201; Zambia, 118, 168–71, 187, 252
Portugal: and Zambian relations with, 48, 69, 76–7, 80–1, 92, 118, 311n39; arms seizure, 77, 78–9, 80, 81, 92, 312n48; Beira airlift, 154, 168–71, 187, 198, 346n127; British diplomatic support, 78, 80, 81, 83, 168, 169; overtures to Lisbon, 77–82, 168–71, 312n52, 348n140; proposed consul, 77, 80, 348nn139, 143; railway holdups, 77
Power pylon, sabotage, 117, 127, 131, 215
Prain, Sir Ronald, 64, 305n21, 359n50, 363n29
Psychological environment, Zambian decision makers, 6, 32, 40; formative influences, 33–5; crisis experiences, 35–7
Public opinion, 28–9, 142–3, 251, 298nn34, 40, 50, 315n89; "meet the people" campaigns, 29, 95, 143; weekly radio reports, 257; white opinion, 28, 143, 153, 187–8, 215, 333n7, 356n24
Puta, Robinson, 310n20
Putterill, Maj.-Gen. Sam, 319n18, 353n188

Quality of Zambian decisions, 240, 370n15; military invasion, difficulties discounted, 231, 368n49; success, 241–4, 287
"Quick kill" strategy, 19, 171, 176–83, 351n173; abandoned, 185, 192, 193, 198–9; impact on Zambia, 178, 180–1; scenario, 178, 180, 182, 352n180; support for Zambia, 178, 180–1, 182; target date, 176, 178, 180, 185, 186, 187, 192, 193, 199, 350n164, 352n185, 356nn28, 29

Racialism, 300n60; Northern Rhodesia, 33–4, 37, 299n49; Rhodesia, 21, 38
RAF in Zambia, 89, 157; air defence, 18, 119, 121, 122, 131, 132, 134, 135–6, 138–9, 143, 178, 212, 330n116, 332nn129, 6; air strike capability, 121, 138, 331n126; British motives, 134, 135, 329n112; cost-sharing, 137–8, 139, 331n125; Javelin fighters, 136, 138, 330n119; RAF Regiment, 136; Zambian motives, 135–6, 214
Railways, 57, 60, 63, 350n159. See also Rhodesia Railways
Rationality in decision making, 9, 40, 239, 243–4, 248, 280–4, 287, 370n12
Reedman, Harry, 308n1
Reid, James, 305n21
Rhodes, Cecil, 20, 74
Rhodesia
– election, 48, 70, 206,

302n2, 361n1; Rhodesian Front, 48, 67, 162; state of emergency, 18, 103–4, 317n2; white paper, 48, 49, 206
- government: cabinet, 68, 103–4, 117; Ministry of External Affairs, 90, 316n98; Security Council, 103
- security services: armed resistance to British, 115, 321n37; intelligence service, 68, 89, 107, 307n39, 309n8, 316n98, 319n12; Rhodesia Light Infantry, 213, 319n19, 321n37; RRAF, 135, 138, 213, 319n19, 331n126

Rhodesia: economic dependence on Zambia, 49, 71, 105, 162, 164, 167, 214, 303n14, 343n100, 344n109; exploitation, 21, 135–6, 294n8; Rhodesian business interests, 164, 165, 193, 344n109

Rhodesia: hostility to Zambia, 48, 103, 359n46
- economic warfare: repatriation of Zambians, 48, 51, 99, 162, 184, 302n4, 303n14, 316n97; threats, 48–9, 50, 52, 68, 70, 83, 117, 162, 246, 322n40; Zambia as hostage, 47, 48–9, 140, 236
- sanctions: arms seizure, 90–2, 99–100, 312n48; ban on UNIP branches, 28, 68; coal royalty, 18, 131, 157, 161, 162–3, 308n53,

343n98, 344n102; financial sanctions, 162, 344n100; oil, 18, 89, 99, 152–3, 155, 157, 167; stocks run-down, 68, 90, 153, 154–5, 313n66, 339nn56, 57
- security threat to Zambia, 107, 109, 111, 124, 213–15, 252, 318n9, 362nn20, 22; air attack, 111, 117, 135, 137, 138, 214, 330n113, 363n25; armed incursion, 106, 111, 132, 135, 213–14, 330n113; Kariba dam, 117, 120, 162, 214–15, 363nn29, 31; occupation, threat discounted, 213; sabotage, 117, 127, 184, 215; troop deployment on border, 18, 106, 108, 117, 213–14, 319nn18, 19. *See also* Zambia: threats to racial harmony
- seeks to neutralize Zambia, 52, 83, 98, 99–100, 162

Rhodesia Railways, 65, 69–74, 90, 150, 152, 188; Board of Management, 69, 70, 72, 73, 130; breakup, 70–4, 310n24; coal royalty, 164; compulsory transfers, 70–1, 73; freight rates, 71, 73, 310n16; Higher Authority for Railways, 69, 70, 72, 73; intergovernmental agreements, 63, 71, 90; joint ownership, 69, 74; payments crisis, 243, 360n65; unitary system, 69, 74

Rhodesians resident in Zambia: defence force,

118, 213, 301n73, 322n46; railwaymen, 19, 70–1, 83, 207, 318n9
Roberts, John, 324n69
Ross, Sir Archibald, 168, 347n134, 348n139
Rothchild, Donald, 249
Rothstein, Robert, 249
Rowland, R.W. ("Tiny"), 26
Royal Navy, 172, 325n77, 349n150
RRAF (Royal Rhodesian Air Force). *See* Rhodesia, security services
RST (Roan Selection Trust), 25–6, 56, 57, 64–5, 305n21, 308n54

Sahnoun, Mohamed, 324n65
Salazar, Antonio, 69, 76, 303n5; Beira airlift, 168–71, 348n139, 365n10
Salima, 101
Sanctions. *See* Britain and Rhodesia; OAU and Rhodesia; "Quick kill strategy"; UN sanctions; Zambia, sanctions
Scots Guards, 242, 353n189
Secrecy: Britain, 57, 63, 82, 89, 307n45; Zambia, 12, 51, 57, 65–6, 89, 169, 303n12
Seers, Dudley, 343n90, 351n172
Shlaim, Avi, 365n19, 366n24, 368n53
Sierra Leone, 335n26
Simbule, Ali, 66, 334n24
Sinoia massacre, 202, 361n63
Sipalo, Munakayumbwa, 296n21
Sklar, Richard, 25–6, 345n116

Slipchenko, Ambassador Sergei, 337n48
Smith, Arnold, 59, 333n12, 335n27, 339nn56, 58
Smith, George Ivan, 334n19, 341n74
Smith, Ian, 38, 135; post-UDI, 133, 149, 162–3, 167, 179, 358n46; pre-UDI, 47, 48, 49, 67, 70, 76, 78, 86, 89, 90–1, 206
Smyth, Ian, 318n4
Snelling, Sir Arthur, 157, 327n87, 342n80, 343n90
Somalia, 335n31, 358n44
Songea, 64, 166, 307n48
Songwe-Kiwire. *See* Songea
South Africa, 20, 34, 300n60, 311n39, 348n137; coal exports, 63, 65, 164, 166, 307n45, 346n119; sanction-busting, 176–7, 181, 201, 241, 357n33; security threat, 115, 118, 124, 213, 253, 363n28; trade, 193, 338n50
South Africans residents in Zambia: defence force, 118, 213, 301n73, 322n46; miners, 19, 301n73
Soviet Union, 34; airlift, 58, 149, 151, 305n22; military intervention, 126, 147, 149, 330n112, 335n33; mission to Moscow, 148, 149–51, 337nn48, 49
Special Air Service Regiment, 213, 319n19, 330n113
Stanleyville (Kisangani) rescue mission, 93, 111, 214, 324n69, 330n113
Stockpiling: coal, 63–4, 65, 308n52; copper, 56, 166, 305n20; essential imports, 188–9, 190, 192; oil, 154–5, 169, 339n57
Stress, crisis-induced, 3, 6, 11, 37, 207–9, 216, 250, 254; collective stress, 208–9, 259; operationalization, 11, 208–9, 210, 257, 262; stress conditions, 209, 211–15, 258–9, 262–3. *See also* Basic values; Military hostilities; Time constraints
Sudan, 197, 324n62, 325n70, 335n31, 358n44

Talmage, Michael, 319n13
Tanzania, 122, 146, 174, 175, 324n62, 325n70, 335n31; access to sea, 68, 83, 92, 187, 221; airlift, 54, 88, 168, 172–3, 222, 349nn148, 150, 151; British forces, 168, 172–3, 326n84, 349nn149, 150, 151; coal deposits, 64, 66, 307nn48, 49; contingency arrangements, 85, 159, 172, 342n87. *See also* Nyerere, Julius
Tanganyika, Lake, 74, 76, 93
Tanzania-Zambia railway, 54, 68–9, 199, 309n15
Telephone communications, 129, 327n90, 341n75
Telli, Diallo, 96, 122
Thermal generators, 56, 62, 306n32
Thixton, John 307n41

Thomson, Ewen, 79
Time constraints, 4, 5, 68, 178, 182, 211–12, 220, 262, 263, 362nn9, 10, 11, 365n20
Tordoff, William, 29
Touré, Sekou, 334n25
Transitional Development Plan: coal deposit survey, 61; Mpulungu, 4. *See also* First National Development Plan
Trans-Zambezia Railway, 101
Trigger events, 6, 47–8, 104, 206–7, 236, 261, 262
Tshombe, Moise, 69, 76, 81, 92–4, 314nn77, 81
Tunisia, 324n69

UDI (Unilateral Declaration of Independence), 3, 67, 206; predictions on:
– date of collapse: British, 19, 86, 120, 158, 161, 176, 178, 185, 323n53; Zambian, 125, 158, 177, 178, 183, 240, 315n87, 318n8, 341n168, 371n16
– date of declaration, 17, 18, 47, 52, 67–8, 86, 101, 103, 104, 293n2, 303n6, 313n60, 318nn4, 7
– economic consequences, 48, 51–2, 100, 303n14, 304n15, 315nn87, 88
Uganda, 324nn62, 66, 335n26, 356n25
UNIP (United National Independence Party), 21, 28, 91, 93, 94; Central Committee, 28, 30–1, 32, 298n37;

National Council, 28, 145, 298n36, 339n55, 341n71; parliamentary caucus, 27–8, 131, 139, 142–3, 145, 332nn129, 6, 334n21; offices abroad, 34; Rhodesia branches, 28, 68; and Tshombe, 93, 94

United Nations, 108, 110, 114, 195
- General Assembly, 321n33; Committee of 24, 77; Security Council, 110, 113–14, 151, 176, 180, 320n25, 350n165; WHO Regional Committee for Africa, 81, 312n52
- sanctions against Rhodesia: Article 50, 111, 320n26, 360n56; economic, 110, 111, 113–14, 150, 151, 320n25; military, 115, 119, 120, 126, 150

United States, 81, 246; airlift, 54–5, 58, 84, 87, 89, 150, 153, 154, 156, 157, 305n22, 313n58, 340n63, 342n77; mission to Washington, 147, 148, 149–50, 335n33, 337nn45, 47; strategic copper reserves, 56, 305n20

Vernon, James W., 341n70, 342n75
Verwoerd, Hendrik, 76, 346n119
Victoria Falls, 73
Vietnam, 58, 87, 150, 246, 305n20

Wankie Colliery Company, 304n14, 344n109. *See also* Coal supplies
Watson, Duncan, 360n62
Williams, Mennen, 313n58
Willoughby, Maj.-Gen. J.E.F., 353n188
Wilson, Harold, 51, 55, 60, 64, 107, 117, 128, 145, 251; Lagos conference, 174–5, 176, 350n163
- and fears of Soviet intrusion, 125, 126, 147, 149, 330n112, 336n38
- and Smith regime: meetings with Smith, 49, 67, 86, 318n7; negotiations, 19, 67–8, 92, 156, 179, 202, 318n7, 352nn177, 178, 360nn60, 62; private communications, 136, 138, 149; warnings to Smith, 48, 313n64
- and use of force in Rhodesia: concern for security of Rhodesian whites, 60, 182, 353n187; possible limited military action, 60, 134, 138, 178, 180, 181–2, 200, 323n49, 352n185, 353n187; protecting Kariba, 132, 327nn94, 96; renounces force, 103, 120, 126, 206

Wilson, confidential revelations to Kaunda on: election date, 181, 195, 353n186; post-election policy, 19, 181, 195, 206; use of force, 60, 138, 178, 181, 352n185. *See also* Kaunda and British Labour government

Wina, Arthur N.L., 30, 31, 299n49, 302n76, 355n17; belief system, 42–3; foreign missions, 105, 150; ministerial consultations, 32, 72, 128, 130, 179, 306n27, 310n22; negotiations with British, 160, 178, 179, 328n102, 341n72; sanctions, 113, 299n43, 315n89; strategy on Rhodesia, 70, 71, 179, 344n103, 345nn113, 118

Wina, Sikota, 31, 299n47, 328n102
World Bank guard for Kariba, 119, 134

Zaire, 314nn72, 80, 324n62, 334n22, 356n25
- access to sea, 55, 69, 76, 92, 93, 199, 314n82; airfield facilities, 93, 154, 187, 305n22
- Zambian relations with: Mobutu regime, 94, 95, 154, 169, 325nn70, 73, 340n65; Tshombe regime, 76, 81, 92–4

Zambia
- access to the sea, 54, 56, 68, 184, 198; Rhodesia Railways, 17, 68, 70, 73, 83, 90
- attributes, 19–20; landlocked, 20, 22, 222, 227, 237, 252
- dependence on Rhodesia, 22, 83, 99, 111, 184, 188
- development: economy, 21–2, 246, 253, 294n11; education, 19, 22, 34; priorities, 18, 62, 65–6, 111, 141, 199, 227
- energy: coal, 18, 22, 56, 60, 83, 99, 162; oil, 18, 22, 99, 152–3; power, 18, 22, 51, 83, 259

- external dependence, 22, 240, 249–50, 252; on Britain, 115, 146, 147, 151, 160, 182, 227, 232–3, 250; on Tanzania, 137, 144–5, 146–7, 154, 168, 171–4; on expatriates, 83, 115, 124, 185, 215
- history, 17, 20; elections, 21, 25, 43; Second Republic, 21, 27; one-party participatory democracy, 21; state of emergency, 106, 108
- threats to racial harmony, 18, 39 47, 50, 106, 124, 143, 184–5, 213, 238–9; destabilization, 207, 318n9, 354n10, 357n31; racism, 143, 259, 318n9
- trade, 112, 151, 189, 191, 193, 338n50, 343n100, 355n17

Zambia Air Force, 135–6

Zambia Airways, 354n9

Zambia and British sanctions policy
- ambivalence, 97, 111; ineffective, 97, 109–10, 111, 129, 151, 177, 217, 320n28; inadequate, 109–10, 152, 180, 196, 246; renewed doubts, 194, 195, 196, 201, 357n34, 358n38
- preference for use of force, 115, 129, 151, 177, 179, 184, 196, 201, 146, 351n168; counter-productive, 97, 111, 200
- support, 182–3, 193–4, 357n32; contingency aid, 114, 151, 152, 180; qualified, 114, 151, 152, 177–8, 180, 201, 321n31, 338nn51, 53, 346n126, 371n17
- time limit on sanctions, 112, 156, 180, 181–2, 341n74

Zambia and OAU, 128, 144, 145–6, 174, 200, 202, 336n44; Accra summit, 89, 96–8, 315nn91, 92, 324n63; Committee of Solidarity for Zambia, 197; Council of Ministers, 98, 125, 129, 131, 132, 134, 137, 175, 194–7, 201, 212, 315n91, 329n107, 342n88; Defence Committee (of Five), 121, 122, 123, 124–5, 130, 131, 195, 323n55, 326n84, 358n30; OAU criticisms of Zambia 97, 145, 197, 334nn24, 25; Zambian criticisms of OAU, 112, 122, 123–4, 125, 222

Zambia and OAU, diplomatic sanctions against Britain: British reaction, 145, 146, 173, 195, 197, 333n14; explanations to OAU members, 128, 144, 146; implications for Zambia, 143–4, 146, 172–3, 333n10, 334n19; non-compliance, 144, 146, 147; perception of resolution, 144, 333n14; support, 143, 333n11, 335n33, 336n39, 358n14
- military intervention in Rhodesia, 42, 96, 108, 121, 122, 124–5, 226, 243, 316n95, 324nn63, 66, 335n33; right to invite non-British troops, 121, 132–3, 134, 137, 147, 316n94, 331nn121, 122; troop offers, 118, 122, 129, 324n64, 325n70, 349n156; Zambian opposition, 98, 115, 118, 119, 121, 122, 123–5, 129, 137, 212, 222

Zambia and oil sanctions against Rhodesia, 151, 153–7, 341nn71, 72
- ineffective, 152, 155, 338n55; unenforced, 152, 241; time limit proposed, 156, 341n74
- oil stocks, 68, 90, 153, 154–5, 168, 173, 313n66, 339nn56, 57, 347n130; petrol rationing, 157, 339n58, 342n76
- Rhodesian counter-sanctions, 18, 89, 99, 152–3, 155, 157, 162–3, 167
- support for, 152, 156; contingency aid, 114, 151

Zambia and the "Quick kill," 228
- acquiescence, 19, 178, 180, 182, 184, 193, 248; political will wanes, 185, 198–9, 200, 201
- consequences: economic, 19, 352n179; fears, 177, 178, 180–1, 198–9
- guarantees sought, 181–2, 352n184; contingency aid, 180–1, 182, 187–9; "Essential Requirements of Zambia," 186–9
- target date, 180, 185, 186, 187, 192, 193, 199, 356n28, 357n30

Zambia and UDI

388 Index

- insights into settler mentality, 35–6, 136, 163, 230, 240, 367n46; coal royalty, 167; irrational, 107, 117, 135, 219
- intelligence sources: pre-UDI, 28, 163, 318nn4, 7; reaction, 104, 106, 108, 318nn8,9

Zambia and UN sanctions, 113–14, 151, 152; Article 50 exemption, 111, 201, 320n26, 360n56; mandatory, 197, 201

Zambia Defence Force, 20, 23, 116; arms imports, 77, 92; Defence Council, 136, 320n20; loyalty of officers, 17, 27, 106, 118, 213, 301n73, 322n46; no invasion of Rhodesia, 118, 322n47; troop deployment, 18, 106, 108–9, 119, 130, 320nn21, 22; Zambia Air Force, 135–6

Zambia, demands British military intervention: to liberate Rhodesia, 18, 39, 59, 98, 104, 114, 115–16, 117, 119, 120, 126, 182, 206, 212, 226, 237, 319n12, 323n55; military feasibility, 59, 115, 182, 231, 241, 321n37, 368n49, 371nn18, 19; to secure Kariba, 18, 116, 117, 119, 120, 121, 126, 127, 128, 133, 134, 138, 140, 143, 149, 215, 323n57, 326n79, 327n91, 329n109, 332n1, 336n40

Zambia, foreign policy, 13

- decision-maker policy predispositions: confrontation, 96, 179; "extremism," 41, 126, 328n97; liberation, 35, 41, 112, 232, 246; nationalism, 35, 41, 60, 97, 134, 137, 141, 155, 157, 166, 179, 315n89; neutralism, 83, 99–100, 141, 146, 160, 227; pan-Africanism, 41–2, 112; realism, 41, 97, 232; risk-taking, 248, 371n24; "Zambia first," 28, 41, 97, 110–1
- lessons learned, 35–6, 227, 230–1, 249–50, 252
- policy objectives, 12, 14–16, 114, 120, 158, 246, 252

Zambia Mineworkers' Union, 29

Zambia Police, 312n51

Zambia, political system, 23–9

- cabinet, 23–4, 30–1, 224, 296nn19, 20; appointments, 23, 34–5, 37, 295n14; committees, 32, 57, 65, 75, 110, 141–2; crises, 187, 199, 354n7, 367n32; controversial issues, 113, 116, 133, 146, 224–5, 323n55, 328n102, 329n110
- civil service, 24, 27, 110, 221, 249; colonial officials, 19, 24, 51, 303n12; committee of permanent secretaries, 142; Ministry of Commerce and Industry, 189; Zambianization, 25, 296n23, 303n12
- Ministry of Foreign Affairs, 22–3, 25, 90, 91, 250, 296n23; diplomatic missions, 25, 218, 334n22
- parliament, 23, 27, 298n33
- presidency, 23–4, 250–1, 253, 295n13

Zambia: relations with Britain, 36; close consultations, 159–60, 164, 221, 222, 344n107, 365n21; colonial responsibilities in Rhodesia, 58, 59, 85, 91, 97, 98, 100, 107, 108, 117, 143, 158, 165, 199, 232, 333n9; conflicting policy assumptions, 86, 114, 117, 126, 152, 158, 246; rejects troop offers, 18, 60, 116, 119, 121, 126–9, 132–4, 181, 182, 214, 224–5, 242–3; search for information from Britain, 84–7, 107, 127, 136, 153–5, 164, 217, 344n107; suspicion of British sellout, 86, 156, 177, 179, 182, 350n170, 360n62

Zambia-Tanzania Road Services, 199

Zambian residents of Rhodesia: forced repatriation threat, 48, 51, 99, 162, 184, 302n4, 303n14, 316n97; UNIP branch, 28, 68

Zambian sanctions against Rhodesia, 97, 109–14, 141, 315n89; declaration of disavowal, 335n13; exemption spurned, 111–12, 201, 320n26, 360n56; financial sanctions, 109, 110, 113, 152, 162, 189,

320n23, 344n101; trade sanctions, 113, 114, 151–2, 177, 191, 321n34, 351n167

Zayat, L., 122, 324n65

Zimbabwe liberation movements, 103, 124, 202; government in exile, 118; Sinoia massacre, 202, 361n63; Zambian criticisms, 41, 111, 118, 119

Zulu, A. Grey, 31, 32, 105, 299n47, 307n48, 308n52, 332n3, 337n45